WITH MORE DELIBERATE SPEED:
ACHIEVING EQUITY AND EXCELLENCE
IN EDUCATION—REALIZING THE FULL POTENTIAL
OF *BROWN V. BOARD OF EDUCATION*

#74809216

LB
5
.N25
105th
pt.2

The *Yearbook of the National Society for the Study of Education* (ISSN 0077-5762, online ISSN 1744-7984) is published in April and September by Blackwell Publishing with offices at 350 Main St, Malden, MA 02148 USA; 9600, Garsington Rd, Oxford, OX4 2DQ, UK; and 550 Swanston Street, Carlton South, 3053 Victoria, Australia.

Society and Membership Office:
The *Yearbook* is published on behalf of the National Society for the Study of Education, with offices at: University of Illinois at Chicago, College of Education (M/C 147) 1040 W. Harrison Street Chicago, IL 60607-7133. For membership information, please visit www.nsse-chicago.org.

Subscription Rates for Volume 105, 2006

	The Americas†	Rest of World‡
Institutional Standard Rate*	$136	£84
Institutional Premium Rate	$150	£92

*Includes print plus online access to the current and previous Volume. †Customers in Canada should add 7% GST or provide evidence of entitlement to exemption.
‡Customers in the UK should add VAT at 5%; customers in the EU should also add VAT at 5%, or provide a VAT registration number or evidence of entitlement to exemption.
For more information about Blackwell Publishing journals, including online access information, terms and conditions, and other pricing options, please visit www.blackwellpublishing.com.
All orders must be paid by check, money order, or credit card. Checks should be made payable to Blackwell. Checks in US dollars must be drawn on a US bank. Checks in Sterling must be drawn on a UK bank.

Volume 105 is available from the publisher for $40 a copy. For earlier Volumes please contact Periodical Service Company, L. P., 11 Main Street, Germantown, NY 12526-5635 USA Tel: (+518) 537-4700, Fax: (+518) 537-5899, Email: Psc@backsets.com or http://www.backsets.com

For new orders, renewals, sample copy requests, claims, changes of address and all other subscription correspondences please contact the Journals Department at your nearest Blackwell office (address details listed above). US office phone 800-835-6770 or 781-388-8206, Fax 781-388-8232, Email customerservices@blackwellpublishing.com; UK office phone +44 (0) 1865-778315, Fax +44 (0) 1865-471775, Email customerservices@blackwellpublishing.com; Asia office phone +65 6511 8000, Fax +44 (0) 1865 471775, Email customerservices@blackwellpublishing.com.

The *Yearbook* is mailed Standard Rate. Mailing to rest of world by DHL Smart & Global Mail. Canadian mail is sent by Canadian publications mail agreement number 40573520.

Postmaster: Send all address changes to *Yearbook of the National Society for the Study of Education*, Blackwell Publishing Inc., Journals Subscription Department, 350 Main St., Malden, MA 02148-5020.

Blackwell Synergy

Sign up to receive Blackwell *Synergy* free e-mail alerts with complete *Yearbook* tables of contents and quick links to article abstracts from the most current issue. Simply go to www.blackwell-synergy.com, select the journal from the list of journals, and click on "Sign-up" for FREE email table of contents alerts.

Copyright 2006 National Society for the Study of Education
All rights reserved. With the exception of fair dealing for the purposes of research or private study or criticism no part of this publication may be reproduced, stored, or transmitted in any form or by any means without the prior permission in writing from the copyright holder. Authorization to photocopy items for internal and personal use is granted by the copyright holder for libraries and other users of the Copyright Clearance Center (CCC), 222 Rosewood Drive, Danvers, MA 01923, USA (www.copyright.com), provided the appropriate fee is paid directly to the CCC. This consent does not extend to other kinds of copying, such as copying for general distribution for advertising or promotional purposes, for creating new collective works, or for resale. Institutions with a paid subscription to this journal may make photocopies for teaching purposes free of charge provided such copies are not resold. For all other permissions inquiries, including requests to republish material in another work, please contact the Journals Rights & Permissions Coordinator, Blackwell Publishing, 9600 Garsington Road, Oxford, OX4 2DQ, UK. E-mail: JournalsRights@oxon.blackwellpublishing.com.

Disclaimer: The Publisher, the National Society for the Study of Education and Editor(s) cannot be held responsible for errors or any consequences arising from the use of information contained in this journal; the views and opinions expressed do not necessarily reflect those of the Publisher, Society or Editor(s).

WITH MORE DELIBERATE SPEED: ACHIEVING EQUITY AND EXCELLENCE IN EDUCATION— REALIZING THE FULL POTENTIAL OF *BROWN V. BOARD OF EDUCATION*

105th Yearbook of the
National Society for the Study of Education

PART II

Edited by
ARNETHA F. BALL,
STANFORD UNIVERSITY

20 NSSE 06

The NATIONAL
SOCIETY for
the STUDY
of EDUCATION

Distributed by BLACKWELL PUBLISHING MALDEN, MASSACHUSETTS

National Society for the Study of Education

The National Society for the Study of Education was founded in 1901 as successor to the National Herbart Society. It publishes an annual two-volume Yearbook, each volume dealing with a separate topic of concern to educators. The Society's yearbook series, now in its one hundred and fifth year, presents articles by scholars and practitioners who are noted for their significant work in critical areas of education.

The Society welcomes as members all individuals who wish to receive its publications and take part in Society activities. Current membership includes educators in the United States, Canada, and elsewhere throughout the world—professors and graduate students in colleges and universities; teachers, administrators, supervisors, and curriculum specialists in elementary and secondary schools; policymakers and researchers at all levels; and any others with an interest in teaching and learning.

Members of the Society elect a Board of Directors. The Board's responsibilities include reviewing proposals for Yearbooks and authorizing their preparation based on accepted proposals, along with guiding the other activities of the Society, including presentations and forums.

Current dues (for 2006) are a modest $40 ($35 for retired members and for students in their first year of membership; $45 for international membership). Members whose dues are paid for the current calendar year receive the Society's Yearbook and are eligible for election to the Board of Directors.

Each year the Society arranges for meetings to be held in conjunction with the annual conferences of one or more of the national educational organizations. All members are urged to attend these meetings, at which the current Yearbook is presented and critiqued. Members are encouraged to submit proposals for future Yearbooks.

Voices for Democracy: Struggles and Celebrations of Transformational Leaders is Part I of the 105th Yearbooks. Part II is *With More Deliberate Speed: Achieving Equity and Excellence in Education: Realizing the Full Potential of* Brown v. Board of Education.

For further information, write to the Secretary, NSSE, University of Illinois at Chicago, College of Education M/C 147, 1040 W. Harrison St., Chicago, Illinois 60607-7133 or see http://www.nsse-chicago.org

Table of Contents

Part One
Looking Back: Historical Perspectives on
CHAPTER *Brown v. Board of Education*

Part Two
U.S. Implications of *Brown v. Board of Education*

Part Three
Comparative Reflections on *Brown v. Board of Education*

Part Four
Looking Forward: Pressing Challenges That Lie Ahead

Introduction

On May 17, 1954, Chief Justice Earl Warren read the unanimous Supreme Court decision that would come to be known as *Brown v. Board of Education*. This landmark decision, sometimes referred to as the defining U.S. legal decision of the 20th century, stated:

We conclude that in the field of public education the doctrine of "separate but equal" has no place. Separate educational facilities are inherently unequal. Therefore, we hold that the plaintiffs and others similarly situated for whom the actions have been brought are, by reason of the segregation complained of, deprived of the equal protection of the laws guaranteed by the Fourteenth Amendment.

More than 50 years ago, *Brown* became one of the most politically significant cases in American constitutional law, holding that racially segregated schools were inherently unequal and violated both the Fifth and the Fourteenth Amendments of the Constitution, striking down the "separate but equal" doctrine of *Plessy v. Ferguson* (1896), and requiring the desegregation of schools throughout the United States. *Brown* focused on ending de jure racial segregation in America's schools and bringing a *legal* end to the inhumane system of American apartheid. Although *Brown* has been used to address discrimination and exclusionary practices on behalf of many historically marginalized groups, the persistent challenge has been full integration in public schools. While some school districts have been able to achieve *desegregation*, or the coexistence of different racial and ethnic groups in a common space, few have succeeded in achieving *integration*, which involves addressing power dynamics in ways that enable equitable status among and between "different" groups of people.

In 2006, young people from diverse racial, cultural, and linguistic groups continue to receive instruction in segregated schools—under far less than excellent or equitable educational conditions. Differences in academic achievement begin early in the academic lives of many students from diverse racial, cultural, and linguistic backgrounds and continue throughout their school years. National Assessment of

1

Educational Progress (NAEP) scores are markedly lower for some students, particularly those from African American, Latino, and Native American backgrounds. Jagers and Carroll (2002), using evidence from the National Center for Education Statistics, note:

Studies have consistently found that African American students from elementary grades through high school are more likely to be placed in remedial and low-track classes, to be retained in grade, and to be suspended from school. Conversely, Black and Brown students are less likely to be placed in gifted and talented, advanced placement, college preparatory, or otherwise high-track classes. (p. 52)

Many of the negative educational outcomes associated with students from diverse racial, cultural, and linguistic backgrounds can be directly linked to the inequitable education they receive.

As has been the tradition of National Society for the Study of Education (NSSE) yearbook authors for the past century, the contributors to this volume speak out on issues that are important for the preservation of democratic education in this country and continue the tradition of chronicling changing educational trends and perspectives in our society. Since their beginning, NSSE yearbooks, often reflecting their societal context, have captured and presented prevailing perspectives on racial and ethnic issues in education. Although rarely confronting race and ethnicity directly, when addressed during NSSE's first decades, the problems of poor educational outcomes of minority students generally reflected a deficit perspective with regard to minority students' rights and academic abilities, an all too common perspective that persists even today (see Davis, 1913; Hollingworth, 1940; Peterson, 1928).

From the mid-20th century through the 1970s, explanations for educational disparity among racial and ethnic groups began to shift to a stronger focus on the home life and community values of the students' families (Havighurst & Dreyer, 1975). In 1967, Barbe, La Brant, Passow, and Witty contended that "inadequate provisions have been made in our schools for two large, overlapping groups: the 'educationally retarded' pupils, who are often neither seriously handicapped, nor greatly retarded; and the 'disadvantaged' pupils of widely varying abilities and potentialities who perform poorly under prevailing conditions" (pp. 1–2). According to these authors, the educationally disadvantaged "may include large ethnic groups (Negro, Mexican, Indian, Puerto Rican) whose backgrounds are often disregarded, even when special opportunities are provided for them" and are also "handicapped by poverty or by the unstimulating conditions characteristic of depressed areas" (p. 2).

Around this time, NSSE authors began to shift the locus of responsibility for minority student failure to institutionalized racism in the schools and the larger society, which resulted in various practices that disadvantaged students of lower socioeconomic status, in particular minority students (Cole & Bruner, 1972; Ervin-Tripp, 1972; Scribner & Knox, 1973). These authors challenged the theorists who focused on the deficits of children, instead suggesting the notion of cultural *difference*, in which nondominant world perspectives and nonstandard dialects were not perceived as inferior, but rather as culturally specific and viable. They called for education that facilitated minority group mastery of the intellectual instruments of the dominant culture and they implicated poverty and racial isolation as the most important problems facing urban schools at the time of their writing. Green (1974) blamed racial segregation for defeatist attitudes and the lowered ambitions of minority students and Wilkinson (1975) outlined structural constraints that consistently limited the educational aspirations of young African Americans. She noted:

Inevitably, the objectives and hopes of young blacks must encounter culturally sanctioned constraints emanating from the society's practices and norms with respect to the race variable. What is important to recognize here is that of all ethnic groupings and socioeconomic groups, white youth never experience the structural handicaps and identity-negating philosophies that every black in the 17–24 age range in America must face, regardless of family social-class background (p. 289).

Since the 1980s, NSSE authors have focused on issues of language and cultural maintenance from a perspective of tapping into students' cultural resources. They have discussed school reforms that change the political and sociocultural nature of schooling to a more equitable system that builds on the strengths of students rather than on deficits (Gradisnik, 1980). Sleeter (1995) documented the emergence of multicultural education, while other authors have discussed educational research, curriculum, and other initiatives that undergird the notion that "all children can learn" (Chasin & Levin, 1995; Oakes & Quartz, 1995; Swanson, Mehan, & Hubbard, 1995).

In recent years, NSSE authors have begun to emphasize policy changes that need to be made to achieve more equitable school structures (Berry & Ginsberg, 1990; Padron, Waxman, & Rivera, 2002) and to meet the comprehensive needs of children for enhanced achievement (Kirst, McLaughlin, & Massell, 1990). Although few, if any, NSSE chapters focused specifically on the topic of desegregation until the 1970s, when the courts began to adjudicate far more school desegregation cases than in previous years, since then the problems of de jure and especially de facto segregation, as well as other social and policy issues regarding inequitable school conditions, have become more salient in NSSE yearbooks (for the most current examples see Herman & Haertel, 2005; Stringfield & Land, 2002).

Despite ongoing legislative and community efforts to eradicate racial stratification, this country has not succeeded in uprooting segregationist practices. We still have not achieved educational excellence and equity for those that *Brown* was meant to impact. As James Anderson points out in his chapter for this volume, despite the many gains in equality under the law, the realities of unequal education today remain complicated and sobering.

Discussions in the Current Volume

This volume views *Brown v. Board of Education* as a starting point to frame discussions about issues of equity and excellence in education from different perspectives and with a particular focus on literacy. It situates *Brown* as an important historical effort that was aimed at *making a difference* in education, in particular having the potential to influence the literate lives of a large number of poor, marginalized, and historically underserved students. One key phrase became obviously significant in terms of working out, in practical terms, the implications of the *Brown* decision. The Court's injunction was that the Board of Education of Topeka, Kansas, and, by extension, all other school districts in the United States, had to "*make a prompt and reasonable start toward full compliance . . . [and to proceed] with all deliberate speed*" to educate children on a nondiscriminatory basis (*Brown v. Board of Education*, 1955, p. 300). According to Ogletree (2004), "While ordering the end of segregation . . . the Court removed much of the force of its decision by allowing proponents of segregation to end it not immediately but with 'all deliberate speed.' Those three words . . . reflect . . . the slow and ultimately unsuccessful effort to eliminate segregated education" (p. xiii).

As we recently celebrated the 50th anniversary of *Brown*, we recognized that we have not yet achieved the goal of equity and excellence in education for all students, particularly as it relates to issues of literacy. When we look at the fields of mathematics and science in education, we see some promising models that are moving in the direction of positive change. However, when we look at the field of literacy education, the picture has been disappointing for poor, marginalized, and underachieving students over the past 50 years, and particularly for students from diverse racial, ethnic, and cultural backgrounds. According to Prendergast (2003),

following *Brown* literacy became one of the most prominent battlegrounds on which struggles over what constituted racial discrimination and remedy were fought in the Supreme Court and in communities . . . If literacy has become the site of the struggle for racial justice since the civil rights movement, it is because it was for so many years the site of racial injustice in America. Throughout American history, literacy has been managed and controlled in myriad ways to rationalize and ensure White domination. In many states, before the Civil War, enslaved African Americans were restricted by law from learning to read and write. After Reconstruction, literacy institutions were closed against freed African Americans, and new forms of deterrence emerged along with segregation to stymie African American efforts to use the literacy they had acquired to exercise their rights as citizens and acquire property and employment. Up until the mid-twentieth century, literacy tests were used widely and often arbitrarily as a tool to disenfranchise African American voters and exclude immigrants configured as racially undesirable . . . The civil rights movement with its legislative mandates for desegregation and voters rights was suppose to end the tradition in America of using literacy to maintain inequities along racial lines. (pp. 1, 3, 4)

Both *Brown* and the Civil Rights Movement were unsuccessful at ending the American tradition of using literacy to maintain inequities along racial lines. Even though we have experimented with numerous campaigns designed to improve the academic literacies of low-income and culturally and linguistically diverse students, we find that neither phonics approaches or whole language approaches to literacy have worked out as anticipated, and even initiatives like the War on Poverty and Head Start have not proven to have the hoped for impact. Fifty-two years after *Brown*, educators and other stakeholders remain concerned that students from diverse racial, ethnic, socioeconomic, and linguistic backgrounds are still failing at disproportionately high rates, with reading scores that are still generally low and dismal writing skills. So the question remains: "What needs to happen before the passage of another 50 years in order for us to fully realize the potential of *Brown v. Board of Education*"? Our contributors, both national and global, remind us that we must move forward *with more deliberate speed.*

Based on what we have seen in the past, we can predict that failure to understand the complex manifestations of racism will most likely result in the absence of a systematic program of transformation. Moreover, by extension, we can predict that things will be much the same 50 years from now unless some critical things change. Using *Brown* as the focal point for beginning the conversation, we ask the question "How does and how should one look at the equity question from different perspectives as it relates to education, excellence, and literacy?" From the perspective of their areas of specialization, we have asked nine eminent scholars in the fields of history, linguistics, sociology, anthropology, language policy, and educational reform to provide contemporary analyses of what needs to happen before the passing of another 50 years for us to realize the full potential of *Brown* as it relates to issues of equity, excellence, and literacy. A responding scholar has then been asked to provide a commentary or reflective essay that expands the senior scholar's discussion. Given the significant topics covered in these chapters and the depth with which these topics are handled, students, teachers, teacher educators, researchers, and policymakers will find this volume an invaluable resource.

The first set of chapters in this volume present historical perspectives on the *Brown* ruling. James Anderson in "A Tale of Two *Browns*: Constitutional Equality and Unequal Education" highlights the amazing educational achievements of blacks and the irony of *Brown*'s undermining of these achievements. He proposes two tales of *Brown*: one a struggle for equality under the law, and the other an unfulfilled promise. He examines the place and meaning of *Brown* in the larger struggle for individual equality and challenges readers to redeem the unfulfilled promises of desegregation and educational equality, reminding us that redemption is not possible unless we are willing to face our past squarely and to commit to changing the deplorable inequalities of the present.

Joy Williamson in "A Tale of Two Movements: The Power and Consequences of Misremembering *Brown*" responds to Anderson's chapter by focusing on the revisionist history and textbooks that have perpetuated a "feel good" version of *Brown* and neglects the reality of the times, asserting, "We must go back and reclaim our past so that we can move forward; so we understand why and how we came to be who we are today." She juxtaposes historiographical tales of *Brown* and the black freedom struggle in the scholarly literature and in high school textbooks, and thus helps us understand the significance of what is unexamined.

Edmund Gordon and Beatrice Bridglall promote "The Affirmative Development of Academic Ability: In Pursuit of Social Justice." In this chapter, Gordon and Bridglall issue a call to scholars and researchers, honoring the legacy of the *Brown* plaintiffs and acknowledging the contributions of social scientist Kenneth Clark, in particular, to the arguments on behalf of *Brown*, to use their resources and prestige as advocates for children. They propose a program of *affirmative development* rather than affirmative action, focusing on ensuring opportunities to "develop and qualify" rather than simply gain admission, as a means of asserting and defending excellence and equity in education as a civil right and a civil liberty.

Carol Lee closes the section with her own tribute to Gordon in "The Affirmative Development of Academic Ability: In Pursuit of Social Justice—A Response to Edmund Gordon." In this chapter, Lee further examines the implications of *Brown* for conceptualizing our demands for social justice in education and for institution building that enhances adult support aimed at encouraging minority youth to develop a lasting sense of heritage and resilience.

Looking at the implications of *Brown* within a national context, John Baugh focuses on "Linguistic Considerations Pertaining to *Brown v. Board*: Exposing Racial Fallacies in the New Millennium." In this chapter, Baugh discusses the unique linguistic legacy of slavery and raises both pedagogical and policy issues around honoring children's home languages in the classroom. Linguistic evidence strongly confirms that race alone can no longer be considered adequate for the purpose of policy or social reform. Baugh calls for a reexamination of our assumptions to better meet the needs of our children.

Arnetha Ball and H. Samy Alim in "Preparation, Pedagogy, Policy, and Power: *Brown*, the *King* Case, and the Struggle for Equal Language Rights" extend Baugh's argument by calling for equal language rights through changes in policy, pedagogy, and teacher preparation. Using the *Martin Luther King Black English* case (1979) as a focal point, they discuss the historically neglected linguistic dimensions of the black American tradition and the educational responses to legal decisions such as *King* that mandate critical language awareness pedagogies and the redefinition of language barriers.

Bernard Gifford and Guadalupe Valdés in "The Linguistic Isolation of Hispanic Students in California's Public Schools: The Challenge of Reintegration" begin with a historical overview of the linguistic isolation of Latino students in California, tracing the evolving hostility toward Spanish and Spanish-speaking immigrants and examining the current policy climate surrounding the education of Latino immigrant students. They persuasively argue that continued segregation of English language learners holds back both Hispanic students and their "majority" classmates from optimal educational achievement.

Robert Jiménez responds to Gifford and Valdés's exposition of California's history of political and educational policy, examining Mexico's and the United States' long and complex relationship. He cautions that willful ignorance of the past and today's global realities is shortsighted, not only for students, but also in terms of the broad economic, political, and cultural consequences likely to result.

Kris Gutiérrez and Nathalia E. Jaramillo in "Looking for Educational Equity: The Consequences of Relying on *Brown*" challenge the belief that educational equity can be mediated by legal measures and federal and local reforms without transformation of the historical practices and ideologies that preserve supremacy and "White innocence"— a racialized analytic concept. They argue that equal access is a necessary but insufficient condition to restructure the policies and practices that support inequity, and they examine the misappropriation of the concept of equal access to support inequitable policies like No Child Left Behind.

Yolanda Majors and Sana Ansari in "A Multivoiced Response to the Call for an Equity-Based Framework" respond to Gutiérrez and Jaramillo with their discussion of black teacher educator–white pre-service teacher dynamics. They argue for an equity-based framework as a curriculum design principle in university classroom contexts to address destructive silences and create spaces for constructive conversations and the development of student awareness.

In the section featuring comparative reflections on *Brown v. Board of Education*, Jonathan Jansen focuses on "The Ties That Bind: Race and Restitution in Education Law and Policy in South Africa and the United States of America." In this chapter, Jansen discusses the history of institutionalized inequality as well as today's continuing struggles in both countries and examines the lessons each has to offer by exposing "the contradictions between law and reality" (de Groof & Lauwers, 2005 cited in Jansen, p. 226).

Chika Sehoole in "The Ties That Bind: A Response to Jonathan Jansen" builds on Jansen's work to examine the experiences of students and educators and the curriculum they experience in desegregated schools, arguing that the efficacy of education policies and laws that promise social justice should be judged by, literally, what actually changes. He draws important and fascinating parallels between the

hopes embodied in *Brown* and apartheid's end and both countries' growing understanding that legislation and policy change cannot compel
acceptance.

Neville Alexander in "*Brown v. Board of Education*: A South African
Perspective" looks at the implications for the shaping of social identities
and for cohesion of the society inherent in the implementation of a
South African affirmative action strategy, arguing against the promotion
of racial identities. Instead, he advocates making a principled decision
to problematize *all* racial categories and, instead, prioritize class as a
measure of disadvantage.

Monica Hendricks in "*Brown v. Board*: With All Deliberate Speed?"
responds to Alexander by arguing that activists must move beyond what
she labels as an "evidential vacuum" to truly confront continued segregation in South African schools. Motivated by her concern about the
quality of South African schooling and children's writing ability in
English, Hendricks considers the extent of integration and access
present in postapartheid schools and education's potential for not only
reproducing the status quo, but also for interrupting its reproduction.

Gloria Ladson-Billings begins the final section of the yearbook,
Looking Forward: Pressing Challenges That Lie Ahead, with a chapter on "The Meaning of *Brown* . . . for Now." Using a critical race
theory lens, she describes three typologies of response to *Brown* and
calls on one type—the "racial realists" who perceive *Brown* as a starting, rather than an ending, point—to mobilize to develop strategies
to confront the ongoing structural concerns that decades of neglect
have produced.

Carla O'Connor in "The Premise of Black Inferiority: An Enduring
Obstacle Fifty Years Post *Brown*" responds to Ladson-Billings by focusing on what she sees as mainstream America's reliance on the "black
pathology" or "acting white" perspectives to excuse a widespread
unwillingness to address racial inequities. She charges that academic,
popular, and professional interest in black pathology undermines any
real effort to make sense of black underachievement and to deliver on
the promise of *Brown*.

Joyce E. King in "'If Justice Is Our Objective': Diaspora Literacy
and Heritage Knowledge in the Praxis of Critical Studyin' for Human
Freedom," discusses the "miseducation" of black children and argues
for culturally relevant curriculum to foster true democratic education
for all students. Diaspora Literacy and Heritage Knowledge, the tools
of Critical Studyin', reference what students can and should know
about their own collective past and present in order to develop hope,

confidence, and a commitment to using their education and skills to benefit their community and humanity.

Maisha Fisher closes out the section with "Building a Literocracy: Diaspora Literacy and Heritage Knowledge in Participatory Literacy Communities." Fisher responds to King with her discussion of alternative knowledge, as embodied in hip-hop music, poetry slams, and other venues, and describes how one teacher and her students educate themselves about their African heritage and their power to both reflect on and change their worlds.

Kenji Hakuta completes the volume with an epilogue on "The Implications of *Brown v. Board of Education* in an Increasingly Diverse Society." As a linguistic minority education scholar, Hakuta notes that he, a beneficiary of *Lau v. Nichols* (1974), has always seen *Brown* as *Lau's* big brother. Hakuta looks back on the impact of *Brown* and ahead to upcoming challenges, writing from a perspective profoundly influenced by these landmark rulings.

Conclusion

The chapters in this volume support Charles Ogletree Jr.'s (2004) contention—"We cannot afford to wait another 50 years to find meaningful remedies to address the problems described in *Brown*" (p. xv)— by illustrating the range of issues that have emerged since the 1954 ruling. The authors in this book contribute meaningful responses to the question "What needs to happen before the passage of another 50 years in order for us to fully realize the potential of *Brown v. Board of Education*?" These responses represent multiple disciplinary perspectives, particularly as they relate to students from culturally and linguistically diverse backgrounds. The hope is that the volume will serve to document the current state of affairs as well as contribute to continuing research and practices that have the potential to fuel successful movement toward achieving our goals of excellence and equity for all students.

I extend my sincere thanks to the authors who have contributed to this volume. I thank them for their thoughtful and provocative contributions, which I hope will provide not only fuel for current and future dialogue on this topic, but also direction for action. I would like to express my deep appreciation to Robert Calfee for his wisdom and support throughout this project and to the members of NSSE who served as reviewers, offering thoughtful comments and insightful suggestions that were quite helpful to the authors as we prepared final versions of the chapters. Most of all, I would like to thank Debra Miretzky at the National Society for the Study of Education (NSSE) for her thorough reviews, patient prodding, helpful editing, and insightful suggestions throughout the project.

REFERENCES

Barbe, W.B., La Brant, L., Passow, A.H., & Witty, P. (1967). Introduction. In M.M. Coulson (Ed.), *The educationally retarded and disadvantaged. The sixty-sixth yearbook of The National Society for the Study of Education*, Part I (pp. 1–7). Chicago: National Society for the Study of Education.

Berry, B., & Ginsberg, R. (1990). Effective schools, teachers, and principals: Today's evidence, tomorrow's prospects. In B. Mitchell & L.L. Cunningham (Eds.), *Educational leadership and changing contexts of families, communities, and schools. The eighty-ninth yearbook of the National Society for the Study of Education*. Part II (pp. 155–183). Chicago: National Society for the Study of Education.

Brown v. Board of Education, 349 U.S. 294 (1955).

Chasin, G., & Levin, H.M. (1995). Thomas Edison accelerated elementary school. In J. Oakes & K.H. Quartz (Eds.), *Creating new educational communities. The ninety-fourth yearbook of the National Society for the Study of Education*, Part I (pp. 130–146). Chicago: National Society for the Study of Education.

Cole, M., & Bruner, J.S. (1972). Preliminaries to a theory of cultural differences. In I.J. Gordon (Ed.), *Early childhood education. The seventy-first yearbook of the National Society for the Study of Education*, Part II (pp. 161–179). Chicago: National Society for the Study of Education.

de Groof, J., & Lauwers, G. (2005). Increasing access to education throughout European society. In C. Russo, J. Beckmann, & J. Jansen (Eds.), *Equal educational opportunities: Comparative perspectives in education law. Brown v. Board of Education at 50 and democratic South Africa at 10* (pp. 35–54). Pretoria, South Africa: Van Schaiks Publishers.

Davis, J. (1913). Supervision of rural schools for Negroes. In S.C. Parker (Ed.), *The supervision of rural schools. The twelfth yearbook of the National Society for the Study of Education*, Part II (pp. 96–110). Bloomington, IL: Public School Publishing.

Ervin-Tripp, S. (1972). Children's sociolinguistic competence and dialect diversity. In I.J. Gordon (Ed.), *Early childhood education. The seventy-first yearbook of the National Society for the Study of Education*, Part II (pp. 123–160). Chicago: National Society for the Study of Education.

Gradisnik, A. (1980). Bilingual education. In F.M. Grittner (Ed.), *Learning a second language. The seventy-ninth yearbook of the National Society for the Study of Education*, Part II (pp.104–127). Chicago: National Society for the Study of Education.

Green, R.L. (1974). Northern school desegregation: Educational, legal, and political issues. In C.W. Gordon (Ed.), *Uses of the sociology of education. The seventy-third yearbook of the National Society for the Study of Education*, Part II (pp. 213–273). Chicago: National Society for the Study of Education.

Havighurst, R.J., & Dreyer, P.H. (Eds.). (1975). *Youth. The seventy-fourth yearbook of the National Society for the Study of Education*, Part I. Chicago: National Society for the Study of Education.

Herman, J., & Haertel, E. (Eds.). (2005). *Uses and misuses of data for educational accountability and improvement. The 104th yearbook of the National Society for the Study of Education*, Part II. Malden, MA: Blackwell Publishing.

Hollingworth, L.S. (1940). The significance of deviates. In G.M. Whipple (Ed.), *Intelligence, its nature and nurture: Comparative and critical exposition. The thirty-ninth Yearbook of the National Society for the Study of Education*, Part I (pp. 43–66). Bloomington, IL: Public School Publishing.

Jagers, R.F., & Carroll, G. (2002). Issues in educating African-American children and youth. In S. Stringfield & D. Land (Eds.), *Educating at-risk students. The 101st yearbook of the National Society for the Study of Education* (pp. 49–65). Chicago: National Society for the Study of Education.

Kirst, M.W., McLaughlin, M., & Massell, D. (1990). Rethinking policy for children: Implications for educational administration. In B. Mitchell & L.L. Cunningham

(Eds.), *Educational leadership and changing contexts of families, communities, and schools. The eighty-ninth yearbook of the National Society for the Study of Education*, Part II (pp. 69–90). Chicago: National Society for the Study of Education.

Lau v. Nichols, 414 U.S. 563 (1974).

Oakes, J., & Quartz, K.H. (Eds.). (1995). *Creating new educational communities. The ninety-fourth yearbook of the National Society for the Study of Education*, Part I. Chicago: National Society for the Study of Education.

Ogletree, C.J. (2004). *All deliberate speed: Reflections on the first half-century of* Brown v. Board of Education. New York: Norton & Company.

Padron, Y.N., Waxman, H.C., & Rivera, H.H. (2002). Issues in educating Hispanic students. In S. Stringfield & D. Land (Eds.), *Educating at-risk students: The 101st yearbook of the National Society for the Study of Education*, Part II (pp. 66–88). Chicago: National Society for the Study of Education.

Peterson, J. (1928). Comparison of white and Negro children in the rational learning test. In L.M. Terman (Ed.), *Nature and nurture: Their influence upon intelligence. The twenty-seventh yearbook of the National Society for the Study of Education*, Part I (pp. 333–342). Bloomington, IL: Public School Publishing Company.

Plessy v. Ferguson, 63 U.S. 537 (1896).

Prendergast, C. (2003). *Literacy and racial justice: The politics of learning after* Brown v. Board of Education. Carbondale, IL: Southern Illinois University Press.

Scribner, J.D., & Knox, O. (1973). The urban elementary school today. In J.I. Goodlad & H.G. Shane (Eds.), *The elementary school in the United States. The seventy-second yearbook of the National Society for the Study of Education*, Part II (pp. 327–349). Chicago: National Society for the Study of Education.

Sleeter, C. (1995). Curriculum controversies in multicultural education. In E. Flaxman & A.H. Passow (Eds.), *Changing populations/Changing schools. The ninety-fourth yearbook of the National Society for the Study of Education*, Part II (pp. 162–185). Chicago: National Society for the Study of Education.

Stringfield, S., & Land, D. (Eds.). (2002). *Educating at-risk students: The 101st yearbook of the National Society for the Study of Education*, Part II. Chicago: National Society for the Study of Education.

Swanson, M.C., Mehan, H., & Hubbard, L. (1995). The AVID classroom: Academic and social support for low-achieving students. In J. Oakes & K.H. Quartz (Eds.), *Creating new educational communities. The ninety-fourth yearbook of the National Society for the Study of Education*, Part I (pp. 53–69). Chicago: National Society for the Study of Education.

Wilkinson, D.Y. (1975). Black youth. In R.J. Havighurst & P.H. Dreyer (Eds.), *Youth. The seventy-fourth yearbook of the National Society for the Study of Education*, Part I (pp. 285–305). Chicago: National Society for the Study of Education.

Part One
Looking Back: Historical Perspectives on *Brown v. Board of Education*

CHAPTER 1

A Tale of Two Browns: *Constitutional Equality and Unequal Education*

JAMES D. ANDERSON

Derrick Bell (2004) begins his recent book on *Brown v. Board of Education* by recounting graduation day at Yale University in May 2002, when his long-standing mentor and friend, Judge Robert L. Carter, received an honorary degree. During the ceremony, Yale's president reminded the audience of Judge Carter's long and distinguished career as a federal judge, National Association for the Advancement of Colored People (NAACP) civil rights attorney, and partner in a large law firm. "When, though," Bell writes, "Yale University president Richard Levin announced that Judge Carter was an important member of the legal team that planned and argued the landmark case of *Brown v. Board of Education* . . . the audience leaped to its feet and, with great enthusiasm, applauded and cheered." As he stood and joined the applause, Bell wondered to himself: "How could a decision that promised so much and, by its terms, accomplished so little, have gained so hallowed a place . . . that its mere mention . . . sparked a contained but very real demonstration" (pp. 1–2).

Derrick Bell is not alone in wondering why *Brown* commands such "awe and respect" in a nation where racial and ethnic groups remain separate and unequal in its public schools. Indeed, the ethnic disparities in academic achievement, the resegregation of public schools, and the

James D. Anderson is a professor in the Department of Educational Policy Studies at the University of Illinois, Urbana-Champaign.

ever-widening disparities in school funding overshadow most of the positive gains made over the past 50 years. Consequently, the various scholarly works commemorating the landmark case emphasize *Brown*'s failure to eliminate racial segregation and inequality. The very titles and subtitles of books and articles, such as "Still Separate and Unequal" and "The Broken Promise of the *Brown* Decision," signify a tale of failure and disappointment rather than a legacy that commands awe and respect (Irons, 2002; Patterson, 2001; Rado, Little, & Aduroja, 2004). Nonetheless, in 2004, Americans commemorated *Brown* as perhaps the Supreme Court's most time-honored decision. Clearly, the 1954 decision has a complex and contradictory legacy (Bell, 2004; Breathett, 1983). Accordingly, this chapter seeks to assess *Brown*'s place in the nation's memory and history, both its undeniably important role in our long struggle for equality under the law and its unfulfilled promises of racial desegregation and educational equality.

This chapter has two basic objectives. First, I examine the place and meaning of *Brown* in the larger struggle for individual and racial equality. Because *Brown* redeemed promises of constitutional equality that had been rejected since the Declaration of Independence, its legal significance is national in scope and its meaning extends beyond the interest of any particular ethnicity, class, or gender. In vital respects, *Brown* achieved a hallowed place in American history and memory because it represents a watershed moment in the nation's quest for constitutional equality, a principle firmly articulated in the Declaration of Independence yet virtually abandoned in the U.S. Constitution until the Reconstruction era. Once Reconstruction ended in the late 1870s, however, equal protection under the law, due process of law for all individuals, and equal access to public accommodations were dealt crippling blows by the U.S. Supreme Court. By the end of the 19th century, southern states, increasingly undergirded by Jim Crow laws, spiraled downward toward extreme segregation and inequality, while northern states designed complex institutional arrangements to sustain day-to-day segregation and racial inequality. The principle of individual and racial equality was reasserted as a fundamental doctrine of American law with *Brown* and the Civil Rights Act of 1964. To be sure, *Brown* did not address important issues of equality, such as equal rights for women. Nonetheless, *Brown*'s direct contribution to the abolition of the racially "separate but equal" principle in American law provided the legal foundation for a significant expansion of democratic rights and changed the social and political terrain on which we continue to win and lose struggles for civil, political, and educational equality.

The second objective of this chapter is to provide an understanding of how the particular implementation of and resistance to *Brown* impacted the struggle for equal education. It is widely acknowledged that *Brown*'s direct impact on school desegregation and unequal education was limited and has become more circumscribed with each passing year. Moreover, the manner in which *Brown* was implemented, particularly in the South, devastated the careers of black educators, placed many black schoolchildren in hostile racial climates, dashed the hopes and dreams of those who expected full equality, and constructed painful memories of the African American experience. The landmark case is now viewed more as a "troubled legacy" than a milestone in achieving educational equality and first class citizenship. Its heritage of constitutional equality represents a pivotal shift in the history of American democracy, while its legacy of unequal public schooling stands, in the words of Jonathan Kozol (2005), as *The Shame of the Nation*. Only a tale of two *Browns* captures both its time-honored place in America's long-standing pursuit of formal equality under the law and its unfulfilled promises of substantive equality in American public education.

The First Tale of *Brown*: A Landmark in Democracy

The tale of formal or constitutional equality begins with the Constitution of 1787. Historian Stanley N. Katz (1988) reminds us that "the word 'equality' appears only once" in the 1787 Constitution, "and it does not apply to individuals" (p. 747). In fact, "constitutional equality, as expressed literally in the text fashioned by the Framers," writes Katz, "was no more than equal representation for all states in the upper house of the national legislature" (p. 747). During "most of American history . . . framers of constitutions, lawmakers and judges avoided committing the nation to the protection of individual equality" (p. 748). Further, Katz contends, "they proclaimed neither formal equality (the appearance of equal treatment of individuals) nor substantive equality (the identical treatment of individuals), for legal equality was not acceptable as a social or political goal before the Civil War" (p. 747).

In view of the Revolutionary ideology of equal rights for all men, an obvious question is, why was there no reference to equality for individuals in the Constitution of 1787? Katz (1988) concludes that American slavery, as much as any factor, precluded the framers from inserting the principle of equality into the body of the Constitution, observing: "Slavery, the 'peculiar institution,' was the most obvious reason why the Framers could not (or would not) write equality into the U.S. Constitution. How could the Constitution pronounce equality a general value when nearly one in every five Americans was enslaved?" (p. 749). Moreover, neither women, Native Americans, nor free persons of color held a legal or political status equal to men. Historian Edmund Morgan (1956) reached similar conclusions; in his words, "When the principle of equality encountered the South's vested interested in slavery, the conflict was irreconcilable, and in the summer of 1787 it was equality that had to give ground" (pp. 141–142). Although sacrificing the principle of equality may have "purchased the continuation of the union and made possible the national government," Morgan contends, the majority of the framers of the American Constitution knew that "they had thrown equality to the wind" (p. 142). Similarly, historian Gary Nash (2005) concludes, "The revolutionary generation's problem was not in its conception of universal rights, as expressed in the declaration, but rather its inability to honor them," especially in the framing of the Constitution (p. 212).

American lawmakers did not begin to honor the principle of individual equality until the immediate post-Civil War period. Out of the crucible of civil war and in the euphoria of abolitionism, Republicans enacted the principle of equality into the body of the Constitution with the passage of the 14th Amendment in 1868. The 14th Amendment established a broad definition of citizenship and required states to provide equal protection under the law and due process to all persons within their jurisdiction. With respect to equal rights, it was the most significant structural provision incorporated into the Constitution since its original framing. The triumph of equality in the immediate post-Civil War period, however, departed from a long tradition of resistance to equal rights. The passage of the 14th Amendment represented the commencement of a long and hotly contested struggle over the meaning of citizenship, equal rights, and due process in American democracy. Indeed, the last third of the 19th century was fraught with conflict and ambiguity over principles of individual and racial equality. Nowhere was this conflict more apparent than in Congress's first attempt to extend equal voting rights to African Americans in the District of Columbia.

The District of Columbia Voting Rights Debate

Early in 1866, Congress proposed a bill to extend voting rights to African Americans in the District of Columbia (Congressional Globe, 1866, p. 175). This highly contested bill and the extensive debate on the floor of the Congress exposed a nation deeply conflicted over the principle of constitutional equality. Two distinctive characteristics of this debate revealed the length and breadth of national ambivalence over equality. First, because the 11 Confederate states remained excluded from Congress, a southern view of racial equality was missing from the debate. Second, because Congress alone held jurisdiction over legislation in the District of Columbia, the debate over voting rights for African Americans was uncluttered by the usual issues of states' rights. The question was not whether a particular state wished to extend voting rights to free men of color, but whether this conception of democracy was favored by the federal government. In short, congressmen from the "free states" were free to consider the broader principle of equality in American democracy without the yoke of southern sectionalism or the constraints of states' versus federal rights. The responses heralded both the short-term victory in favor of equality and the long-term backlash against equality.

The bill and the debate. The proposed bill provided (1) that the word "white" be stricken from all laws prescribing the qualifications of voters for any office in the District of Columbia and (2) that no man could be disqualified from voting at any election in the district on account of color. Benjamin Markley Boyer, a Democrat from Pennsylvania, opposed voting rights for African Americans on several fronts, but primarily because of "the broad general principle that this is, and of right ought to be, a white man's Government" (Congressional Globe, 1866, p. 175). Similarly, Andrew Jackson Rogers, a Democrat from New Jersey, held "that the negroes are not entitled to the exercise of equal political privileges with the white man" (p. 202). John Winthrop Chanler, a Democrat from New York, also viewed the Constitution as a Magna Charter for *Herrenvolk* Democracy, the extension of civil and political equality to those within the dominant white group but not to those without (Fredrickson, 1973; Vickery, 1974). As Chanler stated before the House of Representatives on January 12, 1866,

I claim, sir, that this is a white man's Government, founded by white men to preserve and perpetuate the laws and customs of their race, and to extend the blessing of their civilization to the humblest creature. . . . Although the enjoyment of the benefits of our institutions may be open to all men, still the dominion belongs to the white man alone. It is his Government, to be preserved for his posterity in its purity, and administered with toleration and justice to all races of men who may find a home among us. (Congressional Globe, 1866, p. 202)

Constantly referring to the United States as a "White Democracy" or "White Representative Democracy," Chanler articulated the concept of a hierarchical multiracial democracy, arguing that democracy was a western form of government "held by the white race against all the other sons of Adam" (Congressional Globe, 1866, p. 202). John Adam Kasson, Republican from Iowa, feared that the right to vote would lead to African American domination of selected state governments. Arguing that constitutional equality should be restricted to the white race, he rejected the notion that voting was a natural right to be extended to all male citizens irrespective of color. Samuel Jackson Randall of Pennsylvania, a Democrat elected to the House in 1863, said, "I am unwilling to take any step in this Congress which will place the inferior [negro] race upon an equality with the white men of the country" (p. 261).

On the other side of this question stood the majority of Congressmen. George Washington Julian of Indiana, a Republican, pushed squarely for equality before the law. "Without the ballot," he argued, "no man is really free, because if he enjoys freedom it is by the permission of those who govern, and not in virtue of his own recognized manhood" (Congressional Globe, 1866, p. 256). Thus, declared Julian, "the real test of freedom is the right to share in the governing power" (p. 256), continuing, "Neither color, nor race, nor a certain amount of property, nor any other mere accident of humanity, can justify one portion of the people in stripping another portion of their equal rights before the law, the common master over all" (p. 252).

On January 18, 1866, the House of Representatives voted 116 to 54 (with 12 Representatives' abstentions) to extend suffrage to African Americans in the District of Columbia (Congressional Globe, 1866, p. 311). The proponents of the bill saw themselves less as leaders of a new frontier and more as the rightful heirs to the Revolutionary pledge that "all men are created equal." In the opinion of such congressmen as Sidney Clarke of Kansas, "the fathers affirmed the right of the free colored man to vote and share the Government with the free whites" (p. 303). That post-Revolutionary state constitutions instituted Black Codes denying free blacks the right to vote, according to Clarke, only proved the extent to which state governments had strayed from the ideas of the framers of the Declaration of Independence.

Sumner's crusade. Massachusetts senator Charles Sumner, the avant-garde leader of the post-Civil War congressional movement for equality under the law, explicitly characterized the "equal rights" campaign as a movement to redeem the noble ideas of the Revolutionary generation. Drawing upon the Declaration of Independence and the ideology of the American Revolution as the political and moral foundation for constitutional equality, Sumner sought to insert into the Constitution the ideas of "equality declared by our fathers in 1776" (quoted in Saxton, 1971, p. 36). He insisted that "the rebel states" could not rejoin the Union except "on the footing of the Declaration of Independence, with all persons equal before the law," declaring, "there shall be no discrimination on account of color" (quoted in Du Bois, 1935, p. 199). Although the protection of former slaves was the occasion for his pursuit of constitutional equality, Sumner sought to extend the principle of equality beyond the "rebel states" and to make it the foundation of American democracy. Proclaiming "equality in rights" as "the first of rights" (quoted in Du Bois, 1935, p. 194), he articulated his philosophy of democratic equality to fellow senators in 1866.

Foremost is the equality of all men. Of course, in a declaration of rights, no such supreme folly was intended as that all men are created equal in form or capacity, bodily or mental; but simply that they are created equal in rights. This is the first of the self-evident truths that are announced, leading and governing all the rest. Life, liberty, and the pursuit of happiness are among inalienable rights; but they are all held in subordination to the primal truth. . . . Thus is Equality the Alpha and the Omega, in which all other rights are embraced. . . . I simply insist that all shall be equal before the law, so that, in the enjoyment of this right, there shall be no restriction which is not equally applicable to all. (quoted in Du Bois, 1935, pp. 194–195)

Further proof that Sumner intended to make "equality of all men" the fundamental principle of democracy is evident in his campaign to amend the naturalization clause of the 1790 Immigration Act. The naturalization act passed by the First Congress specified that naturalized citizenship was limited to "any alien, being a free white person" and such restriction still prevailed in 1870 (Vecoli, 1996, p. 10). Sumner argued that the clause violated the principle of equality expressed in the Declaration of Independence and moved to delete "white" as a require-ment for naturalized citizenship. On July 4, 1870, during a congres-sional debate on the status of Chinese in the West, Sumner called for a racially neutral naturalization statute.

It is "all men" and not a race or color that are placed under the protection of the Declaration, and such was the voice of our fathers on the fourth day of July, 1776. . . . Now, Sir, what better thing can you do on this anniversary than to expunge from the statutes that unworthy limitation which dishonors and defiles the original Declaration? . . . The word "white" wherever it occurs as a limita-tion of rights, must disappear. Only in this way can you be consistent with the Declaration (quoted in Saxton, 1971, p. 37).

Sumner's fellow senators, voting 30 to 14 against removing the word "white" from the naturalization act, represented the declining national commitment to equal rights irrespective of race, creed, color, or national origins (Saxton, 1971). The movement to redeem the principle of constitutional equality inherent in the Revolutionary generation and the Declaration of Independence had made important strides (i.e., the Civil Rights Act of 1866 and the 13th, 14th, and 15th Amendments) during the immediate post-Civil War years. After 1870, however, Sumner and fellow reformers found it increasingly difficult to lead the nation to a full-fledged commitment to constitutional equality.

Sensing this backlash, Sumner and his colleagues renewed their efforts to expand individual and racial equality with legislation that specified rights that they believed were not secured explicitly by the Reconstruction Amendments. In May 1870, as a last gasp to stem the tide against constitutional equality, Sumner introduced an act granting equal rights in the use of railroads, steamboats, public conveyances, hotels, restaurants, licensed theaters, public schools, juries, and church organizations or cemeteries incorporated by national or state authority—moving beyond civil and political realms into the arena of what many regarded as "social rights." The original act underwent several revisions before it was finally passed in 1875.

Sumner died in 1874. His Civil Rights Act of 1875 was signed into law, but without a strong commitment to individual and racial equality for all citizens; as McPherson (1965) concluded, the act represented "a hollow achievement," because "its clause outlawing segregation in public schools" and related "social" areas "was stripped away before passage" (p. 493). The gutting of the act was particularly unfortunate, because two years earlier the Supreme Court had severely weakened the Equal Protection Clause of the 14th Amendment. In the *Slaughterhouse Cases* of 1873, interpreting the 14th Amendment to cover only federally guaranteed rights, the Supreme Court "nearly consigned the [14th] amendment to the trash heap" (Kluger, 1975, p. 56). A decade later, the Court's ruling in the *Civil Rights Case* of 1883 signaled additional movement to erode the principle of equality contained in the civil rights acts and constitutional amendments of the Reconstruction era. Defining the Equal Protection Clause of the 14th Amendment narrowly to cover civil and political rights as determined by the judges, the Supreme Court categorized a broad range of "social rights" for racial segregation and inequality (p. 57).

With respect to both racial and individual equality "the *Slaughterhouse* decision was the beginning of a long nightmare" that culminated in *Plessy v. Ferguson* (1896) (Kluger, 1975, p. 57). With *Plessy*, the Supreme Court further nullified the Equal Protection Clause by holding that the Louisiana legislature's policy of racial segregation in public transportation through the provision of comparable, but separate, accommodations was constitutionally "equal." It would be another 58 years before the principle of equal protection would be fully realized in *Brown* (Anderson, 2004). As Katz (1988) persuasively argued, "substantive equality (the notion that there is only one community of rights holders, that everyone is entitled to equal treatment in all aspects of life) came to maturity in constitutional jurisprudence in 1954 in *Brown v. Board of Education*" (p. 758).

In the aftermath of the *Brown* decision, the expansion of the fundamental principle of equality before the law spread quickly to new categories of people, strengthened by the passage of the Civil Rights Acts of 1957, 1960, 1964, and 1968 and the Voting Rights Act of 1965. "Civil rights," as Katz (1988) points out, "now took on a richer range of meaning, extending to employment, public accommodation, education and many new significant realms of public activity" (p. 759). For Americans coming to age in the post-*Brown* era, especially during the last third of the 20th century, "equality had become an operative, meaningful public value" (p. 759). Hence, *Brown* stands as the historical bridge between the principle of equality enacted in the 14th Amendment during the Reconstruction era and the Civil Rights Act of 1964, thereby securing its place in the hallowed halls of American democratic reforms—a "constitutional revolution" (p. 759). For racial and ethnic minorities, women, the handicapped and aged, English as a second language speakers, and children of undocumented immigrants, the *Brown* decision and its progeny redefined equality in American law and set forth a conception of equal rights unprecedented in American history. Without question, it is the watershed moment in the American pursuit of constitutional equality. Generations of progressive American reformers had sought to redeem the equality principle of the Declaration of Independence; that *Brown* achieved this redemption marks it as perhaps the U.S. Supreme Court's greatest contribution to the expansion of American democracy.

The Second Tale of *Brown*: A Double-Edged Sword

The other tale of *Brown* is the history of substantive inequality and of judicial remedies and institutional arrangements designed to address individual and racial equality in everyday life, particularly in public schools. From the outset of the Supreme Court's ruling in *Brown*, African Americans observed the efforts to enforce desegregation with caution and mixed emotions. Nonetheless, in the euphoria of the decision many hoped that the long battle against educational inequality, a process that had cheated their children out of anything resembling a quality education, could be won within a generation or two (Breathett, 1983). Their eyes were focused on equality more than on racial integration. Historically, and despite a limited amount of segregation in the North, public schools across the country had been racially segregated and remained so at the time of the *Brown* decision.

The story of African Americans' struggle for equal education, especially in the South where the vast majority of black children lived at the time of the *Brown* decision, begins, strangely enough, in the context of the relatively equal educational opportunities of the last third of the 19th century. Horace Mann Bond, writing in the 1932 inaugural issue of the *Journal of Negro Education*, documented the dramatic shift in educational resources, along racial lines, that began to undo these advances in the late 19th century. He noted, for example, that in 1890 African American children in Alabama, who comprised 44% of the school-age population, received 44% of public education funds. By 1930, African American schoolchildren, approximately 40% of Alabama's school-age population, received only 11% of the school funds (pp. 49–59). Similarly, African Americans in Mississippi, usually victims of the worst forms of racial subordination, received approximately 35% of the state school funding in 1890 as approximately 60% percent of the school-age population. A half-century later, the funding gap had widened; African Americans, then 57% of Mississippi's school-age population, received only 13% of the annual appropriation for public schools (Anderson, 1990, pp. 50–54). The black-to-white ratio of per pupil expenditures declined in every southern state between 1890 and 1910. In some states (Florida, Mississippi, Virginia, Louisiana), expenditures per black pupil actually fell in constant dollars. In other states, expenditures per black pupil grew at a much slower rate than spending per white pupil (Harlan, 1958). Vast inequalities emerged in every aspect of public education, especially in the construction and maintenance of school property. For example, in 1933, the total value of school property and equipment for African American public schools in Alabama was $4,734,701. The value for white public schools was almost 10 times greater: $49,291,477 (pp. 204–205). The shift from "relative equality" in the late 19th century to gross inequality in the early 20th century could be documented throughout the South (Harlan, 1958; Margo, 1990).

The political disenfranchisement of African Americans coupled with the judicial denial of civil and educational equality (e.g., *Cumming v. Richmond County Board of Education*, 1899, discussed further) precipitated a downward spiral, creating a state of public education that would become the central contention in *Brown* (Kousser, 1980). Massive financial discrimination against conveniently segregated African American schools often left black schoolchildren without tax-supported school buildings. Between 1900–50, discriminatory funding resulted in the diversion of per capita expenditures from African American children and led to the widespread practice of paying for their schools through private contributions of capital, land, and labor, a practice known as "double taxation." In other words, tax-supported school buildings were provided mainly for white children, while African Americans were relegated to a system of quasi-private elementary and secondary education. Such discrimination was most excessive in southern counties heavily populated by African Americans.

In 1915, for example, of the more than 1,000 schoolhouses for African American children in Alabama's "Black Belt," approximately 60% were privately owned. Things did not improve with time; by 1938, 70% of the 2,400 school buildings for African American children in Alabama were privately owned, many of them churches (Knight, 1940). Other southern states pursued a similar path of denying public funds for construction and maintenance of school property for black schoolchildren. In 1940, roughly half of all common schools for black children in Mississippi still met in tenant cabins, lodges, churches, and stores—privately owned structures that under state law could not be improved with public funds, and most of the 90 black high schools were privately owned by African Americans or built through grants from northern foundations. Sunflower County, Mississippi, a Delta county with a sizable black majority, maintained no publicly owned school buildings for African American children in 1950 (McMillen, 1989). In some instances, states even closed high schools or normal schools in order to deny educational opportunities to African American children. In 1904, for example, Mississippi Governor James Vardaman vetoed the appropriation for the State Normal School for Blacks in Holly Springs, arguing that for African Americans, "education only spoils a good field hand and makes a shyster lawyer or a fourth-rate teacher" (quoted in McMillen, 1989, pp. 84–85). As a result, the Holly Springs Normal School, which had trained 2,000 black public school teachers since opening in 1873, was forced to close.

Building a System of Schooling

In the face of such powerful and pervasive denial of educational opportunities to black children, African American communities across the South built an alternative system of universal education that was funded in significant part by private contributions from ordinary black citizens and northern philanthropy, along with some contributions from sympathetic southern whites. Between 1914 and 1932, ordinary African American citizens, despite living and working in cash-poor economies, raised over $4,725,000 to help construct nearly 5,000 Rosenwald Schools (see Anderson, 1988, for an account of this campaign), primarily for the education of black children in elementary schools. The cash total does not include the additional value of voluntary contributions in the form of land, labor, and materials. Moreover, in addition to the initial contributions to construct school buildings, African Americans raised hundreds of thousands of dollars annually to pay for the maintenance and improvement of grounds and buildings and to purchase basic equipment and school supplies (Anderson, 1988).

When the Rosenwald School building program began in 1914, southern states, especially in rural areas, were actively engaged in campaigns to solidify racially separate and unequal public school systems. The Rosenwald program, although unable to bridge the resource gap, did much to stem the tide of rapidly increasing inequality. Black southerners radically transformed the availability of common schools in their communities and, consequently, elementary school attendance increased sharply from 1900 to 1935. Rosenwald schools were built in 66% of the 1,327 southern counties, with their broadest reaches in South Carolina, Alabama, Louisiana, Maryland, North Carolina, and Virginia. By 1935, enough elementary schools had been constructed to accommodate the majority of young African Americans. In one generation, the elementary school attendance of young black children ages 5–14 increased from 36% (in 1900) to 90% (the same percentage as white children of the same age) in the early 1930s. This remarkable transformation rested squarely on the shoulders of ordinary African American men and women who invested their private dollars and waged a grassroots campaign to construct a common school system for black children in spite of state-sponsored racial discrimination (Anderson, 1988).

A parallel campaign to improve educational opportunities at the high school level proved more difficult and ultimately much less successful. The lack of access to public high schools was due in large part to the Supreme Court's ruling in *Cumming v. Richmond County Board of Education* (1899), a case in which the Court made clear that the "equal" in "separate but equal" did not require substantive equality. In 1897, the school board in Richmond County, Georgia, voted to close Ware High School and use the funds to support elementary schools for black children. The case made its way to the U.S. Supreme Court in 1899 and the Court ruled that the closing of Ware High school, the only public high school for African Americans in Georgia at that time, did not violate the Equal Protection Clause of the 14th Amendment. The ruling gave southern states a license to deny public high schools to African Americans. It was not until 1945 when Richmond County funded another full four-year public high school for its black students (Kousser, 1980), while the number of public high schools for white students in Georgia increased from 4 in 1904 to 122 in 1916.

This was not an isolated condition of inequality, but an example of a complex system of racial subordination extending throughout the South. In 1916, Mississippi, South Carolina, Louisiana, and North Carolina had no public high schools for African American children, who made up a significant proportion of each state's high school-age population. Florida, Maryland, and Delaware each had only one public high school for African American students in 1916 (Anderson, 1988). In general, throughout the first half of the 20th century African American youth in the South were largely excluded from public secondary education. On the eve of World War II, 77% of the high school-age black population in the South were not enrolled in public secondary schools and of those who were, few attended on a regular basis. The war worsened this situation as resources and personnel were diverted for military purposes. Between 1940–46, enrollment of African American students in public secondary schools in the South decreased further, and by the 1950s, more than two-thirds of African American high school-age students were still not enrolled in public high schools. The unavailability of public high schools contributed directly to gross inequality in high school graduation rates. Fairfax County, Virginia, had no public high schools for black students as late as 1956, and Sunflower County, Mississippi, had none as late as 1957 (National Education Association and the American Teachers Association, 1954, pp. 35–37).

Migrating North

In view of the appalling conditions of public education in the southern states, many African Americans migrated to the North in hopes of finding not only better jobs and living conditions, but also higher quality education. At the turn of the century, 90% of the country's black population lived in the South. Between 1915 and 1930, about 10% of (approximately 1,500,000) black southerners moved to the North (Douglas, 2005). However, northern schools were not the "promised land" that many of them envisioned. As Douglas has demonstrated, the migration of southern blacks to the North accompanied a rise in white supremacist views that "dismissed blacks as inferior and unfit for full participation in white civilization" (p. 125). As the northern black population grew between 1915 and 1954, so did the intensity of racially segregated public schools. According to Douglas, "by 1954, more northern black children attended predominantly black schools than ever before" (p. 274).

The segregation and subordination of African Americans in northern schools derive from a different history than the southern story. It is a history that is just being written and it deserves to be understood on its own terms. One important regional difference is that northern states in general had been committed to constitutional equality since the late 19th century. During the quarter century following the Civil War, most northern states reversed their pre-Civil War trends toward racially restrictive laws and enacted legislation prohibiting racial discrimination in public accommodations and banning public school segregation. Although the legal devices that drew a color line were discarded after the Civil War, such changes scarcely scratched the surface of the broader and deeper commitment to preserving racial segregation and inequality. In most places, African Americans remained fundamentally as they were before the war—victims of discrimination, social ostracism, segregation, and economic subordination. Hence, in spite of new laws banning school segregation, northern states and local school districts proceeded to develop institutional arrangements and cultural norms that fostered racially segregated schooling (Douglas, 2005). While some northern school segregation could be attributed to residential segregation, much of it, as Douglas documents, resulted from a variety of strategies created by local school boards to deliberately segregate children by race. "The most explicit form of school segregation," according to Douglas, "was the establishment of separate schools for black and white children, with pupil assignments conducted on a racial basis" (p. 141). State officials placed African American children in separate schools, in separate buildings on the grounds of a traditional white school, or in separate classrooms in an otherwise racially mixed school. Some teachers insisted upon racial separation within the classroom, requiring segregated seating arrangements in racially mixed classrooms. Many northern school districts excluded African American children from a variety of extracurricular activities such as athletics, cheerleading, school bands, plays, and talent contests, and from using spaces like swimming pools (Douglas, 2005).

The limited vision and reach of constitutional desegregation was already evident in the lives of many African Americans living in the North during the pre-*Brown* era. Judge Robert L. Carter, a member of the team that planned the strategies and argued the landmark case, knew from personal experience the persistence of educational inequality in states where racially discriminatory schooling was banned by law. As a teenager in Newark, New Jersey's desegregated schools, Carter experienced racial discrimination. Graduating from eighth grade, Carter was pleased to inform his teacher, Miss Vogel, that he had been accepted into the college preparatory curriculum at one of Newark's elite high schools. Normally one's teacher would take pride in such achievement, but Carter's success only served to anger Miss Vogel. As he recalled,

On the last day of school, when I informed Miss Vogel that I had enrolled in the classical college preparatory curriculum at Barringer High School— Newark's elite secondary public school at the time—she expressed anger and impatience. She said I should go to a vocational school and learn a trade. (Carter, 2005, p. 12)

Such an experience provides a glimpse into the underlying institutional practices that sorted African American and Latino students into the lowest curricular levels within northern desegregated schools, foreshadowing the challenges that southern blacks would face in the post-*Brown* era as constitutional equality and institutionalized educational inequality existed side by side. Nevertheless, hardly anyone anticipated such a dichotomy before 1954. Instead, most African Americans in the North and South viewed school desegregation as a means to end unequal education.

The Mixed Effects of Brown

The early post-*Brown* years witnessed significant improvements in school attendance and high school graduation rates for African

American schoolchildren, particularly among those residing in southern states. In 1960, the eighth grade was the terminal grade for the vast majority of the South's African American schoolchildren. Mississippi, with over 80% of its black population having completed fewer than 9 years of school, ranked first in the nation in the denial of high school opportunities to African American children. South Carolina and Georgia, with 79% and 75%, followed. By 1970, however, 31% of African Americans 25 years old and over had graduated from high school, and among younger persons (ages 20–24), 62% were high school graduates. By 1997, 86% of African Americans ages 25–29 were high school graduates, continuing the upward trend. Indeed, between 1987 and 1997, the gap in high school completion between African Americans and whites in the 25–29 group narrowed to the point where there was no significant difference (U.S. Department of Commerce, 1962, 1973). Increased access to public high schools was a direct consequence of *Brown*, although in some southern states improved high school opportunities for African Americans was meant to serve as a way to allay public school desegregation.

Despite these significant gains, setbacks, massive resistance, and, above all else, unfulfilled promises and expectations created feelings of ambivalence, resentment, and disappointment for many. Thus, the legacy of *Brown* continues to contain a tale of despair—the persistence of unequal education largely along racial lines. The post-*Brown* era is marked by a pattern of delay and forced compliance followed by subterfuge and backlash. The moderate and massive resistance campaigns designed to stifle compliance with *Brown* took their toll on African American communities, especially in the South. In the North, a small minority, aware of the limitations of desegregated schools, doubted whether the court's ruling would be enforced. However, among southern African Americans, with virtually no experience with desegregated schools or constitutional equality, very few of them could anticipate the effects of *Brown* on the day-to-day lives of black teachers, students, and parents. They would soon discover that *Brown* was a double-edged sword cutting them in ways they had never imagined.

Desegregation's Unexpected Consequences

Once black southerners acquired access to universal K-12 education, southern states systematically proceeded to dismantle the existing infrastructure that had been traditionally responsible for African American educational achievement. In 1968, after years of resistance, desegregation came suddenly to the South. The large majority of historically black public schools were shut down during the initial stage of school desegregation in the late 1960s and early 1970s. Historian David Cecelski (1994) captured the impact of school closings on the African American community:

Blacks lost important symbols of their educational heritage in this process. When black schools closed, their names, mascots, mottos, holidays, and traditions were sacrificed with them, while the students were transferred to historically white schools that retained those markers of cultural and racial identity. When former black high schools did not shut down, they were invariably converted into integrated junior high or elementary schools. White officials would frequently change the names given the school buildings by the black community and would remove plaques or monuments that honored black cultural, political, or educational leaders. They hid from public view trophy cases featuring black sports teams with those used by the white schools. The depth of white resistance to sending their children to historically black schools was also reflected in the flames of the dozens of these schools that were torched as desegregation approached. (pp. 8–9)

Further, school desegregation devastated an entire generation of black educational leadership and ended the careers of tens of thousands of African American teachers. As Hudson and Holmes (1994) documented, an estimated 38,000 black teachers and administrators lost their jobs in 17 southern and border states between 1954 and 1964. Another 21,515 African American teachers lost their jobs between 1984 and 1989 (pp. 383–393). Similarly, Cecelski (1994) documents the change in the numbers of African American principals in North Carolina's elementary schools, from 620 in 1963 to only 170 in 1970; 209 African American principals had headed high schools in 1963, but less than 10 headed remained in 1970. By 1973, only three black principals had survived the process of wholesale displacement (pp. 8–9).

Between 1967 and 1970, the number of African American principals in Alabama dropped from 250 to 40, and, according to Haney (1978), "Mississippi lost almost all of its black principals during the same period" (p. 94). Kentucky had about 350 African American principals in 1954; the number dropped to 36 by the 1969–70 academic year (Fultz, 2004). Fultz concludes, "The displacement of Black educators was part and parcel of the myriad ways southern white hegemony sought to undermine desegregation and to curtail African-American rights and progress, in order to maintain power and privilege" (pp. 28–29). The cumulative impact of these changes devastated the basic infrastructure of African American education in the South. Many com-

munities faced the daunting task of coping without traditional systems
of support while transitioning into new systems of desegregation that
were poorly organized and resistant to the aspirations of African
American children. The nature of this transition was not inevitable.
Rather, it reflected the thoughtless manner in which states and localities
prepared for desegregation, as well as the continuing resistance by
white-dominated state and local governments to the educational
progress of African American schoolchildren.

Few if any African Americans were prepared for the mass closings
of historically black public high schools that, along with churches, were
the most cherished social and cultural institutions in their communities.
Black principals and teachers were among the most important voices
and role models in local communities. African American neighborhoods
in general were not prepared for a form of school desegregation that
brought with it so many losses and resulted in the placement of their
children into social and academic contexts that were not only culturally
different, but also often hostile. Ultimately, strong feelings of ambivalence and resentment emerged among African Americans in the 1970s,
especially among those students who spearheaded the transition from
segregated schools to desegregated schools. By then, few African
Americans failed to raise objections to school closings and teacher
displacement and many of those who had supported the mid-20th-
century struggle for desegregated schools harbored serious doubts as to
whether any conceivable enforcement of the *Brown* decision could ever
achieve educational equality for African Americans. As the prospects for
desegregation became increasingly bleak in the urban north, particularly following *Milliken v. Bradley*[1] in 1974, African American voices
called for community control and effective schools in what seemed
destined to be predominantly minority school districts. Even today, as
reflected in *Williams v. State of California*,[2] the emphasis is on "adequate
schools" as opposed to "desegregated schools." In significant part, this
shift in focus reflects a profound disbelief in the promise of *Brown*.

The Tale of Two *Browns*

Thus, there remains a "tale of two *Browns*." We revere its democratic victory for equality before the law, even as we are deeply disturbed
with the resulting failure to achieve educational equality.

A recent graduation, ordinarily a joyous occasion, poignantly
reminds us of the scars that *Brown* inadvertently created. As is now well
known, in 1959, rather than comply with the mandate of *Brown*, Prince

Edward County, Virginia, simply shut down its schools for 5 years. Most white students turned to private academies created exclusively for them and funded in part by state tuition grants. Black families in Prince Edward County were devastated, and although some went to other localities and states to receive an education, many students never graduated from high school. On May 16, 2004, about 200 men and women, now in their 50s, donned caps and gowns to receive honorary high school diplomas, a symbolic version of what they were denied approximately 40 years ago. One Prince Edward resident, Clem Venable, reluctantly accepted the honorary degree. "It's of no use, I'm almost 55," says Venable, "I don't need them to give me a piece of paper now. What I needed they can't give me back" (Schouten, 2004, p. 5D).

Venable speaks for generations of Americans. There are times that we cannot relive and debts that cannot be paid. We can only understand and appreciate what happened and then make our own choices about building a better future. As Maya Angelou (1993) states so profoundly, "History, despite its wrenching pain, cannot be unlived, and if faced with courage, need not be lived again." Can Americans face squarely the past of segregation and inequality and their continuing effects? Put another way, can we recognize and understand not only what happened in Prince Edward County, and to all students who were denied a quality education, but also appreciate the consequences for their children and grandchildren? The nation's memory of *Brown* should be a constant call to redeem the unfulfilled promises of desegregation and educational equality. Yet, the historical record suggests redemption is not possible unless we are willing to face our past squarely, commit the resources necessary to changing the deplorable inequalities of the present, and embrace an underlying commitment to substantive equality as opposed to merely celebrating the triumph of constitutional equality.

America remains a nation of racially separate and unequal education. In an analysis of the recent Trends in International Mathematics and Science Study, known as TIMSS 2003, David Berliner (2005) disaggregates test performance by poverty and race. He found that America's white students (without regard for social class) are among the highest performing students in the world. "But our African American and Hispanic students, also undifferentiated by social class, were among the poorest performing students in this international sample" (p. 19). Among 27 industrialized democracies, the white American students ranked third in mathematics achievement, while the average scores for African American and Latino students put them ahead of only Luxembourg and Mexico. Given the nation's long struggle for the essential right of equality and the promise of *Brown*, this state of affairs reflects badly on a nation that is eager to spread "democracy" around the world. Our pride in the advancement of constitutional equality should be matched by our shame regarding the state of unequal education in contemporary institutional life. A nation that celebrates *Brown's* promise of educational equality in a democratic society built on individual and racial equality has every reason to be ashamed of *Brown's* unfortunate legacy of unequal educational opportunities.

NOTES

1. *Milliken v. Bradley* (1974) placed an important limitation on the first major Supreme Court case concerning school busing, *Swann v. Charlotte-Mecklenburg Board of Education* (1971), by holding that such remedies could extend across district lines only where there was actual evidence that multiple districts had deliberately engaged in a policy of segregation. This case effectively ended all hopes of desegregating urban schools via a metropolitan remedy.

2. *Williams v. State of California* (2005) was a statewide class action lawsuit about California's duty to provide every public school student with instructional materials, safe and decent school facilities, and qualified teachers.

REFERENCES

Anderson, J.D. (1988). *The education of Blacks in the south, 1860–1835*. Chapel Hill: University of North Carolina Press.

Anderson, J.D. (1990). Black rural communities and the struggle for equal education during the age of Booker T. Washington, 1877–1915. *Peabody Journal of Education*, 67(4), 46–62.

Anderson, J.D. (2004). The jubilee anniversary of *Brown v. Board of Education*: An essay review. *History of Education Quarterly*, 44(1), 154.

Angelou, M. (1993, January 20). Inaugural poem. Retrieved April 2, 2006, from http://poetry.eserver.org/Angelou.html

Bell, D. (2004). *Silent covenants:* Brown v. Board of Education *and the unfulfilled hopes for racial reform*. New York: Oxford University Press.

Berliner, D.C. (2005). Our impoverished view of educational reform. *Teachers College Record*. Retrieved February 12, 2006, from http://www.tcrecord.org

Bond, H.M. (1932). Negro education: A debate in the Alabama Constitution. *Journal of Negro Education*, 1(1), 49–59.

Breathett, G. (1983). Black educators and the United States Supreme Court decision of May 17, 1954 (*Brown v. the Board of Education*). *Journal of Negro History*, 68(2), 201–208.

Carter, R.L. (2005). *A matter of law: A memoir of struggle in the cause of equal rights*. New York: The New Press.

Cecelski, D.S. (1994). *Along freedom road: Hyde County, North Carolina, and the fate of black schools in the south*. Chapel Hill: University of North Carolina Press.

Congressional Globe. (1866). 39th Congress, House of Representatives, 1st Session (January 11), 202; (January 12), 202; (January 15), 238; (January 16), 261; (January 18), 303.

Cumming v. Richmond County Board of Education, 175 U.S. 528 (1899).

Douglas, D.M. (2005). *Jim Crow moves North: The battle over Northern school segregation*. New York: Cambridge University Press.

Du Bois, W.E.B. (1935). *Black reconstruction in America: An essay toward a history of the part which black folk played in the attempt to reconstruct democracy in America, 1860–1880*. New York: Harcourt, Brace and Company.

Fredrickson, G.M. (1973). *The black image in the white mind: The debate on Afro-American character and destiny, 1817–1914*. New York: Harper and Row.

Fultz, M. (2004). The displacement of black educators post-*Brown*: An overview and analysis. *History of Education Quarterly*, 44(1), 11–45.

Haney, J.E. (1978). The effects of the *Brown* decision on black educators. *The Journal of Negro Education*, 47(1), 88–95.

Harlan, L.R. (1958). *Separate and unequal: Public school campaigns and racism in the southern seaboard states, 1901–1915*. Chapel Hill: University of North Carolina Press.

Hudson, M.J., & Holmes, B.J. (1994). Missing teachers, impaired communities: The unanticipated consequences of *Brown v. Board of Education* on the African American teaching force at the precollegiate level. *The Journal of Negro Education*, 63(3), 388–393.

Irons, P. (2002). *Jim Crow's children: The broken promise of the* Brown *decision*. New York: Viking.

Katz, S.N. (1988). The strange birth and unlikely history of constitutional equality. *The Journal of American History*, 75(3), 747–762.

Kluger, R. (1975). *Simple justice: The history of* Brown v. Board of Education *and black America's struggle for equality*. New York: Vintage Books.

Knight, E.W. (1940). *A study of higher education for Negroes in Alabama*. Series 1, Subseries 3, Box 384, Folder 4013, General Education Board Files. Pocantico Hills, NY: Rockefeller Archives.

Kousser, J.M. (1980). Separate but equal: The Supreme Court's first decision on racial discrimination in schools. *The Journal of Southern History*, *46*(1), 17–44.

Kozol, J. (2005). *The shame of the nation: The restoration of apartheid schooling in America*. New York: Crown Publishing Company.

Margo, R.A. (1990). *Race and schooling in the South, 1880–1950*. Chicago: University of Chicago Press.

McMillen, N.R. (1989). *Dark journey: Black Mississippians in the age of Jim Crow*. Urbana: University of Illinois Press.

McPherson, J.M. (1965). Abolitionists and the Civil Rights Act of 1875. *The Journal of American History*, *52*(3), 493–510.

Milliken v. Bradley, 418 U.S. 717 (1974).

Nash, G.B. (2005). *The unknown American Revolution: The unruly birth of democracy and the struggle to create America*. New York: Viking.

National Education Association and the American Teachers Association. (1954). *Progress of the education of Negroes, 1870–1950*. Washington, DC: National Education Association.

Patterson, J.T. (2001). Brown v. Board of Education: *A civil right's milestone and its troubled legacy*. New York: Oxford University Press.

Plessy v. Ferguson, 63. U.S. 537 (1896).

Rado, D., Little, D., & Aduroja, G. (2004, May 9). Still separate, unequal. *Chicago Tribune*, Section 1, pp. 1, 14–15.

Saxton, A. (1971). *The indispensable enemy: Labor and the anti-Chinese movement in California*. Berkeley: University of California Press.

Schouten, F. (2004, April 28). Town that resisted in '59 tries to right a wrong. *USA Today*, p. 5D.

Swann v. Charlotte-Mecklenburg Board of Education, 402.U.S. 1 (1971).

U.S. Department of Commerce (1962). Bureau of the Census, 1960 Census of Population. Supplementary Report (PC S1-37), *Enrollment and educational attainment for the United States; 1960*. (December 27).

U.S. Department of Commerce (1973). Bureau of the Census, 1970 Census of Population. Supplementary Report, *Educational attainment by age, sex, and race for the United States; 1970*. (April).

Vecoli, R.J. (1996). The significance of immigration in the formation of an American identity. *The History Teacher*, *30*(1), 9–27.

Vickery, K.P. (1974). "Herrenvolk" democracy and egalitarianism in South Africa and the U.S. South. *Comparative Studies in Society and History*, *16*(3), 309–328.

Williams v. State of California, *supra*, 34 Cal. 3d at 26–28 (2004).

CHAPTER 2

A Tale of Two Movements: The Power and Consequences of Misremembering Brown

JOY ANN WILLIAMSON

If, as James Anderson stated, a nation committed to democracy and equality has every reason to be ashamed on *Brown v. Board of Education*'s 50th anniversary, why the commemoration and celebration (this volume, pp. 14–35)? An answer to that question is the mission of this chapter. By revising Anderson's challenge to examine the complex role of *Brown* in the nation's memory and history, the chapter investigates *how* the decision and the broader black freedom struggle are memorialized, *why* the story is told in a particular way, and the *consequences* of that portrayal in understanding the nature of American democracy and equality. An examination of the historiography of the movement and its judicial embodiment, *Brown* offers more than a nuanced understanding of the past; the way we write and understand history often tells us what we want to believe about ourselves in the present. In other words, our interpretations of history expose our conceptions of reality that, in turn, color the way in which we make sense of the world around us. Examining the particular tales of the black freedom struggle and *Brown* is useful in a volume dedicated to the question of what needs to happen before the close of another 50 years. In the spirit of the Akan word, *Sankofa*, "We must go back and reclaim our past so that we can move forward; so we understand why and how we came to be who we are today" ("About Sankofa," n.d.).

To accomplish this task, the first section of the chapter examines two of the historiographical tales of *Brown* and the black freedom struggle in the scholarly literature. The conventional narrative and the revisionist narrative tell very different stories of the origins and goals of the movement, the major players in social reform, and the measures

Joy Ann Williamson is an associate professor (teaching) in the School of Education at Stanford University. Her research focuses on the relationship between social movements and higher educational institutions during the middle 20th century.

of success. Conventional scholars focus on the role of the federal government and a spirit of American goodwill in their story of the black freedom struggle while revisionists focus on local black communities and their ability to mobilize, organize, and coordinate collective action in the face of white intransigence and halfhearted federal support. Both conventional scholars and revisionists recognize the importance of *Brown*, but they position it differently in the black freedom struggle. Conventional scholars portray it as the beginning of the movement and as the codification of the movement's desire for desegregation. Revisionists, on the other hand, position the decision in a broader and longer black freedom struggle that did not begin in 1954 and whose primary aim was not racial integration but political power and human dignity. These two ideological positions on the black freedom struggle are hotly debated in scholarly circles, particularly because historians and social movement scholars understand that interpretations of the black freedom struggle offer a tool to understand social reform, democracy, and the American identity.

The second part of the chapter investigates the treatment of the black freedom struggle and the *Brown* decision in high school history textbooks. While the scholarly community debates the interpretation of the movement, the textbooks portray—for the most part—the conventional story of the movement in which the federal government is considered valiant and the American populous is described as morally righteous and activist. As state regulated and mandated texts, the books and their interpretive framework carry enormous weight and authority. They do not encourage students to understand textbook content as a representation of a particular ideological position. Rather, their tone promotes that students recognize them as "the facts, ma'am, just the facts." Teachers can and do teach against the text, but the textbooks still merit special attention because they represent the decisive, objective, and state sanctioned truth of American history. With regard to the black freedom struggle and the *Brown* decision, the textbooks carry a message to students about the past that intentionally colors the way that students will understand America in the present.

The Two Tales in Scholarly Work

The first tale of the movement, the conventional interpretation, focuses on the central role played by the federal government and national protest organizations. In these accounts, the Supreme Court, presidential mandates, and legislative action take center stage; the movement's national agenda is geared toward judicial and legislative reform; and the movement's successes are measured in federal policies like the *Brown* decision, the 1964 Civil Rights Act, and the 1965 Voting Rights Act. Organizations like the National Association for the Advancement of Colored People (NAACP) and magnetic personalities like Dr. Martin Luther King Jr. are credited with devising an overarching movement strategy and organizing the massive direct-action campaigns taking place in localities throughout the South. Americans were receptive to the agenda of the movement, according to this literature, because elected officials and judges simply formalized the newly liberal, equalitarian, and democratic spirit of the American populous in the wake of World War II (Branch, 1988; Burns, 2004; Farmer, 1985; Lewis, 1970; Meier & Rudwick, 1973; Rosenberg & Karabell, 2003; Schlesinger, 1965; Weisbrot, 1990). As David Levering Lewis states,

Fascism's doctrinal depravity, the solidarism of the war effort, and the trauma of the Holocaust deeply affected the collective American mind. There were not a few white southerners, and probably a majority of white northerners, who would have wished to say to the first sit-in students, as did the woman in the Greensboro Woolworth's, "you should have done this ten years ago" (Sitkoff, 1981, p. 70). (cited in Lewis, 1986, p. 7)

Americans, except for extreme and rabid racists, supported the movement, and a coalition of elite black and white men in Washington, DC, worked in tandem to break the back of segregation.

The conventional interpretation offers a particular version of *Brown*. Blacks, long an aggrieved group in American society, began to grow restless with the racial hierarchy in the South. Where would they turn to have their grievances heard? White southern legislatures had all the political power, and the U.S. Congress had proven it would not divide itself by offending southern congressmen. "There was an avenue, however, through which the advocates of equal rights for blacks could press their cause: the judiciary" (Ravitch, 1983, p. 119). A dedicated and interracial cadre of lawyers in the NAACP Legal Defense Fund chipped away at legally enforced segregation. The litigation eventually wound its way to the U.S. Supreme Court, which heard the "pained depths of the black man's cry for justice" and used its moral authority "to see that justice realized" in the *Brown* decision (Wilkinson, 1979, p. 5). The Court's moral righteousness not only struck dead racial segregation, it birthed the Civil Rights Movement, in that it awoke the slumbering masses of blacks to the desire for equality. Spurred to action, they

organized and continued to use the friendly courts for redress. When
southern whites resisted the march toward equality, the Court, the
federal government, and an interracial group of activists formed "a
mystical, passionate union" (p. 5) toward the "clear and unambiguous
goal . . . [of making] America a color-blind society" (Ravitch, p. 114).
The decision, one of the most important markers of the Civil Rights
Movement's success, stands as a testament to the well-oiled machinery
of democracy.

This type of analysis has received heavy criticism from scholars who
employ different frameworks with which to tell the story of the black
freedom struggle. These scholars, usually called revisionists, argue that
reducing the struggle to a protest movement seeking judicial and legislative redress distorts its broader purpose of achieving equal opportunity, political power, and human dignity. Further, they argue that the
conventional story of the movement overemphasizes the role of
national organizations in mobilizing black southerners, ignores the
lukewarm nature of federal support, minimizes the violent resistance
activists encountered, ignores the role played by local activists in southern communities, and overestimates an American consensus on support
for social reform. Federal policy changes were important and welcome,
particularly because they lent credence and psychological sustenance to
movement activists; but such victories came slowly after years of intense
agitation by black activists and were followed by reluctant (if not non-
existent) federal enforcement. Revisionist scholars believe that focusing
on federal mandates and the ruminations of elite men distorts the
complexity of the historical process and the daily struggle against white
supremacy (Carson, 1986; Morris, 1984; Payne, 1995).

These scholars tell a different story about *Brown*. A relatively new
literature argues that the emergence of the Cold War precipitated
federal policy shifts and overtly influenced the Supreme Court decision
(Dudziak, 2000; Layton, 2000; Plummer, 1996; Skrentny, 1998). Communist countries had harangued the United States for outright hypocrisy and used accounts of intense white resistance to black equality to
discredit America's international agenda. The U.S. government mar-
shaled its forces to combat such media representations but could do
little because southern whites provided ample and violent evidence of
their support for a racial hierarchy. As the Justice Department argued
in an amicus curiae brief supportive of the NAACP's case, "the existence
of discrimination against minority groups in the United States has an
adverse effect upon our relations with other countries. Racial discrimination furnishes grist for the Communist propaganda mills, and it

raises doubts even among friendly nations as to the intensity of our devotion to the democratic faith" (decimal file, cited in Dudziak, 2004). In other words, the repressive and inhumane treatment of African Americans by whites was bad press for a country attempting to sell the concept of democracy abroad. The federal government hoped that the Supreme Court decision would provide an example of the righteousness of the American system of government. This interpretive framework for understanding *Brown* shatters the picture of the federal government as a purely benevolent force enacting the desires of an eager American public. It is also a critique of the lofty position usually assigned to the American legal system in the retelling of *Brown*. As Dudziak (2004) reminds us,

Domesticating the case elevates the role of the legal system as an engine of progressive social change. Law was put to much good use during the civil rights era. But examining the broader forces producing legal change helps us see *Brown's* historical contingency. *Brown* was the product of converging domestic and international developments, rather than an inevitable product of legal progress. (p. 40)

Other revisionist literature on the movement challenges the conventional narrative's use of *Brown* as a starting point for the black freedom struggle. Marking the movement's beginning at 1954 severs it from its antecedents and assumes that integration was its primary goal. Rather, these scholars highlight the continuity of the struggle by examining local southern black organizing efforts and white resistance in the immediate post-World War II era (Chafe, 1980; Dittmer, 1994; Fairclough, 1995; Morris, 1984; Norrell, 1985; Payne, 1995; Raines, 1977; Thornton, 2002). Blacks used churches and created local protest organizations to form an effective wedge against white supremacy and sometimes advocated an agenda distinctly different from the integrationist goals of national organizations like the NAACP. For instance, black activists in Mississippi formed the Regional Council of Negro Leadership in 1951—3 years before *Brown*. The organization focused its efforts on economic interests, eliminating police harassment of black motorists, and voter registration—not the desegregation of Mississippi's schools (Dittmer, 1994; Payne, 1995).

In addition, local NAACP chapters sometimes clashed with the national leadership over the path of the movement and the mechanisms that could be employed to further it. Medgar Evers, the Mississippi Field Secretary of the NAACP, frequently expressed frustration with

the national office's myopia with regard to school desegregation and its
lack of support for local boycotts and demonstrations against economic
injustice (Dittmer, 1994; Evers & Marable, 2005). The involvement of
Martin Luther King Jr. and the support of national organizations in
local direct action campaigns garnered media attention, but crediting
them with making the movement is misguided, according to these
scholars. Local activists, many of them women, had organized an offen-
sive before their arrival and sustained the movement after their departure (Collier-Thomas & Franklin, 2001; Payne, 1995). Similarly, *Brown*
did not awaken the sleeping black masses; they were already in the
process of agitating and organizing. What the decision did was escalate
the movement and place the conflict between the federal government
and the states in stark relief. Viewed in this way, *Brown* remains an
important decision, but it becomes a part of an older tradition of African
American agitation for dignity, equal opportunity, and full citizenship
(Dittmer, 1994; Feldman, 2004; Franklin, 1967; Kelley, 1990; Martin
& Sullivan, 2000).

Revisionist scholars also challenge the conventional narrative's use
of the 1965 Voting Rights Act as an end point for the movement,
particularly when it is used to truncate the black freedom struggle,
position the Black Power Movement against the Civil Rights
Movement, and create two artificially separate movements with different agendas and legitimacy. The conventional narrative characterizes
the good 1960s, nee the Civil Rights Movement, with descriptions of
interracial coalitions and an American consensus on the evils of racism.
The early part of the decade becomes an example of good people
working together in a nonviolent struggle toward greater inclusion in
the American dream. The bad 1960s, nee the Black Power Movement,
are characterized by racially separate groups with racially chauvinist
agendas that precipitated the "disuniting of America" (Schlesinger,
1992; see also Bloom, 1987; Ravitch, 2000). The Civil Rights Movement represented a shining moment in American democracy that went
horribly wrong when it traveled north of the Mason-Dixon Line. At
that point, a movement peopled by middle-class blacks with justifiable
grievances morphed into an urban, radical, and working-class phenomenon geared toward the destruction of the social order.

This artificial split in the movement feeds the conventional narrative's message that moral suasion, normative and institutionalized routes
to social reform, interracialism, and nonviolence are the only valid
means of bringing grievances. Any other type of agitation, according to
particularly conservative scholars, is considered destructive, racist,

unpatriotic, and illegitimate (Bloom, 1987; Ravitch, 1983, 2000; Schlesinger, 1992). Juxtapositions between radical and acceptable are drawn to drive the point home: the Black Panther Party versus the NAACP; the Student Nonviolent Coordinating Committee (from the late 1960s, when it adopted Black Power ideology and ousted whites) versus the Southern Christian Leadership Conference (SCLC); Malcolm X versus Martin Luther King Jr. They are positioned against each other as a way to turn difference into polar opposite. These histories of the movement obscure the fact that *all* these groups and individuals were considered radical in their contemporary contexts, and *none* enjoyed such a broad base of support that they easily won their battles against white supremacy: the state of Alabama outlawed the NAACP; state officials targeted ministers in the SCLC with injunctions and arrests; and COINTELPRO, the federal government's Counter Intelligence Program, sought to discredit and undermine Martin Luther King Jr. (Garrow, 1986; Morris, 1984). Certainly, the activists of the later 1960s juxtaposed themselves against tactically conservative organizations as a rhetorical strategy to gain support, recruit members, and energize the movement (Breitman, 1990; Newton, 1973; Sellers, 1973). So, too, is this a tactic when historians employ such juxtapositions.

The Significance of Interpretation

The fact that the story of the black freedom struggle can be told in different ways is more than an interesting historiography of the literature. It has important implications for how Americans understand racism, social reform, and American democracy. In the conventional interpretation, we are told that legal channels are the most legitimate recourse for grievances, that the federal government is a friend to aggrieved parties, and that the United States is the Mecca of opportunity. Just be patient, these historians say, the democratic ideal is near. In the words of Arthur Schlesinger Jr. (1992), "Our democratic principles contemplate an open society founded on tolerance of differences and on mutual respect. In practice, America has been more open to some than to others. But it is more open to all today than it was yesterday and is likely to be even more open tomorrow than today. The steady movement of American life has been from exclusion to inclusion" (p. 134). An essentialized and mischaracterized *Brown* decision plays a central role in this narrative and is treated as the judicial embodiment of all that is right with America.

However, if, on the other hand, we understand the black freedom struggle from the vantage point of the revisionists, we get a different picture: *Brown* represents a step toward equal opportunity, not a color-blind society; political pressure, not moral suasion, motivates federal intervention; and local action becomes vital to the shape and direction of the movement. As Payne (1998) states, "Far from being the solution, American institutions have always played important roles in the creation and maintenance of racism. What happened in the movement was that civil rights activists were able to maneuver around those institutions to alleviate some of the system's worst features" (p. 99). Rather than wait for the federal government to right historical wrongs or for a charismatic leader to usher directives, these scholars say, look to the power of local indigenous institutions and the revolutionary potential of the black community. The movement toward a democratic ideal exists, but it has moved at a glacial and fitful pace and has been motivated by oppressed groups, not the goodwill of the American government or general populous. The past is far from rosy, and the struggle is far from over.

So, too, does the artificial split in the movement support a particular vision of social reform. In the words of collective memory scholars "the memory of certain events has an aura of transcendence" which, "instead of emanating from the events themselves as embodiments of eternal value, stemmed rather from the positioning of the events relative to other events within collective memory/forgetting process" (Gordon, 1995, p. 347). Such is the case with Civil Rights and Black Power. In the sanitized version of the black freedom struggle story, *Brown*, the 1964 Civil Rights Act, and the 1965 Voting Rights Act take on mythic proportions and represent national and racial reconciliation. Southern racists become easy and ready-made targets. Bull Connor, George Wallace, Ross Barnett, and Orval Faubus are held up for ridicule as ignorant tobacco-chewing rednecks, "an image with which almost no one can identify and which easily supplants more complex and realistic images of racism" (Payne, 1995, pp. 418–419). The systematic, coordinated, and bloody repression of black dignity and humanity is reduced to the actions of a few individuals. This allows the Civil Rights Movement to become an example of Americans grappling with difficult realities and working together to change the system against a few rabid racists. The Black Power Movement cannot fit in a story that has such a happy end. The fact that blacks were not satisfied with the successes of the Civil Rights Movement, employed alternative measures to agitate for equality and justice, and turned away from white liberals preempts a sense of national unity. The Black Power Movement seems almost blasphemous after the victories of a sanitized Civil Rights Movement.

Lastly, the way we understand the movement and *Brown*, in particular, can color the way in which we chart the route to equal educational
opportunity. Conservative pundits who reduce the decision to the desire
for a color-blind society appropriate the language of the decision to
position race-conscious policies against meritocracy. Conservatives
similarly bastardized Martin Luther King Jr.'s (1963) dream of a society
in which his children would "not be judged by the color of their skin
but by the content of their character." Today, the issue is affirmative
action. If *Brown's* mission was to outlaw racial classification then how
can affirmative action be consistent with it, they ask? America's perpetual forward progress in race relations, manifested in *Brown*, has no room
for such race-based policies and programs. We have come a long way,
they say, and the reality of racial equality—defined as color-blindness—
is in sight, if not fully realized. As Justice Sandra Day O'Connor stated
in the *Grutter v. Bollinger* (2003) decision, "We expect that twenty-five
years from now, the use of racial preferences will no longer be necessary
to further the interest approved today." Considering the statistics cited
by James Anderson in the preceding chapter, black children have not
made the kind of advances in the last 50 years that would lead many to
believe that 25 more would be enough to equalize educational opportunity and outcomes. However, by twisting *Brown* into an argument
against racial classification, conservatives can absolve the American
political, economic, social, and educational systems of any role in
African American underachievement. The problem, then, must reside
in the African American community itself (Coleman, 1966; Herrnstein
& Murray, 1996; Ogbu, 1978).

The Tale in the Textbook

How has the misremembering of the black freedom struggle and
Brown been popularized in the American consciousness? Scholarly
books that follow the conventional story, like those discussed above,
perpetuate a particularly top-down picture of the movement. Popular
culture also plays a role. Movies like *Mississippi Burning* or *Malcolm X*
do not pretend to be documentaries, but many audience members
confuse fiction with historical evidence. As one scholar stated, "When
one of the bastard forms of historical mimesis is artful enough, we tend
to excuse the liberties it takes with fact" (Yoder, 1994, p. 207). Another
culprit, and the focus of this section of the chapter, is the high school
history textbook. Textbooks merit special attention because, unlike
books by historians and popular culture creations, they are state sanc-

tioned. Youth may gather much of what they know of the American past from alternative sources (Frisch, 1989), but the influence of the textbook remains (Loewen, 1995; Norton, 1994). Their authoritative tone conveys to students that textbook content is objective knowledge and the truth of American history. In the words of Michael Apple and Linda Christian-Smith (1991), textbooks "participate in creating what a society has recognized as legitimate and truthful. They help set the canons of truthfulness and, as such, also help re-create a major reference point for what knowledge, culture, belief, and morality really *are*" (p. 4).

To this end, high school history textbooks are not merely compilations of particular details like names and dates. Rush Limbaugh may believe that "history is real simple. You know what history is? It's what happened" ("The Rush Limbaugh Show," cited in Nash, Crabtree, & Dunn, 1997, p. 6), but others, including historians and many high school teachers, do not define history as merely the recitation of facts. The study of history is expected to foster comprehension skills that include an understanding of multiple causation, cause-and-effect relationships, continuity and change, and the marshaling of evidence (National Center for History in the Schools, 1996). More broadly, the history classroom is supposed to be one of the places that Americans are made, where the *pluribus* becomes the *unum*. According to the National Center for History in the Schools (1996), the reasons for teaching history are many,

but none are more important to a democratic society than this: *knowledge of history is the precondition of political intelligence.* Without history, a society shares no common memory of where it has been, what its core values are, or what decisions of the past account for present circumstances. Without history, we cannot undertake any sensible inquiry into the political, social, or moral issues in society. Moreover, without historical knowledge and inquiry, we cannot achieve the informed, discriminating citizenship essential to effective participation in the democratic processes of governance and the fulfillment for all our citizens of the nation's democratic ideals. (p. 1)

The same responsibilities are not expected from math, English, or science classrooms. History classes and history textbooks become a form of civic religion in which students are taught the American catechism.

The point here is not to pretend that students read the textbook in isolation or to minimize the teacher's role in the classroom; many teachers use videos like *Eyes on the Prize*, primary sources, library assignments, and the Internet to augment student learning. Nor is it to pretend that external influences like the adoption process, standardized tests, and market concerns do not impact textbook content; "good" history is sometimes sacrificed for these concerns. Still, the textbooks and their content cannot be ignored. Many teachers do use textbooks, and the textbook dominates many classrooms (Loewen, 1995). When teachers teach against the text they face students unable or unwilling to accept alternative interpretations of history. Even textbook writers like Mary Beth Norton (1994), coauthor of the college text *A People and a Nation*, wrestle with "the common student attitude that if it's not in the textbook, it's not important" (p. 29). Put another way, what *is* in the textbook *is* important and, by extension, is considered objective *truth*. Because the scholarly debates over the interpretation of history have barely influenced textbooks (Anderson, 1986; Loewen, 1995), the master narrative of American history becomes a story of perpetual progress and is understood as the only appropriate way to understand the American past.

Textbook treatment of black history, long omitted or maligned in the books, has improved. During the 1960s, the experiences of blacks and other excluded groups made their way into the American tale, but the master narrative of the textbooks—the unwavering pursuit of a democratic ideal—did not shift. Loewen (1995) found that textbooks shoehorned individual examples of successful blacks into the American pageant in the 1990s. Booker T. Washington pulled himself up by his bootstraps! George Washington Carver did wonders with the peanut! The Tuskegee Airmen were heroes in World War II! Yet, blacks as a whole were relegated to the margins of the story. Their important place in American history was often reduced to either the Civil War and Reconstruction (which is when most textbooks focus on the institution of slavery, although it had existed for over 200 years by that time) or the late 1950s and early 1960s (thereby severing the Civil Rights Movement from the Black Power Movement). Even these two bloody battles over white supremacy and black humanity were sanitized. Slavery became a temporary aberration to Jeffersonian democracy whose ramifications were relegated to the distant past, and the Civil Rights Movement stood as a testament to racial liberalism. Several of the most popular textbooks used in secondary school history classrooms of the late 20th century did not even include the word "racism" in their indexes (Anderson, 1986, p. 266). Instead, black radicalism was appropriated and crafted to fit the perpetual progress narrative where democracy works and everybody wins.

Examining Current Texts

Little has changed in the American history textbooks published in the 21st century. For the purposes of this chapter, I reviewed five teacher's editions of textbooks published after the year 2000, and examined their treatment of the black freedom struggle of the middle twentieth century. This is *not* a comprehensive review of high school history textbook content. Rather, it demonstrates the range of treatment of the black freedom struggle in some of the most popular social studies and history texts. The books, all of which have reputable historians as authors, include *American Odyssey: The United States in the 20th Century* (Nash, 2002), *The American Journey* (Appleby, Brinkley, & McPherson, 2003), *Call to Freedom* (Stuckey, Salvucci, & Irvin, 2003), *A History of the United States* (Boorstin & Kelley, 2002), and *The Americans* (Danzer, Klor de Alva, Woloch, & Wilson, 2003). Their discussions of the black freedom struggle range from a highly contextualized and complete story (Danzer, Klor de Alva, Woloch, & Wilson) to a conventional tale with racist undertones (Boorstin & Kelley). The other textbooks represent the middle ground in terms of the treatment of the black freedom struggle. The textbooks represent some progress, but there is still work to be done.

The genesis of the movement. To begin, textbooks often use the *Brown* decision as a marker to launch their discussion of civil rights, thereby severing the black freedom struggle from its antecedents and crediting the Supreme Court ruling with inaugurating the movement (exceptions are Danzer et al., 2003; Stuckey et al., 2003). As the Boorstin and Kelley (2002) book states, "Who had the power to complain if the schools were not really equal? Most blacks were kept from voting in the South, so they had no way of forcing government officials to listen" (p. 738). According to this tale it seems that the Supreme Court itself, rather than a politically active black community, initiated legal proceedings. Also, the textbooks offer only a generalized statement that the schools were not equal and merely hint at the dismal condition of black education (Appleby et al., 2003; Stuckey et al., 2003). Separation and segregation are employed as euphemisms for white supremacy that conceal the fact that, in states like Mississippi, public officials spent money on the education of white children and black children at a ratio of 3:1 (1952 U.S. Census, cited in Dittmer, 1994, p. 34), black high schools were few and far between, and white school boards organized the black school schedule around cotton picking season (Dittmer, 1994).

Similarly, textbooks minimize the ferocity of white resistance and link it to a fear of desegregation rather than an interest in maintaining a racial hierarchy. The drama of Central High School in Little Rock, Arkansas, becomes a testament to the power of an American consensus on the evils of segregation and the morality of the federal government in their triumph over Orval Faubus, the personification of outdated racism. One textbook goes so far as to twist *Brown II* into a civil rights victory: "In 1955 the Court made its ruling stronger, ordering public schools to desegregate 'with all deliberate speed' " (Stuckey et al., 2003, p. 834; see also Danzer et al., 2003, p. 909)—a bizarre claim because the 1955 decision is considered the major stumbling block to timely desegregation (Kluger, 1977). This essentialized story of the good guys versus the bad guys not only masks the intensity of the fight to deseg- regate schools and the NAACP's intent in bringing suit, it leaves high school students with the impressions that *Brown* was an unqualified victory and that the absence of racial classification *is* equal educational opportunity. With such a story, is it any wonder that students may not comprehend why black underachievement continues to exist in a land where meritocracy and equality have reigned for so many years?

Presidential leadership. The triumphal story continues through the lens of morally righteous political elites and a well-functioning demo- cratic machinery. Presidents Harry Truman, Dwight Eisenhower, John Kennedy, and Lyndon Johnson, who figure prominently in the textbook narrative, act on civil rights reform out of personal goodwill and moral conviction. Truman desegregated the military and empowered the Justice Department to prosecute violations of civil rights laws out of principled obligation; students are told: "He knew he lacked the under- standing of foreign policy and the passion for domestic reform of his predecessor, but he had one quality in himself that he trusted supremely: the determination to do the right thing" (Nash, 2002, p. 634). Apparently, domestic pressures from A. Phillip Randolph's League for Nonviolent Civil Disobedience Against Military Segregation and international pressures fueled by the Cold War were non-issues. Eisenhower "had some doubts about the *Brown* decision, [but] he believed it was his duty to enforce the law" (Appleby et al., 2003, p. 840). Eisenhower sent federal troops to Little Rock, but saying that he had "some doubts" is putting it mildly because he only did so grudgingly and as a last resort. Kennedy plays an even more prominent role because he "encouraged blacks" to agitate on a variety of fronts and initiated the southern voting rights campaign by convening a meeting between activists from different protest organizations (Boorstin & Kelley, 2002, p. 790; see also Nash, 2002, p. 684). Kennedy did call a meeting, but he did so as a way to cool the direct action phase of the movement rather than encourage it, and the protection he promised voter registration workers was lukewarm at best (Dittmer, 1994; Payne, 1995). Still, it was Kennedy's dedication to civil rights that Johnson sought to memorialize after his assassination:

"No memorial oration or eulogy," he told Congress, "could more eloquently honor President Kennedy's memory than the earliest possible passage of the civil rights bill for which he fought so long. We have talked long enough in this country about equal rights. We have talked for one hundred years or more. It is time now to write the next chapter—and to write it in the book of law." (Boorstin & Kelley, 2002, p. 798)

Then, as now, these words paint Kennedy as an aggressive rather than reluctant party to the immediate redress of black grievances. In short, the executive branch becomes the hero in the textbook story, and black activists become minor players in their own drama.

The Montgomery bus boycott. Martin Luther King Jr. looms almost as large as the presidents in this narrative and is credited with spearheading the activism that swept the South. The textbook coauthored by Pulitzer Prize-winning Daniel Boorstin (2002), in particular, positions King as the ideological head of the movement. "The nation was ready for the work of Martin Luther King, Jr.," the textbook states, "he was a natural leader, American to the core" (p. 740). When Rosa Parks, "a tired black seamstress," decided not to give up her seat on a public bus to a white passenger, King

agreed with Mrs. Parks that it was time for action. . . . He did not tell people to burn the buses or fight the police. No, he said. All people need to be educated in the ways of peace and decency. . . . So he preached to the blacks in Montgomery. He told them to stop using the buses until the buses gave them their place as Americans. Of course many blacks were angry. But Martin Luther King begged and pleaded with them to keep their heads, and to keep love in their hearts, even while they joined the boycott. . . . In the end the Supreme Court ruled that segregation on buses was illegal. The blacks and all the decent people of Montgomery had won. . . . When the buses ran again, every passenger was treated like all the others. (pp. 740–741)

According to this textbook, the boycott began as an agreement between Dr. King and Mrs. Parks, and Dr. King organized a campaign against inanimate objects—the buses—rather than white racists and the legally established racial hierarchy that are conspicuously absent in the account. Although the description of Mrs. Parks as a tired old woman acting out of fatigue rather than political consciousness has been dispelled in everything from children's books (Adler, 1995; Ringgold, 1999) to scholarly accounts (Gibson Robinson, 1987; Kohl, 2005; Morris, 1984), nowhere are the Women's Political Council (WPC), the NAACP, and the Montgomery Improvement Association (MIA) mentioned as viable and important local movement centers. Rather, the battle in Montgomery marks King's entrance to center stage and relegates the entire black Montgomery community to the periphery.

Boorstin and Kelley's (2002) book is an easy target because its conservative agenda permeates the entire text, but other textbooks also leave something to be desired. Nash (2002) begins his account with the statement "Rosa Parks was tired" (p. 674). With regard to the actual boycott, the Appleby et al. (2003) textbook mentions the NAACP but not the MIA or the WPC. These omissions may seem small, but they are significant. The absence of the WPC—also missing in Stuckey et al. (2003) and Nash—obscures the revolutionary potential of black women. Women as organizers and women as agitators disappear in this retelling of the movement. The actions of Rosa Parks, as an individual woman, become a catalyst that a man, Martin Luther King Jr., translates into a movement. In addition, isolating the actions of Mrs. Parks sets her apart from the black Montgomery community, which already had begun to challenge the constitutionality of segregation on public transportation. Local activists E.D. Nixon, Jo Ann Gibson Robinson, and others in Montgomery used the MIA and the WPC to organize the community and were ready to exploit Mrs. Parks's arrest when it occurred. In short, when Martin Luther King Jr. assumed leadership of the MIA, he led an already organized black community.

The Appleby et al. (2003) volume also omits the fact that other blacks had refused to give up their seats to white passengers prior to Parks's arrest and incorrectly states that Mrs. Parks was seated in a section reserved for whites. The fact that Mrs. Parks was seated in the first row of the colored section, not the last row of the white section, is necessary to include not only because it is accurate. More importantly, it illustrates that blacks had no rights that whites were bound to respect. A black woman sitting in the colored section of the bus still had to give her seat to a white man, woman, or child when the bus filled with white passengers. This seemingly simple fact demonstrates that segregation was not merely about the separation of the races, but the maintenance of white supremacy.

An interracial focus. While some facts are omitted, others are blown out of proportion. For instance, the story of the movement is conspicuously interracial. Textbooks include photographs of black and white freedom riders, sit-in participants, and March on Washington attendees—often with accompanying text that makes their interracial nature explicit in case students cannot discern the black and white faces in the photos. Sympathetic whites even make their way into the story of the Montgomery bus boycott (Stuckey et al., 2003, p. 837) even though no whites were involved in boycotting the busses in Montgomery (Kohl, 2005). Another interracial victory was won when black and white Americans raised their voices in a chorus to force the federal government to act on legislative reform:

The national outrage helped to push the stronger Civil Rights Act of 1964 through Congress in July. Then, even in Mississippi, public places—such as restaurants—began to serve both races. When schools opened there in September, a few white and black children of Mississippi began going to school together. The last strongholds of segregation started to fall. (Nash, 2002, p. 805)

This particular account ignores the intense and rampant violence that followed the passage of the Civil Rights Act, especially in Mississippi. In the 1965–66 academic year—10 years after *Brown II*—only 6% of black children attended desegregated schools, and hostile whites used physical violence and economic sanctions to intimidate any black parent who dared to send his children to previously all-white schools (Curry, 1995; U. S. Commission on Civil Rights, 1967). Nor did the federal government act out of support for some fictionalized black and white American consensus. In fact, a 1963 Gallup Poll found that 51% of whites did not support a bill to desegregate public accommodations, and almost 80% said they would move if a large number of blacks moved into their neighborhood (Payne, 1998, p. 118). Despite these facts, the textbook accounts that foreground interracialism and American liberalism trivialize the tenacity of white supremacy and a political system crafted to maintain a racial hierarchy. Students are left with a consensus history that paints a soothing picture of American togetherness. To say that textbooks tell the story of the freedom struggle in black and white is more than a bad pun.

The Black Power Movement

While the Civil Rights Movement is sanitized, the Black Power Movement is vilified in the textbooks. The bad 1960s become the perfect foil for the good 1960s. Nash (2002) misses the actual goal of the black freedom struggle itself when he states that "[b]lack separatism was the antithesis of the civil rights movement's goal of racial integration" (p. 692). In typical fashion, the Boorstin and Kelley (2002) textbook goes further by using popular figures to personify the supposed dichotomous objectives of the decade: "Stokely Carmichael, a young black radical, began to preach 'Black Power.' Martin Luther King had preached love and human brotherhood. Now the angry champions of 'Black Power' mainly wanted to be able to 'get even.' They wanted their chance to lord it over others" (p. 807).

Not only is this a mischaracterization of the nature and meaning of Black Power, it is a deliberate attempt to color the late 1960s as a tragic time in American history where blacks entertained dangerous and hateful solutions to their grievances. The creation of black community institutions, demands for political power, the development of economic opportunities, and community uplift are never mentioned in these descriptions of Black Power. Rather, Black Power is reduced to directionless annual urban unrest in northern cities when blacks "flailed about" and "went on the rampage, destroying their own neighborhoods and leaving smoking rubble" (Boorstin & Kelley, 2002, pp. 805, 807). The point is driven home by pairing the text with pictures of riots (Boorstin & Kelley; Nash, 2002). Although, as Carson (1986, pp. 27–28) states, "Rather than claiming that a black power movement displaced the civil rights movement, [local activists] would argue that a black freedom movement seeking generalized racial advancement evolved into a black power movement toward the unachieved goals of the earlier movement," the textbooks' mischaracterization of Black Power helps shape, and more importantly, sanitize the historical representation of the Civil Rights Movement. According to textbooks, the later 1960s become the sad dénouement to a valiant struggle.

Why were blacks unsatisfied with the judicial and legislative progress of the 1950s and early 1960s? The textbooks find no credible answers. Therefore, the books have a difficult time explaining the riots in northern cities even though they prominently display pictures of the destruction. According to Nash (2002), "maybe it was the heat and humidity" that provoked the black community in Watts to explode after "rumors of resistance and police brutality" (p. 693). This account trivializes the persistence of racism and political disenfranchisement in this racially segregated and economically depressed section of Los Angeles. Watts residents were unemployed at a rate two to three times that of whites in Los Angeles; police brutality was more than a rumor and often went unpunished; two-thirds of students dropped out of high school; and infant mortality rates were one and a half times that of the citywide average (McCone & Christopher, 1965). The Watts riots were an expression of frustration and blighted opportunity, not merely a combination of temperature and gossip. Even though Nash mentions cultural pride as a component in Black Power, the dominant picture he provides is of Black Power as synonymous with northern, urban, and working-class riots. High school students do not need an apologist version of urban uprisings, but this characterization of Black Power trivializes black revolutionary potential and reduces the movement to an unruly group of discontents bent on disrupting the American system—a system strengthened by judicial and federal mandates for which blacks should have been both content and grateful.

Conclusion

In September 2003, the U.S. Senate convened a hearing on state history standards for high school students. Alarmed by warnings of "The End of History" (Cheney, 1994), and told of *How Pressure Groups Restrict What Students Learn* (Ravitch, 2003), senators blasted high school history textbooks for antipatriotic sentiment. Rather than focusing on heroism and progress, senators found that the textbooks focused too much on the doom and gloom of American history. Senator Judd Gregg (2003), chairman of the committee, warned,

Since September 11, more than at any time in our generation, our country has gone back to school on what it means to be an American, to know our history and the values upon which our Nation was founded. In many American history classrooms, our textbook is the curriculum. . . . So if the textbooks are incomplete, misleading, or blatantly wrong, our children are growing up with a skewed view of our national identity or no idea of our national identity. We have to put a stop to this.

If Senator Gregg wanted a story of the relentless and communal pursuit of democratic perfection, it appears that he has little about which to worry when it comes to the tale of the black freedom struggle.

The conventional narrative of the movement deserves a place in the high school history textbook. So, too, does the revisionist narrative. Positioning the two tales of the black freedom struggle against one another is a useful teaching tool that provides students with the opportunity to engage the material in a more complex way than the memorization of names and dates. A thorough engagement with the historiographical literature demonstrates to students that learning history is a process that involves interpretation and that those interpretations have ramifications for the way in which we explain current social, political, and economic conditions. Including revisionist material in the textbooks, instead of expecting teachers to find additional sources on their own, legitimizes that historical perspective and forces students to think more deeply about the nature of evidence, cause and effect relationships, and continuity and change. After exposure to the revisionist narrative, students may still be persuaded by the conventional narrative's arguments. That is fine. However, current textbooks do not offer students a choice because the revisionist narrative is absent, and the conventional narrative masquerades as truth.

Reclaiming or reframing *Brown* and the black freedom struggle in scholarly texts and high school textbooks is not a panacea for racial, social, and economic inequality. Black America's problems would not disappear with a massive overhaul of textbook content. Nevertheless, it is a start, however small. An introduction to the two tales of the movement can reinvigorate and reorient the conversation about the provision of equal educational opportunity. If we continue to sanitize the decision, consider its mission the creation of a color-blind society, and portray it as an unqualified victory, then blacks are left with little recourse. If, on the other hand, the *Brown* decision is understood as part of a broader black struggle for constitutional rights, equal opportunity, and human dignity that did not begin in 1954 or die in 1965, then the black community's continued agitation—as well as its disappointing gains since the 1954 decision—becomes an important and legitimate vehicle to fuel the quest for a democratic ideal.

In short, historiography can be a powerful weapon in the contemporary context. Frederick Douglass, on April 16, 1888, in his "Address delivered on the twenty-sixth anniversary of abolition in the District of Columbia," told his audience, "Well the nation may forget, it may shut its eyes to the past, and frown upon any who may do otherwise, but the colored people of this country are bound to keep the past in lively memory till justice shall be done them" (reel 16, Frederick Douglass Papers, Library of Congress, Washington, DC, cited in Blight, 1989, p. 1161). That is the role that historians can play more than 50 years after *Brown*. Positioning the decision in a larger movement for liberty and equality reclaims it, resuscitates it, and revolutionizes it. This revisioned *Brown* can then feed the continued struggle.

REFERENCES

About Sankofa (n.d.). Retrieved March 7, 2006, from http://www.sankofa.com/about.shtml

Adler, D. (1995). *A picture book of Rosa Parks*. New York: Holiday House.

Anderson, J.D. (1986). Secondary school history textbooks and the treatment of black history. In D.C. Hine (Ed.), *The state of Afro-American history: Past, present, and future* (pp. 253–274). Baton Rouge: Louisiana State University Press.

Anderson, J.D. (2006). A tale of two *Browns*: Constitutional equality and unequal education. In A. Ball (Ed.), *With more deliberate speed: Achieving equity and excellence in education—Realizing the full potential of* Brown v. Board of Education. *The 105th yearbook of the National Society for the Study of Education*, Part II (pp. 14–35). Malden, MA: Blackwell.

Apple, M.W., & Christian-Smith, L.K. (1991). The politics of the textbook. In M.W. Apple & L.K. Christian-Smith (Eds.), *The politics of the textbook* (pp. 1–21). New York: Routledge.

Appleby, J., Brinkley, A., & McPherson, J.M. (2003). *The American journey* (Teacher's ed.). New York: Glencoe McGraw-Hill.

Blight, D.W. (1989). For something beyond the battlefield: Frederick Douglass and the memory of the Civil War. *Journal of American History*, 75, 1156–1178.

Bloom, A. (1987). *The closing of the American mind*. New York: Simon and Schuster.

Boorstin, D.J., & Kelley, B.M. (2002). *A history of the United States* (Teacher's ed.). Needham, MA: Prentice Hall.

Branch, T. (1988). *Parting the waters: America in the King years*. New York: Simon and Schuster.

Breitman, G. (Ed.). (1990). *Malcolm X speaks: Selected speeches and statements*. New York: Grove Weidenfeld.

Brown v. Board of Education, 347 U.S. 483 (1954).

Brown v. Board of Education, 349 U.S. 295 (1955).

Burns, S. (2004). *To the mountaintop: Martin Luther King Jr.'s sacred mission to save America, 1955–1968*. New York: Harper San Francisco.

Carson, C. (1986). Civil rights reform and the black freedom struggle. In C.W. Eagles (Ed.), *The civil rights movement in America: Essays* (pp. 19–32). Jackson: University Press of Mississippi.

Chafe, W. (1980). *Civilities and civil rights: Greensboro, North Carolina, and the black struggle for freedom*. New York: Oxford University Press.

Cheney, L.V. (1994, October 20). The end of history. *Wall Street Journal*, p. A26.

Coleman, J.S. (1966). *Equality of education opportunity*. Washington, DC: U.S. Department of Health, Education, and Welfare.

Collier-Thomas, B., & Franklin, V.P. (2001). *Sisters in the struggle: African American women in the civil rights and black power movement*. New York: New York University Press.

Curry, C. (1995). *Silver rights*. Chapel Hill, NC: Algonquin Books.

Danzer, G.A., Klor de Alva, J.J., Woloch, N., & Wilson, L.E. (2003). *The Americans* (Teacher's ed.). Evanston: McDougal Littell.

Dittmer, J. (1994). *Local people: The struggle for civil rights in Mississippi*. Urbana: University of Illinois Press.

Douglass, F. (1888, April 16). Address delivered on the twenty-sixth anniversary of abolition in the District of Columbia. Reel 16, Frederick Douglass Papers, Library of Congress, Washington, DC.

Dudziak, M.L. (2000). *Cold War and civil rights: Race and the image of American democracy*. Princeton, NJ: Princeton University Press.

Dudziak, M.L. (2004). *Brown* as a Cold War case. *Journal of American History*, 91, 32–42. Retrieved January 12, 2006, from http://www.historycooperative.org/journals/jah/91.1/dudziak.html

Evers, M., & Marable, M. (Eds.). (2005). *The autobiography of Medgar Evers: A hero's life and legacy revealed through his writings, letters, and speeches*. New York: Basic Civitas Books.

Fairclough, A. (1995). *Race and democracy: The civil rights struggle in Louisiana, 1915–1972*. Athens: University of Georgia Press.

Farmer, J. (1985). *Lay bare the heart: An autobiography of the civil rights movement*. New York: Arbor House.

Feldman, G. (Ed.). (2004). *Before Brown: Civil rights and white backlash in the modern south*. Tuscaloosa: University of Alabama Press.

Franklin, J.H. (1967). *From slavery to freedom: A history of Negro Americans*. New York: Vintage Books.

Frisch, M. (1989). American history and the structures of collective memory: A modest exercise in empirical iconography. *Journal of American History, 75*, 1130–1155.

Garrow, D.J. (1986). *Bearing the cross: Martin Luther King, Jr., and the Southern Christian Leadership Conference*. New York: William and Morrow.

Gibson Robinson, J.A. (1987). *The Montgomery bus boycott and the women who started it: The memoir of Jo Ann Gibson Robinson*. Knoxville: University of Tennessee Press.

Gordon, D. (1995). [Review of Hutton, P. (1993). History as an art of memory. Hanover: University Press of New England.] *History and Theory, 34*, 340–354.

Gregg, J. (2003, September 24). Prepared statement. In *What is your child reading in school? How standards and textbooks influence education*. Committee on Health, Education, Labor, and Pensions, Senate Hearing no. 108–272. Retrieved December 12, 2005, from http://frwebgate.access.gpo.gov/cgi-bin/getdoc.cgi?dbname=108_senate_hearings&docid=f:89644.pdf

Grutter v. Bollinger, 539 U.S. 306 (2003).

Herrnstein, R.J., & Murray, C. (1996). *The Bell Curve: Intelligence and class structure in American life*. New York: Simon and Schuster.

Kelley, R.D.G. (1990). *Hammer and hoe: Alabama communists during the Great Depression*. Chapel Hill: University of North Carolina Press.

King, M.L., Jr. (1963, August 28). I have a dream. Retrieved January 12, 2006 from http://www.americanrhetoric.com/speeches/Ihaveadream.htm

Kluger, R. (1977). *Simple justice: The history of* Brown v. Board of Education *and black America's struggle for equality*. New York: Vintage Books.

Kohl, H. (2005). *She would not be moved: How we tell the story of Rosa Parks and the Montgomery bus boycott*. New York: New Press.

Layton, A.S. (2000). *International politics and civil rights policies in the United States, 1941–1960*. New York: Cambridge University Press.

Lewis, D.L. (1970). *King: A critical biography*. New York: Praeger Publishers.

Lewis, D.L. (1986). The origins and causes of the Civil Rights Movement. In C.W. Eagles (Ed.), *The civil rights movement in America: Essays* (pp. 3–17). Jackson: University Press of Mississippi.

Limbaugh, R. (1994, October 4). *The Rush Limbaugh Show*.

Loewen, J.W. (1995). *Lies my teacher told me: Everything your American history textbook got wrong*. New York: New Press.

Martin, W.E., & Sullivan, P. (Eds.). (2000). *Civil rights in the United States*. New York: Macmillan.

McCone, J., & Christopher, W.M. (1965). *Violence in the city: An end or a beginning? A report of the governor's Commission on the Los Angeles Riots*. Los Angeles: Commission on the Los Angeles Riots.

Meier, A., & Rudwick, E. (1973). *CORE: A study in the civil rights movement, 1942–1968*. New York: Oxford University Press.

Morris, A. (1984). *The origins of the civil rights movement: Black communities organizing for change*. New York: Free Press.

Nash, G.B. (2002). *American odyssey: The United States in the twentieth century* (Teacher's ed.). New York: Glencoe McGraw-Hill.

Nash, G.B., Crabtree, C., & Dunn, R. (1997). *History on trial: Culture wars and the teaching of the past.* New York: A.A. Knopf.

National Center for History in the Schools. (1996). *Significance of history for the educated citizen. National Standards for History.* Retrieved January 12, 2006, from http://nchs.ucla.edu/standards/dev-5-12a.html

Newton, H.P. (1973). *Revolutionary suicide.* New York: Harcourt, Brace, and Jovanovich.

Norrell, R. (1985). *Reaping the whirlwind: The civil rights movement in Tuskegee.* New York: Vintage Books.

Norton, M.B. (1994). Rethinking American history textbooks. In L. Kramer, D. Reid, & W.L. Barney (Eds.), *Learning history in America: Schools, cultures, and politics* (pp. 25–43). Minneapolis: University of Minnesota Press.

Ogbu, J.U. (1978). *Minority education and caste: The American system in cross-cultural perspective.* New York: Academic Press.

Payne, C.M. (1995). *I've got the light of freedom: The organizing tradition and the Mississippi freedom struggle.* Berkeley: University of California Press.

Payne, C.M. (1998). The view from the trenches. In J.T. Patterson (Ed.), *Debating the civil rights movement, 1945–1968* (pp. 99–136). Lanham, MD: Roman and Littlefield.

Plummer, B.G. (1996). *Rising wind: Black Americans and U.S. foreign affairs, 1935–1960.* Chapel Hill: University of North Carolina Press.

Raines, H. (1977). *My soul is rested: Movement days in the deep south remembered.* New York: Penguin Books.

Ravitch, D. (1983). *The troubled crusade: American education, 1945–1980.* New York: Basic Books.

Ravitch, D. (2000). *The great school wars: A history of the New York City public schools.* Baltimore, MD: Johns Hopkins University Press.

Ravitch, D. (2003). *The language police: How pressure groups restrict what students learn.* New York: Knopf.

Ringgold, F. (1999). *If a bus could talk: The story of Rosa Parks.* New York: Simon and Schuster.

Rosenberg, J., & Karabell, Z. (2003). *Kennedy, Johnson, and the quest for justice: The civil rights tapes.* New York: Norton.

Schlesinger, A.M., Jr. (1965). *A thousand days: John F. Kennedy in the White House.* Boston: Houghton Mifflin.

Schlesinger, A.M., Jr. (1992). *The disuniting of America.* New York: W.W. Norton.

Sellers, C. (1973). *The river of no return: The autobiography of a black militant and the life and death of SNCC.* New York: Morrow.

Sitkoff, H. (1981). *The struggle for black equality, 1954–1980.* New York: Hill and Wang.

Skrentny, J.D. (1998). The effect of the Cold War on African-American civil rights: America and the world audience, 1945–1968. *Theory and Society, 27*(4), 237–285.

Stuckey, S., Salvucci, L.K., & Irvin, J. (2003). *Call to freedom* (Teacher's ed.). New York: Holt, Rinehart and Winston.

Thornton, J.M., III. (2002). *Dividing lines: Municipal politics and the struggle for civil rights in Montgomery, Birmingham, and Selma.* Tuscaloosa: University of Alabama Press.

U.S. Census Bureau. (1952). *United States Census, 1950, Volume II, Part 24, Mississippi.* Washington, DC: Government Printing Office.

United States Commission on Civil Rights (1967). *Southern school desegregation, 5–9.* Washington, DC: Government Printing Office.

Weisbrot, R. (1990). *Freedom bound: A history of the civil rights movement in America.* New York: Norton.

Wilkinson, J.H., III. (1979). *From Brown to Bakke: The supreme court and school integration, 1954–1978.* New York: Oxford University Press.

Yoder, E.M., Jr. (1994). Reflections on the crisis in history. In L. Kramer, D. Reid, & W.L. Barney (Eds.), *Learning history in America: Schools, cultures, and politics* (pp. 201–211). Minneapolis: University of Minnesota Press.

CHAPTER 3

The Affirmative Development of Academic Ability: In Pursuit of Social Justice

EDMUND W. GORDON AND BEATRICE L. BRIDGLALL

The chapter that follows is adapted from the address that inaugurated the American Educational Research Association annual lecture series commemorating the anniversary of the 1954 Supreme Court decision in the case *Brown v. Board of Education*. Three related ideas are advanced.

- The reduction of racial isolation via desegregation is an insufficient condition for the achievement of equally high levels of educational attainment across the social divisions by which people are classified in our society.
- In a society where members have unequal access to education-relevant forms of capital, the deliberate or affirmative development of academic ability may be indicated.
- The pedagogical sciences community should replicate the action of the social scientists who more than 50 years ago deliberately used findings from their research to influence the U.S. courts and ultimately public policy.

A Tribute to Kenneth B. Clark

We begin this chapter by paying tribute to Kenneth Bancroft Clark, who led the distinguished group of pedagogical and social scientists who

Edmund W. Gordon is the John M. Musser Professor of Psychology, Emeritus at Yale University, Richard March Hoe Professor, Emeritus of Psychology and Education, and Senior Scholar in Residence at the College Board.

Beatrice L. Bridglall has a joint appointment as Research Scientist & Editor in the National Center for Children & Families and the Institute for Urban and Minority Education at Teacher's College, Columbia University. She is also an Adjunct Assistant Professor of Health Education in the Department of Health and Behavior Studies at Teachers College.

The authors acknowledge with appreciation the support of the College Board in the development of this chapter.

did the intellectual work that was foundational to the judicial, legislative, and public policy work of which the *Brown* decision of 1954 is symbolic. Professor Clark and this group of scholars prepared what has been referred to as the defining brief, synthesizing the research findings that became the basis for the 1954 decision. To the best that many of us have been able to determine, this was the first time that social science research concerning education had been used to inform a decision of the U.S. Supreme Court. You may recall that reference was made to this work by then Chief Justice Earl Warren in the body of the decision he wrote. This chapter's senior author heard of the work initially during his first year as a graduate student at Columbia University. The late professor Herbert Birch called to ask if he would join a group of scholars who were helping a young assistant professor named Clark with the further development of a literature review he and others had submitted to the Supreme Court of the United States in support of the claim that racially segregated schools were unconstitutional. He does not recall playing a significant role and certainly was not among the group of scholars who were signatories to the report that Clark prepared. However, many prominent social scientists signed the report. Among them were several names that were readily recognizable, such as Jerome Brunner, Isodor Chein, Mamie Clark, Allison Davis, Otto Kleinberg, and Ira Reid. These scholars represent the ideal role of the scientist in society—science in the service of humankind and social justice. Kenneth B. Clark was such a scholar.

A Reprise of the 1954 Decision and Social Science Evidence

Three lines of argument based on educational and social science research were advanced in the brief that Professor Clark and his associates presented. They argued that

- state-sponsored racial segregation in public schooling has a deleterious impact on black children;
- state-sponsored segregation in public schooling had a less clear but implicitly negative impact on white children; and
- when structural factors in the social context force changes in human behavior, changes in attitudes follow, thus challenging the traditional belief that changes in attitudes had to precede changes in behavior. (Clark, 1950)

These educational and social scientists advised the Court that science is not always as exact and precise as we would like and that the evidence in support of these findings was, indeed, uneven. In addition to reporting the empirical research evidence, they also reported findings from a survey of several prominent social science scholars of that time. These findings supported the conclusions drawn from the empirical evidence by the scholars who had signed the report.

This synthesis of the knowledge base was completed before 1952, but anticipates the problems that we face today concerning warrants for evidence in support of our research claims. The problem that Clark and his colleagues faced is reflected in the current debates concerning the privileging of the random assignment of subjects to controlled experimentation as the gold standard in knowledge production and decision making relative to policy and practice. Here, some 50 years ago, these scholars respectfully considered the uneven findings drawn from empirical evidence and complemented the findings with reflexive human judgment. They reflected the best expression of an admonition Gordon once heard from Urie Bronfenbrenner, who reminded us that the human brain is one of our most powerful research tools when used in the service of sense making. Knowledge can be produced by observation, enumeration, experimentation, and reflexive interpretation (Gordon, 2000).

In the middle of the 20th century, the U.S. Supreme Court determined that segregation by race in educational institutions was inconsistent with the rights of citizenship protected by the Constitution. This action effectively reversed an earlier decision (*Plessy v. Ferguson*, 1896) in which the Court decided that separate but equal arrangements *were* consistent with that Constitution. Since the momentous decision of 1954, most of the institutions within our society have strived to comply with the spirit of the declaration that segregation by race creates an inherently unequal condition. So powerfully is that principle imprinted on modern American society that even a conservative Supreme Court, at the beginning of the 21st century, has ruled in favor of race-sensitive affirmative action to redress the imbalance that has been created by the disadvantages associated with caste-like ethnic/racial status in this country (*Grutter v. Bollinger*, 2003). This despite Justice Sandra Day O'Connor's hope that such an interpretation would be unnecessary by the end of another 25 years. However, the struggle is not over.

The State of Black America

Overall, our nation made considerable progress in the education of African American students during the 20th century. Educational opportunities and academic achievement for some persons of African descent in the United States appear to be on the rise judging from several of the findings outlined by the National Center for Education Statistics Report, *Status and Trends in the Education of Blacks* (Hoffman, Lieges, & Snyder, 2003). The percentage of black children whose mothers have obtained a high school education has increased significantly since 1954. The proportion of black students who have completed high school and gone on to college has increased. Blacks seem to have reached a plateau, however, with respect to gains made in the 1960s, 1970s, and 1980s in academic achievement.

For example, most black students attend public schools where minorities represent the majority of the student body. Seventy-three percent of black 4th grade students were enrolled in schools with more than one-half of the students eligible to receive a free or reduced price lunch (Hoffman et al., 2003). Nationally, too few African American students are proficient at reading and math. In reading, only 12% of African American 4th graders reach proficient or advanced levels; 61% are not at basic levels. A similar proportion of African American 8th graders fall below the basic achievement level in math, and only 7% reach the proficient level or above on the National Assessment of Educational Progress.

By the end of high school, African American students have math and reading skills that are comparable to white 8th graders (African American Achievement in America, n.d.). Long-term trends in National Assessment of Educational Progress scores do show increased performance in reading, math, and science for black students between 1971 and 1999, however. While black high school graduates completed more academic courses in 1998 than in 1982, their academic credit totals remained lower than those of whites in 1998. Blacks' vocational credit totals were higher than those of whites, and black students were less likely than white students to take advanced mathematics and science courses and less likely than Hispanic students to take advanced foreign language classes (Hoffman et al., 2003).

In 1999–2000, the proportion of associate degrees earned by blacks was greater than the proportion of bachelor's degrees earned by blacks. Nearly one-quarter of all bachelor's degrees earned by blacks in 1999 were earned at historically black colleges and universities. The proportion of blacks completing college increased between 1975 and 2000; however, blacks still remained less likely than whites to earn degrees (Hoffman et al., 2003). Overall and perhaps most troublesome is the fact that significant gaps in academic achievement continue between

Asian American and European American students and their African American, Latina or Latino, and Native American peers (College Board, 1999).

The Limitations of *Brown* and Single Issue Public Policy

During 2004, many of us gathered at points across the country to commemorate the 50th anniversary of *Brown*, but it is obvious that, despite this celebrated decision, excellence and equity in educational opportunity and achievement have not been achieved. Despite the enormous gains from the emphasis on racial justice in the *Brown* decision and in the Civil Rights Movement, the attack on racism, in general, was a necessary but insufficient solution to the problem of integrating excellence and equity in education. If the goals were equal access to excellent educational opportunities and equal representation among those who achieve academic excellence, the *Brown* decision was clearly insufficient.

Consider for a moment the possibility that W.E.B. Du Bois may have been correct. Gordon recalls his argument that one of the more destructive things that white America has done to black people was to get their attention so focused on race that the dominant society was free to run away with the entire store. In their focus on race, racial isolation, and segregation, they have ignored the possibility that the problem may be *caste* and its concomitant constraints on access to the educationally relevant forms of capital that appear to be correlates of high academic achievement (Miller, 1995). The framing of the problem of inequality in education as caused by racial segregation may contribute to our ignoring the following:

- Du Bois's shift from his primary focus on the "color line" as the problem of the 20th century to his focus on the division of the world's population between the haves and the have nots as the problem of the 21st century (Lewis, 2000);
- William Julius Wilson's (1978) claim for "the declining significance of race." Wilson claimed that in the latter part of the 20th century race was a lesser deterrent to social mobility than were money, isolation, underdeveloped skills, and the absence of hegemonic cultural capital;
- Bourdieu's (1986) iteration of the forms of educationally relevant capital necessary for investment in education and other human resource development enterprises, such as cultural, fiscal, health, human, and social capitals, and polity capital (Miller, 1995);

- Coleman's (1990), Jaynes and Williams's (1989), Piven and Cloward's (1971), and Sexton's (1969) findings showing the association between family income (SES) and academic achievement; and

- Wolf's (1966) and Mercer's (1973) findings concerning the association between family environmental supports for academic learning and quality of academic achievement. Achievement test data indicates increases in academic achievement, regardless of ethnic identity, when quality of life and opportunity to learn are improved.

Intellective Competence: The Universal Currency of Technologically Advanced Societies

Apparently competencies in critical literacy, critical numeracy, and critical orality enable the achievement of intellective competence, defined as the developed abilities and dispositions to perceive critically, to explore widely, to bring rational order to chaos, to bring knowledge and technique to bear on the solution of problems, to test ideas against explicit and considered moral values and against empirical data, and to recognize and create real and abstract relationships between concrete and imaginary phenomena. In other words, intellective competence essentially reflects the effective orchestration of affective, cognitive, and situative mental processes in the service of sense making and problem solving, which is less focused on what we want learners to know and know how to do than on what it is that we want learners to become and be, that is, compassionate and thinking interdependent members of humane communities.

We use *intellective* to distinguish our concerns—the variety of cognitive, affective, situative processes that are integral to daily functioning and problem solving—from both *intelligent* and *intellectual* behavior. The term *intelligent* may be too closely associated with *intelligence*, which is often thought of as something measured by IQ tests. Intellectual behavior seems too easily confused with the work or habits of intellectuals and professional scholars. How then, can we begin to frame the construct "intellective competence"? We can start by defining pedagogy as the "art and science of teaching." This definition is not incorrect, but it is narrower than the conception we choose to advance. We prefer to think of pedagogy (inclusive of teaching, learning, and assessment) as dialectical and transactive components of a maieutic process that enables the development of problem solving abilities and sense making.

From our perspective, "to teach" is to enable and empower through directed learning experiences, guided exploration, structured problem and question posing, mediated problem solving, and explicated modeling of examples. In contrast to earlier notions of teaching as primarily involving the transfer of knowledge, skills, and values, our perspective casts the teacher as guide, as coach, as model, and as resource person who respects the fact that learning is something that one does for oneself and cannot be done *for* someone else. Our reference to learning is bifocal, and references the assimilation and accommodation of that which is old and the active construction and integration of that which is new. While not rejecting the traditional emphasis on such processes as attending to, associating, memorizing, and retrieving data, our vision of human learning privileges situative social processes that require constructive, hermeneutic, and transformative engagement, by learning persons, with data that are or become one's own—no matter the source. The product of such encounters— education that cultivates intelligence (see Martinez, 2000)—results in the achievement of intellective competence (Gordon & Bridglall, in press).

Affirmative Development

Until recently, our society has accepted the assignment of preferential treatment to designated categories of persons as special rewards for service to the nation, as compensation for unusual prior disadvantage, or simply as the entitlement associated with one's status. These various forms of affirmative action are currently under increased attack largely because of their public and colloquial association with minority group membership privilege. In all candor, affirmative action is also under attack because of the perception of abuses in its practice. Instead of an effort to ensure that qualified persons are not disqualified because of ethnicity or gender, affirmative action is often perceived as a program to privilege "unqualified" persons over those who are "qualified." The preoccupation with race may be a part of the problem. In a racist society, all social arrangements are designed to reflect racist values. In addition, explicit efforts to subvert those racist values are bound to come up against open resistance.

We propose a few adjustments. Rather than targeting ethnic or gender groups for affirmative action, let us target larger and more diverse groups: those that are low on wealth and wealth-derived capital resources. Education and employment opportunities could be regarded as instruments of human resource development rather than as avenues for the credentialing and rewarding of the "ablest." Rather than protecting the opportunity to enter, let us ensure the opportunity to develop and qualify. In addition to a program of affirmative action, we are proposing a program of *affirmative development*.

The G.I. bill. The largest affirmative action effort in the history of the United States was our veterans' preference program, which began in the aftermath of World War II. The components of that program ensured that veterans had ample opportunities to improve their economic, education, and health status. They were a protected group with respect to vocational skills development and employment. They were assisted in the acquisition of wealth through subsidized business and home ownership. The social ethos even gave them privileged positions in the political arena, where they were enabled to access political capital through the jingoistic and patriotic biases of the populists. This national effort may have begun as a reward for service in the nation's defense establishment, but in reality it was a massive *human resource development endeavor* that positioned the nation's labor force for the economic and technological expansions of the latter half of the 20th century. The affirmative development of the nation's underdeveloped human resources proved to be in the best interest of the entire United States.

The Affirmative Development of Academic Ability

Almost 75 years ago, Du Bois (1940) warned against the neglect of gifted and talented minority students. Current attention, however, is primarily focused on the overrepresentation of minorities on the underachieving end of the academic attainment distribution to the neglect of those on the exceptional end. Concerns include a persistent gap between minority and majority students, in general; a larger gap between high-achieving minority and high-achieving majority students; and the tendency of traditional indicators of high academic achievement to overpredict the subsequent academic achievement of many minority students. These often ignored findings were first reported in the 1980s and 1990s by Willingham (1985), Durán (1983), and Ramist, Lewis, and McCamley-Jenkins (1994).

The National Task Force on Minority High Achievement[1] concluded that these problems require a national commitment to the *affirmative development* of academic ability. Academic ability is one expression of human intellective competence that, increasingly, is recognized as the universal currency of societies that are technologically advanced. Academic ability references such capabilities as the following:

- critical literacy and numeracy;
- mathematical and verbal reasoning;
- creating, recognizing, and resolving relationships;
- classification of information and stimulus material;
- problem solving from both abstract and concrete situations as in deductive and inductive reasoning;
- sensitivity to multiple contexts and perspectives;
- accessing and managing disparate bodies and chunks of information;
- resource recognition and utilization (help-seeking); and
- self-regulation (including metacognitive competence and meta-componential strategies).

These capabilities appear to be the products of exposure to the demands of specialized cultural experiences—schooling being the most common—that interact with a wide variety of human potentials (Cole & Scribner, 1974; Cole, Gay, Glick, & Sharp, 1971; Hunt, 1966; Martinez, 2000; Sternberg, 1994). This suggests that academic ability is a developed ability—the quality of which is not primarily a function of one's biological endowment or fixed aptitudes. With this recognition, the Study Group on the Affirmative Development of Academic Ability, a small group of researchers convened by the North Central Regional Education Laboratory for a yearlong study on issues related to closing academic achievement gaps among groups of children, began with the assumption that closing the gaps between groups of students from different social divisions (class, ethnicity, gender, and language) would require the affirmative development of ability in a wide range of individuals through certain interventions in our homes, communities, and schools.

The Major Findings of the Study Group

The Study Group reviewed extant research, commissioned six review papers, and reported the results of their deliberation. The major findings were published under the title *All Children Reaching the Top* (National Study Group for the Affirmative Development of Academic Ability, 2004). They are the following:

- The development of academic ability requires that various forms of education-related capital be invested in the educational and personal development of the learner. Among these forms of capital that appear to be foundational to academic success are cultural, financial, health and nutritional, human, institutional, polity, and social capital (Bourdieu, 1986; Coleman, 1966; Miller 1995).

- Learners and teachers need to experience feelings of trust in the school as an institution and in those who seem to represent the interests of that institution (administrators, staff, and especially teachers) (Bryk & Schneider, 2003; Mendoza-Denton & Aronson, in press; Steele & Aronson, 2000).
- Early and continuing exposure to pleasurable and progressively more rigorous learning experiences that are relevant to the knowledge, skills, and understandings that are part of the repertoire of educated persons are critical (Bloom, 1984; Everson & Dunham, 1996; Hunt, 1966; Lee, in press).
- Effort and time devoted to and engaged in learning tasks are important (Carroll, 1989; Lee, in press; Resnick, 1987).
- Acquiring factual knowledge that in turn enables the organization of knowledge in ways that facilitate retrieval and application is necessary (Bransford, Brown, & Cocking, 1999; Everson, in press; Greeno, 1991; Lee, in press).
- Metacognitive and metacomponential competencies and agentic behaviors and dispositions that are focused on academic learning must be developed (Bandura, 2001; Flavel, 1979; Greeno, 1991; Sternberg, 1994).
- The most effective pedagogy involves opportunities to engage in teaching and learning encounters that are grounded in one's zone of proximal development (a point just beyond the learner's zone of learning comfort or current level of mastery) combined with guidance in the utilization of instructional scaffolding of the new material to be learned (Lee, in press; Vygotsky, 1978).
- The exchange of distributed knowledge that is made available through cooperative and expeditionary learning in which the learner is encouraged to think about and evaluate what is being experienced is important (Fullilove & Treisman, 1990; Greeno, 1991).
- Socialization to and/or explication (giving emphasis to) of the unique demands of scholarly work and repeated exposures to exemplars of the standards that are operative has great value (Gordon, 1999).

- Students benefit from access to a wide range of supplementary education experiences that support both intellective and social competencies (Gordon, Bridglall, & Meroe, 2005; Steinberg, Brown, & Dornbusch, 1996).
- The politicalization of academic learning in the lives of minority student learners is necessary so that they can more readily see that academic learning is compatible with the ends that they seek. Learning task engagement, time on task, and resource utilization are seen as being related to such compatibility (Ianni, 1988).
- Students need freedom to concentrate on academic tasks without constant concern about the relationship between one's cultural identity and "prejudice apprehension" or "stereotype confirmation" (Mendoza-Denton & Aronson, in press; Steele & Aronson, 1995).

Science and Human Society

The findings of the Study Group on the Affirmative Development of Academic Ability represent a sampling of the rich knowledge base that is available to inform public policy and professional practice concerning education. None of us believe that extant policies, practices, and resources relative to education are adequate or are the best that we can do. It may be time to assert and defend excellence and equity in education as a civil right and a civil liberty. The challenge to those of us who produce knowledge and utilize it in our professional practice is to find ways to honor the cardinal values of our profession—agency based on knowledge, technique, judgment, reason, and justice—in our personal, professional, and public lives.

NOTE

1. The College Board organized the National Task Force on Minority High Achievement in 1997 to study and make recommendations for addressing a crucial national issue: the chronic shortage of African American, Latino, and Native American students who achieve at very high levels academically. For additional information see http://www.collegeboard.com/about/association/academic/taskforce/taskforce.html

REFERENCES

African American Achievement in America (n.d.) *The Education Trust*. Retrieved March 3, 2006, from http://www2.edtrust.org/NR/rdonlyres/9AB4AC88-7301-43FF-81A3-EB94807B917F/0/AfAmer_Achievement.pdf

Bandura, A. (2001). Social cognitive theory: An agentive perspective. *Annual Review of Psychology, 54*(1), 1–26.

Bloom, B. (1984). *Developing talent in young people*. New York: Ballantine Books.

Bourdieu, P. (1986). The forms of capital. In J. Richardson (Ed.), *Handbook of theory and research for the sociology of education* (pp. 241–258). Westport, CT: Greenwood.

Bransford, J., Brown, A., & Cocking, R. (Eds.). (1999). *How people learn: Brain, mind, experience and school*. Washington, DC: National Academies Press.

Brown v. Board of Education. 347 U.S. 483 (1954).

Bryk, A.S., & Schneider, B. (2003). Trust in schools: A core resource for school reform. *Educational Leadership, 60*(6), 40–45.

Carroll, J.B. (1989). The Carroll model: A 25-year retrospective and prospective view. *Educational Researcher, 18*(1), 26–31.

Clark, K.B. (1950). *Effect of prejudice and discrimination on personality development*. Paper presented at the Mid-century White House Conference on Children and Youth, Washington, DC.

Cole, M., & Scribner, S. (1974). *Culture and thought*. New York: Wiley.

Cole, M., Gay, J., Glick, G., & Sharp, D. (1971). *Cultural contexts of learning and thinking*. New York: Basic Books.

Coleman, J.S. (1990). *Families and schools*. Cambridge, MA: Harvard University Press.

Coleman, J.S., Campbell, E., Mood, A., Weinfeld, E., Hobson, D., York, R. et al. (1966). *Equality of educational opportunity*. Washington, DC: Government Printing Office.

The College Board (1999). *Reaching the top: A report of the National Task Force on Minority High Achievement*. New York: The College Board.

Du Bois, W.E.B. (1940). *Dusk of dawn*. New York: Harcourt, Brace and Co.

Durán, R.P. (1983). *Hispanics' education and background: Predictors of college achievement*. New York: College Entrance Examination Board.

Everson, H.T., & Dunham, M.D. (1996). *Signs of success: Equity 2000—Preliminary evidence of effectiveness*. New York: College Board (ERIC document reproduction Service No. ED 455 109).

Everson, H.T. (In press). The problem of transfer and adaptability: Applying the learning sciences to the challenge of the achievement gap. In E.W. Gordon & B.L. Bridglall (Eds.), *The affirmative development of academic ability*. Lanham, MD: Rowman and Littlefield.

Flavel, J.H. (1979). Metacognition and cognitive monitoring: A new area of cognitive developmental inquiry. *American Psychologist, 34*, 906–911.

Fullilove, R.E., & Treisman, P.U. (1990). Mathematics achievement among African American undergraduates at the University of California, Berkeley: An evaluation of the mathematics workshop program. *Journal of Negro Education, 59*(3), 463–478.

Gordon, E.W. (1999). *Education and justice: A view from the back of the bus*. New York: Teachers College Press.

Gordon, E.W. (2000). Production of knowledge and pursuit of understanding. In C.C. Yeakey (Ed.), *Producing knowledge, pursuing understanding*. Stanford, CT: JAI Press. (pp. 301–318)

Gordon, E.W. (2004). State of black education in America. In L.A. Daniels (Ed.), *The State of black America 2004* (pp. 97–113). New York: National Urban League.

Gordon, E.W., & Bridglall, B. (Eds.). (in press). *Affirmative development: The cultivation of academic ability*. Lanham, MD: Rowman and Littlefield.

Gordon, E.W., Bridglall, B.L., & Meroe, A.S. (Eds.). (2005). *Supplementary education*. Landham, MD: Rowman and Littlefield.

70 AFFIRMATIVE DEVELOPMENT OF ACADEMIC ABILITY

Greeno, J. (1991). Number sense as situated knowing in a conceptual domain. *Journal for Research in Mathematics Education, 22*(3), 170–218.
Grutter v. Bollinger. (02-241) 539 U.S. 306 (2003).
Hoffman, K., Lieges, C., & Snyder, T. (2003). *Status and trends in the education of blacks.* Washington, DC: National Center for Education Statistics.
Hunt, J.M. (1966). Black genes—white environment. *Transaction, 6,* 12–22.
Ianni, F.A.J. (1988). *The search for structure: A report on American youth today.* New York: The Free Press.
Jaynes, G.D., & Williams, R.M. (Eds.). (1989). *A common destiny.* Washington, DC: National Academies Press.
Lee, C.D. (in press). The educability of intellective competence. In E.W. Gordon & B.L. Bridglall (Eds.), *The affirmative development of academic ability.* Lanham, MD: Rowman and Littlefield.
Lewis, D.L. (2000). *W.E.B. Du Bois: The fight for equality and the American century, 1919–1963.* New York: Henry Holt and Company.
Martinez, M.E. (2000). *Education as the cultivation of intelligence.* Mahwah, NJ: Lawrence Erlbaum.
Mendoza-Denton, R., & Aronson, J. (in press). Making the pinnacle possible: Psychological processes associated with minority students' achievement. In E.W. Gordon & B.L. Bridglall (Eds.), *The affirmative development of academic ability.* Lanham, MD: Rowman and Littlefield.
Mercer, J.R. (1973). *Labeling the mentally retarded: Clinical and social system perspectives on mental retardation.* Berkeley: University of California Press.
Miller, L.S. (1995). *An American imperative: Accelerating minority educational advancement.* New Haven, CT: Yale University Press.
National Study Group for the Affirmative Development of Academic Ability (2004). *All students reaching the top: Strategies for closing academic achievement gaps.* Naperville, IL: Learning Point Associates.
Piven, F.F., & Cloward, R.A. (1971). *Regulating the poor: The functions of public welfare.* New York: Pantheon Books.
Plessy v. Ferguson. 163 U.S. 537 (1896).
Ramist, L., Lewis, C., & McCamley-Jenkins, L. (1994). *Student group differences in predicting college grades: Sex, language, and ethnic groups.* New York: The College Board.
Resnick, L.B. (1987). Learning in school and out. *Educational Researcher, 16*(9), 13–20.
Sexton, P. (1969). *Income and education.* New York: Basic Books.
Steele, C.M., & Aronson, J. (1995). Stereotype threat and the intellectual test performance of African-Americans. *Journal of Personality and Social Psychology, 69,* 797–811.
Steele, C.M., & Aronson, J. (2000). Stereotype threat and the intellectual test performance of African Americans. In C. Stangor (Ed.), *Stereotypes and prejudice: Essential readings* (pp. 369–389). Philadelphia: Psychology Press/Taylor & Francis.
Steinberg, L., Brown, B.B., & Dornbusch, S.M. (1996). *Beyond the classroom: Why school reform has failed and what parents need to do.* New York: Simon & Schuster.
Sternberg, R.J. (Ed.). (1994). *Encyclopedia of human intelligence.* New York: Macmillan.
Vygotsky, L.S. (1978). *Mind and society: The development of higher mental processes.* Cambridge, MA: Harvard University Press.
Willingham, W.W. (1985). *Success in college: The role of personal qualities and academic ability.* New York: The College Board.
Wilson, W.J. (1978). *The declining significance of race: Blacks and changing American institutions.* Chicago: University of Chicago Press.
Wolf, R. (1966). The measurement of environments. In A. Anastasi (Ed.), *Testing problems in perspective* (pp. 491–503). Washington, DC: American Council on Education.

The Affirmative Development of Academic Ability: A Response to Edmund Gordon

CAROL D. LEE

I too must begin my response with a tribute.

Professor Edmund W. Gordon represents the scholar-activist, a renaissance man in terms of breadth of intellect and commitment. It is fascinating to listen to him talk about working with Kenneth Clark and having discussions with W.E.B. Du Bois and Paul Robeson in Harlem. Throughout his career, he has promoted "science in the service of humankind and social justice." There is probably no significant issue of social justice in the last 50 years that Dr. Gordon has not influenced either directly through his research or through his own advocacy. He speaks a difficult truth that is sometimes hard to hear, but one always knows that in his heart his criterion is "How does this wrestle promote social justice for those most in need?" I am honored to know him, to call him my friend, to work on occasions with him on projects, and to be able to respond to his chapter with Beatrice Bridglall in this extraordinarily important volume.

I would like to place my comments in a historical context. First, as Drs. Gordon and Bridglall so aptly point out, the *Brown v. Board of Education* case was the result of decades of preparation by esteemed scholars in the fields of law, psychology, and education and the commitments of key institutions such as the Howard University Law School (where Charles Hamilton Houston was dean) and the National Association for the Advancement of Colored People (NAACP) and their staff

Carol D. Lee is Professor in the School of Education and Social Policy (SESP), Professor of African-American Studies, and the co-coordinator of SESP's Spencer Research Training Program at Northwestern University. She is also a founder and chairman of the Board of Directors of the Betty Shabazz International Charter Schools in Chicago.

of legal activists such as Thurgood Marshall and Constance Baker Motley. It was also the result of coordination across a number of community-based institutions that worked in concert with formal educational institutions such as Howard University. Educational historian Vanessa Siddle-Walker (2005) documents how professional groups of teachers in Georgia, as well, weighed in on the issues on which the case focused. To address the challenges of what Gordon and Bridglall call the "affirmative development of academic ability," *Brown* points to the need for institutional infrastructures working in coordination over time. Our present tendency to rely almost solely on public good will and public policy to address the inequalities in life opportunities, including the opportunity to learn, may be naïve in light of history (Orfield & Eaton, 1996). In addition, understanding the limitations of *Brown*, in part a reflection of limitations in what *Brown I* and *Brown II* called for, may also direct us to examine what it is that we advocate for from different perspectives (Bell, 1980). Thus, in my response to Drs. Gordon and Bridglall's chapter, I want to further examine the implications of *Brown* for institution building and for conceptualizing our demands for social justice in education.

Reconceptualizing Our Demands for Social Justice in Education

Gordon and Bridglall (this volume, pp. 58–70) summarize the three lines of argument in the brief presented to the Supreme Court as follows:

- state-sponsored racial segregation in public schooling has a deleterious impact on black children;
- state-sponsored segregation in public schooling has a less clear but implicitly negative impact on white children; and
- when structural factors in the social context force changes in human behavior, change in attitudes follow, thus challenging the traditional belief that change in attitudes must precede change in behavior. (Clark, 1950, cited in Gordon & Bridglall, this volume)

The Harvard Civil Rights Project documents the persistence of segregated schools, 50 years after the *Brown* Supreme Court decision (Orfield & Eaton, 1996). The persistence of segregated schools as the norm in most urban school districts suggests that it is difficult in the United States to force schools to integrate (Ladson-Billings, 2004). Decades of court mandates and sanctions on school districts by and large have not changed the color concentrations of U.S. schools. Chicago, where I live, has been under court mandate for decades to desegregate schools, but today, the population of self-identified white students in Chicago public schools is less than 10%. In fact, a recent newspaper article on the impact of No Child Left Behind in Chicago reported the low probability of a student of color having access to an integrated school, in large part because there are so few white students in the system (Olszewski, 2005). Ironically, many of them are concentrated in magnet and special admissions schools, leaving few opportunities to truly integrate neighborhood schools. Chicago has expended tremendous effort over the decades in employment practices that favor integrating school faculties as well as in creating magnet and other school options that permit students to attend schools outside their immediate neighborhoods. This strategy of creating school options outside neighborhoods of residence is the plan of action in Chicago because most neighborhoods are highly segregated. Moreover, even though one finds fewer patterns of residential segregation in coastal cities like Los Angeles and New York, there is still substantial segregation by race, ethnicity, and of course class in these cities as well. Thus, I would argue that structural changes in policy in one domain are insufficient to change behaviors that are rooted in deeply held belief systems.

Thus, the question that this raises around opportunity to learn and public policy is not so much about whether students of color get to sit next to white students in order to either affect attitudes or increase the likelihood of receiving a "good" education based on enrollment in an integrated school. Rather, it is about having equal access to resources that increase the likelihood of having robust opportunities to learn, and about how to provide such resources for students from "minority" and low-income communities without restricting access to students from "majority" and higher income communities. This has important and challenging implications for how schools are funded. For example, in Illinois, funding schools from the local tax base of districts results in huge discrepancies in per pupil funding. Discrepancies between elementary schools can range from $4,340 to $18,193 per student; between high schools, they can range from $6,509 to $17,291 per student (Finkel, 2004). These discrepancies reflect national patterns (Education Trust, 2005).

At the same time, we know that equal access to opportunity to learn is accounted for only in part by issues of funding. While the No Child Left Behind legislation does offer financial incentives for achieving equitable outcomes in academic achievement, it does not equalize per pupil funding. While it does bring public attention to the proportion of qualified teachers in a school (as defined by certification), it does not assure equitable salaries for teachers across school districts. Perhaps most importantly, it does not assure equitable rigor in expected outcomes across states, nor does it require a robust medium through which students are expected to display competence. Recent reports have documented how students in a state like North Carolina meet No Child Left Behind standards based on the state assessment yet score below levels of proficiency on the National Assessment of Educational Progress (RAND Corporation, 2005). While some make excuses that there are differences in sampling across the state and national assessments, others argue that the two assessments examine fundamentally different forms of knowledge (Wolf, Bixby, Glenn, & Gardner, 1991). Thus, clarifying *what* knowledge goals students are educated to meet remains an important question. This is the question that those of us advocating for social justice goals in education must work very carefully to articulate and to organize toward. The question of what kinds of knowledge are necessary for equalizing life opportunities within a democracy is not the question that *Brown* raised. It is, however, an important question that Gordon and Bridglall address in their chapter.

Gordon and Bridglall, in addressing this question, report differential educational and life course outcomes between blacks, Latinos, other people of color, and whites. They conclude that many discrepancies can be explained by class, and that perhaps we should focus more of our attention on the challenges posed by class differences than by race. While I fundamentally agree with the sentiment of their argument— namely, that class is extremely important in our analysis—I wish to offer two caveats. First, race, ethnicity, and class are highly correlated in the United States (Bell, 1992; Mills, 1997). It is much more likely that you will have lower income and all that entails if you are black or brown than if you are white. Second, as they point out, one still finds differential outcomes between middle-class blacks and whites on almost all measures of achievement (Ferguson, 2002), on graduation rates (Kaufman, Alt, & Chapman, 2004), and on salary with equal background training (Urban League, 2005). Thus, I argue that we need a dual focus on both race and class because they are so highly correlated and because issues of race surface even when poverty is not a factor. I will discuss some of the ways I believe we need to think about both in relation to opportunities to learn.

Why We Need a Focus on Race in Understanding and Responding to the Achievement Gap

I argue here that a focus on race in understanding and responding to the achievement gap is needed in the realm of public policy (Walters, 2003), in pedagogy (King, 1990), and in the African American community's internal responses to this persistent challenge (Hilliard, 1995; Madhubuti, 1990; Nobles, 1985).

Public Policy

A focus on race in public policy is needed because we continue to find differential outcomes in achievement, in high school graduation rates, in college completions, in health outcomes (Byrd & Clayton, 2000), and in equity in the job market across fields that are predicted by both race and class. The predictions from race hold across socioeconomic status. The Minority Student Achievement Network (MSAN) is a consortium of racially integrated (although typically majority white) suburban school districts. While MSAN continues to make concerted efforts to equalize achievement outcomes between majority and minority students, these differences are persistent. Ron Ferguson (2002) of Harvard University has worked for several years with MSAN in conducting surveys and interviews to disentangle possible sources of these discrepancies. On the one hand, Ferguson finds that black and white students spend equal amounts of time, on average, on homework. On the other hand, he finds that high-achieving black students are less likely to be enrolled in advanced placement courses and are most likely to have as friends other black students who may not be high achieving.

He also finds that students' perceptions of their relationships with their teachers, as well as how they believe their teachers perceive them and their capabilities, matter more to black students than to white students. These data suggest that the fields of human development and social cognition may offer relevant research related to this dilemma. Why are these black students earning lower grades and achieving at lower rates on standardized assessments if they are spending as much time studying at home as their white peers? This suggests that the desire to achieve and the willingness to expend effort to learn are not the issues here (Graham & Taylor, 2002).

The Role of Perceptions and Social Relationships in Learning

The field of social cognition focuses on what is entailed in how people learn to read the internal states and motivations of other people, as well as the demands of participating in activity settings (Bandura, 2001; Kunda, 1999). Personal identity influences how we socially read the world. Graham, Taylor, and Hudley (1998) present empirical evidence that racial identity and motivation are indeed related. In addition, research on stereotype threat indicates that displays of competence can be compromised by the anticipation of being stereotyped (Steele & Aronson, 1995). Additional research in the area of cognition and emotion document the importance of perceptions on emotional states and of emotional states on cognition (Dai & Sternberg, 2004; Pintrich & DeGroot, 1990). Together, these bodies of research strongly suggest that attention to the social significance of race is important for teacher knowledge, for the organization of schools, and for how families and communities organize to socialize youth. The psychological literature refers to this as *racial socialization* (Cross, 1991).

For decades, African American psychologists, in particular, have documented the protective roles that racial socialization can play for African American youth and adults (Boykin & Bailey, 2000; Nobles, 1980). Bowman (1989) has empirically demonstrated how the kinds of role strains that African American men face change across the life course and how different forms of social supports are useful for preparing them to adapt to these changing circumstances. It is important, however, to add a note of caution: This research does not imply that every African American will share common experiences, knowledge, values, or perceptions. The implication for practice is that schools need to consider students' perceptions, the presence and effects of possible stereotyping, and the social relationships among students and between students and teachers as these are influenced by race. We have good reason to believe that the presence of African American teachers can be a useful resource (Foster, 1994), but this in no way suggests that black teachers are a panacea, nor that white teachers cannot effectively teach black students (Ladson-Billings, 1994).

Spencer and her colleagues (Spencer, 1995; Spencer et al., 2006) offer a powerful framework for helping us understand the need for racial socialization and its possible relationship to academic achievement: the Phenomenological Variant of Ecological Systems Theory (PVEST), which is based on the fundamental premise that social context matters for human development. Learning to read, shape, and adapt to the environments we meet in ways that fulfill our goals—be they adaptive or maladaptive—are the fundamental tasks of human development. Research in human development suggests that the needs to belong, to be competent, and to experience one's perceptions (which are often a community's perceptions) of emotional well-being are universal human goals (Bandura, 1977; Maslow, 1970). However, the paths to achieving these states and the criteria for what makes such states viable are culturally variable (Boykin & Bailey, 2000; Greenfield & Cocking, 1994; Rogoff, 2003). Weisner (2002) has argued "the cultural pathways in which human development occurs constitute the single most important influences shaping development and developmental outcomes" (p. 276). Cultural pathways to development for youth of African descent living in the United States are more often than not racialized in important ways, that is, influenced by social, political, and economic manifestations of race (Lee, Spencer, & Harpalani, 2003; Spencer, 1987; Spencer et al., 2006).

Spencer (1987) argues that all humans face risks as they engage in the normative tasks of life course development. For example, adolescence is typically marked by physiological changes and in Western societies by transitions from schools that are generally smaller and more closely knit to high schools that are generally larger and more impersonal and where subject matter is more removed from everyday experience. Adolescence is also a period in which youth are beginning to negotiate new roles with parents and family in preparation for adult roles outside the immediate family and a period in which negotiating social relationships with peers is paramount and sexual and gender identities are being negotiated. All of these negotiations involve risk because what makes for success is rarely clear and unambiguous and success is never assured. Spencer (1999) asserts that in addition to these normative tasks of adolescence, some youth have additional risks associated with racial or ethnic group membership, poverty, gender, disability, and body type, among others. There is an abundance of empirical data to document the prevalent risks associated with each of these social markers (Jencks & Mayer, 1990; McLoyd, 1998).

In Spencer's (1999) paradigm, our internal phenomenological experience of both the normative and additional risks is less about the objective reality of these risks than about the nature of the kinds of supports that we have for making sense of them and negotiating them. The racial socialization literature (Cross, 1991; McAdoo & McAdoo, 1985) would indicate that preparation for understanding how racism and class prejudices manifest themselves in our daily lives (Baron, Tom, & Cooper, 1985; Ladson-Billings & Tate, 1995; Oakes, 1990); the internalization of belief systems about efficacy and resilience (Dweck & Goetz, 1978; Pajares, 1996; Spencer, 1987); and the availability of institutional resources that can scaffold the processes of adaptation over time provide the kinds of supports that black, brown, and poor youth need to respond in ways that are adaptive and promote healthy life course outcomes (Lee, 2005b, in press; Lee et al., 2003).

My point here is that one of the assets in the African American community that has been neglected post-*Brown* is the attention to racial socialization in families and in schools (Irvine, 1990; Irvine & Irvine, 1983). Segregated schools today are a different animal than the segregated schools of the pre-*Brown* era (Tate, Ladson-Billings, & Grant, 1993), where racial socialization was more of a focus (Anderson, 1988; Siddle-Walker, 1996). There are many reasons for this. Wilson (1987) points out that the African American community has become more internally segregated by class. In the pre-*Brown* era, one would more likely find the children of doctors and blue-collar workers attending the same school. This new class segregation within the African American community demonstrates the argument by Gordon and Bridglall about our lack of sufficient focus on class and the problems of poverty. I want to be clear that I totally agree with their argument in that regard; however, I also believe that the data on the differences in outcomes and opportunities, even controlling for class, suggest that in our lives both race and class matter.

My purpose in this discussion so far is to raise questions about what we must articulate as goals for our youth in a very complex and dangerous post-*Brown* world. Our children do not live in a pre-1954 world in which the boundaries and interests of nation-states were clearly defined. They must compete with young people from across the globe in terms of jobs and economic production, but they must also collaborate with people from across the globe to sustain the ecosystems of Mother Earth on which we all depend. Across the globe, people of African descent continue to face persistent challenges related to education, health, and economic competitiveness (America, 1990; Rodney, 1974).

Thus, I argue that as people of African descent, we have particular and pressing problems that require coordinated analyses and deep institutional forms of collaboration, which include programs of racial and ethnic socialization for our youth—not for purposes of exclusion from the world community, but more so to understand what we as a people have given to the world community and to be inspired to continue the legacy of those on whose shoulders we stand. Our goal should be to produce more scholars like Edmund Gordon, who throughout his professional career has combined community-based social activism with profound scholarship, like Du Bois before him. I have argued elsewhere that in terms of education we should be pushing our young people—in the United States, in Latin America, in Europe, and across Africa—to pursue careers in fields like economics, business, medicine and public health, engineering, architecture, communications, law and international relations, and education. These are fields in which skill and commitment to use knowledge for social justice ends—that is, to help humans in need—can only have a positive impact on community development. This is a very different goal than the pursuit of academic achievement to simply make money. Making money and plenty of it is clearly a good thing; but the accumulation of wealth and the disbursal of that wealth are very political issues. With the former, your name will be forgotten; with the latter, you will live for eternity, remembered for your good deeds.

The Class Question: Implications for Teaching and Learning

In this section, I would like to address the discussion of what Drs. Gordon and Bridglall call "the affirmative development of academic ability." I have connected my response in this area to the class question, in part, to address some of the ways that I think class plays out in the development of this ability. Gordon and Bridglall make reference to the Coleman Report of 1966, which not only documented inequitable outcomes and allocation of resources, but also concluded that a "culture of poverty" posed problems that schools would have great difficulty addressing. Around the same time, Moynihan (1965) wrote an influential report in which he claimed that the family structure of low-income African Americans was disintegrating because of this culture of poverty and the resulting "tangle of pathology." This spurred a torrent of research that was essentially class-based (McLoyd, 1998) and offered up a portrait of the disadvantaged (read: black) child who does not enter school prepared to learn (Bereiter & Engelmann, 1966; Deutsch & Brown, 1964; Hess & Shipman, 1965). More recent studies, however, have documented that resources invested in schools (teacher quality, per pupil funding, class size) do matter substantively for achievement outcomes (Greenwald, Hedges, & Laine, 1996; Nye, Hedges, & Konstantopoulos, 2000).

Everyday Cognition

Gordon and Bridglall say that academic ability is "a developed ability—the quality of which is not primarily a function of one's biological endowment or fixed aptitudes" but "appear to be the products of exposure to the demands of specialized cultural experiences—schooling being the most common" (this volume, p. 319), citing the groundbreaking work on everyday cognition by people like Sylvia Scribner and Michael Cole (1981). Research in everyday cognition (Rogoff & Lave, 1984) has documented the kinds of reasoning in which ordinary people, in nonacademic settings, engage in every day. Such research demonstrates that learning in these nonacademic settings may look very different from either the traditional ways we conceive of pedagogy or more liberal conceptions of constructivist and inquiry pedagogies.

For example, Rogoff (2003) documents one way of organizing learning that she calls *intent participation*. Studying Guatemalan mothers teaching their daughters to weave, Rogoff found that in this and other settings in which children took part as peripheral participants in adult activity, mothers did not give didactic instructions and children did not push for questions to be answered. Rather, children learned largely through intent observation of adult activity. This social organization of learning is very different from most Western societies, where children are largely segregated from adult life and work. The important point is that the range of ways of organizing learning and the range of contexts that support "the affirmative development of ability" are much broader than "formal schooling" addresses or even imagines.

Thus, I argue that one of the positions we need to examine in this post-*Brown* era is how schools can leverage the range of intellective repertoires and ways of socializing learning routines that youth experience *out of school* as resources for enhancing formal schooling. This is a long-standing question posed in a variety of ways by those who call for culturally responsive curriculum, instruction, and teacher preservice and professional development (Gay, 2000; Ladson-Billings, 1994; Warren, Ballenger, Ogonowski, Rosebery, & Hudicourt-Barnes, 2001). It appears more likely that out of school experiences of youth from low-income backgrounds are considered deficits, rather than resources. The use of African American Vernacular English (AAVE) as a medium of communication perhaps has the longest history of attack. In 1996, when the Oakland, California, school board voted to incorporate AAVE into instructional planning, they were subject to a fierce national negative response (Perry & Delpit, 1998), despite the fact that linguists have consistently argued that AAVE represents a systematic and logical language system (Ball & Lardner, 2006; Mufwene, Rickford, Bailey, & Baugh, 1998; Smitherman, 1977) and is one of the many dialects of English spoken within the United States (Ferguson & Heath, 1981; Wolfram, 1981).

The Cultural Modeling Framework

I have attempted to address this challenge of what it means to leverage the everyday knowledge, ways of using language, and everyday practices of youth from minority and low-income communities to promote complex subject matter-specific forms of reasoning (Lee, 1993, 2006). The Cultural Modeling Framework is a tool for analyzing how to leverage such knowledge in relation to the demands of subject matters (Lee, 2001, 2005a, 2005b). My work has focused primarily on literacy, specifically the response to literature at the secondary level. We have demonstrated that in the act of signifying, speakers of AAVE comprehend and produce satire, irony, hyperbole, and symbolism (Lee, 1995). We have analyzed hip-hop lyrics that require the same types of sophisticated thinking; for example, the song "The Mask" by the Fugees features characters who, we are told, wear masks. No youth listening to that song thinks that the guy at the Burger King is wearing a literal, physical mask; they all understand the mask is symbolic. However, this knowledge is typically tacit. Through what we call metacognitive instructional conversations, students are helped to make public how they recognize these tropes as other than literal, and how they reason to infer a warrantable interpretation.

We have done similar work in narrative composing at the elementary school level (Lee, Rosenfeld, Mendenhall, Rivers, & Tynes, 2003), drawing on students' stores of knowledge about African American English rhetorical features and the everyday scripts of events in their worlds to scaffold the composition of well-developed narratives. There is a body of research documenting how instruction in a range of subjects can be organized to leverage what youth of varied (often low-income) backgrounds know and value to support precisely the kinds of academic competencies that Gordon and Bridglall describe as well as the capabilities articulated by the Study Group on the Affirmative Development of Academic Ability (Foster, 1994; Gay, 2000; Nasir et al., 2006; Tharp & Gallimore, 1988).

Thus, I think the question is not whether we have a sufficient knowledge base for such teaching, nor whether we have ample evidence of its efficacy. Rather, our biggest questions are how to help adults learn to teach in this way; how to help school administrators and district leaders organize learning environments for adults; and whether those with vested interests in dismantling this web of inequity have the will, the courage, the organizational abilities, and the political acumen to bring about the kinds of political changes that will be necessary to create schools and neighborhoods where all our children can thrive. How we conceptualize the problems will be crucial to their solutions. We know that the battle for *Brown* required long-term collaboration and institutional resources and that the articulated goals were in response to both the knowledge base and the political constraints of the time.

Our question is whether we can organize ourselves in the ways that Kenneth Clark and Thurgood Marshall and others did—engaging both the academy, other professions, and community organizations such as the NAACP and the Urban League—and equally whether we can read the opportunities and challenges of our times to articulate a program of action that can move us forward. We must in that work anticipate the limitations of *Brown*, including the ways in which the positive outcomes of the *Brown* decision ultimately acerbated class distinctions within the African American community.

The Role of Institution Building

It is my belief that Edmund Gordon and his wife, Dr. Susan Gordon, established the Harriet Tubman Clinic on St. Nicholas Avenue in Harlem in the early 1950s because they saw the need to develop institutions within the community that would support healthy outcomes for youth—that would offer what the PVEST model refers to as protective factors for navigating environmental risks. I think it is for the same reason that nearly 5 decades later, Dr. Gordon has established the Institute for Urban and Minority Education on 125th Street and Adam Clayton Powell Boulevard in Harlem, even though he could have easily housed the institute at his institutional home, Teachers College Columbia.

In a similar vein, I worked with colleagues in Chicago to form the Third World Press in 1966, the Institute of Positive Education in 1969, New Concept School in 1974, and the Betty Shabazz International Charter Schools in 1998 (now with three campuses). Over the past 40 years, these institutions have provided models of educational excellence rooted in an African-centered pedagogy (Lee, 1994; Murrell, 2002); classes for adults focused on wrestling with key issues of the day; the publication of books that have informed political movements; and support for community empowerment efforts. Similar collaborations can be found across the country, but are often invisible to the public and media (Ratteray-Davis, 1994; Warfield-Coppock, 1994).

Because our challenges are grave and persistent, we must always work on multiple levels simultaneously. While we organize and advocate for changes in public policy regarding access to resources that facilitate the affirmative development of academic ability, we must simultaneously organize within our communities, neighborhoods, extended family networks, and homes. I have called for the establishment of a National Rites of Passage program for youth of African descent, with parallel efforts in local communities (Madhubuti, 1990; Warfield-Coppock, 1994). Such an initiative should avoid a uniform, scripted program. In each major urban area and in smaller and more rural towns, my goal is to enable a form of community social organization, providing youth with long-term mentoring from caring adults in addition to their parents and extended family. One component of such efforts needs to be the kind of racial socialization I have described earlier, preparing young people for the world they are about to enter and helping them to internalize positive habits and belief systems about their own efficacy, their responsibilities to themselves and others, and their capacity to pick themselves up when they inevitably get knocked down. I call for a network of socializing institutions that will advocate for advanced placement courses in schools that do not have them; for the increased representation of youth of color and low-income youth in such classes and in other settings that will expose them to work and professional opportunities; and for tutoring and support for children who are failing in school, along with continued advocacy to ensure that schools fulfill their roles more effectively.

This is the tradition that we have inherited from the efforts to bring *Brown* into being and the efforts for community empowerment that preceded *Brown* by hundreds of years (Bennett, 1964; Bethune, 1939; Du Bois, 1992; Harding, 1981). We know that people of African descent, forced into enslavement in the United States, fought in the courts from at least the 18th century forward for legal equity and citizenship (Ladson-Billings, 2004). However, they did not depend solely on the courts or the legislatures. During what many of us call the Holocaust of Enslavement, Africans understood that if you learned to read, you had a responsibility to teach others. After 1865, they formed an array of self-help groups and over 500 schools and 1,500 Sabbath schools (Anderson, 1988). When blacks in Philadelphia could not use the public library system, they developed their own societies that provided access to books (Porter, 1936). These internal efforts at community building typically have a ripple effect. Du Bois and Dill (1911) credited the development of a southern public education system for poor whites to black citizens' efforts to develop public schools. During the 1960s, the evolution of the movement for black studies in universities spawned similar efforts to form Chicano and Chicana studies, Puerto Rican studies, Asian American studies, and Native American studies (Karenga, 1993). Together these ethnic studies programs created an intellectual space within university curriculums for the inclusion of a wider array of contributions to human knowledge, beyond the restricted vision of a Euro-centered context.

While a focus on ethnicity can be exclusive and divisive (as the European-centered focus has indeed been), it can also be liberating and expansive. The world will not be a better place because we all homogenize into a sameness, but rather because we respect and nurture the diversity that is the social ecology of human development, the hybridity out of which new knowledge and insights into the human experience can occur.

REFERENCES

America, R.F. (1990). *The wealth of races: The present value of benefits from past injustices.* NY: Greenwood Press.

Anderson, J.D. (1988). *The education of blacks in the South, 1860–1935.* Chapel Hill: University of North Carolina Press.

Ball, A., & Lardner, T. (2006). *African American literacies unleashed: Vernacular English and the composition classroom.* Carbondale: Southern Illinois University Press.

Bandura, A. (1977). *Social learning theory.* Englewood Cliffs, NJ: Prentice-Hall.

Bandura, A. (2001). Social cognitive theory. *Annual Review of Psychology, 54*(1), 1–26.

Baron, R., Tom, D., & Cooper, H. (1985). Social class, race and teacher expectations. In J.B. Dusek (Ed.), *Teacher expectations* (pp. 251–269). Hillsdale, NJ: Erlbaum.

Bell, D. (1980). *Brown* and the interest-convergence dilemma. In D. Bell (Ed.), *Shades of Brown: New perspectives on school desegregation* (pp. 90–106). New York: Teachers College Press.

Bell, D. (1992). *Faces at the bottom of the well: The permanence of racism.* New York: Basic Books.

Bennett, L. (1964). *Before the Mayflower: A history of the Negro in America, 1619–1964.* Chicago: Johnson Publishing Company.

Bereiter, C., & Engelmann, S. (1966). *Teaching disadvantaged children in pre-school.* Englewood Cliffs, NJ: Prentice Hall.

Bethune, M.M. (1939). The adaption of the history of the Negro to the capacity of the child. *Journal of Negro History, 29*, 9–13.

Bowman, P. (1989). Research perspectives on black men: Role strain and adaptation across the adult life cycle. In R. Jones (Ed.), *Black adult development and aging* (pp. 117–150). Berkeley, CA: Cobbs & Henry.

Boykin, A.W., & Bailey, C.T. (2000). *The role of cultural factors in school relevant cognitive functioning: Synthesis of findings on cultural contexts, cultural orientations, and individual differences.* (Research Report No. 42). Washington, DC: Center for Research on the Education of Students Placed at Risk.

Brown v. Board of Education, 347 U.S. 483 (1954).

Brown v. Board of Education, 349 U.S. 295 (1955).

Byrd, W.M., & Clayton, L. (2000). *An American health dilemma: A medical history of African Americans and the problem of race.* New York: Routledge.

Clark, K.B. (1950). Effect of prejudice and discrimination on personality development. Paper presented at the Midcentury White House Conference on Children and Youth, Washington, DC.

Coleman, J.S., Campbell, E.Q., Hobson, C.J., McPartland, J., Mood, A.M., Weinfeld, F.D. et al. (1966). *Equality of educational opportunity.* Washington, DC: U.S. Department of Education.

Cross, W. (1991). *Shades of black: Diversity in African American identity.* Philadelphia: Temple University Press.

Dai, D.Y., & Sternberg, R. (2004). *Motivation, emotion, and cognition: Integrative perspectives on intellectual functioning and development.* Mahwah, NJ: Lawrence Erlbaum.

Deutsch, M., & Brown, B. (1964). Social influences in Negro-White intelligence differences. *Journal of Social Issues, 20*, 24–35.

Du Bois, W.E.B. (1935/1992). *Black reconstruction in America, 1860–1880.* New York: Macmillan.

Du Bois, W.E.B., & Dill, A.G. (1911). *The common school and the Negro American.* Atlanta: Atlanta University Press.

Dweck, C.S., & Goetz, T. (1978). Attributions and learned helplessness. In J. Harvey, W. Ickes, & R. Kidd (Eds.), *New directions in attribution research* (pp. 157–179). Hillsdale, NJ: Lawrence Erlbaum.

Education Trust (2005). *The funding gap 2005: Low income and minority students shortchanged by most states.* Washington, DC: The Education Trust.

Ferguson, C., & Heath, S.B. (1981). *Language in the USA*. New York: Cambridge University Press.

Ferguson, R.F. (2002). *What doesn't meet the eye: Understanding and addressing racial disparities in high-achieving suburban schools*. Learning Point Associates/NCREL. Retrieved January 30, 2006, from http://www.ncrel.org/gap/ferg/

Finkel, E. (2004, April). *Resolved: State taxes should be raised to improve school funding*. Retrieved February 12, 2006, from http://www.catalyst-chicago.org/arch/04-04/0404debate.htm

Foster, M. (1994). Educating for competence in community and culture: Exploring views of exemplary African-American teachers. In M. Shujaa (Ed.), *Too much schooling, too little education: A paradox of Black life in White societies* (pp. 221–244). Trenton, NJ: Africa World Press.

Gay, G. (2000). *Culturally responsive teaching: Theory, research, and practice*. New York: Teachers College Press.

Gordon, E.W., & Bridglall, B. (2006). The affirmative development of academic ability: In pursuit of social justice. In A. Ball (Ed.), *With more deliberate speed: Achieving equity and excellence in education—Realizing the full potential of* Brown v. Board of Education. *The 105th yearbook of the National Society for the Study of Education*, Part II (pp. 58–70). Malden, MA: Blackwell.

Graham, S., & Taylor, A. (2002). Ethnicity, gender, and the development of achievement values. In A. Wigfield & J. Eccles (Eds.), *Development of achievement motivation* (pp. 121–146). San Diego: Academic Press.

Graham, S., Taylor, A., & Hudley, C. (1998). Exploring achievement values among ethnic minority early adolescents. *Journal of Educational Psychology, 90*(4), 606–620.

Greenfield, P.M., & Cocking, R.R. (1994). *Cross-cultural roots of minority child development*. Hillsdale, NJ: Erlbaum.

Greenwald, R., Hedges, L.V., & Laine, R.D. (1996). The effect of school resources on student achievement. *Review of Educational Research, 66*, 361–396.

Harding, V. (1981). *There is a river: The Black struggle for freedom in America*. New York: Harcourt Brace Jovanovich.

Hess, R., & Shipman, V. (1965). Early experience and the socialization of cognitive modes in children. *Child Development, 36*, 869–886.

Hilliard, A.G. (1995). *The maroon within us: Selected essays on African American community socialization*. Baltimore, MD: Black Classic Press.

Irvine, J.J. (1990). *Black students and school failure*. New York: Praeger.

Irvine, R.W., & Irvine, J.J. (1983). The impact of the desegregation process on the education of Black students: Key variables. *Journal of Negro Education, 52*(4), 410–422.

Jencks, C., & Mayer, S. (1990). The social consequences of growing up in a poor neighborhood: A review. In M. McGeary & L. Lynn (Eds.), *Inner city poverty in the United States* (pp. 111–186). Washington, DC: National Academies Press.

Karenga, M. (1993). *Introduction to Black Studies*. Los Angeles: University of Sankore Press.

Kaufman, P., Alt, M.N., & Chapman, C.D. (2004). *Dropout rates in the United States: 2001*. Washington, DC: National Center for Education Statistics.

King, J.E. (1990). In search of African liberation pedagogy: Multiple contexts of education and struggle. *Journal of Education, 172*(2), [special issue].

Kunda, Z. (1999). *Social cognition: Making sense of people*. Cambridge, MA: MIT Press.

Ladson-Billings, G. (1994). *The dreamkeepers*. San Francisco: Jossey-Bass.

Ladson-Billings, G. (2004). Landing on the wrong note: The price we paid for *Brown*. *Educational Researcher, 33*(7), 3–13.

Ladson-Billings, G., & Tate, W. (1995). Toward a critical race theory of education. *Teachers College Record, 97*(1), 47–68.

Lee, C.D. (1993). *Signifying as a scaffold for literary interpretation: The pedagogical implications of an African American discourse genre*. Urbana, IL: National Council of Teachers of English.

Lee, C.D. (1994). The complexities of African centered pedagogy. In M. Shujaa (Ed.), *Too much schooling, too little education: A paradox in African-American life* (pp. 295–318). Trenton, NJ: Africa World Press.

Lee, C.D. (1995). A culturally based cognitive apprenticeship: Teaching African American high school students' skills in literary interpretation. *Reading Research Quarterly, 30*(4), 608–631.

Lee, C.D. (2001). Is October Brown Chinese: A cultural modeling activity system for underachieving students. *American Educational Research Journal, 38*(1), 97–142.

Lee, C.D. (2005a). Double voiced discourse: African American Vernacular English as a resource in cultural modeling classrooms. In A. Ball & S.W. Freedman (Eds.), *New literacies for new times: Bakhtinian perspectives on language, literacy, and learning for the 21st century*. New York: Cambridge University Press.

Lee, C.D. (2005b). *Taking culture into account: Intervention research based on current views of cognition and learning*. In J.E. King (Ed.), *Black education: A transformative research and action agenda for the new century*. Mahwah, NJ: Lawrence Erlbaum (with AERA).

Lee, C.D. (2006). Every good-bye ain't gone: Analyzing the cultural underpinnings of classroom talk. *Qualitative Studies in Education, 19*(3), 305–327.

Lee, C.D. (in press). *The role of culture in teaching and learning academic literacies: Conducting our blooming in the midst of the whirlwind*. New York: Teachers College Press.

Lee, C.D., Rosenfeld, E., Mendenhall, R., Rivers, A., & Tynes, B. (2003). Cultural modeling as a framework for narrative analysis. In C. Dauite & C. Lightfoot (Eds.), *Narrative analysis: Studying the development of individuals in society*. Thousand Oaks, CA: Sage Publications.

Lee, C.D., Spencer, M.B., & Harpalani, V. (2003). Every shut eye ain't sleep: Studying how people live culturally. *Educational Researcher, 32*(5), 6–13.

Madhubuti, H. (1990). *Black men: Obsolete, single, dangerous?* Chicago: Third World Press.

Maslow, A.H. (1970). *Motivation and personality*. New York: Harper and Row.

McAdoo, H.P., & McAdoo, J.L. (1985). *Black children: Social, educational and parental environments*. Beverly Hills, CA: Sage Publications.

McLoyd, V. (1998). Children in poverty: Development, public policy and practice. In I.E. Sigel & A. Renninger (Eds.), *Handbook of child psychology: Social, emotional and personality development* (Vol. 4, pp. 135–210). New York: John Wiley & Company.

Mills, C. (1997). *The racial contract*. Ithaca, NY: Cornell University Press.

Moynihan, D.P. (1965). *The Negro family: The case for national action*. Washington, DC: U.S. Department of Labor.

Mufwene, S., Rickford, J., Bailey, G., & Baugh, J. (1998). *African-American English: Structure, history and use*. New York: Routledge.

Murrell, P. (2002). *African-centered pedagogy: Developing schools of achievement for African American children*. Albany: State University of New York Press.

Nasir, N., Rosebery, A.S., Warren, B., & Lee, C.D. (2006). Learning as a cultural process: Achieving equity through diversity. In K. Sawyer (Ed.), *Handbook of the learning sciences* (pp. 489–504). New York: Cambridge University Press.

Nobles, W. (1980). African philosophy: Foundations for Black psychology. In R.L. Jones (Ed.), *Black psychology* (2nd ed., pp. 23–36). New York: Harper & Row.

Nobles, W. (1985). *Africanity and the Black family: The development of a theoretical model*. Oakland, CA: The Institute for the Advanced Study of Black Family Life and Culture.

Nye, B., Hedges, L.V., & Konstantopoulos, S. (2000). The effects of small classes on academic achievement: The results of the Tennessee class size experiment. *American Educational Research Journal, 21*(2), 127–142.

Oakes, J. (1990). *Multiplying inequalities: The effects of race, social class and teaching.* Santa Monica, CA: RAND.

Olszewski, L. (2005, December 2). School fight brewing. *The Chicago Tribune,* Metro Section, p. 1.

Orfield, G., & Eaton, S. (1996). *Dismantling desegregation: The quiet reversal of* Brown v. Board of Education. New York: The New Press.

Pajares, F. (1996). Self-efficiency beliefs in achievement settings. *Review of Educational Research, 66,* 543–578.

Perry, T., & Delpit, L. (Eds.). (1998). *The real Ebonics debate: Power, language and the education of African-American children.* Boston: Beacon Press.

Pintrich, P.R., & DeGroot, E.V. (1990). Motivational and self regulated learning components of classroom academic performance. *Journal of Educational Psychology, 82,* 33–40.

Porter, D. (1936). The organized educational activities of Negro literary societies, 1828–1846. *Journal of Negro Education, 5*(4), 555–576.

RAND Corporation. (2005). *Meeting literacy goals set by No Child Left Behind: A long uphill road.* Santa Monica, CA: Author.

Ratteray-Davis, J. (1994). The search for access and content in the education of African-Americans. In M. Shujaa (Ed.), *Too much schooling, too little education: A paradox of black life in white societies* (pp. 123–142). Trenton, NJ: Africa World Press, Inc.

Rodney, W. (1974). *How Europe underdeveloped Africa.* Washington, DC: Howard University Press.

Rogoff, B. (2003). *The cultural nature of human development.* New York: Oxford University Press.

Rogoff, B., & Lave, J. (1984). *Everyday cognition: Its development in social context.* Cambridge: Harvard University Press.

Scribner, S., & Cole, M. (1981). *The psychology of literacy.* Cambridge: Harvard University Press.

Siddle-Walker, E.V. (1996). *Their highest potential: An African-American school community in the segregated South.* Chapel Hill: University of North Carolina Press.

Siddle-Walker, E.V. (2005). Organized resistance and black educators' quest for school equality. *Teachers College Record, 107*(3), 355–388.

Smitherman, G. (1977). *Talkin and testifyin: The language of black America.* Boston: Houghton Mifflin.

Spencer, M.B. (1987). Black children's ethnic identity formation: Risk and resilience in castelike minorities. In J. Phinney & M. Rotheram (Eds.), *Children's ethnic socialization: Pluralism and development* (pp. 103–116). Newbury Park, CA: Sage.

Spencer, M.B. (1995). Old issues and new theorizing about African American youth: A phenomenological variant of ecological systems theory. In R.L. Taylor (Ed.), *Black youth: Perspectives on their status in the United States* (pp. 37–70). Westport, CT: Praeger.

Spencer, M.B. (1999). Social and cultural influences on school adjustment: The application of an identity-focused cultural ecological perspective. *Educational Psychologist, 34*(1), 43–57.

Spencer, M.B., Harpalani, V., Cassidy, E., Jacobs, C., Donde, S., Goss, T., et al. (2006). Understanding vulnerability and resilience from a normative development perspective: Implications for racially and ethnically diverse youth. In D. Chicchetti & E. Cohen (Eds.), *Developmental psychopathology* (pp. 627–672). Hoboken, NJ: Wiley Publishers.

Steele, C.M., & Aronson, J. (1995). Stereotype threat and the intellectual test performance of African Americans. *Journal of Personality and Social Psychology, 69*(5), 797–811.

Tate, W., Ladson-Billings, G., & Grant, C. (1993). The *Brown* decision revisited: Mathematizing social problems. *Educational Policy, 7,* 255–275.

Tharp, R., & Gallimore, R. (1988). *Rousing minds to life: Teaching, learning, and schooling in social context.* New York: Cambridge University Press.

Urban League (2005). *The state of black America.* New York: Urban League.

Walters, R.W. (2003). *White nationalism, Black interests: Conservative public policy and the Black community.* Detroit: Wayne State University Press.

Warfield-Coppock, N. (1994). The rites of passage: Extending education into the African-American community. In M. Shujaa (Ed.), *Too much schooling, too little education: A paradox of Black life in white societies* (pp. 375–393). Trenton, NJ: Africa WorldPress.

Warren, B., Ballenger, C., Ogonowski, M., Rosebery, A.S., & Hudicourt-Barnes, J. (2001). Rethinking diversity in learning science: The logic of everyday sense-making. *Journal of Research in Science Teaching, 38,* 529–552.

Weisner, T. (2002). Ecocultural understanding of children's developmental pathways. *Human Development, 45*(4), 275–281.

Wilson, W.J. (1987). *The truly disadvantaged: The inner city, the underclass, and public policy.* Chicago: University of Chicago Press.

Wolf, D., Bixby, J., Glenn, J., & Gardner, H. (1991). To use their minds well: Investigating new forms of student assessment. In G. Grant (Ed.), *Review of research in education* (pp. 31–74). Washington, DC: American Educational Research Association.

Wolfram, W. (1981). Varieties of American English. In C. Ferguson & S.B. Heath (Eds.), *Language in the USA* (pp. 44–68). New York: Cambridge University Press.

Part Two
U.S. Implications of *Brown v. Board of Education*

CHAPTER 5

Linguistic Considerations Pertaining to Brown v. Board: *Exposing Racial Fallacies in the New Millennium*

JOHN BAUGH

Brown v. Board reminds me, as a linguist, of the linguistic diversity among black Americans, be they descendants of enslaved Africans—as I am proud to be—or Africans who escaped slavery. There is as much linguistic diversity among our race as among any other racial or ethnic group in the United States.

Of course, a statement like that begs the question: What does *Brown* have to do with linguistics? The case attempted to overturn the system of de jure racial segregation and educational apartheid that flourished under the ruse of "separate but equal" public facilities for whites and blacks, as established by an earlier Supreme Court decision, *Plessy v. Ferguson* (1896). At issue in both cases was the relationship between race and public resources, not language, right? However, that is just it. When the Supreme Court handed down its landmark decision, *Brown* was hailed as the case that would lead to educational equality for all African Americans. That vision, however, has yet to be realized. In part, that is because, since *Brown*, we have come to understand that racial segregation was only one obstacle standing in our way. There are

---

John Baugh is the Margaret Bush Wilson Professor in Arts and Sciences at Washington University in St. Louis, where he also directs the African and African-American Studies Program.

numerous other obstacles not acknowledged by the Supreme Court's decision, nor adequately dealt with since. Among the most important of these are the tremendous linguistic divisions between those who trace their ancestry to African slaves and those who do not, divisions that grew out of nearly 500 years of slavery, officially sanctioned segregation, and substandard schools—divisions that continue to affect current attitudes about the linguistic practices of African Americans. America still struggles with racial reconciliation in our collective quest to level the educational playing field so that talent, rather than privilege, will determine each child's prospects, regardless of race. This discussion seeks to introduce some neglected linguistic dimensions into this realm, with particular attention to the *Brown* ruling and the growing linguistic diversity of black America.

The Linguistic Legacy of the African Slave Trade

The linguistic legacy of slave descendants of African origin differs from that of every other immigrant group that has come to the United States (Baugh, 1983, 1999, 2000; Labov, 1972; Rickford & Rickford, 2000; Smitherman, 2000; Wolfram & Thomas, 2002). Whereas the vast majority of immigrants to the United States came here in poverty speaking languages other than English, they typically did so as a group, bringing the language and customs of their homeland with them. Once here, they could build their own communities, profit from their own labor, maintain their own families, and gradually adapt to the dominant language of their new country. For slaves, the situation was much different. Linguistically isolated upon capture, they were intentionally grouped with strangers who did not speak the same language to restrict communication. Once here, they were subject to immediate sale, a practice that dispersed families and eliminated the possibility of gradually transitioning between the old language and the new. It is a remarkable fact that no African languages survived the Atlantic crossing to be preserved in America. All were phased out as slaves were forced to adopt the tongues of their captors to survive. However, the adoption was neither conventional nor complete because slaves were statutorily denied access to schools and literacy. Even when access was finally granted, it was only in a limited fashion and in racially segregated schools with inferior resources. These circumstances and others collectively produced significant differences between the linguistic practices of slaves, slave descendants, and other Americans—differences that still exist in some form to this day.

As we consider the historical impact of the *Brown* ruling, and the unavoidable lack of linguistic consideration that it reflects, we should note that U.S. residents of African origin fall, like all Americans, into one of three linguistic categories:

1. native speakers of Standard (American) English (SEN);
2. native speakers of Nonstandard (American) English (NNE); and
3. those for whom English is not native (ENN).

Dillard (1972) speculated that nearly 80% of U.S. slave descendants fit within category 2, those for whom English is their mother tongue, but Standard (American) English is not their native dialect. We will not delve here into specific linguistic and dialectical differences that distinguish African American Vernacular English (AAVE) from Standard (American) English because those differences have been described at length elsewhere (Baugh, 1983, 1999, 2000; Labov, 1972; Smitherman, 1977). For our purposes here, let us simply say that the native, nonstandard dialect of many U.S. slave descendants is sufficiently different from the prevailing European American standard to represent a barrier to full participation and achievement in school, the workplace, and other areas. Nonstandard dialect speakers differ from their ENN counterparts substantially in their capacity to comprehend spoken Standard English. Comprehension alone, however, in the face of other language barriers and linguistic discrimination, does not mean that nonstandard dialect speakers enjoy the same advantages as those who speak Standard English natively.

It should come as no surprise that the linguistic behavior of U.S. slave descendants has always been criticized when compared to the corresponding European American standard. Nor is the United States alone in this regard. Linguistic controversies about black language usage abound in Brazil, Canada, Mexico, and the Caribbean, among other places where slave descendants of African origin currently reside. However, because so many people, including some slave descendants themselves, have come to view "black" language usage as synonymous with "improper" usage, the unique linguistic and historical reasons for those usage differences have been overlooked in many legal and educational circumstances where such information should be fundamental.

Surely, Thurgood Marshall and his colleagues could not foretell the future significance of linguistic evidence. As in many Supreme Court cases, the issue under judicial review in *Brown* was narrowly focused, and there was no compelling legal need in the course of the trial to stress the unique linguistic consequences of slavery. With other things at stake, such as equal access to public schools, such considerations might have seemed moot. Indeed, few people were even thinking along these lines. A noteworthy exception exists in the work of Lorenzo Dow Turner (1949), who documented extensive Africanisms in the Gullah dialect found in South Carolina and Georgia. Turner's work, while pioneering and highly innovative, tended to be overlooked in his own time by many traditional anthropologists and historical linguists, to say nothing of civil rights attorneys or concerned African American parents in search of quality public education for their children. Be that as it may, there can be no doubt that extensive linguistic barriers confront many students who are African slave descendants in the United States and throughout other nations in North and South America.

Historical Hardship, Immigration Status, and Affirmative Action

The reader will note that I have tried to cast this discussion on an international scale. This is necessary to fully comprehend the relevant linguistic impact of slavery, as well as the lingering consequences of racism that have restricted opportunities for slave descendants of African origin disproportionately when compared with opportunities available to voluntary immigrants to countries that once imported African slaves.

Ogbu (1978) calls attention to "involuntary, caste-like minorities" without overt reference to race, and additional linguistic evidence further suggests that policies once based solely on race—be they legal, educational, or otherwise—are outdated and sorely in need of reform if they are to meet their historical goal of helping descendants of former African slaves gain the competitive educational and entrepreneurial skills that are the hallmark of success among Americans.

Ogbu's work proved to be highly controversial among anthropologists, educators, and linguists for different reasons. In the cases of anthropological and educational critiques, scholars found that his three classifications—that is, the voluntary, involuntary, or autonomous historical status of one's ancestors—proved to be more complicated, if not inaccurate. (He initially classified Native Americans and Mexican Americans as "involuntary immigrants," which is simply wrong.) Some scholars defended Ogbu, while others rejected his paradigm. Its relevance here is to acknowledge his important observation regarding immigrant patterns based on *voluntary* immigration. Unlike many U.S. residents who know their linguistic ancestry, the vast majority of U.S.

slave descendants cannot retrace their precise family origin, as did Alex Haley (1976) on his monumental quest in *Roots*.

Why, then, after so many years, should we reconsider the *Brown* ruling in light of new linguistic facts? A brief thought experiment regarding alternative means to calculate an individual's historical hardship may prove useful. Let us consider a modified version of Ogbu's (1978) caste-like classifications combined with sex and linguistic background.

This experiment calls for you to classify yourself in terms of your personal history. If you are not a U.S. resident, this will not apply. However, if you are, you must describe yourself in terms of sex, language background, and the relative voluntary or involuntary status of your ancestors. In this instance, I have modified Ogbu's original categories to include those whose ancestors were Native American, involuntary immigrants (slave descendants, as well as descendants of indentured servants transported to America against their will), and voluntary immigrants (all those who came to America of their own volition).

As a first order of business, were the majority of your ancestors (e.g., your four grandparents) Native American, involuntary Americans, or voluntary Americans? Some readers will no doubt have grandparents of mixed racial or ethnic heritage, in which case you should concentrate on your four grandparents (i.e., if their personal ancestry is known to you), and their heritage status with respect to native, involuntary, or voluntary immigration. Second, what is your linguistic background? Are you a native speaker of Standard American English (SEN), or would you classify yourself as a native speaker of Nonstandard English (NNE)? If neither of these categories applies to you, then English is not your mother tongue, and you would classify yourself as ENN (English is not native). Finally, are you a man or a woman? With rare exceptions, men have historically had more opportunities than women of comparable social standing. Although we have not included race within this experiment, to avoid further controversies on that subject, we recognize that there are circumstances in which racial differences might justifiably fit within this type of historical calculation. However, because racial classification can be highly complicated, we have chosen to delay its inclusion at this time.

In Figure 1, we have provided a ranking of your relative historical privilege or hardship (somewhat arbitrarily using the Greek letters alpha and omega to illustrate the range from most privileged group to least privileged, respectively). As mentioned earlier, men will tend to have greater opportunities than women of similar social standing.

FIGURE 1

HISTORICAL HARDSHIP INDEX, BASED ON HERITAGE, SEX, AND LINGUISTIC
BACKGROUND.

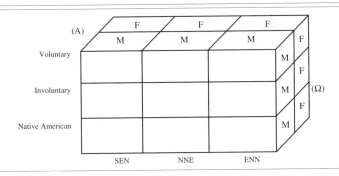

Native speakers of Standard English will have advantages over those for whom Standard English is not native, although native speakers of Nonstandard English will have advantages (again, in the U.S. context), over those who lack basic proficiency in English. Lastly, we argue that those whose ancestors came here voluntarily have advantages over those whose ancestors were forced to immigrate. Moreover, we feel that those who trace the majority of their ancestry to Native Americans fare least well with respect to full participation in American society.

We recognize that the ultimate calibration of these scales is subject to modification, growth, and change (ideally suited to immediate local circumstances), but they call attention to linguistic problems associated with the *Brown* ruling, because it was based exclusively on race. The justices who wrote the ruling did so with America's history of overt racial segregation firmly in mind. At the time, and in the context of Jim Crow segregation, voluntary black migration to the United States was extremely limited and virtually all black Americans were descended from slaves. The number of immigrants gradually increased with the advent of the Civil Rights Movement and with efforts to provide greater opportunities for African Americans. Today, African immigrants continue to arrive in the United States, as well as from Haiti, Brazil, and other nations where people of African descent reside.

However, in light of those historical circumstances, it is easy to see how affirmative action programs that rely exclusively on race could give a black voluntary immigrant who is a native speaker of Standard English undue consideration that, in actuality, had been intended to assist slave descendants toward overcoming past discrimination. Just as we acknowledge that important linguistic dimensions have been overlooked in the past, so too must we take care to distinguish between those whose ancestors suffered under the excruciating yoke of slavery and those of African descent whose ancestors were never enslaved.

Similarly, whereas the typical black person in America is frequently presumed (correctly or not) to be a slave descendant, it is less common for the typical white resident to be presumed a descendant of former slave owners. Descendants of American slave owners, almost without exception, have remained conspicuously silent regarding the multifarious ways they benefited from inheritances derived substantially, if not entirely, from slavery. It is to their collective shame that such people are not more visible or forthcoming in efforts to assist slave descendants toward educational opportunities that will provide today's slave descendants with access to world-class education, health care, and jobs that are competitive in the current global economy.

It is my opinion that slave owner descendants' collective debt to slave labor helps to explain the ongoing controversy about financial reparations for slave descendants, or other forms of racial restitution that are often deemed unfair by more recent U.S. immigrants whose ancestors had nothing to do with slavery. Nevertheless, recent immigrants and U.S. slave descendants find themselves in stiff competition with all other Americans for limited access to higher education and the good-paying jobs that we pray will remain in existence for our children and our children's children.

Although we will not fully resolve all racial conflicts or identify infallible remedies for past American racial afflictions, we can acknowledge that some children have historical economic and linguistic advantages that others do not have. In addition, substantial linguistic evidence confirms that the vast majority of students who trace their ancestry to former enslaved Africans could benefit greatly from effective educational, medical, legal, and social interventions that were unavailable to their ancestors (Baugh, 1998; Denham & Lobeck, 2005).

Although conditions are now more equitable than they ever have been, we have far to go before we can claim that no child will suffer from any form of racial discrimination. Many contributors to this volume have devoted their personal and professional lives to leveling the educational, social, and racial playing field, and they have done so being mindful of the limited or inadequate resources that restrict the right to learn (Darling-Hammond, 1997), as well as the importance of literacy among students of African descent (Ball, 1992, 1998, 2006; Baugh, 1983, 1999; Labov, 1972). Most teacher education programs either ignore the linguistic legacy of the African slave trade or else treat it superficially on their way to bilingual education for ENN students classified as "English Language Learners."

Elsewhere (Baugh, 1998), I have called for reforming the linguistic classification of students, particularly in the wake of the global Ebonics controversy that erupted in Oakland, California, when members of the local school board passed a notorious resolution claiming that 28,000 African American students within that school district spoke "Ebonics." Although the crafters of the Oakland resolution had the commendable intention of improving Standard English proficiency among their students, they did not anticipate the firestorm of protest that would greet their claim that blacks in America speak a language other than English. Indeed, it was partly this tactic of classifying nonstandard dialect speakers as foreign language speakers that caused the Oakland resolution to backfire. If slave descendants speak a language other than English, then they are entitled to access to bilingual education funding just like every other ENN group, according to the 1976 Supreme Court *Lau v. Nichols* ruling that compelled school districts to make special accommodations for students whose mother tongue is not English. As a means of obtaining funds for improving Standard English proficiency, this approach did not work, and for good reason. To be sure, U.S. slave descendants who speak a nonstandard dialect of English are not considered "English language learners," nor should the two be confused. However, neither are they native speakers of Standard English, and the fact remains that not all dialects are perceived as equal from a social or educational point of view. Therein lies the necessity for educational policies targeted to the needs of nonstandard dialect speakers.

Although the educational issues that emerged during the Ebonics episode were not resolved, they are directly relevant to *Brown* in that they highlight the inadequacy of using race as the sole criterion for evaluating our progress toward educational equity for all Americans. Surely, the *Brown* ruling is of limited relevance to recent voluntary black immigrants. Moreover, important ethical considerations are glossed over by policies that allow affluent immigrants (of any racial background) to displace those whose ancestors suffered long-standing historical hardship in the United States, such as Native Americans, white descendants of indentured servants, or my fellow slave descendants of African origin. Racial classification alone cannot tease out these important historical differences, but educational programs based on evaluations of students' cultural and linguistic backgrounds could be more precise and overcome some of the problems posed by social remedies that now rely exclusively, or primarily, on race. The ultimate decision on whether to consider race in affirmative action will remain controversial because it is such a highly personal matter. Affirmative action decisions may need to be determined on a case-by-case basis, if for no other reason than the tremendous complexity of racial classification.

Although the strongest economic and sociological evidence with which I am familiar confirms Cornell West's (1993) admonition that race still matters, a thesis buttressed by the independent efforts of Sears, Sidanius, and Bobo (2000), it has been useful to consider alternatives to race when pondering the task of racial reconciliation. While it may seem counterintuitive to exclude race from models intended to overcome past racial afflictions, the linguistic evidence strongly confirms that race alone can no longer be considered adequate for the purpose of policy or social reform. One exception to this rule is medicine, an area in which racial considerations remain critical to basic research. Because genetic ancestry is often linked to propensity for disease, efforts to advance color-blind medical research typically constitute retrograde steps toward providing high-quality medical care to a socially stratified nation of (in)voluntary immigrants with disparate access to wealth.

On the whole, however, efforts aimed at overcoming past racial discrimination that are based exclusively on race—like the *Brown* ruling—should be reexamined to ensure that taxpayer funds are effectively serving those students most in need of help. This ranking is visually depicted in Figure 1, where those in the upper left quadrant may be thought of as socially privileged in contrast to those who are in the lower right quadrant. They are most in need of help, whether in the form of affirmative action or other means that will guarantee every child, from every background, an education that will allow them to reach their full potential as a citizen of a compassionate nation that strives to advance the well-being of all.

These general observations about historical trends belie an important personal dimension that is vital to every individual's linguistic journey in life. That dimension has to do with personal linguistic aspirations. Within the United States, as elsewhere, young adults strive to adopt the same linguistic behavior exhibited by persons they respect and wish to impress. Because young adults vary greatly regarding those they seek to impress, the pressures effecting ongoing linguistic changes within the general populace look much like our national weather map, with constant and contextual fluctuations as we move between formal, informal, private, and public discourse. Some individuals or families are sticklers for linguistic precision, and they do all they can to avoid excessive colloquialisms. Others from nearly identical backgrounds may choose to embrace their historical vernacular, and to do so with considerable pride, despite the awareness that others seek to diminish their way of speaking. The elastic quality of our speech, when combined with personal linguistic aspiration, cannot be artificially constrained; rather, we are a product of the linguistic exposure that we encounter throughout life. In some instances, we are displeased with our linguistic plight, while in others we are delighted, as when we find our linguistic skills to be of value, if not a source of power.

Within a given day, we are each likely to face competing linguistic forces within our families, at school, or on the job. The linguistic adjustments that we display in our day-to-day lives become more complicated, at least within U.S. contexts, for those who lack proficiency in the dominant linguistic culture. Some people for whom Standard English is not native devote tremendous effort to "accent reduction," which might more accurately be called "accent replacement." They know that others, typically native English speakers, find fault with their English, and they devote time, money, and great effort to gain as much fluency as possible. Others, again from nearly identical circumstances, will choose linguistic paths of less arduous resistance, and this may often be to their credit and economic benefit, depending on their personal circumstances. Vendors who speak languages other than English frequently attempt to build networks with customers who share their cultural, linguistic, and/or religious backgrounds. I mention the value of heritage languages other than English for two reasons: Some people simply have difficulty mastering a second language. I would argue that it is also difficult to master a second dialect of one's first language.

Educational Challenges

The *Brown* decision is, from a linguistic point of view, devoted to students who have been asked to master Standard English as a secondary dialect of their native vernacular African American English. As such, they are typically drilled on pronouncing "ask" rather than "aks," and they are told to replace "ain't" with "doesn't," "didn't," or "don't," as necessary. These grammatical and pronunciation matters are but the tip of an educational iceberg that lurks beneath the surface of most teacher preparation programs.

The challenges that continue to impede effective education for U.S. slave descendants of African origin are enormous, and the complexities of funding, teacher preparation, class size, charter schools, educational malpractice, and much more have yet to be adequately resolved. The *Brown* ruling made a monumental first step by confirming that educational apartheid in America was unfair to black students in segregated schools. However, because the unique linguistic legacy of slavery was not well understood at that time, many educators (and politicians) underestimate the significance of linguistic barriers that impede academic progress among students for whom Standard American English is not native.

When personal proclivities, peer pressure, and the emergence of the global impact of hip-hop are taken into account, there can be little doubt that educators will encounter considerable linguistic defiance in the classroom. Ironically, the global growth of hip-hop provides many traditional educational opportunities that can help close existing educational achievement gaps (Alim, 2003; Baugh, 1999). Educators can tap into the existence of urban verbal battles or poetry slams that thrive on vernacular innovation. Most people find language to be a fascinating subject, and popular lyrics and other forms of nonprofane language can be used for educational purposes by creative teachers who are willing to acknowledge the value of those languages that students bring with them from their home communities.

By building linguistic scaffolds that begin with children where they are (see Alim, 2003; Ball, 1998; Foster, 1997; Gadsden & Wagner, 1995; King, Hollins, & Hayman, 1997; Lee, 1993; Lewis & Hoover, 1979; Morgan, 2002; Smitherman, 1977, 2000), we are likely to provide students access to the necessary linguistic machinery to produce fluent documents in Standard American English, without calling undue attention to matters of pronunciation that are otherwise inconsequential to the individual AAVE speaker in his or her day-to-day life.

We remain ever thankful to those who broke down the artificial racial barriers that flourished under Jim Crow, and we are both humbled and honored to offer these modest linguistic insights that affirm the unique linguistic heritage of American slave descendants of African origin. Let us acknowledge the importance of respecting our students' home language while at the same time motivating them to employ professional linguistic norms to their economic benefit.

AUTHOR'S NOTE

I would like to acknowledge the generous support of the Ford Foundation regarding my research on inequality and injustice in American education and society. Aaron Welborn, Charla Baugh, Arnetha Ball, and Debra Miretzky provided helpful and substantial contributions to this article, as did three anonymous reviewers who called on me to clarify the linkage between language and race as it pertains to the education of U.S. slave descendants. I benefited greatly from their collective advice and guidance, and all limitations herein are my own.

REFERENCES

Alim, H.S. (2003). *You know my steez: An ethnographic and sociolinguistic study of styleshifting in a black American speech community*. (Publication of the American Dialect Society No. 89). Durham, NC: Duke University Press.

Ball, A.F. (1992). Cultural preference and the expository writing of African-American adolescents. *Written Communication, 9*, 501–532.

Ball, A.F. (1998). Evaluating the writing of culturally and linguistically diverse students: The case of the African American Vernacular English speaker. In C.R. Cooper & L. Odell (Eds.), *Evaluating writing: The role of teachers' knowledge about text, learning, and culture* (pp. 225–248). Urbana, IL: National Council of Teachers of English Press.

Ball, A.F. (2006). Teaching writing in culturally diverse classrooms. In C.A. MacArthur, S. Graham, J. Fitzgerald (Eds.), *Handbook of writing research* (pp. 293–310). New York: Macmillan.

Baugh, J. (1983). *Black street speech: Its history, structure, and survival*. Austin: University of Texas Press.

Baugh, J. (1998). Linguistics, education, and the law: Educational reform for African-American language minority students. In S. Mufwene, J. Rickford, G. Bailey, & J. Baugh (Eds.), *African-American English: Structure, history, and use* (pp. 282–301). London: Routledge.

Baugh, J. (1999). *Out of the mouths of slaves: African American language and educational malpractice*. Austin: University of Texas Press.

Baugh, J. (2000). *Beyond ebonics: Linguistic pride and racial prejudice*. New York: Oxford University Press.

Darling-Hammond, L. (1997). *The right to learn: A blueprint for creating schools that work*. San Francisco: Jossey-Bass.

Denham, K., & Lobeck, A. (Eds.) (2005). *Language in the schools: Integrating linguistic knowledge into K-12 teaching*. Mahwah, NJ: Lawrence Erlbaum Associates.

Dillard, J.L. (1972). *Black English*. New York: Random House.

Foster, M. (1997). *Black teachers on teaching*. New York: New Press.

Gadsden, V., & Wagner, D.A. (1995). *Literacy among African-American youth: Issues in learning, teaching, and schooling*. Cresskill, NJ: Hampton Press.

Haley, A. (1976). *Roots*. Garden City, NY: Doubleday.

King, J.E., Hollins, E.R., & Hayman, W.C. (1997). *Preparing teachers for cultural diversity*. New York: Teachers College Press.

Labov, W. (1972). *Language in the inner city: Studies in the Black English Vernacular*. Philadelphia: University of Pennsylvania Press.

Lau v. Nichols, 414 U.S. 563 (1974).

Lee, C.D. (1993). *Signifying as a scaffold for literary interpretation: The pedagogical implications of an African American discourse genre*. Urbana, IL: National Council of Teachers of English.

Lewis, S.A.R., & Hoover, M.R. (1979). *Teacher training workshops on Black English and language arts teaching*. Stanford, CA: Center for Research and Development in Teaching.

Morgan, M.H. (2002). *Language, discourse and power in African American culture*. New York: Cambridge University Press.

Ogbu, J. (1978). *Minority education and caste: The American system in cross-cultural perspective*. New York: Academic Press.

Plessy v. Ferguson, 163 U.S. 537 (1896).

Rickford, J.R., & Rickford, R. (2000). *Spoken soul: The story of Black English*. New York: John Wiley & Sons.

Sears, D.O., Sidanius, J., & Bobo, L. (2000). *Racialized politics: The debate about racism in America*. Chicago: University of Chicago Press.

Smitherman, G. (1977). *Talkin and testifyin: The language of Black America*. Boston: Houghton Mifflin.

Smitherman, G. (2000). *Talkin that talk: Language, culture, and education in African America*. New York: Routledge.

Turner, L.D. (1949). *Africanisms in the Gullah dialect*. Chicago: University of Chicago Press.

West, C. (1993). *Race matters*. Boston: Beacon Press.

Wolfram, W., & Thomas, E.R. (2002). *The development of African American English*. Oxford, UK: Blackwell Publishers.

CHAPTER 6

Preparation, Pedagogy, Policy, and Power: Brown, *the* King *Case, and the Struggle for Equal Language Rights*

ARNETHA F. BALL AND H. SAMY ALIM

This case is a judicial investigation of a school's response to language, a language used in informal and casual oral communication among many blacks but a language that is not accepted as an appropriate means of communication among people in their professional roles in society. . . . The problem posed by this case is one which, the evidence indicates, has been compounded by efforts on the part of society to fully integrate blacks into the mainstream of society by relying solely on simplistic devices such as scatter housing and busing of students. Full integration and equal opportunity require much more and one of the matters requiring more attention is the teaching of the young blacks to read Standard English. . . . Some evidence suggests that the teachers in the schools that are "ideally" integrated such as King do not succeed as well with minority black students in teaching language arts as did many of the teachers of black children before integration. The problem, of course, is multidimensional, but the language of the home environment may be one of the dimensions. It is a problem that every thoughtful citizen has pondered, and that school boards, school administrators and teachers are trying to solve. (*Memorandum Opinion and Order, Martin Luther King Elementary School Children v. Ann Arbor School District Board*, 1979)

The crisis is not about education at all. It is about power. Power is threatened whenever the victim—the hypothetical victim, the victim being in this case, someone defined by others—decides to describe himself. It is not that he is speechless; it is that the world wishes that he were. (Baldwin, 1981)

Arnetha F. Ball is Associate Professor of Education at Stanford University. Her research focuses on writing and writing instruction and the preparation of teachers to work with poor, marginalized, and underachieving students.

H. Samy Alim is an Assistant Professor in UCLA's Department of Anthropology and author of *Roc the Mic Right: The Language of Hip Hop Culture* (2006) and *You Know My Steez* (2004). His research interests include language and race, global Hip Hop Culture, and diversifying approaches to language and literacy development.

As scholars concerned with educational issues, the year 2004 gave us pause to reevaluate the successes and failures of 50 years of court-ordered segregation since *Brown v. Board of Education* (1954). Taking an action-oriented approach toward social change, all of the authors in this volume are responding to the question: What needs to happen before the close of another half-century in order for us to realize the full potential of *Brown*? Many of the authors in this volume have children, and some of our children have children as well. For us, reexamining *Brown* is not merely a professional exercise. It has personal meaning because we recognize the urgency involved. We realize that our children cannot afford to be subjected to unequal educational opportunities for another 50 years without dire consequences.

For scholars of literacy and educational linguistics, the years 2004 and beyond have given us cause to not only revisit racial issues 50 years after *Brown*, but also to revisit 25 years of language and racial politics since "the Martin Luther King Black English case." This chapter discusses what needs to happen now—with *more* deliberate speed—as we reflect on the years since these two cases were decided and their impact on language education in the United States. As people of color continue to struggle for equal language rights in the United States, we are calling for an agenda that focuses on policy, pedagogy, and preparation. In our view, three major action points should be placed high on the language education agenda for the next half-century: the development and implementation of (1) inclusive, comprehensive, systemic reform in language education policy; (2) critical language pedagogies; and (3) teacher preparation programs in language and literacy education. Before we get to these action points, however, it is necessary to understand some of the historical contexts of this continuing struggle for equal rights. We will discuss the historically neglected linguistic dimensions of the black American tradition; the legal contexts and consequences of *Brown* and *King*; and the educational responses to the rulings. In the final section, we consider the challenges that remain.

The Historically Neglected Linguistic Dimensions of the Black American Tradition

In his thought-provoking chapter (this volume, pp. 90–103), "Linguistic Considerations Pertaining to *Brown v. Board*: Exposing Racial Fallacies in the New Millennium," John Baugh paid particular attention to the historically neglected linguistic dimension of the black American experience in light of the currently neglected issue of linguistic and

cultural diversity in black America. Citing substantial evidence from the
work of sociolinguists on black language in the United States, Baugh
begins with the premise that the linguistic legacy of slave descendants
of African origin differs from that of *every other* immigrant group.
Despite this unique linguistic heritage, or perhaps because of it, the law
has never fully addressed the language issues faced by many black
Americans. As involuntary immigrants (Ogbu, 1978, 1992), black
Americans differ from voluntary immigrants in that, in addition to
suffering the cruel and obvious indignities of chattel slavery, they were
abruptly and systematically cut off from their linguistic heritage. As
Baugh writes elsewhere, not only were they "isolated from other speakers of their native language, which was a practice employed by slave
traders to prevent revolts," they were also simultaneously "denied statutory access to schools, literacy or judicial relief in the courts" (Baugh,
2000a, pp. 108–109). Through the manipulation and control of access
to language and literacy, European slavemasters hoped to situate blacks
as a permanent underclass. These efforts, however, also provided the
sociolinguistic conditions that fostered the development of a unique
black language—alternatively known as Ebonics, Black English, African
American Vernacular English (AAVE), and African American Language, among other labels.

Baugh points out that within the context of the ever-diversifying
black population in the United States (which includes immigrants
from North and South America and Caribbean slave descendants, as
well as continental Africans) all of the above terms for the language of
slave descendants may not exactly fit the bill. In other words, the labels
that are currently being used do not adequately or accurately describe
the full range and complexity of the linguistic diversity represented
in the black language community today. While the black population in
the United States is far more diverse than is often noted, the languages
of most black slave descendants in the Americas do share two very
important qualities. First, all of the "New World" hybrid languages are
the result of contact between African and European languages (e.g.,
Wolof, a West African Niger language, and English). Second, all of
these languages, without fail, have been viewed as lesser versions of
their European counterparts (to put it mildly), and they have suffered
under the laws, practices, and ideologies of linguistic supremacy and
white racism (Alim, 2004a, 2004b). It is the ideology and practice of
linguistic supremacy—that is, the false, unsubstantiated notion that
certain linguistic norms are inherently superior to the linguistic norms
of other communities, and the practice of mapping those "superior"

norms onto the "language" of "schooling," "intellectual pursuits," "economic mobility," and "success"—that we, along with Baugh, seek to dismantle. Our collective aim is to recognize and acknowledge the unique linguistic legacy of the African slave trade and to propose a social action agenda that is based on policy, pedagogy, and teacher preparation to address the long-neglected sociolinguistic reality of black Americans.

In addressing this unique sociolinguistic situation, particularly within the educational context, we must begin with the question: When did speaking black language come to be seen as a problem? According to Baugh, this has always been a problem; however, the fact that there was a vast proliferation of sociolinguistic studies of black language in the 1960s leads us to an expanded response to this question. As a result of *Brown*, America underwent what was often a tumultuous process in attempting to integrate many of its schools. For the first time, no matter how reluctantly, white teachers were faced with the opportunity to teach black students, many of whom were speakers of black language. It was forced interaction between two very different social and cultural worlds that provided the context for the proliferation of public and scholarly discourse about the existence of a "black language." Hypothetically, we could ask: What did the black child speak before his language became known as "Nonstandard Negro English"? In other words, what was the language education experience of the black child in the pre-integration era? Professor Richard Wright provided an insightful response to these questions during a television discussion about the Oakland school board's Ebonics resolution, describing his own childhood education experience in racially segregated schools in Texas. His comments touch on a critical issue that is central to every chapter in this volume concerning racism in American schooling. He notes,

The whole problem of black children going to school and not learning Standard English is a relatively recent phenomenon. . . . I went to school during the 1940s and 50s. We didn't go to school as speakers of black English. . . . Since desegregation you've had to deal with the weight of color. When we went to school, we just went to school. You didn't go to school as a black child, you just went to school as a child. . . . I did not go to a black school, I just went to school. . . . You were simply going to school and the assumption was that you were going to school because you had something to do there you couldn't do away from school, and that's learn something . . . but [now] what we need to understand is that there is an environment in school in which race is something you have to deal with while you're trying to learn something. (Quoted in Baugh, 2000, pp. 109–110)

In this dialogue, we see that public discourse about the language education of black youth in the United States often incites discourse about racism and race relations, underscoring the fact that racism is still a significant issue in American schooling. Further, we see that linguistic concerns, in the minds of many Americans, are often linked to issues of race. In the next section, we take time to reflect on the *Brown* decision—a decision mainly about race—in relation to *Memorandum Opinion and Order, Martin Luther King Elementary School Children v. Ann Arbor School District Board* (1979)—a decision mainly about language. While these two cases have often been discussed separately in the scholarly literature, a joint understanding of the cases should prove useful in our more deliberate movement toward access and equal educational opportunity for all students.

The Legal Context and Its Consequences: The (Re)segregation of Schools, Speech Communities, and *Brown* and *King* in Comparative Perspective

Brown, which many refer to as "the single most honored opinion in the Supreme Court's corpus" (Balkin, 2001), effectively overruled *Plessy v. Ferguson* (1896), which sanctioned separate but equal facilities for blacks and whites. In the years of struggle leading up to the case, many blacks and their supporters, fully aware that white facilities were usually better funded and better resourced by local and state governments, argued that the doctrine of "separate but equal" was inherently unequal and that de jure segregation helped to reinforce the ideology of white supremacy. As we witnessed only one decade ago in the heated "Ebonics controversy" of Oakland, California, in 1996–97 (where the Oakland school board called for teachers to respect the legitimacy and richness of "Ebonics" while teaching "English"), "race and schooling" have remained a cause for concern. However, amidst the firestorm of discussion that emerged around blacks and their language, almost no one mentioned the fact that America has silently become a resegregated society (Orfield & Yun, 1999).

Witnessing the massive white American resistance to court-ordered desegregation, Gillespie-Hayes (1981) noted that "Twenty-five years after *Brown v. Board of Education*, the desegregation of schools 'with all deliberate speed' has resulted in more deliberation than speed in the dismantling of dual school systems. The crucial word for black people in the *Brown* mandate was 'speed,' while the Southern school boards accentuated 'deliberation'" (p. 259). One of the greatest ironies of the *Brown* decision is that students at the beginning of the 21st century are once again separated by race and language in U.S. schools, only this time the segregation is caused by an increasingly complex array of social, economic, and legal issues (Frankenberg & Lee, 2002). The resegregation of American society—not just of some, but of all communities—has resulted in a situation where most black and brown children attend racially segregated schools. De facto segregation is in full effect in almost every major urban area and the increasing resegregation of American cities is strongly correlated with poverty levels: "Although only 5% of segregated white schools are in areas of concentrated poverty, over 80% of black and Latino schools are" (Balkin, 2001, p. 6). Along with teachers throughout the United States, we can testify to the presence of de facto segregation, as there has been a gradual relaxing of the need to comply with court-ordered desegregation since the 1970s (see Balkin's [2001] discussions of *Board of Education of Oklahoma City v. Dowell* [1991], *Freeman v. Pitts* [1992], and *Missouri v. Jenkins* [1995]). While the Kerner Commission (National Advisory Commission on Civil Disorders, 1968, p. 1) feared the development of "two societies, one black, one white—separate and unequal," some sociolinguists feared the development of two separate languages, one black, the other white (Labov & Harris, 1986; also see the debate in Fasold's 1987 special issue of *American Speech*). This, they argued, would mean that the language of some blacks in resegregated America would be growing further and further away from the "language of schooling," possibly halting black American educational progress.

The Martin Luther King Black English Case

In 1979, a federal district court handed down a decision in favor of 11 African American children, residents of a scatter-site low-income housing project in Ann Arbor, Michigan, and students at Martin Luther King Jr., Elementary School, holding the Ann Arbor School district board responsible for failing to adequately prepare the King School teachers to teach children whose home language was African American English (see Ball & Lardner, 1997). Like *Brown*, the *King* case drew national as well as international attention. *King* focused on the role of language variation in the education of black children, the language barriers created by teachers' unconscious negative attitudes toward these students' language use, and the negative effect these attitudes had on student learning. Ball and Lardner noted that the *King* case is significant because it associated low educational achievement not with shortcomings within learners, but with inadequate, ineffective curricular and pedagogical routines, and it held the school district and teachers responsible for rethinking pedagogy and curriculum in light of extant information about AAVE. Stating that a major goal of a school system is to teach reading, writing, speaking, and understanding standard English (Memorandum 1391), Judge Charles Joiner wrote that "when teachers fail to take into account the home language" (Memorandum 1380) of their students, "some children will turn off and not learn" (Memorandum 1381). In the *King* case, the Court ruled that the teachers' unconscious but obvious attitudes toward the African American English used by the plaintiff children constituted a language barrier that impeded the students' educational progress (Memorandum 1381).

In the *King* decision, Joiner explicitly makes the connection between language barriers and segregation (see this chapter's opening quote). *King* represents the first test of applicability of 1703(f), the language provision of the 1974 Equal Educational Opportunity Act, to speakers of black language (Smitherman, 1981, 2000).

Critical to this chapter, the judge was also influenced by sociolinguistic testimony that dually attributed the continued existence of black language to external, social factors (such as the historical and enduring isolation of blacks from "mainstream" America and its institutions) and internal, community factors (such as the recognition of black language as an important cultural symbol of black ethnic identity and group solidarity). Unfortunately, while there is much to celebrate as a result of the *King* case, it is also important to note that the elements of the decision that directly address language barriers and African American English have yet to be cited as a precedent in other cases aimed at school policy. Furthermore, the Court's final *Memorandum Opinion and Order* explicitly and unequivocally positions African American English in a subordinate relationship to the mainstream, stating that

Black English is not a language used by the mainstream of society—black or white. It is not an acceptable method of communication in the educational world, in the commercial community, in the community of the arts and science, or among professionals. (Memorandum 1378)

In the aftermath of both the *King* decision and the Oakland "Ebonics controversy" (Baugh, 2000a; Rickford & Rickford, 2000), the majority of the American public deemed it irrational to expect teachers to use existing knowledge on African American English to better educate AAVE speaking students. However, the dialogue on the right of black students to their own language that took place among scholars following both cases presented important questions for educators to consider: What are the rational ways by which teachers can take black language into account when teaching black students? What is the state of "existing knowledge" on the subject? How can we prepare teachers who have the knowledge, skills, and disposition to teach all students effectively? In the remainder of this chapter, we examine the state of educational language policy for speakers of black language and suggest ways in which we can revisit and rethink pedagogical approaches that take students' language into account while also considering the interconnectedness of language within a larger sociopolitical and sociohistorical context that helps to maintain unequal power relations in a still segregated society. In addition, we address the issue of teacher preparation.

The Educational Response to the Legal Decision: Systemic Educational Language Policy Reform for All "Language Minority Students"

Although not mentioned in the prior chapter, perhaps the most comprehensive ideas on creating systemic educational language policy reform were formulated by its author (Baugh, 1995, 1998) when he drew on the "African American language minority student" as a point of departure and as a case in point in his discussion of "language minority students." Traditionally, this term had been used as a code phrase that actually referred to English language learners (ELLs) or those students for whom English is not their native language. Using Judge Joiner's decision in the *King* case, Baugh redefined linguistic parameters in innovative ways that adjusts educational policy so the linguistic classification "Language Minority Students" included black American students. He noticed how in the *King* case, Joiner drew upon *Lau v. Nichols* (1974), a Supreme Court ruling that called upon school districts to address the linguistic needs of ELLs (in this case, Chinese-speaking students in San Francisco) to bolster his decision. This precedent had significant implications for the linguistic reclassification of speakers of black language. For Baugh, the key dimension of Joiner's reasoning was the fact that he called upon education agencies "to take appropriate action to overcome *language barriers* that impede equal participation by its students in its instructional programs" (see 1703[f] above; author's emphasis). For the first time, the barriers faced by black

American students who spoke a variety of English known as "Black English" were given the same attention as those barriers faced by ELLs (that is, students traditionally referred to as "language minority students").

Baugh further drew some comparisons between the black American and Hawaiian sociolinguistic situations, wherein both groups share a history of "creolized English," both are "'involuntary caste-like' minorities, both have been denied the use of the languages of their ethnic background, and both have performed poorly in schools once they were given the opportunity to attend schools" (Baugh, 1998, p. 294). In Hawaii, however, categorical programs in bidialectal education exist and their success can be partially attributed to Hawaiian native language revitalization efforts and the *respect* that is afforded these students' home language. This overt respect stands in obvious contrast to the black language situation, in which AAVE is afforded little or no respect in most educational contexts. This lack of respect may very well be the primary reason why cases like *King* and incidents like "the Ebonics controversy" continue to emerge.

In his analysis, Baugh also reformulated the two traditional categories of "language minority students" into three linguistic subdivisions: (1) students who are native speakers of Standard English; (2) students who are native speakers of Nonstandard English; and (3) students for whom English is not native (see Baugh, 1998, p. 296). Under 1703(f) and Title VII, the second and third groups would receive funding from the federal government to address the "language barriers" that they confront in school (e.g., most Spanish-speaking Latinos fall under the "Bilingual Education Act" [1968]). The question remains: While this reclassification makes all the sense in the world, why has such a classification been resisted and rejected by policymakers?

Historically, in the bureaucratic world of educational policy, blacks were excluded from any funds for linguistic purposes based on their receipt of Title I funds for poverty, while Latinos and other ELLs were excluded from funds designated to fight against poverty, based on their receipt of Title VII funds as ELLs. This is a strange situation, particularly because poverty and English language learning are highly correlated variables. Under Baugh's reformulation, the two policies did not have to be seen as mutually exclusive. Baugh supported efforts that called for the extension of Title I (poverty) funds to ELLs who were also poor, but added that black Americans and other speakers of "Non-standard English" should receive funding from a federal source to address language barriers to educational success. While Baugh's forward-looking, comprehensive policy recommendations offered a way for the American upper middle class to recognize their privilege and level the linguistic playing field in a sincere effort to leave no child behind, his recommendation was met with great resistance. If implemented, such a policy would have secured federal funding for all linguistically and culturally diverse students who face language barriers that limit their chances at educational success.

Now, more than ever, it is time to forge a language policy alliance between scholars, education reformers, and advocates for the rights of all linguistically and culturally diverse students. Together, these constituencies can present a united front that calls for the formulation of a national language policy for all students who speak a language variety other than Standard English—that would include, for example, Vietnamese ELLs in the San Francisco Bay Area, Jamaican Creole speakers in the Bronx, Chicano English speakers in East Los Angeles, isolated white Appalachian English speakers in the mountains of the northeast, Gullah speakers on the Carolina Sea Islands, Lumbee English speakers in southeastern North Carolina, and Arabic-dominant Palestinian ELLs in New Jersey—to name a few. This broad-based coalition could argue for the cultural, social, and economic value of additive language policies that foster the development of "Standard English" while maintaining, respecting, and building upon the home languages of the students that we teach. While black Americans have long been the most vocal leaders of the struggle for civil rights in the United States, which every "minority" group has benefited from, this broad-based coalition would give added strength and momentum to the struggle, particularly in light of growing antibilingual sentiment and legislation, and in light of the public furor over Ebonics and the proposed establishment of anti-Ebonics laws (Richardson, 1998, p. 14), which prohibit the use of black language in the classrooms—even as a means of acquiring Standard English.

The Conference on College Composition and Communication has adopted a national language policy that includes three main points: (1) it reinforces the need for teachers to teach students mainstream academic language varieties; (2) it reaffirms the legitimacy of nonmainstream languages and dialects and promotes instruction in mother tongue as a coequal language of instruction along with the predominant academic language variety; and (3) it promotes the acquisition of one or more foreign languages, preferably a language spoken by persons in the Third World, such as Spanish, because of its widespread use in this hemisphere.

Along with the widespread adoption of such policies, we need to develop ways to improve language pedagogies and teacher preparation programs that prepare teachers to work with culturally and linguistically diverse students.

Pedagogies of Power, Critical Language Awareness Pedagogies, and the Redefinition of "Language Barriers"

Examining the Power of Language

In redefining the regulatory definition of "language minority students," Baugh (1998) also posited a rather unique and insightful redefinition of "language barriers" to refer not only to the academic struggles faced by linguistically marginalized students, but also to those experienced by students classified as members of the linguistic majority who may experience language barriers as well. Baugh does not neglect native speakers of Standard English, either, asserting that they need a different kind of linguistic training: "*They must learn to be tolerant of those who do not speak Standard English*" (p. 297; emphasis in the original). Specifically, these students "must learn that they have a linguistic heritage that places them at considerable advantage in this society, and that the longstanding attitudes of linguistic elitism among politically powerful speakers of American Standard English have restricted opportunities for less fortunate citizens from other linguistic backgrounds" (p. 297).

Teachers and students alike should learn about the relationship between language and discrimination in American society. Linguistic training should teach about the diversity of American English dialects so as to combat ideologies of linguistic prejudice as well as internalized feelings of linguistic shame. For example, linguists have been involved in the production of a set of documentaries that can serve as excellent resources for students engaged in learning about the deconstruction of linguistic elitism. One film, *American Tongues* (Alvarez & Kolker, 1987), can be used in teacher education programs and in secondary schools to generate discussions on the topic of language and discrimination. Participants could share their opinions about the issues raised in the film and discuss some of the perspectives that are shared, such as these:

It's easy to figure out which dialects are more desirable and which dialects are less desirable—just look at which groups are more desirable and which groups are less desirable. We tend to think of urban as better than rural. We tend to think of middle class as better than working class. We tend to think of white as better than black. So if you are a member of one of those stigmatized groups, then the way you talk will also be stigmatized. This goes on all over the United States—in every community.

There's the feeling that anybody who talks like that can't be very smart. And if I don't talk like that I must be smarter than you, and I don't want anybody who's not very smart representing my company. And those kinds of folks tend to have a hard time getting a job. So their speech is very, very important.

Participants can relate the video to their own life experiences and the way people have responded to the way they talk. Experienced facilitators would know that these discussions should be approached with sensitivity.

Critical Language Awareness Pedagogies

In considering critical language awareness pedagogies that combat linguistic discrimination, facilitators could draw on the work of scholars who disprove the notion that the language and literacy practices of students from linguistically marginalized groups are "deficient." According to Labov (1972),

The view of the black speech community which we obtain from our work in the ghetto areas is precisely the opposite from that reported by Deutsch or by Bereiter and Engelmann. We see a child bathed in verbal stimulation from morning to night. We see many speech events which depend upon the competitive exhibition of verbal skills—sounding, singing, toasts, rifting, louding—a whole range of activities in which the individual gains status through his use of language . . . We see no connection between verbal skill in the speech events characteristic of the street culture and success in the schoolroom. (pp. 212–213)

Many scholars have utilized ethnography of communication to provide evidence that students on the margins of school success often use "different, not deficient" language and literacy practices in their home communities. Heath's (1983) classic, decade-long study showed how families from black and white working class communities socialize their children into different "ways with words," some of which are closer to school norms than others. Scholars have demonstrated the language resources students bring into the classroom (Ball, 1992, 1995, 1998) or focused on bridging the out-of-school language and literacy practices of black students with classroom practices (Ball, 2000; Ball & Lardner, 2005; Dyson, 2003; Foster, 2001; Lee, 1993), while others have examined the inventive and innovative language and literacy events of black youth involved in hip-hop culture (Alim,

2004a, 2004b, 2006; Cooks, 2004), spoken word poetry (Fisher, 2003; Jocson, 2005), and other verbal activities (Mahiri & Sutton, 1996; Richardson, 2003).

New Literacy Studies scholars, such as Gee (1996) and Street (1993), situate literacies within the social and cultural practices that are constitutive of everyday life (Hull & Schultz, 2002). Exploring what Ball and Freedman (2004) refer to as "new literacies for new times," the New Literacy Studies pull away from the generally noncritical American sociolinguistic tradition by drawing upon contemporary social and cultural theorists, and thus more closely align with the British tradition of Critical Language Awareness (CAF) (Fairclough, 1995; Wodak, 1995). CAF views educational institutions as helping to maintain the sociolinguistic status quo, and works to identify the ways in which the dominant ideology (and the resulting social control) is perpetuated through language. Both CAF and New Literacy Studies foreground the examination and interconnectedness of identities, ideologies, histories/herstories, and the hierarchical nature of power relations between groups. Research in this area attempts to make the invisible *visible* by examining the ways in which well-meaning educators sometimes silence diverse languages in white public space by inculcating speakers of heterogeneous language varieties into what are, at their core, white ways of speaking and seeing the word/world—that is, the norms of white, middle-class, heterosexist males (Alim, 2004c, 2006). Importantly, a critical approach is not concerned with the study of decontextualized language, but rather with the analysis of "opaque and transparent structural relationships of dominance, discrimination, power and control as manifested in language" (Wodak, 1995).

While American sociolinguistic research has certainly been helpful in providing detailed descriptions of language variation and change, this is often where it stops (Lippi-Green, 1997). Most American suggestions about pedagogy on language attitudes and awareness tend to discuss linguistic stigmatization in terms of *individual* prejudices, rather than as discrimination that is part and parcel of the *socio-structural fabric of society*, which serves the needs of those who currently benefit the most from what is portrayed as the "natural" sociolinguistic order of things. Fairclough (1989, pp. 7–8) argues that the job of sociolinguists should be to do more than ask, "What language varieties are stigmatized?" Rather, we should be asking, "How, in terms of the development of social relationships to power, was the existing sociolinguistic order brought into being? How is it sustained? And how might it be changed to the advantage of those who are dominated by it?"

Research conducted by the Linguistic Profiling project at Stanford University (Baugh, 2000b, 2003; Purnell, Idsardi, & Baugh, 1999) attempts to apply findings of studies on language-based discrimination to educational practice by working with black, Chicano, and Pacific Islander youth in a diverse working-class city in northern California. One goal is to develop a Freireian critical pedagogy (Freire, 1970) of language that aims to educate linguistically profiled and marginalized students about how language is used and, importantly, how language can be used against them (Alim, 2004d). Questions central to the project are: "How can language be used to maintain, reinforce, and perpetuate existing power relations?" and "How can language be used to resist, redefine, and possibly reverse these relations?" By learning about the full scope of their language use (through conducting ethnographic and sociolinguistic analyses of their own communicative behavior) and how language can actually be used against them (through linguistic profiling and other means; see Bertrand & Mullainathan, 2003), students become more conscious of their communicative behavior and the ways by which they can transform the conditions under which they live. The project moves beyond traditional sociolinguistic and educational rhetoric like "respect for diversity" and "all languages are equal" that continually defaults a "standard language" over all other varieties.

Research conducted by the Literacies Unleashed Project at Stanford University (Ball, Ellis, & Wilson, 2004) drew on a sociocultural framework to investigate linguistically diverse students as active learners, capable of reasoning, problem solving, and higher order thinking skills, particularly when provided with adequate support or scaffolds within the zone of proximal development (Vygotsky, 1978). This line of work used writing as the focal medium of literacy to investigate students' higher order thinking skills inside and outside of schools and contributed to our understanding of both the role of others in extending students' learning and the relationship between formal and informal teaching and learning. Realizing the critical role writing plays in the development of higher order thinking skills, researchers questioned why writing does not play a more central role in efforts aimed at closing the achievement gap in our nation's schools.

The research was conducted in a class of 23 students: 13 Latino/as, four African Americans, five Pacific Islanders, and one Filipino—with the majority of them assessed at the lowest quartile of achievement in language arts. The questions guiding the research asked: What is the nature of the home- and community-based literacies that culturally and linguistically diverse adolescents practice when they are away from school? What observable achievement gains do students experience in a writing-intensive class where the curriculum is explicitly based on their home and community literacy practices? Using interview data, surveys, and text analysis, the researchers found that when students' home and community literacy practices are honored in the classroom and allowed to grow along with academic literacies, students experienced not only increased classroom attendance and increased levels of interest in writing over the school year, but they also experienced minimal disciplinary problems in the classroom (unlike in other classrooms), increased lexical density and complex development of ideas in their writing, and the development of generative literacy practices such as multiple representations of ideas through visual literacies, performances, and increased uses of technology-based literacies. More research on the writing of linguistically diverse students is needed if we are serious as a nation about moving, with more deliberate speed, toward closing the achievement gaps in our schools.

Teachers' Attitudes as "Language Barrier": Teacher Preparation for Linguistically and Culturally Diverse Students

Ball and Lardner (1997) discussed the structural and nonstructural barriers to the classroom success of students who are speakers of AAVE. As demonstrated in the *King* case, the teachers' failure to recognize that AAVE is a rule-governed language system led to negative attitudes toward the children who spoke it. In effect, their attitudes constituted a "language barrier" impeding students' educational progress. Then as now, research on language attitudes consistently indicates that teachers perceive speakers of AAVE to be slow learners or uneducable; their speech is often considered to be unsystematic and in need of constant correction and improvement.

In the *King* case, the Court identified teachers' language attitudes as a significant impediment to children's learning, noting that "Research indicates that the black dialect or vernacular used at home by black students in general makes it more difficult for such children to read because teachers' unconscious but evident attitudes toward the home language causes a psychological barrier to learning by the student" (1381). The Court called for the Ann Arbor school district board to develop a program to help the teachers understand the problem, provide them with knowledge about the children's use of African American English, and suggest ways and means of using that knowledge in teaching the students to read (1381). In a court-ordered, 20-hour in-service program for King School teachers, experts in reading and sociolinguistics furnished teachers with information on these topics. In spite of the wealth of information delivered to teachers, the district's report of the results of this in-service program concluded that, although teacher respondents felt positively about all substantive issues, they were somewhat less positive about their understanding of the pedagogical issues.

The nonstructural barriers resulting from negative attitudes were the focus of the Ann Arbor case, and they remain a challenge to successful practice and to our students' educational progress today. Ball and Muhammad (2003) documented the voices of preservice teachers who continue to reflect an attitude of "zero tolerance" about the use of language variation in classrooms. The comments expressed by some of our nation's future educators indicated that there might continue to be very little tolerance for linguistic diversity and the expression of ideas from diverse cultures in many future classrooms. Exploring why these attitudes persist, Ball and Muhammad reported the findings of an Internet study that revealed the lack of required courses in language diversity in most teacher preparation programs. They also concluded that the enrollment of preservice teachers in available courses on language variation is typically low because the curriculum sequence for preservice teachers is loaded with other required courses. After describing one course that was designed to give preservice teachers opportunities to consider the role and function of language and literacies in their lives and in the lives of others, and to consider how language and literacies could be used to teach diverse students more effectively, the researchers concluded that well-designed courses that address issues of linguistic diversity in substantial ways do result in students reexamining their language attitudes and understandings of language, literacy, and linguistic diversity as issues of power and privilege (Ball, 2006; Ball & Muhammad, 2003). They recommend that at least one course—but ideally a three-course series—on the ideologies, pedagogies, and policies of linguistic diversity be required of all teachers.

We call for further efforts that will help us develop future teachers who have a broadened understanding of and respect for linguistic diversity in their classrooms. We call for the preparation of future teachers who will grow to become agents of change within current reform efforts to improve our nation's schools (Ball, 2006; Ball & Lardner, 2005). Research on teacher efficacy suggests that effective teachers develop strong human bonds with their students, have high expectations, focus on the total child, and are able to use communication styles familiar to their students. Exemplary African American teachers in Ball's (1995) community-based organizations were able to draw, to varying degrees, on the rhetorical modes and discourse-level strategies of African American English in shaping interactive discourse as the medium of instruction with their students. Their practice in this regard stands as a model for other teachers to reflect on as they consider expanding their own pedagogical repertoires. Ball argues that the practices of these teachers demonstrate ways of focusing on student participation patterns in interactive discourse to raise teacher awareness of the possible links between their own styles of communication and their students' responsiveness in classroom exchanges. Having high expectations and good intentions is not enough; these intentions and expectations need to be evident to students in observable or, we might say, *audible* behaviors in the classroom.

Challenges That Remain: Realizing the Full Potential of *Brown*

Today, several years after *Brown* has turned 50 and *King* has turned 25, we find ourselves still at a turning point in the journey toward realizing the full potential of these rulings. As was the case with *Brown*, it is clear that the *King* case left many questions unanswered, including the most pressing question of how teachers are to respond to the linguistic and cultural diversity of their students. At the heart of the *King* decision was the recognition of the need for policies, pedagogies, and teacher preparation that reflected sensitivity to students' uses of African American English and responsiveness to racial and linguistic difference. The *King* case raised a question that continues to perplex educators even today: How can policymakers and educators accomplish the necessary but complicated task of assimilating new knowledge about race and language and translating that knowledge into effective pedagogical practices? In ordering the defendant school board to invest time and money in a staff development program for the King School teachers, the Court disrupted the institutional status quo by holding the school district accountable for the inadequate educational progress of their black students. From this perspective, the *King* case can be viewed as a turning point in the history of educational justice for African American children. At the heart of both decisions was the recognition of the need for schools to become sensitive and responsive to the needs of diverse students; Judge Joiner's Memorandum and the court order clearly signaled that recognition.

In this chapter, we have proposed three major action points that move us beyond mere recognition of the problem and in the direction of responding to the question "How can policymakers and educators accomplish the necessary but complicated task of assimilating new knowledge about race and language and translating that knowledge into effective pedagogical practices?" We have proposed that, to effectively address this question over the next half-century, we must place high on the language education agenda the development and implementation of (1) an inclusive, comprehensive, systemic reform in language education policy, (2) critical language pedagogies, and (3) teacher education programs that are specifically designed to prepare teachers to teach in culturally and linguistically diverse classrooms. If we are to realize the full potential of *Brown*, we must continue to disrupt the institutional status quo by aggressively pursuing these action points as we strive to support schools in their efforts to become sensitive and responsive to the needs of diverse student populations.

REFERENCES

Alim, H.S. (2004a). *You know my steez: An ethnographic and sociolinguistic study of styleshifting in a black American speech community*. Publications of the American Dialect Society, no. 89. Durham, NC: Duke University Press.

Alim, H.S. (2004b). Hip hop nation language. In E. Finegan & J. Rickford (Eds.), *Language in the USA: Perspectives for the 21st century* (pp. 387–409). Cambridge: Cambridge University Press.

Alim, H.S. (2004c). Hearing what's not said and missing what is: Black language in White public space. In C.B. Paulston & S. Keisling (Eds.), *Intercultural discourse and communication: The essential readings* (pp. 180–197). Malden, MA: Blackwell.

Alim, H.S. (2004d). *Combat, consciousness, and the cultural politics of communication: Reversing the dominating discourse on language by empowering linguistically profiled and marginalized groups*. Paper presented at the annual meeting of the American Dialect Society, Boston, MA.

Alim, H.S. (2006). *Roc the mic right: The language of hip hop culture*. London & New York: Routledge.

Alvarez, L., & Kolker, A. (Producers/Directors). (1987). *American tongues* [Motion Picture]. New York: The Center for New American Media.

Baldwin, J. (1981). Rap session. In G. Smitherman (Ed.), *Black English and the education of Black children and youth: Proceedings of the National Invitational Symposium on the King decision* (pp. 84–92). Detroit, MI: Wayne State University, Center for Black Studies.

Balkin, J.M. (Ed.). (2001). *What* Brown v. Board of Education *should have said: The nation's top legal experts rewrite America's landmark civil rights decision*. New York: New York University Press.

Ball, A.F. (1992). Cultural preference and the expository writing of African-American adolescents. *Written Communication, 9*(4), 501–532.

Ball, A.F. (1995). Community-based learning in urban settings as a model for educational reform. *Applied Behavioral Science Review, 3*(2), 127–146.

Ball, A.F. (1998). Evaluating the writing of culturally and linguistically diverse students: The case of the African American Vernacular English speaker. In C.R. Cooper & L. Odell (Eds.), *Evaluating writing: The role of teachers' knowledge about text, learning, and culture* (pp. 225–248). Urbana, IL: National Council of Teachers of English Press.

Ball, A.F. (2000). Empowering pedagogies that enhance the learning of multicultural students. *Teachers College Record, 102*(6), 1006–1034.

Ball, A.F. (2006). *Multicultural strategies for education and social change: Carriers of the torch in the U.S. and South Africa*. New York: Teachers College Press.

Ball, A.F., Ellis, P., & Wilson, J. (2004). *Literacies unleashed: Investigating the writing of culturally and linguistically diverse students*. Research Project funded by the Spencer Foundation, Research Training Grant.

Ball, A.F., & Freedman, S.W. (Eds.). (2004). *Bakhtinian perspectives on language, literacy, and learning*. New York: Cambridge University.

Ball, A.F., & Lardner, T. (1997). Dispositions toward literacy: Constructs of teacher knowledge and the Ann Arbor Black English case. *College Composition and Communication, 48*(4), 469–485.

Ball, A.F., & Lardner, T. (2005). *African American literacies unleashed: Vernacular English and the composition classroom*. Carbondale: Southern Illinois University Press.

Ball, A.F., & Muhammad, R.J. (2003). Language diversity in teacher education and in the classroom. In G. Smitherman & V. Villanueva (Eds.), *Language diversity in the classroom: From intention to practice* (pp. 76–88). Carbondale: Southern Illinois University Press.

Baugh, J. (1995). The law, linguistics, and education: Educational reform for African American language minority students. *Linguistic and Education, 7*(2), 87–105.

Baugh, J. (1998). Linguistics, education, and the law: Educational reform for African-American language minority students. In S.S. Mufwene, J.R. Rickford, G. Bailey, & J. Baugh (Eds.), *African-American English: Structure, history and use* (pp. 282–301). London: Routledge.

Baugh, J. (2000a). *Beyond Ebonics: Linguistic pride and racial prejudice*. New York: Oxford University Press.

Baugh, J. (2000b). Racial identification by speech. *American Speech*, 75(4), 362–364.

Baugh, J. (2003). Linguistic profiling. In S. Makoni, G. Smitherman, A.F. Ball, & A.K. Spears (Eds.), *Black linguistics: Language, politics and society in Africa and the Americas*. London: Routledge.

Baugh, J. (2006). Linguistic considerations pertaining to *Brown v. Board*: Exposing racial fallacies in the new millennium. In A. Ball (Ed.), *With more deliberate speed: Achieving equity and excellence in education—Realizing the full potential of* Brown v. Board of Education. *The 105th yearbook of the National Society for the Study of Education*, Part II (pp. 90–103). Malden, MA: Blackwell.

Bertrand, M., & Mullainathan, S. (2003). *Are Emily and Greg more employable than Lakisha and Jamal? A field experiment on labor market discrimination*. (NBER Working Paper No. 9873). Cambridge, MA: National Bureau for Economic Research.

Bilingual Education Act. (Reauthorization of ESEA; P.L. 90–247) (1968).

Board of Education of Oklahoma City v. Dowell, 498 U.S. 237 (1991).

Brown v. Board of Education of Topeka, Kansas, 347 U.S. 483 (1954).

Cooks, J. (2004). Writing for something: The nexus among raps, essay, and expository organizational patterns among AA adolescents. *English Journal*, 94(1), 72–76.

Dyson, A. (2003). *The brothers and sisters learn to write: Popular literacies in childhood and school cultures*. New York: Teachers College Press.

Fairclough, N. (1989). *Language and power*. New York: Longman.

Fairclough, N. (1995). *Critical discourse analysis: The critical study of language*. London and New York: Longman.

Fasold, R.W. (1987). Are Black and White vernaculars diverging? *American Speech*, 62, 3–5.

Fisher, M. (2003). Open mics and open minds: Spoken word poetry in African diaspora participatory literacy communities. *Harvard Educational Review*, 73(3), 362–389.

Foster, M. (2001). Pay Leon, pay Leon, pay Leon, Paleontologist: Using call-and-response to facilitate language mastery and literacy acquisition among African American students. In S. Lanehart (Ed.), *Sociocultural and historical contexts of African American English* (pp. 281–298). Philadelphia: John Benjamins.

Frankenberg, E., & Lee, C. (2002). *Race in American public schools: Rapidly resegregating school districts*. Harvard University: Civil Rights Project of Harvard University. Retrieved January 12, 2006, from http://www.civilrightsproject.harvard.edu/research/deseg/reseg_schools02.php

Freeman v. Pitts, 112 S.Ct. 1430 (1992).

Freire, P. (1970). *Pedagogy of the oppressed*. New York: Continuum.

Gee, J. (1996). *Social linguistics and literacies: Ideology in discourses*. Bristol, PA: Falmer.

Gillespie-Hayes, A. (1981). More deliberation than speed: The educational quest. In G. Smitherman (Ed.), *Black English and the education of Black children and youth: Proceedings of the national invitational symposium on the* King *decision* (pp. 259–271). Detroit: Wayne State University, Center for Black Studies.

Heath, S.B. (1983). *Ways with words: Language, life, and work in communities and classrooms*. Cambridge: Cambridge University Press.

Hull, G., & Schultz, K. (Eds.). (2002). *School's out! Bridging out-of-school literacies with classroom practice*. New York: Teachers College Press.

Jocson, K. (2005). "Taking it to the mike": Pedagogy of June Jordan's poetry of the people in partnership with an urban high school. *English Journal*, 37(2), 44–60.

Labov, W. (1972). *Language in the inner city: Studies in the Black English vernacular.* Philadelphia: University of Pennsylvania Press.

Labov, W., & Harris, W.A. (1986). De facto segregation of Black and White vernaculars. In D. Sankoff (Ed.), *Diversity and diachrony* (pp. 1–24). Amsterdam: John Benjamins.

Lau v. Nichols, 414 U.S. 563 (1974).

Lee, C.D. (1993). *Signifying as a scaffold for literary interpretation: The pedagogical implications of an African American discourse genre* (Research Report Series). Urbana, IL: National Council of Teachers of English.

Lippi-Green, R. (1997). *English with an accent: Language, ideology and discrimination in the United States.* London: Routledge.

Memorandum Opinion and Order, Martin Luther King Elementary School Children v. Ann Arbor School District Board. Civil Action No. 7-71861. 473 F. Supp. 1371 (1979).

Mahiri, J., & Sutton, S.S. (1996). Writing for their lives: The non-school literacy of California's urban African American youth. *Journal of Negro Education, 65,* 164–180.

Missouri v. Jenkins (93-1823), 515 U.S. 70 (1995).

National Advisory Commission on Civil Disorders. (1968). *The Kerner Report.* Commission Chair, Illinois Governor Otto Kerner, Washington, DC.

Ogbu, J. (1978). *Minority education and caste: The American system in cross-cultural perspective.* New York: Academic Press.

Ogbu, J. (1992). Understanding cultural differences and school learning. *Education Libraries, 16*(3), 7–11.

Orfield, G., & Yun, J. (1999). *Resegregation in American schools.* Report published by the Civil Rights Project of Harvard University. Retrieved January 12, 2006, from http://www.civilrightsproject.harvard.edu/research/deseg/reseg_schools99.php#fullreport

Plessy v. Ferguson, 163 U.S. 537 (1896).

Purnell, T., Idsardi, W., & Baugh, J. (1999). Perceptual and phonetic experiments on American English dialect identification. *Journal of Language and Social Psychology, 18*(1), 10–30.

Richardson, E. (1998). The anti-Ebonics movement: "Standard" English-Only. *The Journal of English Linguistics, 26*(2), 156–169.

Richardson, E. (2003). *African American literacies.* New York: Routledge.

Rickford, J., & Rickford, R. (2000). *Spoken soul.* New York: John Wiley & Sons.

Smitherman, G. (Ed.). (1981). *Black English and the education of Black children and youth: Proceedings of the National Invitational Symposium on the King Decision.* Detroit, MI: Wayne State University, Center for Black Studies.

Smitherman, G. (2000). *Talkin that talk: Language, culture, and education in African America.* New York: Routledge.

Street, B. (1993). *Cross-cultural approaches to literacy.* New York: Cambridge University Press.

Vygotsky, L.S. (1978). *Mind in society: The development of higher psychological processes.* Cambridge, MA: Harvard University Press.

Wodak, R. (1995). Critical linguistics and critical discourse. In J. Verschueren, J. Ostman, & J. Blommaert (Eds.), *Handbook of pragmatics* (pp. 204–210). Philadelphia: John Benjamins.

CHAPTER 7

The Linguistic Isolation of Hispanic Students in California's Public Schools: The Challenge of Reintegration

BERNARD R. GIFFORD AND GUADALUPE VALDÉS

According to Frankenberg, Lee, and Orfield (2003), segregation for black students declined substantially after the landmark 1954 U.S. Supreme Court decision, *Brown v. Board of Education*, reaching its lowest point 30 years later. Since this low point, however, because of changing policies governing school desegregation (e.g., the termination of desegregation orders in many areas of the country) as well as increasing residential segregation, American public schools have increasingly become *resegregated* as the proportion of black students in majority white schools has decreased. In the 2000–01 school year, for example, black students in Atlanta and Chicago attended schools in which white students were only 3% of the students enrolled.

By comparison, Latino students have experienced "steadily rising segregation since the 1960s" (Frankenberg & Lee, 2002, p. 2). Unlike black students who have been the focus of desegregation orders and Office of Civil Rights enforcements, Latinos have remained segregated both because of limited policy efforts on their behalf and because of their increasing numbers (a result of increased immigration and high birth rates) in public schools (Frankenberg et al., 2003).

In this chapter, we focus on the educational challenges of linguistic isolation for Latino students by examining the case of California. We first provide a historical overview of Spanish in California, tracing the climate of evolving hostility toward Spanish and Spanish-speaking

Bernard R. Gifford is a Professor in the Division of Education in Mathematics, Science, Technology, & Engineering and Faculty Director of the UC-Berkeley/CSU Joint Doctoral Program in Leadership for Educational Equity at the University of California, Berkeley.

Guadalupe Valdés is the Bonnie Katz Tenenbaum Professor of Education and Professor of Spanish and Portuguese at Stanford University.

immigrants and describing the challenges of achieving equity for Latino students segregated by language. We then address four objectives that are of paramount importance in the challenge of reintegration. The first objective is to summarize the dramatic changes occurring in the racial, ethnic, and linguistic composition of the California public schools, with a special focus on the consequences of these changes for Hispanic students. By design, this summary is considerably more granular than previous efforts (cf. Carroll, Krop, Arkes, Morrison, & Flanagan, 2005; Tienda & Mitchell, 2006a, 2006b). Our conclusions will explain why we believe it is shortsighted to conceive of the challenge of improving the academic achievement of Hispanic students as subsidiary to the larger policy objective of promoting systemic educational reform. Separating these objectives from one another may make for tidy policy discussions, but in light of the demographic and linguistic realities of California's public schools, treating these two objectives as if they were actually divisible is not feasible.

The second objective is to examine the connection between these demographic changes and the corresponding seismic shifts in the linguistic landscape of the California public schools. A better understanding of these interdependent transformations will make it evident why we believe so strongly that any educational initiative that claims to be capable of promoting significant improvements in the academic achievement of Hispanic students must address the challenge of accelerating the acquisition of English among Hispanic English language learners (ELLs). It is only through language acquisition that students can become full participants in their community. We are not suggesting that all Hispanic students are ELLs; in fact, many have sufficient proficiency in English to participate in all–English mainstream classrooms. However, in instances where such fluent English-speaking Hispanic students attend schools populated mainly by Hispanic ELLs, they face a burden that few other students must deal with: functioning as English language informants, models, and mentors to their classmates while performing as exemplary students themselves.

The third objective of this article is to examine the distribution of Hispanic students, particularly ELLs, within the California public schools. As we have noted, a system in which the ELL students are highly concentrated within a limited number of schools, largely populated by other monolingual Spanish-speaking students, makes the task of promoting proficiency in English among Hispanic ELLs much more difficult. The nature of this linguistic isolation[1] will be described, and the relationship between this isolation in school contexts and the economic status of these students' households will be examined. The correlation between this isolation and student academic achievement will be explored by making extensive use of the Academic Performance Index (API), a composite indicator of school-level academic achievement developed by the California Department of Education (CDE)[2] to analyze the progress made by schools in meeting the Annual Yearly Progress (AYP) requirements of the No Child Left Behind Act of 2001 (NCLB).

Our fourth and last objective is to situate our statistical findings within a policy context that acknowledges the legacy of *Brown v. Board of Education*, but seeks to further expand upon this legacy. Unlike the situation facing African Americans, the highly problematic circumstances currently facing Hispanic students enrolled in the California public schools is not the result of 200-plus years of state-sanctioned racism and oppression. Rather, they stem from the federal government's failure to acknowledge the consequences of its schizophrenic immigration policies on the public schools; specifically, U.S. officials' inability or unwillingness to craft an immigration policy that acknowledges the reality of the integrated character of the U.S.–Mexico economy or the larger possibilities of an integrated common market of North and South American countries, spurred by the movement of people across national borders.

Current U.S. immigration policy has and continues to encourage the movement of large numbers of "unauthorized resident" workers into California, principally from Mexico and other Latin American nations, while penalizing these individuals once their families become members of the new community. These workers are attractive to many U.S. employers because they are inexpensive, willing to take on work that U.S. citizens will not do, isolated from other workers and the larger polity, and usually too frightened to defend themselves against predatory employers. They are attracted to the United States because they live in countries plagued by corrupt politicians, underdeveloped economies, and discrimination against "Mestizos" and women (Nazario, 2006). Although children born into the households of these "unauthorized residents" are legal U.S. citizens, they are not exempt from the dangers and uncertainties that afflict their "unauthorized" family members, including high rates of household poverty, poor schools, inadequate health care, and limited employment prospects.

Frustratingly, the U.S. immigration policies that have both encouraged and permitted school-age children of unauthorized residents to

enter the California public schools also treat them as if they are unin-
vited dinner guests who have exhausted the generosity of their hosts, at
best, and at worst as criminals, guilty of stealing educational benefits
they do not deserve. It is likely that these schizophrenic policies have
fed the sentiments that produced the series of propositions California
voters enacted to express their frustration with the character of U.S.
immigration policies in the last 25 years.

Spanish Speakers in California: A Historical Overview[3]

Currently, Spanish is spoken in California by 8.1 million of
California's residents over age five, out of a total population of 33.8
million (U.S. Census, 2003). Because recent immigrants often struggle
with the English language (Hill & Hayes, 2002), many English-
speaking, monolingual Californians view Spanish as a persistent threat
to English, a language of the undocumented and the uneducated that
has little value for ordinary Americans who do not plan to work in
immigrant communities.

The Spanish language entered California in 1542 with Juan
Rodríguez Cabrillo's arrival at the port of San Diego and was established as the language of interaction and imposed on the native people
(Schiffman, 1996). According to Mar-Molinero (2000), three types of
pressures led to the imposition of Spanish during the colonial period:
the pressure toward centralization, the belief that the native people
would not adopt Christian values as long as they spoke their original
languages, and the belief that other tongues could not convey Christian
beliefs.

The Imposition of the English Language

In 1823, after a bitter war of independence with the mother country,
the provinces of New Spain, including California, became provinces of
the new Republic of Mexico. For *Californios* who had not been involved
in the war of independence, the change was a difficult one. They did
not see themselves as Mexicans and deeply resented changes made by
Mexican government officials, especially the secularization of the mis-
sions. *Californios* subsequently resented the Mexican government even
more when they learned that California had ceded to the United States
as an outcome of the Mexican War.

The English language arrived officially in California in 1846 when
Sloat raised the American flag in Monterrey, the capital of California.
In 1848, Mexico and the United States signed the Treaty of Guadalupe

Hidalgo. According to Schiffman (1996), the treaty included guarantees of the rights of the citizens within the ceded territories, including customs, religion, and language. The first California Constitution, ratified in 1849, interpreted the language of this treaty as ensuring that Mexican citizens would receive the same freedom and privileges granted to other citizens of the United States, and convention delegates accepted the proposal of delegate Noriega from San Luis Obispo, which established that:

All laws, regulations, and provisions emanating from any of the three supreme powers of this State, which from their nature require publication, shall be published in English and Spanish. (Constitution of the State of California 1849, Article VI, Section 21)

Historical accounts of the period after 1846 suggest that, as had been the case with the first conquerors of California (the Spanish), the Anglo-Americans also viewed themselves as racially and culturally superior to the vanquished population. Anglos who arrived in California felt great disdain for the wealthy and aristocratic *Californios*, seeing them as indolent, unproductive, and lazy (Haas, 1995; Mapes, 1992). Accounts of the lifestyles of wealthy ranchers written by Easterners traveling in California (e.g., Mapes, 1992; Pitt, 1998) emphasize differences between Anglo-Protestant values stressing frugality and hard work and their perception of the ranchers as irresponsible with their land, exploitative of the native people, and ostentatious.

Unfortunately, by 1878, as Crawford (1992a) points out, not a single Spanish-speaking delegate was present at the Constitutional Convention that revised the 1849 document. Perhaps as a result, the Constitution of 1879 revoked its earlier policy on publishing laws in English and Spanish and limited the publication of all official state proceedings to English. During the convention debates, proponents of the English-only stance argued that *Californios* had had 30 years to learn English, and that the Treaty of Guadalupe Hidalgo was not an implied contract to protect language rights.

The English-only, anti-Mexican stances that influenced the new Constitution also influenced the daily lives of the Spanish-speaking population of California. According to Macías (2001), by 1855 the State Bureau of Public Instruction decreed that all schooling, public and private, should be conducted exclusively in English. Up until that time, Spanish was used in 18% of private and Catholic schools. In 1870, a second state law was passed requiring English as the only language of

instruction in all schools. Macías concludes (p. 347) that by the beginning of the 20th century, California had subjugated non-English languages, especially Spanish. English was the official language of
instruction in the schools, English literacy was required for voting, and
English was the language for administration of government.

The Segregation of Spanish-Speaking Students

The early segregation of Mexican-origin students in California
schools is an example of a policy directed, in theory, at providing
language services, through special instruction and programs, for
English learners. However, an examination of school segregation in
California as it has impacted African American, Asian, and Mexican
children revealed that "throughout the state's history there has been a
conflict between those who have seen the schools as universal and
unifying institutions and those who have seen the schools as particular-
ist and separated institutions" (Wollenberg, 1976, p. 6).

In the case of Mexican students in California, Wollenberg (1976)
presents evidence of the routine segregation of children of Mexican
workers beginning in 1910. By the 1920s, 10% of the state's total school
population consisted of Mexican-origin students. This increased enrollment of Mexican children led to the opening of separate Mexican
schools in many areas of the state as well as segregated swimming pools,
theatres, and restaurants. Schools segregated children largely in
response to the demands of white parents who feared educational retardation for their own children.

It was not until 1945 that Mexican parents took legal action against
the schools. The 1946 case of *Mendez v. Westminster* held that the State
Education Code did not provide for the segregation of children of
Mexican origin and that no clear valid educational reason justified their
segregation (Wollenberg, 1976); however, although the plaintiffs prevailed in the appeal, the decision had an impact only on de jure and not
on de facto segregation.

Bilingual Education Policy

In 1976, the California legislature approved the passage of the
Chacon-Moscone Bilingual-Bicultural Education Act (1976), which
made it legal to give non-English-speaking students access to the curriculum through their primary language. Macías (2001) argues that
federal policies (e.g., the Civil Rights Act of 1964 and the Bilingual
Education Act of 1968) and the 1974 *Lau v. Nichols* U.S. Supreme Court
decision had created a context in which states like California were

encouraged to repeal existing laws limiting or prohibiting the use of non-English languages in education. Chacon-Moscone required schools to provide pupils who were limited- or non-English speaking with equal educational opportunities. In 1980, the Bilingual Education Improvement and Reform Act mandated schools to provide bilingual education to limited English-speaking students.

These two statutes, however, expired (or sunsetted) in 1987 and were not renewed. By that time, controversies surrounding the vagueness of the language of the *Lau* decision had provoked a debate around the country about the types of remedies considered legitimate in providing equal educational opportunities to ELLs.[4] As a language policy, Chacon-Moscone overtly dealt with the implementation of instruction in non-English languages, and as a civil rights policy, it obligated the state of California to provide a meaningful and equitable education for all students. However, to some degree, California's Bilingual Education and Reform Act (1980) could be seen as a covert exclusionary policy. It allowed Spanish-speaking students to be educated separately from other students, and it justified this separation— as was done in the case of *Mendez v. Westminster*—by arguing that the special language needs of certain groups of students required the development of unique educational programs designed to meet their special needs.

For those concerned about segregation, bilingual education appeared to be a language policy that masked exclusion. For those concerned about the futility of educating students in a language that they did not understand, bilingual education was a compensatory education policy that focused on language, the condition that prevented students from accessing the curriculum. Finally, for those concerned about providing too many benefits to an undeserving population, bilingual education was an employment boon for Spanish-speaking teachers, an expensive drain on state resources, a Spanish language program designed to prevent students from learning English, and a manifestation of new immigrants' refusal to become American. Over time, negative views about bilingual education resulted in the passage of a number of anti-immigrant, anti-Spanish-speaking, and anti-Mexican legislative initiatives during the 1980s and 1990s in California.[5]

From 1976 to 1995, immigration to California increased dramatically, and by 1994, one-third of the foreign-born population in the United States resided in California (Population Resource Center, 2004). The political climate toward Spanish-speaking people is a hostile one in California, and disputes about education continue. No Child Left Behind rhetoric permeates discussions about the schooling of ELLs while budgetary constraints have led to per pupil spending that is well below the national average in an environment replete with challenges caused by changing demographics (i.e., relative youth of the population, racial/ethnic diversity, number of English language learners, and the geographic redistribution of the population) (Carroll et al., 2005), which we examine now.

Demographic Changes in the Hispanic and English Learner Population

Our examination of recent demographic shifts begins with the "scissor graph" plotted in Figure 1.

Beginning with the 1996–97 school year, the proportion of Hispanic public school students exceeded the proportion of non-Hispanic white students enrolled in the California public schools, and this trend has since continued. The proportion of Hispanic students in 2004–05 (46.8%) exceeded that of non-Hispanic whites (31.3%) by more than one-half. The data compiled in Table 1 enable us to examine the micro-demographic forces responsible for the downward bend in the lower blade of the scissors graph in Figure 1.

The recorded data show that during the period 1999–2000 to 2004–05, the growth in the K-12 student population was three-quarters of the total for the previous period (371,000 versus 484,000 students). This drop was fueled by a 9.8% decline in the non-Hispanic white student population, along with a lesser decline in the African American student

FIGURE 1

CHANGES IN THE PROPORTION OF HISPANIC AND NON-HISPANIC WHITE K-12 STUDENTS ENROLLED IN THE CALIFORNIA PUBLIC SCHOOLS: 1995–96 TO 2004–05.

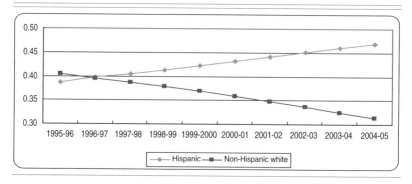

TABLE 1
CHANGES IN CALIFORNIA'S PUBLIC SCHOOL'S STUDENT POPULATION SEGMENTS BETWEEN 1995–96 TO 2004–05

Segment	School Years			Changes: 1995–95 to 1999–2000			Changes: 1999–2000 to 2004–05		
	1995–96	1999–2000	2004–05	Number	%	Distribution	Number	%	Distribution
Hispanic	2,118,028	2,513,453	2,961,101	395,425	18.7	81.6	447,648	17.8	120.8
White	2,209,717	2,195,706	1,981,597	(14,011)	(0.6)	(2.9)	(214,109)	(9.8)	(57.8)
Asian	449,725	479,073	510,450	29,348	6.5	6.1	31,377	6.5	8.5
African American	478,912	509,637	505,215	30,725	6.4	6.3	(4,422)	(0.9)	(1.2)
Filipino	131,820	141,045	163,149	9,225	7.0	1.9	22,104	15.7	6.0
American Indian	47,697	50,750	51,822	3,053	6.4	0.6	1,072	2.1	0.3
Pacific Islander	31,325	37,995	39,634	6,670	21.3	1.4	1,639	4.3	0.4
Multiracial/Other		23,953	109,214	23,953		4.9	85,261		23.0
Totals	5,467,224	5,951,612	6,322,182	484,388	8.9	100.0	370,570	6.2	100.0

Note: Tables prepared by authors from California Department of Education data files.

population.[6] These declines were more than offset by a dramatic increase in the Hispanic student population. Between 1995–96 and 2004–05, California's public schools increased their enrollment by 856,000 students, 843,000 (98.6%) of them Hispanic—a number higher than K-12 enrollment in 31 states, including Delaware, Indiana, Missouri, and Minnesota. The cumulative effects of these sharp declines in the non-Hispanic white population and the substantial increases in the Hispanic K-12 population accounts for the downward bend in the lower blade of the scissor graph in Figure 1.

Figure 2 traces changes in the proportion of Hispanic K-12 students enrolled in the California public schools at three grade levels: K-5, 6–8, and 9–12. The line graph for K-5 Hispanic students shows that, for the first time ever, the proportion of K-5 Hispanic students in the total school populations exceeded 50% during the 2004–05 school year.

The New Linguistic Landscape

In Figure 3, the percent of Hispanic students designated by school authorities as ELLs is presented. These are students whose current level of fluency in English makes it difficult for them to keep up with their classmates in classrooms in which English is the primary language of instruction.

Assessed strictly in terms of the challenge confronting California's public schools, the good news in Figure 3 is that the proportion of Hispanic ELLs at the K-5 grade level shows signs of declining. This falloff may be caused by the growth in the numbers of K-5 Hispanic students born in the United States. The bad news, in terms of the

FIGURE 2

CHANGES IN THE PROPORTION OF HISPANIC K-12 STUDENTS AT THREE GRADE LEVELS ENROLLED IN THE CALIFORNIA PUBLIC SCHOOLS: 1995–96 TO 2004–06.

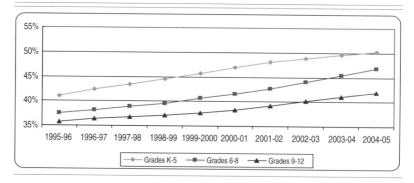

FIGURE 3

PERCENT HISPANIC ENGLISH LEARNERS AT THREE EDUCATIONAL LEVELS ENROLLED
IN THE CALIFORNIA PUBLIC SCHOOLS: 1995–96 TO 2004–06.

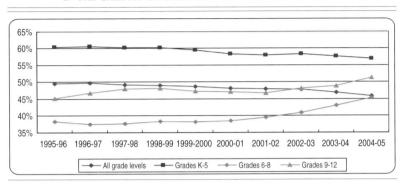

availability of an adequate supply of role models and mentors, is that in recent years the proportion of Hispanic ELLs in grades 6–8 and 9–12 has increased rapidly, likely caused by increased rates of immigration of older children from Spanish-speaking countries and/or the failure of California's public schools to facilitate the acquisition of critical levels of English language fluency among Hispanic middle and high school pupils.

Table 2 provides a microdemographic portrait of these shifts in the linguistic landscape of the California public schools. A notable feature of the data is the light they shed on the divergence in the ELL landscape. The Spanish-speaking ELL population has continued to increase and the non-Spanish-speaking population has declined significantly.

From 1995–96, the rate of growth in Hispanic enrollment exceeded the rate of growth in Spanish-speaking ELLs at every educational level, consistent with a demographic scenario in which the growth in Hispanic students, fueled by children reaching school age and by the migration of Hispanic students from other states, exceeds the rate of growth of Hispanic students immigrating to California from Spanish-speaking countries. From 1999–2000 to 2004–05, the growth in Spanish-speaking ELLs exceeded the growth in Hispanic students. This pattern is consistent with a scenario in which the growth in the Hispanic public school population is fueled largely by the immigration of school-age children from Spanish-speaking countries.

The 1995–96 to 1999–2000 rate of growth of non-Hispanic K-12 students increased while the rate of the non-Spanish-speaking ELL

TABLE 2

CHANGES IN CALIFORNIA'S HISPANIC ENGLISH LANGUAGE LEARNER (ELL) POPULATION: 1995–96 TO 1999–2000 AND 1999–2000 TO 2004–05

Segment	School Years			Changes: 1995–95 to 1999–2000			Changes: 1999–2000 to 2004–05		
	1995–96	1999–2000	2004–05	Number	%	Distribution	Number	%	Distribution
Hispanic Students	2,118,028	2,513,453	2,961,105	395,425	18.7	100.0	447,652	17.8	100.0
Grades K–5	1,098,459	1,312,969	1,439,515	214,510	19.5	54.2	126,546	9.6	28.3
Grades 6–8	483,067	559,062	708,904	75,995	15.7	19.2	149,842	26.8	33.5
Grades 9–12	536,502	641,422	812,686	104,920	19.6	26.5	171,264	26.7	38.3
Spanish-Speaking ELLs	1,051,125	1,222,809	1,357,778	171,684	16.3	100.0	134,969	11.0	100.0
Grades K–5	663,231	782,207	819,116	118,976	17.9	69.3	36,909	4.7	27.3
Grades 6–8	200,045	231,831	270,916	31,786	15.9	18.5	39,085	16.9	29.0
Grades 9–12	187,849	208,771	267,746	20,922	11.1	12.2	58,975	28.2	43.7
Non-Hispanic Students	3,349,196	3,438,159	3,361,085	88,963	2.7	100.0	(77,074)	(2.2)	100.0
Grades K–5	1,581,833	1,558,978	1,430,265	(22,855)	(1.4)	(25.7)	(128,713)	(8.3)	167.0
Grades 6–8	805,643	817,111	806,520	11,468	1.4	12.9	(10,591)	(1.3)	13.7
Grades 9–12	961,720	1,062,070	1,124,300	100,350	10.4	112.8	62,230	5.9	(80.7)
Non-Spanish-Speaking ELLs	272,642	257,718	233,747	(14,924)	(5.5)	100.0	(23,972)	(9.3)	100.0
Grades K–5	154,939	144,209	138,702	(10,730)	(6.9)	71.9	(5,507)	(3.8)	23.0
Grades 6–8	55,503	50,428	41,877	(5,075)	(9.1)	34.0	(8,551)	(17.0)	35.7
Grades 9–12	62,200	63,081	53,168	881	1.4	(5.9)	(9,913)	(15.7)	41.4

population declined at nearly double the rate. The 1999–2000 to 2004–05 enrollment of non-Hispanic K-12 students fell, as did the non-Spanish-speaking ELL population numbers. This pattern shows that the majority of growth in the ELL population is caused by Spanish-speaking ELLs, with significant decreases in the non-Spanish-speaking ELL population.

Clustering the Hispanic Elementary School Population

To better characterize the growth of the Hispanic and Spanish-speaking ELL population, we focus on examining the characteristics of the Hispanic population enrolled in the 5,537 elementary schools in California. We begin by analyzing the distribution of these students within these schools, rank ordering them by their percent Hispanic enrollment. We then subdivide the results of this ordering scheme into 20 clusters, according to the percent Hispanic in those schools. While not as sophisticated as the cluster allocation schemes reviewed in Bailey (1975), Bryson and Phillips (1975), or Yun and Moreno (2006), our method is consistent with approaches commonly used to generate indices of student segregation and isolation (Reardon & Firebaugh, 2002). The principal advantage of our approach is that it does not require that we situate this exploratory data analysis within the context of a specific explanatory theory. Rather, our method generates the data one needs to construct plausible causal theoretical relationships. The outcomes of these procedures, in terms of the mean percent Hispanic students, the number of schools, and the mean total number of students, as well as the mean number of students associated with each cluster, are summarized in Table 3.[7]

Table 4 tabulates the number of students in each of the population segments assessed in conjunction with the API.

The Hispanic and non-Hispanic white students represented here show a strong inverse relationship between these two segments, and is indicative of a high degree of segregation between Hispanic and non-Hispanic white students in those clusters (Figure 4).

Using the data tabulated in Table 4, we created Figure 5. The height of the bar graphs in Figure 5 represents the proportion of students in a particular population segment enrolled in the corresponding cluster of elementary schools.

Referring to Tables 3 and 4, the first cluster consists of 350 schools in which the Hispanic enrollment is between 0–4.9 percent. These schools enroll 4% of the 2.2 million elementary school stu-

TABLE 3

DESCRIPTIVE STATISTICS ASSOCIATED WITH 20 CLUSTERS CREATED BY RANK-ORDERING ELEMENTARY SCHOOLS BY THEIR PERCENT HISPANIC ENROLLMENT

(1) Group	(2) Group Range Percent Hispanic	(3) Mean Percent Hispanic	(4) Std Error	(5) Std Dev	(6) Num of Schools	(7) Distrib	(8) Mean Number of Tested Students	(9) Std Error	(10) Std Dev	(11) Mean Number of Hispanic Students	(12) Std Error	(13) Std Dev
1	0–4.9	3.18	0.084	1.579	350	6.32	251.9	9.27	173.43	8.3	0.38	7.12
2	5–9.9	8.02	0.066	1.428	474	8.56	323.3	7.90	172.05	24.2	0.63	13.79
3	10–14.9	12.85	0.066	1.404	447	8.07	329.3	8.53	180.27	39.4	1.08	22.73
4	15–19.9	18.02	0.073	1.395	364	6.57	359.3	8.71	166.22	59.3	1.44	27.48
5	20–24.9	23.02	0.076	1.402	342	6.18	367.3	9.20	170.20	78.0	2.02	37.34
6	25–29.9	27.83	0.082	1.359	275	4.97	375.5	10.59	175.62	95.9	2.71	44.88
7	30–34.9	32.93	0.088	1.449	270	4.88	382.9	10.98	180.39	115.3	3.33	54.77
8	35–39.9	37.85	0.094	2.133	241	4.35	384.8	11.80	183.17	132.5	4.07	63.17
9	40–44.9	43.01	0.087	1.427	269	4.86	381.5	10.83	177.67	150.8	4.31	70.76
10	45–49.9	47.95	0.095	1.400	219	3.96	390.3	11.04	163.36	170.5	4.74	70.13
11	50–54.9	52.78	0.085	1.353	252	4.55	411.0	10.50	166.75	198.3	5.10	80.98
12	55–59.9	58.00	0.097	1.421	215	3.88	408.1	12.11	177.62	215.5	6.33	92.75
13	60–64.9	62.96	0.102	1.412	192	3.47	420.5	13.77	190.78	241.6	7.94	110.01
14	65–69.9	68.00	0.088	1.350	237	4.28	453.5	12.16	187.23	282.3	7.54	116.06
15	70–74.9	73.03	0.094	1.339	204	3.68	447.5	12.47	178.15	299.7	8.33	118.99
16	75–79.9	77.98	0.102	1.436	197	3.56	459.6	12.94	181.56	329.1	9.44	132.51
17	80–84.9	82.95	0.094	1.470	247	4.46	467.9	13.03	204.71	358.2	10.13	159.27
18	85–89.9	87.89	0.100	1.506	226	4.08	468.0	13.28	199.70	378.6	10.83	162.81
19	90–94.9	93.04	1.400	1.400	263	4.75	500.3	13.88	225.13	430.4	12.04	195.22
20	95–100	97.79	0.080	1.272	253	4.57	533.5	17.36	276.17	487.6	16.15	256.94
		44.54	0.404	30.038	5,537	100.0	394.0	2.66	198.11	179.5	2.36	175.96

Grades 2–8
Std error, standard error; Std dev, standard deviation; Num of Schools, number of schools; Distrib, distribution.

TABLE 4
DISTRIBUTION OF THE EIGHT CALIFORNIA POPULATION SEGMENTS IN 20 CLUSTERS OF ELEMENTARY SCHOOLS

Group	% Hispanic	Hispanic Students	White	Asian	African American	Filipino	American Indian	Pacific Islander	Multiracial / Other
1	0–4.9	2,906	55,041	19,377	2,683	1,089	1,414	298	5,362
2	5–9.9	11,462	96,621	22,350	7,543	3,238	2,190	654	9,167
3	10–14.9	17,599	83,069	18,449	10,084	5,537	1,624	934	9,881
4	15–19.9	21,585	67,494	14,407	10,833	4,115	1,397	980	9,983
5	20–24.9	26,684	55,656	15,307	11,793	4,949	1,099	995	9,124
6	25–29.9	26,376	43,633	11,222	7,926	4,398	988	859	7,860
7	30–34.9	31,129	37,506	10,741	9,622	3,346	1,067	989	8,993
8	35–39.9	31,936	29,874	7,817	9,344	3,808	925	750	8,288
9	40–44.9	40,566	29,621	8,271	10,555	3,641	841	831	8,305
10	45–49.9	37,337	22,944	6,291	7,529	2,350	634	561	7,840
11	50–54.9	49,968	22,641	7,364	9,981	2,826	612	875	9,309
12	55–59.9	46,323	15,996	4,692	8,584	2,476	677	715	8,285
13	60–64.9	46,386	11,574	3,806	8,636	1,705	472	525	7,634
14	65–69.9	66,910	13,287	5,332	8,998	2,016	602	674	9,665
15	70–74.9	61,135	8,781	3,710	6,850	1,713	434	519	8,158
16	75–79.9	64,836	7,650	2,788	5,198	1,362	286	361	8,060
17	80–84.9	88,487	6,948	2,578	5,275	1,718	380	365	9,809
18	85–89.9	85,562	4,222	1,973	3,303	1,229	267	244	8,960
19	90–94.9	113,206	2,851	1,326	2,198	995	253	219	10,533
20	95–100	123,373	825	369	689	268	164	94	9,186
TOTAL	0–100	993,766	616,244	168,170	147,624	52,779	16,326	12,442	174,402

FIGURE 4

PERCENT ELEMENTARY SCHOOL ENROLLMENT BY POPULATION SEGMENT IN THE 20
CLUSTERS INFORMING OUR EXPLORATORY DATA ANALYSIS: 2004–05.
API, ACADEMIC PERFORMANCE INDEX.

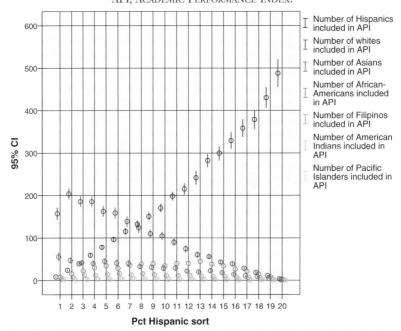

FIGURE 5

DISTRIBUTION OF THE FOUR LARGEST ELEMENTARY SCHOOL STUDENT POPULATION
SEGMENTS, BY PERCENT HISPANIC STUDENTS: 2004–05.

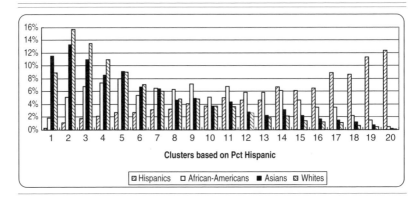

dents in grades 2–8 assessed during the 2004–05 school year. The enrollment of Hispanic and African American students in this cluster totaled 2,900 and 2,700, or approximately 0.3% and 1.8% of the total Hispanic and African American student populations. The enrollment and distribution figures for Asian and white students tell a very different story regarding the degree of contact among students. Nearly 12% of the total Asian population attends schools where Hispanic students make up no more than 5% of the total student population; this figure is even greater than the 8.9% of white students enrolled in these schools.

The 478 schools corresponding to clusters 9 and 10, the two clusters with the most equally heterogeneous populations, enrolled 8.6% of the elementary student population. These schools also enrolled 7.9%, 8.5%, 8.6%, and 12.2% of the total number of the state's Hispanic, white, Asian, and African American elementary school population.

The 253 schools in the 20th cluster, the most heavily Hispanic cluster, enrolled 6.2% of the elementary students assessed in 2004–05. The number of Hispanic students attending these schools, 123,400, made up 14.4% of the total Hispanic enrollment. The figures for African American, Asian, and whites were, respectively, 0.5%, 0.2%, and 0.1%.

Distribution of ELLs

Table 5 provides additional data on the distribution of Hispanic, ELL, and socioeconomically disadvantaged (SD) students. Again, the clusters from Table 3 of the mean percent Hispanic of the students tested are used, and the percent of each group is given.

The data in columns three and four indicate that the concentration of Spanish-speaking ELLs is even higher than the concentration of Hispanic students. For example, 23.8% of California's Hispanic elementary students attend schools that are 85% or greater Hispanic, compared to 29.8% of the state's native Spanish-speaking ELLs.

Hispanic Student Concentration and Academic Performance

Figures 6a to 6d show the performance of non-SD and SD Hispanic students and ELL students on the standards-based examinations in English language arts (ELA) and mathematics administered to elementary school students. These exams are used to compute school-level API scores.

TABLE 5
DISTRIBUTION (IN PERCENT) OF ELEMENTARY SCHOOL ENGLISH LANGUAGE LEARNERS ACROSS 20 CLUSTERS

(1) Group	(2) % Hispanic	(3) % Hispanic Students	(4) % Spanish ELL	(5) % Non-Hispanic Students	(6) % Non-Spanish ELL	(7) % All Students	(8) % Hispanic	(9) % ELL
1	0–4.9	0.29	0.10	7.18	5.07	0.87	0.04	0.16
2	5–9.9	1.15	0.41	11.93	8.23	2.36	0.25	0.42
3	10–14.9	1.77	0.82	10.91	9.00	2.74	0.46	0.60
4	15–19.9	2.17	1.13	9.19	8.75	3.06	0.73	1.13
5	20–24.9	2.69	1.57	8.33	8.95	3.37	1.06	1.49
6	25–29.9	2.65	1.65	6.47	7.38	3.18	1.30	1.72
7	30–34.9	3.13	2.27	6.08	7.31	3.79	1.96	2.26
8	35–39.9	3.21	2.32	5.12	5.39	3.65	2.14	2.15
9	40–44.9	4.08	3.20	5.22	5.98	4.47	3.21	3.20
10	45–49.9	3.76	2.86	4.05	4.30	3.93	3.17	2.86
11	50–54.9	5.03	4.60	4.51	5.93	5.43	4.78	4.62
12	55–59.9	4.66	4.46	3.49	4.09	4.85	4.90	4.63
13	60–64.9	4.67	4.65	2.89	3.11	4.82	5.00	4.63
14	65–69.9	6.73	7.06	3.42	4.39	6.55	7.29	7.12
15	70–74.9	6.15	6.46	2.54	2.97	5.71	6.69	6.42
16	75–79.9	6.52	7.12	2.16	2.54	5.96	7.37	7.08
17	80–84.9	8.90	9.72	2.28	2.57	7.79	10.20	9.69
18	85–89.9	8.61	9.75	1.70	1.99	7.41	10.17	9.88
19	90–94.9	11.39	13.74	1.55	1.48	9.68	13.89	13.94
20	95–100	12.41	16.08	0.98	0.58	10.38	15.37	15.99
TOTAL		993,766	864,026	1,187,987	147,648	1,174,750	831,502	623,779

Note: The entries for Spanish-speaking and non-Spanish-speaking English language learners (ELLs) include students enrolled in grades K–1. The API elementary school data in this table, as well as the others in this article, include students in grades 2–8.

GIFFORD AND VALDÉS   143

FIGURE 6

STUDENT PERFORMANCE ON THE STANDARDS-BASED ENGLISH LANGUAGE ARTS
(ELA) AND MATH ASSESSMENTS ADMINISTERED BY THE CALIFORNIA DEPARTMENT
OF EDUCATION TO COMPUTE SCHOOL-LEVEL ACADEMIC PERFORMANCE
INDEX SCORES.

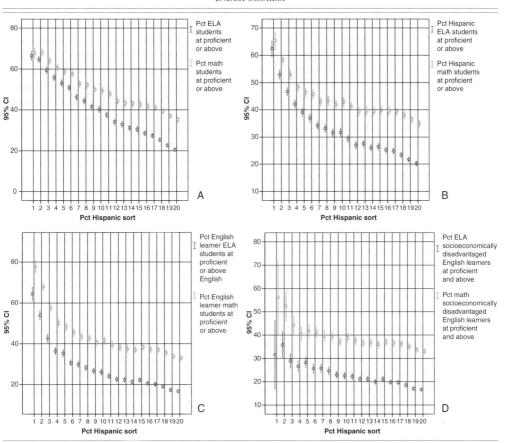

The student performance data plotted in Figures 6a to 6d permit
us to track student learning in ELA and mathematics across our 20
clusters. The results are anything but encouraging. Students enrolled
in schools with large numbers of students from these population segments do not perform as well on these exams, particularly those who
are SD.

Hispanic Student Concentration and the No Child Left Behind Act
of 2001

NCLB requires that students in Grades 2–9 be measured yearly
against a set of standards to determine student "proficiency" in English
language arts (ELA) and mathematics and to track adequate yearly
progress (AYP). If a school does not meet AYP goals, it goes into
Program Improvement (PI) during which remediation must take place.
PI Years 1 and 2 are considered School Improvement years and a Local
Educational Agency (LEA) provides technical assistance and professional development to the school staff to develop and implement a
school plan and teacher professional development activities. In Year 3,
the Corrective Action year, the LEA replaces school staff, implements
new curriculum, or provides some other type of corrective action. In
Years 4 and 5, the Restructuring years, the school is restructured, which
can mean reopening as a charter school, replacing the school staff, or
other major restructuring; professional development and other school
improvement activities continue.

We wished to look at not only the percentage of Hispanic students
in PI and non-PI schools, according to status of the school, not in PI
or in PI (denominator number of students not in PI or in PI schools),
but also the percentage of Hispanic students not in PI and in PI schools
when looking at the total number of Hispanic students in California
(denominator number of students in population segment). When looking at California students, using data provided by the California State
Department of Education, we see that 53% of Hispanic students are
not in PI schools and 42% are in PI schools; yet looking solely at the
percentage of Hispanic students in PI schools, 72% are Hispanic and
only 11% are white.

The State of California identifies schools that have (1) never been
in PI, (2) have been in PI and exited, and (3) are currently in PI and for
how many years. We organize the data as a time series, beginning with
those schools that have been in PI the longest (Year 5; entered PI in
2001). Figure 7 shows Hispanic students as the highest proportion of
each PI status group. While the curve heads up for whites, with the
largest proportion of whites in schools that have never been in PI, the
curve heads down for Hispanics, with the largest proportion of Hispanics nearly reaching 80% in schools in Year 5 of PI. Barely 50% of the
students in schools that have never been in PI are Hispanic.

This creates an extremely challenging set of circumstances for
Hispanic students in California schools. Not only are they segregated

FIGURE 7

PERCENT OF AFRICAN AMERICAN, HISPANIC, AND WHITE STUDENTS IN CALIFORNIA
SCHOOLS BY PROGRAM IMPROVEMENT (PI) STATUS AND NUMBER OF YEARS.

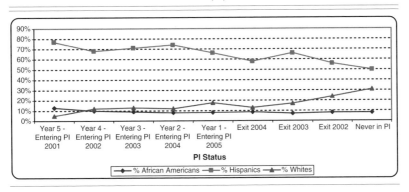

from the mainstream population, but they are also attending schools in need of program improvement—schools that have a greater proportion of free and reduced price lunch participants than non-PI schools, a greater proportion of English learners, and less highly qualified teachers.

Linguistic Isolation and Education: A Policy Challenge

Recent media coverage of the challenges created by a growing influx of new immigrants (e.g., Thornburgh, 2006) makes evident that there is an increasing concern among ordinary citizens about Latino immigration—both legal and illegal. Whether coverage involves vigilantism on the Mexican border (Redeker, 2005) or responses to legislation designed to penalize individuals who aid undocumented residents (Williams, 2006), American public opinion appears to support immigration reform legislation that will address the many perceived economic and security problems. In 2006, the U.S. Senate began reviewing the issue of comprehensive immigration reform, and at this writing, it is unclear whether new legislation will lean heavily towards enforcement, as proposed by H.R. 4437 (the Border Protection, Antiterrorism and Illegal Immigration Act of 2005), or true immigration reform provisions. What is evident is that there are strong feelings about providing amnesty to "unauthorized migrants"[8] and about providing pathways to citizenship to those who have broken the law. At the same time, it is also clear that business groups favor a solution that will allow them to fill jobs they contend Americans will not or cannot fill.

Hispanic immigrants are—because of their numbers—at the center of the current immigration debate. According to *Hispanics and the Future of America* (Tienda & Mitchell, 2006b), Hispanics are unlike other ethnic and racial groups because of their age, their low education levels, their employment in unskilled jobs, their language, and the presence of large numbers of individuals who are here illegally. Contributing authors explore these differences and how successfully Hispanics are assimilating into the U.S. mainstream. In a companion volume called *Multiple Origins, Uncertain Destinies* (Tienda & Mitchell, 2006a), the authors conclude that the most profound risk facing this population is "failure to graduate from high school" (p. 7). Concerned about the importance of English language proficiency for Hispanic students, they add, "Hispanic students who fail to master English before leaving school incur considerable costs. English proficiency is mandatory for success in the labor market and is vitally important for navigating the health care system and for meaningful civic engagement. How to ensure proficiency in English remains highly controversial; there is no consensus on how best to teach non-English-speaking students across the grade spectrum" (pp. 7–8).

For the 3 million Hispanic students currently enrolled in California schools, who constitute 20% of the school population and whose numbers continue to grow, the future is here. Non-Hispanic white and non-Spanish-speaking ELLs are decreasing in absolute numbers and as a proportion of the school population, and Spanish-speaking ELLs are increasing in number. Whether legislators vote to develop a coherent immigration policy or not, the challenge to California schools is clear. We must educate the children who are now in California so that we can ensure their and our long-term economic and social well-being, and we must abandon nativist fears and unrealistic separatist illusions about reclaiming the original lost territories of Aztlan as we work to address this challenge.

Our analysis of the hypersegregation of Hispanic students, and particularly Spanish-speaking ELLs, suggests that little or no attention has been given to the consequences of linguistic isolation for a population whose future depends on the acquisition of English. Unfortunately, segregation of ELLs from both their white and black English-speaking peers has profound consequences for their acquisition of English. For ELLs, interaction with ordinary English-speaking peers is essential to their English language development and consequently to their acquisition of academic English, "the English used to obtain, process, construct and provide subject matter information in spoken and written form" (Valdés, 2004, p. 19).

It is not difficult, therefore, to imagine that schools in financially stressed and disadvantaged communities with high numbers of immigrants face particularly urgent crises when their students are among the most disadvantaged and vulnerable. As we have pointed out, the school clusters with the highest number of Hispanic students tend to also have a higher proportion of African American students and a lower proportion of non-Hispanic white and Asian students. This places the educational futures of the students in these clusters further at risk: curriculum suffers and budgets are strained because academic resources must be diverted to provide for the increased demand and accommodations for ELLs and these resources require funding. These crises are real, and they are also difficult to examine because of the strong opinions and emotions expressed by opponents and proponents of public education to newly arrived immigrants.

Moving Forward

In moving forward, we suggest that the larger message of *Brown v. Board of Education* compels us to explore ways in which we might achieve the reintegration of American society and the original vision of the common public school (Tyack, 2003). Although flawed and often surrounded by "winner-take-all policy conflicts," Tyack argues that public schools "have had a public mandate to teach children about civic and moral life" (p. 183) and that "democracy in education and education in democracy are not quaint legacies from a distant and happier time" (p. 185). Immigrant children and their families have long been contributors to the American system of public schooling as well as beneficiaries, largely because of the opportunities presented by attending school with other youngsters who represent the diversity of their new homeland. However, as the data shows, this integration is not currently happening in California.

Ideally, the policy conversation about the education of Hispanic ELLs will carefully consider the federal role in educating all children, states' roles in ensuring the quality of education, and local responsibility in making schools less homogeneous. Since the 1980s, civic and political groups in states with large numbers of unauthorized migrants have engaged in contentious arguments over who was responsible for providing essential health care, education, and social welfare services to "undocumented immigrants." Some of these groups contend that the federal government should fund such services, on the grounds that these costs, already burdensome, will continue to increase as a result of ongoing national failures to reconcile espoused policies on immigration with enforcement strategies and to address the insatiable desire of U.S. employers for inexpensive immigrant labor. Other groups hold that the solution to the gap between espoused and enacted immigration policies is not more federal funding but a stepped up commitment on the part of the federal government to prevent individuals from traversing U.S. borders without official permission.

The debate over who should pay for the essential services needed by unauthorized migrants, and whether or not such services should be provided at all, has been particularly divisive in California, Florida, and Texas. In California, for example, this polarization has resulted in the passage of a number of popularly sponsored ballot measures mandating that state agencies deny services to "undocumented immigrants." In some instances, the courts have found these measures to be in gross violation of U.S. civil rights laws, but these decisions have not dampened the fires of political discontent. In fact, they appear to have increased the hostility of some groups to the notion that state governmental agencies have a fundamental moral responsibility to address the basic needs of their state's least advantaged residents, even if they have entered the country without the approval of the U.S. immigration authorities, and have resulted in state residents being increasingly unwilling to vote to raise taxes to pay for these services.

This gap between the federal government's *espoused* and *enacted* immigration policies, though, presents an opportunity for states with large new immigrant populations to make a case for desperately needed funding. Specifically, this policy gap can and should be exploited in a manner that turns the question of federal financial assistance into an opportunity for public schools to seek funding to provide much needed assistance for both Hispanic students and SD students. Issues, evidence, and precedents related to the financial responsibilities and obligations of the federal government to public schools must be analyzed and examined. The aim is to produce solid, clear, and unbiased research and analysis of federal immigration policies and legislation with regard to education for school-age children residing in immigrant households— both legal resident immigrant households and households headed by undocumented immigrants.

The Arguments for Educating

Providing education to unauthorized migrants is ethical in a nation that values unauthorized migrants as a productive workforce. It is to the advantage of the national and state economies to support the education of children of unauthorized migrants as a means for them to become contributing members of society and to sustain the maintenance of a healthy social fabric in communities where unauthorized migrants live, work, and socialize and where their children play and learn.

Education is a resource that is universally accepted and recognized as a necessity in our society. The argument must therefore underscore the fairness of providing "unauthorized resident" children access to education while their parents provide labor. Twenty years ago, *Plyler v. Doe* (1982) upheld the right of unauthorized migrant children to receive a public school education, holding that a "statute which withholds from local school districts any state funds for the education of children who were not 'legally admitted' into the United States, and which authorizes local school districts to deny enrollment to such children, violates the Equal Protection Clause of the 14th Amendment" (p. 222), further noting that "the deprivation of education takes an inestimable toll on the social, economic, intellectual, and psychological well-being of the individual, and poses an obstacle to individual achievement" (p. 223).

Education specialists thus clearly stand on strong legal ground when arguing that if states are responsible for the education of "unauthorized resident" children, the federal government bears the responsibility not to make this financially impossible by delegating the responsibility and financial burden to individual states, regardless of these states' resources and proportion of unauthorized migrants in their population.

Educational tourism. Educational policymakers and education specialists must further argue that the provision of education to the children of unauthorized migrants is not the motivation behind unauthorized entrance into the United States. "Educational tourism" is a myth. In fact, many "unauthorized resident" parents face enormous difficulties enrolling their children in U.S. schools. Many speak poor English, have low levels of education, and fear risking deportation because of enrolling their students in public schools. They often feel intimidated by educational institutions, finding it difficult to articulate their educational needs to teachers, principals, and supervisors.

Migrants, both legal and unauthorized, leave their homes, their communities, and their countries of origin in search of better working and living conditions, not to enroll their children in American schools. As researched by Portes and Rumbaut (1996), "individual migration is determined by . . . two different types of social structures: those linking sending and receiving countries and those linking communities and families in places of origin and destination" (p. 272). As migrants leave their homes of origin, they do not choose their destinations randomly; they choose on the basis of close networks of relatives and friends who are in a position to provide them with valuable information regarding housing and work opportunities.

Strengthening communities. Similarly, educational policymakers and education specialists must make it clear that providing federal funding to public schools with unauthorized migrant children would significantly strengthen the social fabric of these communities. As *Plyler v. Doe* states, "[p]ublic education has a pivotal role in maintaining the fabric of our society and in sustaining our political and cultural heritage" (p. 230). Denying "unauthorized resident" children access to public schools would increase already existing social tensions—not only within immigrant communities, but also between these communities and communities that consider themselves nonimmigrant.

The impact of NCLB. Another argument that education specialists may choose to consider is how the educational "reforms" of NCLB are affecting the priorities and prospects of public schools. NCLB requires that schools be assessed and evaluated annually using student test data; it also requires that schools implement educational interventions to raise the achievement of students in different demographic segments.[9] Unfortunately, as the sanctions imposed by NCLB increase in severity, the implications become ominous for schools with large numbers of immigrant children. Sanctioned schools are given 5 years in PI status to raise the scores of the students or face restructuring, and these are the schools with the highest number of Hispanic students; each year in PI results in a higher percentage of Hispanic students in these schools as well.

The reality of NCLB is that school districts in communities with children with special needs, such as ELL children, generally lack the quantity and quality of expertise and resources needed to foster significant improvement. Assisting such schools is clearly necessary, because as children of unauthorized migrants continue to enroll in schools, legal Hispanic resident children find themselves at additional risk. Primarily

Hispanic schools are vulnerable to closure because of their inability to raise scores, since many are underfunded "majority minority" schools with uncredentialed teachers, but closing these schools would have an adverse impact on their communities as well as on the future of both the unauthorized and resident Hispanic children.

In a report entitled *Who's Left Behind*, Consentino de Cohen, Deterding, and Clewell (2005) argue that NCLB, because it holds schools accountable for the academic performance of ELLs, must examine the ways in which such learners are educated. They point out, as we have above, that a large percentage of ELLs (70%) are concentrated in 10% of what they call high limited English proficient (High LEP) schools. They also argue "the segregation of LEP students results in their isolation from the educational mainstream and the attendant loss of the benefits of interacting with English-speaking classmates" and "a loss for English-dominant students" (p. 16).

California, with its increasing Hispanic population, presents a special challenge in terms of contending with the reduced achievement level of this population. We too argue that for ELLs, the intense and sustained linguistic isolation that results from racial and ethnic segregation is one of the central factors of this challenge and is critical to address. As we imagine the future, we agree with Tienda and Mitchell (2006a) as they point out,

During the first quarter of the 21st century, the Hispanic age bulge will offer a unique opportunity to improve the common good by attenuating the social and economic costs of an aging majority population while enhancing national productivity and global competitiveness. Realizing this potential will require educational investments that position future entrants into the labor force to compete for high-paying jobs in a service and information economy. . . . Given the projected growth of the Hispanic population over the next quarter century, compromising the future economic prospects of Hispanics by underinvesting in their education will likely compromise the nation's future as well. (pp. 126–127)

NOTES

1. The census defines linguistically isolated households as those in which everyone over the age of 14 speaks English less than "very well." We use the term linguistic isolation as synonymous to linguistic segregation.

2. All raw data are from California Department of Education, http://www.cde.ca.gov/ta/

3. This section draws significantly from Valdés, Fishman, Chavez, & Perez (in press).

4. For a discussion of the debates surrounding the *Lau* remedies, see Crawford (1992a).

5. Proposition O in 1983 urged the federal government to amend the Voting Rights Act; Proposition 63 in 1986 named English as the official language of California; Proposition 187, from 1994, called upon school and health and welfare agencies to ask students and clients to prove their legal status before receiving services; Proposition 209 in 1996 urged an end to affirmative action through constitutional amendment; and in 1998, 61% of voters agreed to dismantle bilingual education by supporting Proposition 227. For further information see Adams and Brink (1990) and Crawford (1992a, 1992b) for Proposition 63; Herrera (1995) and McLaughlin et al. (1995) for Proposition 187; Gibbs and Bankhead (2001) for Proposition 209; and Butler, Orr, Gutierrez, and Hakuta (2000) and Garcia and Curry-Rodriguez (2000) for Proposition 227.

6. It is possible that the falloffs in the non-Hispanic white and African American student segments may in fact be significantly lower than the totals listed in Table 1 because of the explosive increase in the number of students who identify themselves as "Multiracial/Other." If students elect to classify themselves as such, the bottom blade in the scissor graph in Figure 1 would reflect this change with a downward bend.

7. To determine the "mean Hispanic percent" we divided the "mean number of Hispanic students" by the "mean number of tested students" and then clustered the schools by the "mean Hispanic percent." The mean total number of students tested in grades 2–8 is 394 students (with standard error and deviation of 2.66 and 198, respectively).

8. Passel (2006) uses the term "unauthorized migrants" to refer to individuals who reside in the United States but who are not U.S. citizens or persons admitted to the U.S. for permanent residency or persons authorized to work or reside in the United States on a temporary basis.

9. NCLB requires that school districts maintain achievement data for students according to their gender, ethnicity, socioeconomic status, mobility level, English language proficiency level, and disability status, as well as according to the percentage in schools employing teachers who are fully credentialed and the percentage in schools employing teachers who hold emergency credentials.

REFERENCES

Adams, K.L., & Brink, D.T. (Eds.). (1990). *Perspectives on official English: The campaign for English as the official language of the USA*. Berlin: Mouton de Gruyter.

Bailey, K.D. (1975). Cluster analysis. *Sociological Methodology, 6*, 59–128.

Bilingual Education Act. (reauthorization of ESEA; P.L. 90-247). (1968).

Bilingual Education Improvement and Reform Act of 1980. (Ed. Code 52163-52170). (CAC 3934-4310).

Border Protection, Antiterrorism and Illegal Immigration Act of 2005. H.R. 4437 (proposed).

Bryson, K.R., & Phillips, D.P. (1975). Methods for classifying interval-scale and ordinal-scale data. *Sociological Methodology, 6*, 171–190.

Butler, Y.G., Orr, J.E., Bousquet Gutierrez, M., & Hakuta, K. (2000). Inadequate conclusions from an inadequate assessment: What can SAT-9 scores tell us about the impact of Proposition 227 in California? *Bilingual Research Journal, 24*(1–2), 141–154.

Carroll, S.J., Krop, C., Arkes, J., Morrison, P.J., & Flanagan, A. (2005). *California's K-12 public schools: How are they doing?* Santa Monica, CA: RAND Corporation.

Chacon-Moscone Bilingual-Bicultural Education Act of 1976. (Ed. Code, § 52160 et seq.).

Civil Rights Act of 1964, PL 88-352. 88th Congress, H.R. 7152. (1964).

Consentino de Cohen, C., Deterding, N., & Clewell, B.C. (2005). *Who's left behind? Immigrant children in high and low LEP schools*. Washington, DC: The Urban Institute.

Constitution of the State of California. Annotated by D. L. Hearing. Los Angeles. Chas. W. Palm, 1985.

Crawford, J. (Ed.). (1992a). *Language loyalties: A source book on the official English controversy*. Chicago: University of Chicago Press.

Crawford, J. (1992b). *Hold your tongue: Bilingualism and the politics of English only*. Reading, MA: Addison Wesley.

Frankenberg, E., & Lee, C. (2002). *Race in American public schools: Rapidly resegregating school districts*. Cambridge, MA: The Civil Rights Project.

Frankenberg, E., Lee, C., & Orfield, G. (2003). *A multiracial society with segregated schools: Are we losing the dream?* Cambridge, MA: The Civil Rights Project.

Garcia, E.E., & Curry-Rodriguez, J.E. (2000). The education of limited English proficient students in California schools: An assessment of the influence of Proposition 227 in selected districts and schools. *Bilingual Research Journal, 24*(1–2), 15–35.

Gibbs, J.T., & Bankhead, T. (2001). *Preserving privilege: California politics, propositions, and people of color*. Westport, CT: Praeger.

Haas, L. (1995). *Conquests and historical identities in California 1769–1936*. Berkeley: University of California Press.

Herrera, L.Q. (1995). *Majority will v. minority rights: Proposition 187 and the Latino community*. Unpublished honors thesis in Political Science, Stanford University, CA.

Hill, L.E., & Hayes, J.M. (Eds.). (2003). *California's newest immigrants* (2nd ed., Vol. 5, No. 2), p. 20. San Francisco: Public Policy Institute of California.

Lau v. Nichols, No. 72-6520, 414 U.S. 56 (1974).

Macías, R. (2001). Minority languages in the United States with a focus on California. In G. Extra & D. Gorter (Eds.), *The other languages of Europe: Demographic, sociolinguistic, and educational perspectives* (pp. 332–354). Clevedon: Multilingual Matters.

Mapes, K.A. (1992). *Race and class in nineteenth century California*. Unpublished master's thesis, Michigan State University, Lansing, MI.

Mar-Molinero, C. (2000). *The politics of language in the Spanish-speaking world: From colonization to globalization*. London and New York: Routledge.

McLaughlin, K., Kramer, P., & Legon, J. (1995). Judge guts core of Prop. 187. *San Jose Mercury News*, p. 1A.

Mendez v. Westminster. (1946). 64 F. Supp. 544.

Nazario, S. (2006). *Enrique's journey: The story of a boy's dangerous odyssey to reunite with his mother*. New York: Random House.

No Child Left Behind Act of 2001, Pub. L. No. 107-110, 115 Stat. 1425 (2002).

Passel, J.S. (2006). *The size and characteristics of the unauthorized migrant population in the U. S.* Washington, DC: PEW Hispanic Center.

Pitt, L. (1998). *The decline of the Californios: A social history of the Spanish-speaking Californians, 1846–1890*. Berkeley: University of California Press.

Plyler v. Doe. 457 US 202 (1982).

Population Resource Center (2004). Immigration to California. Retrieved March 20, 2006 from http://www.prcdc.org/summaries/immigrationca/immigrationca/html

Portes, A., & Rumbaut, R.G. (1996). *Immigrant America: A portrait* (2nd ed.). Berkeley: University of California Press.

Reardon, S.F., & Firebaugh, G. (2002). Measures of multigroup segregation. *Sociological Methodology, 32*, 33–67.

Redeker, B. (2005). "Minutemen" volunteer to watch U.S. border. *ABC News, World News Tonight*. Retrieved March 20, 2006, from http://abcnews.go.com/WNT/US/story

Schiffman, H.F. (1996). *Linguistic culture and language policy*. London: Routledge.

Thornburgh, N. (2006). Inside the life of the migrants next door. *Time, 167*, 34–45.

Tienda, M., & Mitchell, F. (2006a). *Multiple origins, uncertain destinies: Hispanics and the American future. Committee on Transforming Our Common Destiny: Hispanics in the United States*. Washington, DC: National Academies Press.

Tienda, M., & Mitchell, F. (Eds.). (2006b). *Hispanics and the future of America*. National Research Council. Washington, DC: National Academies Press.

Tyack, D. (2003). *Seeking common ground: Public schools in a diverse society*. Cambridge, MA: Harvard University Press.

U.S. Census. (2003). Census 2000 PHC-T-37. Ability to speak English by language spoken at home. [Table 6, California]. Retrieved from http://www.census.gov/population/cen2000/phc-t37/tab06a.xls.

Valdés, G. (2004). Between support and marginalization: The development of academic language in linguistic minority children. *International Journal of Bilingualism and Bilingual Education, 7*(2 &3), 102–132.

Valdés, G., Fishman, J.A., Chavez, R., & Perez, W. (in press). *The development of language resources: Lessons from the case of California*. Clevedon: Multilingual Matters.

Williams, J.J. (2006, March 20). Immigration bill draws criticism. *Baltimore Sun*. Retrieved April 3, 2006, from http://www.baltimoresun.com/news/opinion/ideas/bal-immigrant0320,0,57703.story?coll=bal-ideas-headlines

Wollenberg, C. (1976). *All deliberate speed*. Berkeley: University of California.

Yun, J.T., & Moreno, J.E. (2006). College access, K-12 concentrated disadvantage, and the next 25 years of educational research. *Educational Researcher, 35*(1), 12–19.

CHAPTER 8

A Response to "The Linguistic Isolation of Hispanic Students in California's Public Schools"

ROBERT T. JIMÉNEZ

In their chapter "The Linguistic Isolation of Hispanic Students in California's Public Schools: The Challenge of Reintegration," Gifford and Valdés consult the historical record concerning English-speaking Anglo contact with Spanish-speaking *Californios* in 19th-century North America and provide statistical evidence of the resegregation currently being experienced by Latino students (this volume, pp. 125–154). They describe how, shortly after the Mexican government ceded California to the United States in 1848, an ideology of racial, cultural, and linguistic superiority led to the enactment of English-only legislative and educational policy, as well as, ultimately, a segregated system of schooling. These highly respected and influential scholars thus demonstrate one of the uses of history for the purposes of contemporary educational research, that is, the pedagogical value of providing lessons from the past.

In the current frenetic national debate on immigration—framed by the media as almost entirely about Mexican immigrants—those most opposed to more open immigration policies also raise the issue of the United States' historical relationship with Mexico (Gorman, 2006). Their charge is that Mexico is "reclaiming" territory lost in 1848 through the politics of mass immigration. The not-so-subtle intent is to stake out a position of conflict between *them* and *us* . . . *They* are mounting an invasion and *we* are under attack. Individuals driven by opposing ideological agendas thus frame history's lessons. What *is* undeniable is that the United States and Mexico share a unique and special relationship that spans more than a century and a half, as well as a border that is nearly 2,000 miles long. Geography and time, then, are both involved in highly influential ways in the current association

---

Robert T. Jiménez is a professor of language, literacy and culture in the Department of Teaching and Learning at Peabody College, Vanderbilt University.

between the two countries. Gifford and Valdés remind us of this relationship and how it continues to influence our thinking at this moment.

In an essay discussing the importance of history in the field of
literacy research, Moore, Monaghan, and Hartman (1997) identify a
number of ways that history enriches our understanding and thus our
ability to take action in the field of education. Moore identifies the use
of history as both an aid to viewing the present in alternative ways as
well as a stimulus for envisioning alternative futures. Monaghan argues
that knowledge of history is useful in its own right, just as is knowledge
of music and art. She posits that the past matters because "It is the
collective memory of the human race" (p. 93). Monaghan also points
out that history promotes interdisciplinarity and that it can help us
avoid the dangerous propensity to repeat the mistakes of the past,
something that she claims occurs regularly in the field of education. She
counsels the reader that to reap history's benefits, we have to learn how
to "do history better."

Doing History Better

A problem with doing history better is that few researchers who
specialize in issues like those presented in Gifford and Valdés's work—
the English language learning of Latino students—also have professional expertise in the field of historiography. Instead, academicians in
this area are often experts in areas such as applied linguistics, literacy,
multicultural education, or other content specializations. There is significant value in adding a historical perspective in these areas. Without
a historical perspective, Tuchman (1994) argues, social science researchers run the risk of badly misunderstanding their topic of study:

One needs knowledge of the main lines of dispute . . . Accordingly, the
researcher's first task is to acquire the necessary background—not only to learn
the dates, names, and key events, but also to master the controversies among
historians about whether, how, and why those dates, names, and events matter.
(p. 314)

Tuchman (1994) thus furthers our understanding by providing guidance to social science researchers seeking deeper and more sophisticated
understanding of their chosen topic. She recommends engaging in
careful and extensive reading on relevant issues. Furthermore, Tuchman
tells researchers to become familiar with the interpretive frameworks
used by historians to approach their work. Gifford and Valdés provide
a good or optimal example of how social science researchers can incor-

porate historical understandings and information into discussions of current controversies and pressing concerns. They do this by outlining the historical treatment of the Spanish language in California, including how Spanish was marginalized following the signing of the Treaty of Guadalupe Hidalgo in 1848 and its ultimate banishment from schools in 1855 as a result of legislation. They continue by detailing how English-speaking Anglos legislated privilege and dominance for themselves. This privilege and dominance then became part of what Bourdieu (1998) calls "the obviousness of ordinary experience."

The question, then, is how can one use Tuchman's (1994) recommendations to develop this kind of deeper historical understanding? While her recommendations begin to provide methodological guidance for educational researchers who want to incorporate a historical perspective into their research studies, there are calls to provide even more historical context to research studies in general. In my own field of literacy research, David Barton and his colleagues argue, "We need a historical approach for an understanding of the ideology, culture and traditions on which current [literacy] practices are based" (Barton & Hamilton, 2000, p. 13).

It makes sense, then, to understand how California's history of language policy played a role in creating the context that culminated in the *Mendez v. Westminster* (1946) case. Donato (1997) describes how this case was influenced by *Alvarez v. Owen* (1931), which was the first successful lawsuit against segregation in the United States. Both cases involved Mexican American students and their families. In *Mendez*, Mexican American parents successfully sued a school district in California for segregating their children into inferior schools. This case served as an important precedent for the *Brown v. Board of Education* (1954) decision, and key individuals in *Brown*, such as Thurgood Marshall and Earl Warren, played important roles in *Mendez*—Marshall filed an amicus brief on behalf of the plaintiffs and Warren was then governor of California (San Miguel, 1987).

While the addition of historical content may appear to be of obvious value, there is still the matter of how to use such material in a way that furthers the goals of the researcher. Although Barton and Hamilton (2000) make a very strong case for the importance of historical understanding in literacy research, they do not offer explicit recommendations for doing so. In earlier work that focused on the literacies of Lancaster, England, Barton and Hamilton (2000) make a statement that typifies this lack of specificity: "In this paper we will provide some historical details of literacy in Lancaster in earlier times," (p. 23) in other words, no report of how they went about finding this information, chose relevant examples, or shaped their account for the project at hand. This lack of specificity is common in educational research. In a very brief description of historical case studies, Merriam (2001) tells us that an understanding of historical events can enhance analytical interpretation if the researcher understands "the context of the [historical] event, the assumptions behind it, and perhaps the event's impact on the institution or participants" (p. 35). Once again, these are good suggestions, but hardly the sort of information that a novice researcher could put to use in a straightforward and methodical manner.

Adding a historical component to research studies in education requires the researcher to cross disciplinary lines in a field that is already inherently transdisciplinary. Knowledge of the past, not surprisingly, often helps explain the present. There are examples, though, of how knowledge of the past can disrupt and trouble contemporary, taken-for-granted ways of thinking (Kamberelis & Dimitriadis, 2004). For example, in a discussion of Vietnamese literacies, Lo Bianco (2000) establishes that "new Available Designs . . . always carry the messages of the old system in the bruises and shapes of the new forms" (p. 103). Lo Bianco thus goes somewhat beyond Barton and Hamilton (2000) to raise the possibility of history as a methodological tool that directs our attention not only to the overall importance of understanding the history, but also more specifically to what one can expect to find after careful study of contemporary practices. In other words, he claims that careful study of contemporary practices *should* reveal historical influences. One of the contributions of Gifford and Valdés's work is that they bring to light a number of the "bruises and shapes" of past events that underlay and inhabit contemporary events involving Latino students and their trajectories through U.S. schools.

As a result, they demonstrate not only how California's history of political and educational policy helped shape current realities, but also hint at how careful examination of these realities reveals how history is embodied and practiced in our everyday thinking and linguistic interactions and in the relationships between groups. These relationships include those between ethnic groups and those between nations. For example, the long and complex history of relations between the United States and Mexico needs to be understood to make sense of how things got to be the way they are today. The constant drumbeat of cries of "illegality" in association with Mexican-origin immigrants (or any immigrants for that matter) needs to be accompanied by more accurate portrayals of the Mexican American War (1846–48) and its aftermath, as well as other key events that occurred involving the United States and Mexico. Not to do so casts contemporary White America in the role of victim and innocent bystander in much the same way that such an image was consciously shaped vis-à-vis indigenous America during westward expansion. This too is one of the lessons of the past. An examination of the present state of relations between the two nations, though, would seem to indicate either ignorance of this past and this geography, or a magician-like attempt to erase and hide these inconvenient and embarrassing realities.

Demagoguery Concerning Immigrants

At present, multiple events have created a situation in which the lines between foreigners, terrorists, and immigrants—particularly those of Mexican origin, and regardless of their legal status—have been blurred (Barlett & Steele, 2004; Figueroa, 2002). These events include the terrorist attacks of 9/11 on New York City and Washington, DC, the U.S. government's war on terror, and conservative reaction to efforts to curb racial profiling, generally directed at persons considered "foreign," which has seen a resurgence since the terrorist attacks (Lamm, n.d.). While many claim to make a distinction between "legal" and "illegal" immigrants, in practice, such distinctions are far too often overlooked (Robbins, 1998; Wilson, 2001).

The confluence of these events and the deliberate positioning and alignment of immigrants with foreign "enemies" has been facilitated by recurring themes found within the media. Throughout 2005 and 2006, for example, the news media have reported on crises at the U.S.-Mexican border (Blumenthal, 2005; Pollack, 2005). Stories have focused on armed vigilante groups searching for "illegal" immigrants (Mansfield, 2005; Stewart, 2005); deportation hearings for high school graduates raised almost entirely in the United States (Billeaud, 2005; Mabin, 2005; Wilkie, 2005); and the effects that English language learners (ELLs) exert on local and state test scores (Winerip, 2005, 2006). These education-related stories almost always conclude that ELL students depress test scores and impose serious problems on schools. Other writers have dealt with legislation aimed at reforming immigration policies and what to do with undocumented immigrants already in the United States (O'Neil & Holusha, 2006). In the process, a way of thinking about immigrants, about who they are and why they are here, has taken shape and rooted itself deep within "that which everyone knows."

As already noted, Bourdieu (1998) calls this kind of thinking "the obviousness of ordinary experience." He goes on to explain that this common wisdom is not neutral, natural, or without political consequences. There are those who benefit from these ways of thinking (and understanding) and those who are excluded, marginalized, and scapegoated. Whether we are aware of it or not, all of us take part in the larger conversation about immigrants and English language learners. We all have a stake in the outcome of this conversation because who "they" are also plays a part in who "we" are. "They" are presented as illegitimate, illegal, criminal, undesirable, and unwanted, and Honig (1998) argues that this labeling of immigrants reflects "public anxiety about national identity and unity"(pp. 192–193).

Powerful images have been communicated through the words that accompany news reports and commentaries—words like *illegal, criminals, repeat offenders, violence, trespass, smuggling, kidnapping, murder*, and *deportation*. All of these words appeared in just one newspaper article about immigrants (Blumenthal, 2005). If this were a list of vocabulary items used to describe terrorists or convicted felons not many people would be surprised, but these are words used in stories about men, women, and children looking for a better life, looking for jobs, looking for opportunities, looking to contribute to society, and looking for an education for their children. These are individuals who want to work in factories, construction, and agriculture; people who want to work in hotels, restaurants, and hospitals; who are willing to work in a thousand other low-paying jobs. In short, these are people very much like earlier generations of those who came to find a better life in the United States, a place that previously was referred to as "a nation of immigrants."

Although the present work is not intended to advocate unregulated mass immigration, it seems odd that so much attention is being paid to this issue at this specific point in time, especially since immigration has been increasing at substantial rates for at least the past 15, if not 30, years. Could it be that all of this attention to immigration, while ostensibly related to creating "fair" and comprehensive national policy, is actually generating a mental template for permanently sorting and categorizing immigrants (as well as anyone who looks like an immigrant)? Are we witnessing a struggle over whether to include or exclude immigrants as possible future citizens? In other words, are we part of a much larger effort to determine the future status of millions of people?

Or do these reports reflect real contradictions among those with political and economic power? Without a doubt, some want to continue reaping the profits from immigrants' cheap labor, while others see these same individuals as a threat to national unity, undesirable, forever "illegal," and always as foreigners because of their racial/ethnic and linguistic backgrounds (National Research Council, 2006). There are yet others who desire immigrants' political support, as measured by their votes. Is it possible that such thinking, conflicted as it may be, also affects what happens in schools? Might these reports influence how schools allocate resources for English-language learners and how teachers and other educators see and treat children who come from immigrant families?

Bourdieu (1989) helps explain what is happening in the United States as well as around the world given the massive flow of peoples from less developed nations to those in Europe, North America, and certain countries in Asia:

To change the world, one has to change the ways of world-making, that is, the vision of the world and the practical operations by which groups are produced and reproduced. Symbolic power, whose form par excellence is the power to make groups. . . . The power to impose and to inculcate a vision of divisions, that is the power to make visible and explicit social divisions that are implicit, is political power par excellence. It is the power to make groups, to manipulate the objective structure of society. (p. 23)

While the debate rages over what our official government response ought to be and will be concerning future immigration, one thing is fairly certain: Latinos in the United States are in the process of being defined, labeled, and categorized. Of course, the power "to make groups" is now being met by resistance and counterefforts at self-definition, as surprising numbers of people are just now beginning to voice their disagreement with mainstream efforts to criminalize their existence. The nation may well be on the verge of a political movement to reframe the terms of this debate (Watanabe & Becerra, 2006). The mobilization of thousands, perhaps millions of individuals in support of immigrant rights is an interesting development, quite unexpected but entirely reasonable in the face of unrelenting scapegoating. It remains to be seen just how influential this movement will be, but it appears that there are at least *some* effects on politicians in the states with the most significant numbers of both Latinos and immigrants (Kirkpatrick, 2006). The motivating force for change here, of course, is the threat of losing votes.

Latino Students and Schooling

The mainstream discourse calling for removal of immigrants, primarily Latino immigrants, from the United States has been superimposed on a long and rather depressing history of exclusion and marginalization of Latino students from access to academic opportunity (Valencia, 1991). Unfortunately, Latino students have experienced disproportionate problems with their academic achievement throughout their history of contact with Anglo America, stretching back to the conflicts over the language of instruction in schools from the mid-1800s.

Surprisingly, and perhaps somewhat paradoxically, there are few groups that believe as strongly in the U.S. educational system as fervently as recent immigrants. The fact that so many Latino students and their families are first- or second-generation immigrants is a potentially significant strength that educators have yet to fully appreciate. Many Mexican (and other Latino) parents hold U.S. schools in high esteem primarily because U.S. schools receive more financial support than do their counterparts in Latin America (Nieto, 2000a). The general public in the United States, including many educators, often wrongly assume that Latino parents do not value education, and this assumption has been used as justification for denying Latino students quality instruction.

Such unexamined beliefs cause difficulties for many Latino students. Conversations with Latino parents that elicit their opinions concerning schooling, learning, and their children's futures almost always reveal a deep respect for teachers and learning (e.g., Barrera & Jiménez, 2001). So, in spite of the fact that U.S. schools often fail to provide meaningful educational opportunity to Latino students, their families and communities still maintain hope that schooling will allow their children to achieve more than the previous generation.

Some theorists, like Macedo (2000), have argued that the so-called failure of U.S. schools concerning Latino students is not a failure at all, but rather the intended outcome of a system that was never designed to provide these students with a quality education. While some might question the conspiratorial tone of such a charge, far too much effort has gone into finding fault with Latino students, their families, and their teachers, rather than into examining how larger systems predetermine and constrain students' opportunity. Deeper questions concerning how lack of adequate health care, worthwhile economic opportunity, and the relationships these issues have to instructional quality have most often been ignored, despite the fact that these issues were raised by Latino educators like George Sánchez (1940) over 60 years ago and are now being revived by a new generation of scholars who refuse to separate and disconnect material conditions from schooling (Luke, 2003; Macedo, 1994). Of course, perhaps not so surprisingly, the shift in the debate from equity to that of the *right to exist*, as dictated by our current national discourse around immigration, has pushed these concerns off the table and out of sight. Instead of examining how our schools fail students who are English language learners or culturally and linguistically diverse, many in the media focus their ire on issues such as why Latino students are admitted into U.S. institutions of higher learning.

A History of Neglect

What this means, to use a sports metaphor, is that the goal posts have not only been moved. . . . they have been placed on an entirely different field. This new field, however, is familiar territory when situated in a historical context. Segregation of Latino students was accomplished by establishing separate programs, ostensibly to "Americanize" students with respect to language and culture. The language and culture of Latino students was purposely excluded from the official curriculum (Carter & Segura, 1979; San Miguel, 1984). These programs had the effect of denying Latino students access to the curriculum of power and to instruction that might lead to enhanced economic opportunity.

An additional complicating but important factor is that political and economic forces have created residential patterns that result in schools in which Latino and other minority students constitute a segregated majority (Frankenberg, Lee, & Orfield, 2003). It is perhaps no coincidence that an acrimonious anti-immigrant movement is occurring at the same time that increased attention is being paid to Latino students and their academic achievement, through research efforts and because of the data generated by No Child Left Behind disaggregating of student achievement scores. The danger is that the attention of policymakers and voters will continue to be shifted from how to improve educational opportunities for Latino and other immigrant students to how these students can be removed altogether from the educational system.

Economic Factors and Latino Students

Preceding the debates on immigration, policymakers legislated increased demands for student academic performance. Ironically, considering the intense nature of the current debate over immigration, we must remember that culturally and linguistically diverse students are now and will be the workers of tomorrow (National Research Council, 2006). The economy depends on these individuals, but there are contradictory forces at work within our economic system. A demand for cheap labor contrasts with the need for highly skilled, knowledgeable individuals. And we are entering a period in which both types of workers are increasingly viewed as expendable, as "raw materials" who exist only to serve economic interests. When the needs of workers clash with those of employers and their profits, jobs are often simply exported to locations that provide more profit by way of less costly labor. Latino students and their families, especially, are seen as a readily available workforce that can be disposed of when no longer needed through deportation and/or the denial of basic human rights. These contradictions are embarrassingly evident when states pass special legislation to allow temporary workers into the country because they are necessary to sectors such as agribusiness, while at the same time legislate policies that deny basic human rights such as jobs, health care, education, and the use of their languages to immigrants (Cheah & Robbins, 1998).

In the past, the struggles of students from linguistically and culturally diverse backgrounds were simply ignored by schools. These students were provided with only a shadow of the curriculum and instruction provided to students from mainstream backgrounds, and few worried much when they failed to graduate from high school (Reyes & Halcón, 2001). If Valencia (1991) is correct when he claims that Latino students have faced difficulties wherever they happen to be found in the United States, then we may be facing a massive new wave of problems given the combination of low expectations and the potentially insidious discourse of "border control." The fact is, Latino immigrants are moving into places where they traditionally have not resided—places like rural Nebraska, Iowa, and downstate Illinois. Large communities of Latinos can be found in much of the Southeast, in Georgia, North and South Carolina, and Tennessee (National Research Council, 2006).

School districts in rural areas seldom are prepared, in terms of personnel and materials, to support students from linguistically diverse backgrounds. Many of the ineffective practices employed in a previous era in the Southwest may once again be instituted in these new settings. The difference, however, will be that ineffective instructional practices will coexist with calls for immigrant removal. Such a combination does not bode well for how schools will respond to the challenges of teaching an increasingly diverse student population.

Legislation targeting immigrants may be an indication of where federal and state policy is headed. Georgia, for example, has enacted harsh legislation that will "require employers to maintain valid employment authorization documents for employees in order to claim a tax deduction for wages . . . lawmakers [added] a 6% withholding of wages for contract workers without a valid taxpayer identification or social security number" (Cowan, 2006). The subtitle of the article claims that the proposed law "would slam the door on undocumented workers."

These penalties are reminiscent of the "foreign miner's tax" levied on predominantly Mexican Californians in 1850 (Acuña, 1988), which had the unintended consequence of severely disrupting California's economy. Rather than paying the tax, huge numbers of "foreign" miners abandoned their work. One has to wonder how Georgia's proposed legislation may end up affecting the "Hispanic market" of $10.6 billion within that state. One also has to wonder how the system of schooling in places that enact such legislation will view and subsequently teach students whose families are the victims of such laws.

A World That Demands Immigration

It is telling that anti-immigrant legislation and English-only educational policies are recurring and related events in U.S. history. Ironically, English-only schooling imposed after military conquest and/or colonial acquisition typically leaves those affected without either English proficiency *or* necessary levels of literacy. Crawford (1995) points to the experiences of several groups including French-speaking Louisianans, Spanish-speaking southwesterners, Cherokee-speaking Native Americans, Hawaiian-speaking islanders, and Spanish-speaking Puerto Ricans to support this claim. Legislated demands that certain groups must learn English have proven to be notoriously ineffective. It takes little historical understanding to grasp this, but, be that as it may, the U.S. Senate went so far as to approve a measure designating English as the country's official language in May 2006 (Fountain, 2006).

One issue unaddressed by Gifford and Valdés involves the continuing U.S. involvement in the politics and economies of many immigrant-sending countries such as Mexico and other Latin American nations and Puerto Rico, which continues to support situations in which vast numbers of individuals must consider the option of emigration out of their home countries (Nieto, 2000b; Walsh, 1998). This involvement has taken the form of military invasions, political manipulations, and economic domination. Workers, for example, have been forced by the lack of jobs or the poor working conditions and extremely low pay of the *maquiladoras* (assembly plants near the United States–Mexico border) to consider working in the United States if they hope to feed themselves and their families. Such a situation constantly reinforces the urgency of both internal and external migration (Levinson, 2001). Schooling, theoretically a way to better oneself, is not always available in nations like Mexico, due at least in part to the huge sums of money these nations must pay on their national debts to foreign banks (Cockcroft, 1998).

Even in the United States, schooling is not always available for immigrant students. Although not often acknowledged, the combination of factors such as low-quality instruction, the danger of violence, unavailability due to lack of space, or difficult rules and regulations associated with school enrollment conspire to deprive many students of a worthwhile education or of any education at all (Carger, 1996). This situation is difficult and uncomfortable to confront head on—because of prevailing egalitarian and meritocratic mythologies in the United States, class differences created through historical and economic means are not supposed to hinder or otherwise restrict one's eventual place in society.

At present, failing politicians are only too happy to blame Latino and other immigrant students for overall declining economic and educational conditions and outcomes. Latinos have been blamed before; for example, they were blamed for joblessness during the Great Depression of the 1930s and many were deported to Mexico during that time, whether they were citizens or not (Acuña, 1988). It seems reasonable to posit that the relationship between students' class backgrounds and their racial/ethnic backgrounds is a powerful force shaping their access to literacy, their desire to learn English, and their dispositions in general concerning schooling (Ferdman, 1990). Macedo (2000) asked the question: Do material conditions that foster human misery adversely affect academic development (p. 19)? Without a doubt, current and prevailing political conditions will do nothing to improve student achievement and will most likely have the effect of demoralizing students who are learning English even more than is currently the case.

The Reality of National Boundaries

Perhaps closely related to the issues of history and economics is the transnational character of literacy for many Latino students, both those currently residing in their countries of origin and those living in the United States. Gifford and Valdés argue that "U.S. officials have proven themselves unable or unwilling to come up with an immigration policy that acknowledges the reality of the integrated nature of the U.S.-Mexico economy" (p. 20). As has been already pointed out, large numbers of families move about the world in search of the basic necessities in life; this movement is not simply one way. For some Latinos, specifically those of Puerto Rican origin, issues of citizenship are irrelevant and migration and reverse migration is as simple as purchasing airfare. For those of Mexican and Central American background, a return to their native country can be achieved through jet travel or a long drive. The point is that many Latino students and their families will not, as has been the case with some earlier immigrant groups, view the United States as their only option for residence. This perspective on immigration—the idea that returning to the home country is a real option, even if only sporadically—is probably true for many of the immigrant groups currently making their way to the United States. The psychology behind this global view, or dual-national perspective, may be less important for our purposes, however, than its effects on how students view language and literacy.

The transnational nature of students' lives is, in some ways, a reflection of the neocolonial relationship between their homeland and their destination (Grinberg & Saavedra, 2000). At the very least, better understanding of the transnational nature of students' lives may help researchers and educators grasp why knowledge of the Spanish language and literacy are still important for many students, as well as how their neocolonial status creates a continuing struggle between the forces of assimilation and those of identity maintenance (Walsh, 1998).

The nature of students' transnational lives opens up new lines of thought concerning the future of the *Brown* decision. For example, what influence should this reality have on curriculum selection, instructional methods, and linguistic mode of instruction? One could also question many of the underlying goals and objectives for schooling, especially as these pertain to Latino students, but also in terms of European American students. In what ways do monocultural, monolingual instructional practices and curriculum materials handicap *all* students—not just "foreigners"? What opportunities are lost because linguistic and cultural capital is squandered by current educational policies? How do the substantial flows of individuals from within the nation as well as from without it question and destabilize the assumptions (of relatively settled populations living in close proximity) upon which the original *Brown* decision was established?

In other words, do earlier notions of segregation need to be reconceptualized in more complex ways, less in terms of a binary, and further, take into consideration the multiplicity of populations, geographies, and differences within groups?

Where Do We Go From Here?

Gifford and Valdés identify the fears of white parents who worry about the effects Latino children would have on their own children's educational progress (p. 8). These fears motivated the establishment of a segregated school system in an earlier era, and as the authors suggest, it may also contribute to the intense and sustained linguistic isolation that is a result of today's racial and ethnic segregation. And the more successful the efforts to segregate Latino students, the more likely it is that they will not learn English, at least not the kind of English needed to make academic progress, contributing to a vicious cycle. Such predictable outcomes of backward and insular reactions to immigration call into question the motives behind the unceasing demand that immigrants must learn English. This demand is prominently displayed in all current attempts at legislation designed to address immigration policy (Goolsbee, 2006). Of course, these proposals do nothing to actually help people learn English—no funding is included to prepare teachers to work with English learners, no plan for teaching English has been proposed, and no thought toward how to provide individuals with more English language input has been offered.

Globalization has unleashed a new virulent strain of tribalism that seeks to quite literally build walls to keep others out of territory for which they are considered unworthy (Reynolds & Gaouette, 2006). On the other hand, new technologies and corporate capitalism have erased boundaries that were once considered final and inviolate. As always, changes like these have upset established patterns of thinking about space and time that many found comforting (and others viewed as barriers to progress). *Brown* unsettled, albeit in a rather mild manner, previous patterns of power and privilege. New developments, grounded as always in our history and shaped by physical boundaries established by treaties from previous centuries, promise to unsettle the world of schooling a great deal more. Mainstream backlash, a newfound sense of voice and empowerment within the immigrant community, and continued economic and political instability across the globe but especially among governments in the Caribbean and to the south of the United States, will continue to challenge us to live up to what *Brown*, however minimally, began.

REFERENCES

Acuña, R. (1988). *Occupied America: A history of Chicanos* (2nd ed.). New York: Harper Collins.

Alvarez v. Owen, slip. op. at 5 (San Diego County Super. Ct., March 30, 1931).

Barlett, D.L., & Steele, J.B. (2004, September 20). Who left the door open? *Time*. Retrieved, June 3, 2006, from http://www.time.com/time/magazine/article/ 0,9171,995145,00.html

Barrera, R.B., & Jiménez, R.T. (2001). Bilingual teachers speak about the literacy instruction of bilingual Latino students. In B.M. Taylor & P.D. Pearson (Eds.), *Teaching reading: Effective schools and accomplished teachers* (pp. 335–357). Mahwah, NJ: Erlbaum.

Barton, D., & Hamilton, M. (2000). Literacy practices. In D. Barton, M. Hamilton, & R. Ivanic (Eds.), *Situated literacies* (pp. 7–15). New York: Routledge.

Billeaud, J. (2005, July 22). Deportation case against students dropped. *Comcast News*. Retrieved April 3, 2006, from http://www.comcast.net/news/national/index. jsp?cat=DOMESTIC

Blumenthal, R. (2005, August 23). For one family, front row seats to border crisis. *NYTimes.com*. Retrieved, February 13, 2006, from http://www.nytimes.com/2005/ 08/23/national/23border.html?ex=1282449600&en=a618d45274008587&ei=5088& partner=rssnyt &emc=rss

Bourdieu, P. (1989). Social space and symbolic power. *Sociological Theory*, 7(1), 14–25.

Bourdieu, P. (1998). *Practical reason*. Stanford, CA: Stanford University Press.

Brown v. Board of Education, 347 U.S. 483 (1954).

Carger, C.L. (1996). *Of borders and dreams*. New York: Teachers College Press.

Carter, T.P., & Segura, R.D. (1979). *Mexican Americans in school: A decade of change*. New York: College Entrance Examination Board.

Cheah, P., & Robbins, B. (1998). *Cosmopolitics: Thinking and feeling beyond the nation*. Minneapolis: University of Minnesota Press.

Cockcroft, J.D. (1998). *Mexico's hope: An encounter with politics and history*. New York: Monthly Review Press.

Cowan, C. (2006, March 31). In Georgia, immigration is no peach. *Businessweek Online*. Retrieved March 31, 2006, from http://www.businessweek.com/bwdaily/dnflash/ mar2006/nf20060331_6208.htm

Crawford, J. (1995). *Bilingual education: History, politics, theory and practice*. Los Angeles: Bilingual Educational Services.

Donato, R. (1997). *The other struggle for equal schools: Mexican Americans during the civil rights era*. Albany, NY: SUNY Press.

Ferdman, B. (1990). Literacy and cultural identity. *Harvard Educational Review*, 60(2), 181–204.

Figueroa, K. (2002). Immigrants and the civil rights regime: Parens Patriae standing, foreign governments and protection from private discrimination. *Columbia Law Review*, 102(2), 408–470.

Fountain, H. (2006, May 21). In language bill, the language counts. *The New York Times*, section 4, p. 2.

Frankenberg, E., Lee, C., & Orfield, G. (2003). *A multiracial society with segregated schools: Are we losing the dream?* Cambridge, MA: The Civil Rights Project, Harvard University.

Gifford, B.R., & Valdés, G. (2006). The linguistic isolation of Hispanic students in California's public schools: The challenge of reintegration. In A. Ball (Ed.), *With more deliberate speed: Achieving equity and excellence in education—Realizing the full potential of Brown v. Board of Education. The 105th yearbook of the National Society for the Study of Education*, Part II (pp. 125–154). Malden, MA: Blackwell.

Goolsbee, A. (2006, June 22). ECONOMIC SCENE; Legislate learning English? If only it were so easy. *The New York Times*, Section C, p. 3.

Gorman, A. (2006, March 29). Flag's meaning is in the eye of the beholder. *Los Angeles Times*, p. A11.

Grinberg, J., & Saavedra, E. (2000). The constitution of bilingual/ESL education as a disciplinary practice: Genealogical explorations. *Review of Educational Research, 70*(4), 419–442.

Honig, B. (1998). Ruth, the model émigré. In P. Cheah & B. Robbins (Eds.), *Cosmopolitics: Thinking and feeling beyond the nation* (pp. 192–215). Minneapolis: University of Minnesota Press.

Kamberelis, G., & Dimitriadis, G. (2004). *On qualitative inquiry: Approaches to language ad literacy research*. New York: Teachers College Press.

Kirkpatrick, D.D. (2006, March 30). G.O.P. Risking Hispanic votes on immigration. *NYTimes.com*. Retrieved March 30, 2006, from http://www.nytimes.com/2006/03/30/politics/30hispanics.html?ex=1301374800&en=a5fde43d7fd314c5&ei=5088&partner=rssnyt&emc=rss

Lamm R.D. (n.d). *Terrorism and immigration: A decision memorandum*. The Foundation for the Defense of Democracies. Retrieved May 10, 2006, from http://www.defenddemocracy.org/usr_doc/terrorism-immigration_2.pdf

Levinson, B.A.U. (2001). *We are all equal: Student culture and identity at a Mexican secondary school, 1988–1998*. Durham, NC: Duke University Press.

Lo Bianco, J. (2000). Multiliteracies and multilingualism. In B. Cope & M. Kalantzis (Eds.), *Multiliteracies: Literacy learning and the design of social futures* (pp. 92–105). London: Routledge.

Luke, A. (2003). Literacy and the other: A sociological approach to literacy research and policy in multilingual societies. *Reading Research Quarterly, 38*(1), 132–141.

Mabin, C. (2005, December 30). Immigration judge halts deportation hearings of high school student. *The Beacon Journal*. Retrieved December 30, 2005, from http://www.ohio.com/mld/beaconjournal13512493.htm

Macedo, D. (1994). *Literacies of power*. Boulder, CO: Westview.

Macedo, D. (2000). The colonialism of the English only movement. *Educational Researcher, 29*(3), 15–24.

Mansfield, D. (2005, July 18). Migrant "patrols" take root nationally. *Arizona Daily Star*. Retrieved July 18, 2005, from http://www.azstarnet.com/dailystar/dailystar/84560

Mendez v. Westminster, 64 F. Supp. 544 (S.O. Cal. 1946).

Merriam, S.B. (2001). *Qualitative research and case study applications in education*. San Francisco: Jossey-Bass.

Moore, D.W., Monaghan, E.J., & Hartman, D.K. (1997). Values of literacy history. *Reading Research Quarterly, 32*, 90–102.

National Research Council. (2006). *Multiple origins, uncertain destinies: Hispanics and the American future*. Washington, DC: National Academies Press.

Nieto, S. (2000a). *Affirming diversity* (3rd ed.). New York: Addison Wesley/Longman.

Nieto, S. (2000b). Puerto Rican students in U.S. schools: A brief history. In S. Nieto (Ed.), *Puerto Rican students in U.S. schools* (pp. 5–37). White Plains, NY: Erlbaum.

O'Neil, J., & Holusha, J. (2006, March 27). Senate debates citizen eligibility for immigrants. *The New York Times*. Retrieved June 27, 2006, from http://www.nytimes.com/2006/03/27/national/27cnd-immig.html?hp&ex=1143522000&en=ad0f089e26191399&ei=5094&partner=homepage

Pollack, A. (2005, August 19). 2 illegal immigrants win Arizona ranch in court. *The New York Times*, section A, p. 16.

Reyes, M.L., & Halcón, J. (2001). *The best for our children: Critical perspectives on literacy for Latino students*. New York: Teachers College Press.

Reynolds, M., & Gaovette, N. (2006, March 29). Senators delay immigration debate to work behind the scenes. *Los Angeles Times*, A16.

Robbins, B. (1998). Comparative cosmopolitanism. In P. Cheah & B. Robbins (Eds.), *Cosmopolitics: Thinking and feeling beyond the nation* (pp. 246–264). Minneapolis: University of Minnesota Press.

Sánchez, George I. (1940). *Forgotten People: A Study of New Mexicans*. Alberquerque, N.M.: The University of New Mexico Press.

San Miguel, G. (1984). The origins, development, and consequences of the educational segregation of Mexican Americans in the Southwest. In E.E. García, F.A. Lomelí, & I.D. Ortiz (Eds.), *Chicano studies: A multidisciplinary approach* (pp. 195–208). New York: Teachers College Press.

San Miguel, G. (1987). *"Let all of them take heed": Mexican Americans and the campaign for educational equality in Texas, 1910–1981*. Austin: University of Texas Press.

Stewart, M. (2005, May 21). Volunteers recruited to help catch illegal immigrants in east Tennessee. *WBIR.com*. Retrieved March 25, 2006, from http://www.wbir.com/news/archive.aspx?storyid=25845

Tuchman, G. (1994). Historical social science: Methodologies, methods, and meanings. In N.K. Denzin & Y.S. Lincoln (Eds.), *Handbook of qualitative research* (pp. 306–323). Thousand Oaks, CA: Sage.

Valencia, R.R. (1991). *Chicano school failure and success: Research and policy agendas for the 1990s*. New York: Falmer Press.

Walsh, C. (1998). "Staging encounters": The educational decline of U.S. Puerto Ricans in [post]-colonial perspective. *Harvard Educational Review, 68*(2), 218–243.

Watanabe, T., & Becerra, H. (2006, March 26). 500,000 pack streets to protest immigration bill. *Los Angeles Times*, p. A1.

Wilkie, J. (2005, July 4). High school graduate faces deportation. *The Epoch Times International*. Retrieved March 27, 2006, from http://www.theepochtimes.com/news/5-7-4/30002.html

Wilson, T.C. (2001). Americans' views on immigration policy: Testing the role of threatened group interests. *Sociological Perspectives, 44*(4), 485–501.

Winerip, M. (2005, November 2). Are schools passing or failing? Now there's a third choice. Both. *The New York Times*, Section B, p. 9.

Winerip, M. (2006, January 11). Bitter lesson: A good school gets an "F.". *The New York Times*, Section B, p. 7.

CHAPTER 9

Looking for Educational Equity: The Consequences of Relying on Brown

KRIS D. GUTIÉRREZ AND NATHALIA E. JARAMILLO

Those who are racially marginalized are like the miner's canary: their distress is the first sign of the danger that threatens us all (Guinier & Torres, 2002, 11).

Race, as Guinier and Torres (2002) remind us, is our miner's canary—a constant measure of the state of race relations in our country, a measure of our humanity. As we wrote this piece, we found ourselves in the midst of another historical moment when our inhumanity, undergirded by a legacy of racist and classist practices, was nakedly exposed for the world to see. The public and private discourse around the tragedies of hurricane Katrina revealed shock and awe as many learned that the poorest in our country, predominantly African American, had been left to languish, suffer, and die by the richest, most powerful nation in the world. The media pundits have engaged in analysis about how such neglect or delayed responses could occur when racial inequities have improved so dramatically in the decades after the hard-fought battles of the civil rights movement. . . . or so the story goes. And today we have another existence proof of the persistence of inequality in our country. At this historical moment, millions of immigrants whose labor forms the backbone of the U.S. economy fight for their dignity and human rights.

This chapter attempts to begin a conversation about how so many of us in the educational and academic communities have come to believe that educational equity could be mediated by legal measures and federal

Kris D. Gutiérrez is Professor of Social Research Methodology in the Graduate School of Education and Information Studies at the University of California at Los Angeles.

Nathalia E. Jaramillo is a Ph.D. candidate in the Division of Urban Schooling in the Graduate School of Education and Information Studies at the University of California, Los Angeles.

and local reforms without transformation of the historical practices and
ideologies that preserve supremacy and "White innocence"—a racialized analytic concept we adapt from Gotanda (2004). We focus on the
landmark *Brown v. Board of Education* (1954) decision, the theme of this
volume, as the context for a discussion of how race and race relations
in this country continue to signal a need for race-conscious practices
that go beyond the limitations of legal remedies and their monitoring
apparatus. Central to this discussion is the important distinction
between an equity-minded agenda versus one that considers equal
opportunity as the single organizing principle of reform (Crosland,
2004). Put simply, while remaining faithful to the goal of equal opportunity, we argue that equal access is a necessary but insufficient
condition to restructure the very policies and practices that create the
inequities in the first place. Moreover, as we will elaborate in this
chapter, the equal access and opportunity concept has been appropriated by neoconservatives and serves as the organizing principle for the
"sameness as fairness" principle in current educational policy and practice (p. 3). We examine the *Brown* decision from this standpoint.

Brown: *Reconsiderations From the Present*

In this chapter we argue that the *Brown* decision addressed the issue
of segregation in educational settings but was never intended as a means
for remediating general and more fundamental educational disparities
and other legal racial segregations. We discuss briefly the historical
context of *Brown*, posit some reasons for the prominent role of *Brown*
in issues of equity and equality in educational communities, and propose
a race conscious, equity-oriented agenda for transformative education.
We focus on the undereducation of children in California for whom
English is not the home language as an illustrative case of the effects
of new race-based educational practices instituted via language and
literacy policies. Here language becomes a proxy for race and ethnicity
and serves as the tool for organizing schooling around a "sameness as
fairness" principle that is ensuring new forms of segregation. Finally, in
this era of high-stakes accountability, we argue for an accountability
framework that begins to dismantle inequality and ensures that educational reform and its instantiations in practice are organized around
robust learning practices that are simultaneously race-conscious and
equity-oriented.

We begin by focusing on *Brown*, long held by members of the
educational community as the touchstone case for educational equity
and equality, thus, long considered the legal arm for educational and

social redress. In fact, we have come to rely on *Brown* as the primary basis for race-conscious educational policies. We have poured money into its remedies, operating under the assumption that integration would mediate cross-cultural relations, perceptions, and historical inequities. The public and the educational community have come to understand and rely on the *Brown* decision as our standard for race relations and as the backdrop for educational equality and equity.

How did we come to place so much hope on the Court? And what are the consequences of relying so heavily on *Brown* and other legal decisions to regulate a nation's moral consciousness around race relations and to ensure equity for students from nondominant groups, especially in these times?

Historical Context

The 1954 *Brown* decision reversed the legacy of the "separate and equal" doctrine established by *Plessy v. Ferguson* (1896). While *Plessy* applied to all public services in the United States, *Brown* pertained only to public schools, and therefore did not have the capacity or the legal jurisdiction to fully dismantle the application of "separate" or "segregated" public services. Of significance, neither *Plessy* nor *Brown* applied to de facto segregation, and the narrow scope of *Brown* only outlawed de jure segregation, leaving intact the vast apparatus of de facto segregation.

While the scope of *Brown* was limited, the case did compel the Court to address a deeply fundamental question: "Does segregation of children in public schools solely on the basis of race, even though the physical facilities and other 'tangible' factors may be equal, deprive the children of the minority group of equal education opportunities?" (*Brown v. Board of Education*, 1954). Chief Justice Earl Warren addressed this issue directly in the Court's majority opinion, stating, "We believe that it does" (*Brown v. Board of Education*, 1954).

Theoretically, the Court imparted a notion of educational equity that dealt with the underlying pathology of the forced separation of children on the basis of race. Citing a series of new research studies that demonstrated the negative psychosocial stigmas experienced by segregated Black youth (see Kluger, 1975), the court affirmed that "separate" educational facilities violated students' constitutional right to equal protection under the 14th Amendment, a point to which we will return shortly.

This decision signaled a telling and unprecedented shift in legal doctrines, as *Brown* mandated a set of race-conscious remedies intended to reverse an era of court-approved race-conscious segregation legalized by *Plessy*, and continues to serve for many in this country as a foundational building block toward establishing an "interracial democracy" (Street, 2004).

However, as Street (2004) has argued, an interracial democracy is difficult to achieve without directly confronting white supremacist ideologies that were *not* overturned by *Brown*. And although *Brown*'s intent was to dismantle dual school settings to ensure equal educational opportunity for nondominant students, the ruling's framers and supporters did not adequately account for the degree to which "White supremacy and racism were instantiated in the U.S. cultural model" (Ladson–Billings, 2004, p. 5).

It comes as no surprise, then, that attempts to overturn decades of segregation and accompanying commonplace racist practices through mandated integration were met with serious resistance. *Brown*'s limited success in a few Southern school districts, for example, is best understood in relation to the historical practices and dominant class interests of Southern communities. Derek Bell's (2004) notion of "interest convergence" is particularly useful here to better understand changes in civil rights in historical context. According to Bell, "Black rights are recognized and protected when and only so long as policy makers perceive that such advances will further interests that are their primary concern" (p. 49). The construct of interest convergence serves as a useful analytical tool that helps us unpack the complex sociopolitical, economic, and cultural shifts vis-à-vis race relations in this country.

The Role of *Brown* in Educational Change

We begin this section asking: To what extent has *Brown* contributed to school reform in the United States? We should be clear here that we do not dispute the importance of the *Brown* decision and its legacy. Clearly, the law plays a pivotal and instrumental role in establishing policies that have the capacity to move the country toward more egalitarian objectives. Judicial intervention is now considered one of the main mechanisms for transforming K-12 schooling as well as institutions of higher learning (Reed, 2001). As Reed suggests, *Brown*'s "profound legacy" is found in the "continuing relationship between courtrooms and classrooms" (p. 37). For example, in the realm of affirmative action, school funding, and more recently, the implementation of equal opportunity to learn standards (see *Williams v. State of California*, 2004), the law has demonstrated its capacity to redefine access and to redistribute resources. But in doing so, the law has also confirmed its limitations, as does this line of analysis.

The court is partial to extant systems of economic and racial hierarchies and is motivated by its inherent inclination to protect dominant class interests. Following Bell (1987, 2004), Lawrence (1995) asserts, "the legal establishment has not responded to civil rights claims that threaten the superior social status of upper and middle class whites" (p. 254). Without taking into consideration the underlying narratives and historical agents left to enact or react to such policies, the law retains a limited function in ratifying "progressive" or "equity minded" school reform in the long term—especially when such rulings crash against the tide of the political and social economy. In fact, throughout the past two decades, the nation has witnessed a rollback of affirmative action policies, such as Proposition 209 in California, the dismantling of primary language instruction, Proposition 227 (Gutiérrez, Asato, Santos, & Gotanda, 2002; Gutiérrez, Baquedano-Lopez, & Asato, 2001), and a more strict (if not untenable) interpretation of discriminatory "intent" under the Fourteenth Amendment equal protection clause (see discussion of intent in Brown, 1994; Welner & Oakes, 1996).

A Call for New Analyses

Despite *Brown's* contributions, we are concerned, as Delgado and Stefancic (1995) note, that *Brown's* legacy is often measured along a temporal axis that focuses narrowly on changes in a limited sphere of the social context of race relations that both preceded and followed *Brown*. Such analyses are organized around questions that ask: Did *Brown* benefit Blacks in any way? Did the ruling make any difference in improving race relations (Delgado & Stefancic)? This notion of progress in race relations examines the "situation that prevailed before *Brown*, and that after, and looks for signs that *Brown* brought about changes" (p. 5).

At issue here is that change as a measure of incremental social progress is insufficient in gauging transformation in the nation's moral and social fabric vis-à-vis the legacy of racial, social, and economic inequity and hierarchies. Instead, a due consideration of *Brown* includes an analysis of the ruling's "gravitational field"—that is, a sociohistorical analysis of meanings and social interpretations, social practices, and the role of narratives against which *Brown* would be forced to operate (Delgado & Stefancic, 1995). Such an analysis, we believe, would illuminate existing and fundamental contradictions and would better orient us toward transformative action and a new moral discourse that reinvokes the so-called American ideal of equality that framed the U.S. Constitution and specifically, the 14th Amendment—the basic building block from which *Brown* was argued.

Of relevance to our argument in this chapter, *Brown* largely ignored the historical and fundamental relations that led to the segregation of schoolchildren, leaving a legacy of post-*Brown* educational initiatives that remained faithful to the latent objectives associated with the Court's ruling. Moreover, it appears that many have interpreted *Brown* as a "return to" those basic principles of equality, an interpretation that we believe misses the mark as the dismantling of the legacy and structural effects of racism—the underlying logic of segregation—were not in question under *Brown*. More fundamental to our point, in legal terms, no moral argument was advanced at the time of *Brown*'s ruling (Gotanda, personal communication, July 2005).

We believe if we are to achieve educational equity today, a proactive and concerted effort to dismantle the constitutive elements of racism that reflects a different and contemporary moral imperative is in order. As Guinier and Torres (2002) argue, we are in need of a new moral grammar that compels us to move beyond the conventional and more restrictive legal analysis around race. Such a focus on the underlying moral dimensions of educational equity should remind us that while the *Brown* plaintiffs argued that legal racial segregation caused educational disparities, the Court only addressed the issue of segregation in educational settings. Moreover, while the Court subsequently used this landmark case as a legal precedent—a form of blanket desegregation for subsequent desegregation cases—the Court did not legislate a new moral stance or ethic among the people toward educational equity.

Moving Toward Equity

Several years ago, Kristin Crosland (2004) advanced a race-sensitive analysis that illustrated how a focus on racial equity instead of the reform du jour (in her case, decentralization) leads to dramatically different agendas and outcomes. To illustrate this argument, Crosland wrote:

> The equity agenda focuses on eliminating racial discrimination in schooling by confronting it at its source, by guaranteeing equalized educational opportunities through compensatory programming, and by developing multicultural curricular and pedagogical approaches that offer meaningful, rigorous curricula to diverse students. In contrast, the decentralization agenda strives to improve school quality through market notions of "consumer choice," to radically alter

the bureaucratic structure of schooling for increased local control, and to establish standards and accountability practices to inform consumers' choices. (p. 3)

Drawing on Crosland's analysis, equity and desegregation and educational opportunity, as in the case of *Brown*, reflect very different goals and values. Of significance, as Crosland elaborates, race-based equity reforms focus on the source of the problem—the underlying historical practices that have contributed to the inequity.

However, as we have written elsewhere, the discourse of equity has become so powerful and persuasive that it has been co-opted in recent years by those seeking to turn back the small gains in civil rights of previous decades (Gutiérrez, Asato, Santos, & Gotanda, 2002; Gutiérrez et al., 2001). By proposing new forms of equal educational opportunity through color-blind, merit-based interventions, a "sameness as fairness" argument has come to dominate the rhetoric of educational reform—obscuring the link between economic disparities, asymmetrical power relations, and historically racialized practices (Bobo, Oliver, Johnson, & Valenzuela, 2000; Crosland, 2004; Gutmann, 1996, as cited in Crosland, 2004).

Consider for example, former Secretary of Education Rod Paige's (2002) appropriation of *Brown* to champion the No Child Left Behind Act of 2001 (NCLB), characterizing NCLB as *Brown*'s "logical next step" and "one of the legacies of *Brown v. Board of Education*" (p. 1). For Paige and the Bush Administration, educational opportunity is achieved through a concerted effort in applying the same "high standards" to racially and economically segregated schools—a form of the "sameness as fairness" framework—without regard to the historical and present structures that gave rise to and sustain deeply rooted inequities. Paige and other supporters of the accountability mechanisms established through NCLB argue that a strict system of disaggregated test scores by race, ethnicity, language status, and disability ensures that the "American ideal" is distributed evenly across student populations. With an evangelical allegiance to testing and high stakes accountability, NCLB and its supporters attempt to make the case that such measures will eliminate the separate and unequal instruction nondominant student populations and their more affluent counterparts experience. Integration is no longer a viable or necessary remedy within this educational framework.

Language as the New Proxy for Race

Language and notions of ability serve as discursive surrogates for the larger categories of race and intelligence. Of relevance to the larger argument of this chapter, we will focus on language policies in California as they constitute a telling case both for the limits of legal interventions designed to insure equal opportunity and, as we will discuss later in this chapter, for the ways resurrected English-only polices both recreate and sustain separate and unequal educational practices under the refurbished neoconservative mantra of equal access and opportunity.

For example, in California and states with increasing immigrant populations, language rights and practices continue to be at the heart of the current contested social and educational terrain as language in this post-civil rights era becomes the new proxy for race and ethnicity. Consider the 1998 California voter initiative, Proposition 227, that legislated English-only instruction by selling equal opportunity as the outcome of English-only practices. We provide a key segment of the proposition's text to illustrate this point:

(b) Whereas, Immigrant parents are eager to have their children acquire a good knowledge of English, thereby allowing them to fully participate in the American Dream of economic and social advancement; and

(c) Whereas, The government and the public schools of California have a moral obligation and a constitutional duty to provide all of California's children, regardless of their ethnicity or national origins, with the skills necessary to become productive members of our society, and of these skills, literacy in the English language is among the most important; (italics in the original)

Undergirded by anti-immigrant policies and language ideologies, the legislation also served as a wedge to fracture cultural communities and as a means of preserving the status quo and linguistic hegemony (Gutiérrez et al., 2002). We will return to effects of the sameness as fairness principle at work in language policies shortly.

The Discursive Construction of Sameness

The existing vulnerability of English learners is exacerbated by marketplace practices such as high stakes assessment programs, assessment-driven curricula, and English-only laws that legislate instructional practices for English learners. As previously articulated, such practices discourage and prohibit, respectively, the use of the students' complete linguistic, sociocultural, and academic repertoires in learning processes and events (Crossland & Gutiérrez, 2003; Gutiérrez, 2004b). Further, these marketplace practices require the sorting and labeling of students in which new devices once again marginalize groups of students and categorize them by racial, ethnic, and linguistic groups as a means of distributing educational treatments categorically (Gutiérrez, 2002, 2004a).

In the case of English learners, their homogenization, that is, the characterization of students' academic needs, potential, and trajectories by a single measure (i.e., their language status), satisfies several mutually reinforcing social and educational policies organized around an anti-immigrant and nationalist agenda: (1) the sorting of students for a single educational treatment; (2) the sorting of students by ethnic and racial categories to identify immigrant status; and (3) the sorting of students and their test scores as primary determinants of individual and school "failure" (i.e., "underperforming student" and "underperforming school"). This labeling and sorting of English learners has contributed to their participation in separate and unequal educational practices through the establishment of English-only policies and practices, and standards-based and literacy reforms that claim the goal of equal access and opportunity.

No Child Left Behind and its constitutive reforms rely on such gross demographics about students and their abilities to facilitate the implementation of curricular and assessment programs that are key elements of sweeping national reform. This, of course, makes sense if we understand that the "marketplace" reforms under NCLB bring business principles of accountability, efficiency, quality, and choice to the educational agenda. Such reforms rely on the "sameness as fairness" principle—making it easier to mandate and monitor one-size-fits-all literacy and language programs that are assessment driven.

Considering the Consequences

Our studies document that larger numbers of poor immigrant Latino/a children in California receive a substantially inequitable education as compared to their peers (Gutiérrez et al., 2001). Even when we hold poverty constant across student populations, English learners are less likely to enroll in schools that provide adequate facilities and curricular materials and are less likely to participate in academic programs organized around productive pedagogies and rigorous coursework. Their inferior educational experience is further complicated by less instructional time devoted to meeting their educational needs, assessments that do not adequately measure their learning needs and achievement, and their overrepresentation in remedial, special education, and other pullout programs (Artiles, Rueda, Salazar, & Higareda, 2002; Gandara, Rumberger, Maxwell-Jolly, & Callahan, 2003; Gutiérrez, 2004a).

We also found that the kind of instructional community in which English learners participated was correlated with several factors—their socioeconomic status and their membership in particular cultural communities. Moreover, we see an increased level of segregation in California schools, most notably in the lowest performing (Decile 1) schools, comprised largely of poor students, many of whom are English learners (Education for Democracy, 2002–03). In sum, economically poor students who are also English learners in California are most likely to attend inferior, underresourced, and highly segregated schools that privilege reductive literacy programs, test preparation, and English-language instruction (Gutiérrez, Asato, Zavala, Pacheco, & Olson, 2004).

We argue that the dramatically unequal education of English learners must be understood within a matrix of sociopolitical, economic, and educational policies and a legacy of historical racist practices that legislate a particular kind of learning for poor children from nondominant groups. But we must ask: How can the separate and unequal educational experience of English learners be understood vis-à-vis the *Brown* decision that outlawed segregation as detrimental to nondominant students? We turn to race-based equity strategies as one means of addressing such injustice.

Equity as a Cornerstone

Bell (2004) has argued that a race-based equity remedy and a genuine commitment to *Brown*'s promise would have been accompanied by a series of mandates to ensure relief for nondominant student populations. These include an equalization of resources, racially balanced representation in governing authorities such as school boards, and the proper enactment of judicial oversight and monitoring committees to ensure that integration goals were fully met. Such measures are central to creating and sustaining rich learning communities, a cornerstone of equity-oriented education. The key notion here, however, is that like Bell, we argue that the legal remedy must also include multiple and sustained strategies and approaches organized around equity. Relying on a singular and limited remedy limits the possibility of achieving the desired outcome of equality and redressing historical inequities in our society.

An Equity Framework as a Design Principle

Like the miner's canary that detects the presence of poisonous gases in the mineshaft, a robust equity framework with appropriate indicators will help detect policies and practices that fail nondominant students by maintaining their current separate and unequal education. In this framework, equity serves as the organizing principle for the development, instantiation, and evaluation of policies and practices vis-à-vis nondominant students, in this case English learners. In contrast to neoliberal notions of equal opportunity that are devoid of the function of critique (Crosland, 2004), a focus on equity is instrumental to design, as well as to ongoing critical analysis from the perspective of the nondominant community (Gutiérrez, in press). Of significance, in this framework the theoretical lens of *White innocence* functions as the primary analytical tool for providing a racialized understanding of the social, cognitive, and political consequences or effects of a range of policies designed to remediate inequity—ranging from legally mandated policies such as *Brown* to national and local educational policies and practices.

White innocence and Brown. This analytical lens is particularly relevant to our proposed analytical framework as it served as the standpoint from which Gotanda (2004) examined racial ideology in the *Brown* decision. In his analysis, Gotanda argues that the U.S. Court was engaged in defending and maintaining White innocence by explaining the decision to overturn segregation as the result of new scientific evidence of the detrimental psychological effects of segregation on blacks. Specifically, by claiming that the "new" empirical findings regarding psychological damage constituted previously unavailable scientific information, the Court was able to claim "who knew?" and absolve itself of a legacy of racist practices.

This "who knew?" or "aha moment" (Santos, 1992) preserves the status quo, circumvents any complicity, and, in the case of *Brown*, allowed the Court to remain *innocent*. Of significance to our argument in this chapter, maintaining innocence requires no fundamental structural change in the legacy of cultural, social, and institutional racism in the United States. As a consequence, there is no compelling moral obligation for the innocent to acknowledge and challenge the underlying logic of the inhumanity and inequity that fuels racism and racist practices. We believe such was the case in *Brown*.

Through the White innocence lens, we can begin to understand the limits of *Brown* to challenge the structural apparatus that upholds supremacy and to incite a new moral order. Moreover, we also can begin to understand how new legal, social, and educational remedies similarly preserve innocence by detaching the remedy from historical, moral, social, economic, and political ties to racialized practices and ideologies.[1]

A White innocence lens is fundamental to the equity-minded framework we are proposing, as it requires a race-conscious sociohistorical analysis of the explicit and implicit constructs and logics that drive the remedy du jour. A White innocence analysis also requires a race-conscious critical analysis of the role of equity in defining and remediating the specific problem of injustice; how issues of equity have been addressed in the design and theory of action; and how issues of equity have fared throughout the implementation and evaluation processes. Such race-conscious analyses help ensure that equity is the object of the ongoing activity of remediating the injustice to racialized persons and communities.

Language Practices

Let's return to current language practices to consider what happens when a focus on equity drops out of the reform equation. The recent English-only movement in California was ostensibly designed to help English learners participate more quickly in mainstream education (Unz & Tuchman, 1997). Here "equal opportunity" was advanced as part of the rationale to require students of other languages to become immersed in English-only instruction. In other words, equal opportunity was the purported object of English-only instruction.

However, an historical analysis of how English learners have fared under English-only instruction reveals long-standing educational inequity for the non-English-speaking student, despite the legal remedies provided under *Lau v. Nichols*. In 1973, the Amicus Brief filed by the Mexican American Legal Defense Fund with the U.S. Supreme Court on behalf of the *Lau* plaintiffs described the inequities:

This suit was brought on behalf of approximately 1,800 non-English speaking students of Chinese origin in the San Francisco Unified School District who are excluded from receiving the benefits of public school education. Such benefits are denied since the school system does not offer them instruction that allows them to participate in the school program. The issue before the Court is: Does the school district have an obligation under the equal protection clause of the Fourteenth Amendment and Title VI of the Civil Rights Act of 1964 to provide non-English speaking students with instruction that would enable them to benefit from classes taught in English?

This denial of an equal educational opportunity presently taking place in the Chinese community in San Francisco is but a microcosm of the situation facing Spanish speaking communities in the United States today. From towns as diverse as Laredo, Texas to New York City, Spanish surnamed children come to school with little or no ability to speak the English language; with a cultural heritage entirely different than that of Anglo Americans. (*Brief of Amici Curiae*, pp. 4–5)

In response to this case more than three decades ago, the Supreme Court argued that English learners must receive the same instruction as their English-speaking peers:

There is no equality of treatment merely by providing students with the same facilities, textbooks, teachers, and curriculum: for students who do not understand English are effectively foreclosed from any meaningful education. (*Lau v. Nichols*, 1974)

In the 1974 *Lau* decision, instruction in the students' home language was one effective remedy toward an equal education. However, *Lau* was just that—an important but limited remedy that did not restructure the significantly inferior schooling conditions of English learners, as we discussed earlier in this chapter. And while we would argue for the importance and possibilities of bilingual education, we also would argue that bilingual education alone could not transform the sociopolitical and educational contexts in ways that would ensure an equitable education for English learners; nor could it rupture existing sentiments and ideologies about language and corresponding language communities. The *Lau* litigation and its aftermath, taken together, are but one example.

Today the new language policies, undergirded by the same ideology that precluded instruction in the students' native language prior to *Lau*, ignores the historical conditions that mandated a legal remedy in the first place, and makes it easier to employ the "sameness as fairness" principle at work in one-size-fits-all instructional policies and practices (Gutiérrez et al., 2001; Gutiérrez, et al., 2002). In prohibiting students' use of their complete linguistic toolkit in the service of learning, students have little access to the kind of instruction mandated in *Lau*. More central to this analysis, focusing exclusively on English-language instruction while ignoring the structural issues of discrimination in language and educational policies sets up the conditions that sustain inequity for English learners. Moreover, without conscious reflection and discussion around race-conscious, equity-oriented remediation, there is limited opportunity to engage in ways that incite a moral "turn" in individuals and policymakers.

Our central argument, then, is that if race-conscious, equity-oriented principles and analyses do not inform and guide educational remedies and interventions, legal and otherwise, then the double binds that members of nondominant communities find themselves in as a result of limited rulings will remain intact. Consider that under NCLB English learners are made the object of color-blind reform *and* are categorized according to racial and ethnic subgroups. Chang and Aoki (1997) explain the double bind which minorities experience in public policy:

We might question legal doctrines such as equal protection and their role in producing racialized identities while simultaneously mandating color-blindness on the part of public actors. (p. 313)

Moreover, nondominant communities are both the objects of reform and of purported academic failure without any substantive or meaningful activities underway to remedy the structural and historical relations and practices that have resulted in their prolonged marginalization in public schools. We are reminded daily of the need to examine educational practices within the broader equity-oriented agenda that we set forth in this chapter to understand how "separate and equal" has fared in nondominant communities, particularly culturally and linguistically complex communities.

Consider, for example, the case of Zach Rubio, a 17-year-old student suspended from his alternative high school in a small community in Kansas for uttering the phrase "no problema" outside the classroom context to a peer who asked "me prestas un dolar? (can I borrow a dollar?)" School officials maintained the legitimacy of their decision because "it is not the first time we have [asked] Zach and others to not speak Spanish at school" (Reid, 2005, p. 1). In other words, officials did not question the profoundly discriminatory and illegal nature of the suspension, but rather saw the action as due course for a student's lack of compliance with a language policy rooted in inequity and racial inequality. Such practices are linked to larger discourses dedicated to making English America's official language and eliminating the use of languages other than English in public affairs. Jim Boulet, executive director of English First, a nonprofit organization, defended the school's decision by enveloping his argument in post-9/11 xenophobic sentiments: "Let's face facts here; if the kid had been saying in Spanish, 'the bomb is around the corner' the school would be held liable for not knowing that" (Brown & Parker, 2005, p. 1). Speaking Spanish not only was an act of rebellion and noncompliance, according to an informal code of language "ethics" imposed by the school, but it was further conceptualized in terms of maintaining the national security of the United States.

Zach's father filed a legal suit against the school, the district, and its officiaries, and the school district officially rescinded the suspension. Nonetheless, the case of Zach Rubio serves as sober reminder that pre-civil rights era racist beliefs and practices have not been deluded by legal mandates to desegregate and to regulate equalitarian language practices in schools. Given the new forms of racism emerging in an era exacerbated by the "fear factor"—when every citizen is increasingly becoming conditioned to fear the foreign or the "other" as a threat both to safety and national security—Zach's case is not an idiosyncratic one, but instead is increasingly normative, both historically and in the present context. When the fundamental principles of inequity remain unrecognized and uncontested in everyday practices as well as in educational and reform policies, such ideologies and practices like those evidenced in the Rubio case and those that led to the *Brown* ruling become normalized and rationalized as appropriate and necessary behavior. We argue the need to make such practices visible in order to contest them and their historical antecedents and present instantiations. A race-conscious equity accountability framework is the miner's canary that can help make such inequities visible, so that they become the engines of deep change.

NOTE

1. In this discussion, the racialized notion of *White innocence* does not refer to the racial category of whiteness but rather to the dominant subject position that preserves racial subordination and the differential benefits for the *innocents* who retain their own dominant position. From this perspective, we are all implicated in some way in maintaining *White innocence*.

REFERENCES

Artiles, A.J., Rueda, R., Salazar, J., & Higareda, I. (2002). English-language learner representation in special education in California urban school districts. In D. Losen & G. Orfield (Eds.), *Racial inequity in special education* (pp. 117–136). Cambridge, MA: Harvard Education Press.

Bell, D. (1987). *And we are not saved.* New York: Basic Books.

Bell, D. (2004). *Silent covenants.* Oxford: Oxford University Press.

Bobo, L.D., Oliver, M.L., Johnson, J.H., & Valenzuela, A. (2000). Analyzing inequality in Los Angeles. In L.D. Bobo, M.L. Oliver, J.H. Johnson, & A. Valenzuela (Eds.), *Prismatic metropolis: Inequality in Los Angeles* (pp. 3–50). New York: Russell Sage Foundation.

Brief of Amici Curiae Mexican American Legal Defense and Educational Fund, American G. I. Forum, & League of United Latin American Citizens Association of Mexican American Educators. (1973). Lau v. Nichols, 1973 WL 172365 (August 2, 1973).

Brown, F. (1994). *Brown* and educational policy making at 40. *Journal of Negro Education, 63*(3), 336–348.

Brown, J., & Parker, J. (2005, December 14). English First advocate feels school rightly suspended student for speaking Spanish. *Agape Press.* Retrieved November 12, 2005, from http://headlines.agapepress.org/archive/12/142005c.asp

Brown v. Board of Education of Topeka, 347 U.S. 483 (1954).

Chang, R., & Aoki, K. (1997). Centering the immigrant in the inter/national imagination. *La Raza Law Review, 10,* 309–361.

Crosland, K. (2004). *Color–blind desegregation: Race neutral remedies as the new "equal opportunity."* Paper presented at the annual meeting of the American Educational Research Association, San Diego, California.

Crosland, K., & Gutiérrez, K. (2003). Standardizing teaching, standardizing teachers: Educational reform and the deprofessionalization of teachers in an English-only era. *Educators for Urban Minorities, 2*(2), 24–40.

Delgado, R., & Stefancic, J. (1995). The social construction of *Brown v. Board of Education*: Law reform and the reconstructive paradox. *William and Mary Law Review, 36,* 547–570.

Education for Democracy. (2002–03). A teacher qualification index for California's schools. Retrieved January 15, 2006, from http://www.edfordemocracy.org/TQI/page2a.asp

Gandara, P., Rumberger, R., Maxwell-Jolly, J., & Callahan, R. (2003). *English learners in California schools: Unequal resources, unequal outcomes.* Education Policy Analysis Archives. Retrieved November 15, 2005, from http://epaa.asu.edu/epaa/v11n36/

Gotanda, N. (2004). Reflections on *Korematsu, Brown* and White innocence. *Temple Political and Civil Rights Law Review, 13,* 663.

Guinier, L., & Torres, G. (2002). *The miner's canary.* Cambridge, MA: Harvard University Press.

Gutiérrez, K. (2002). Studying cultural practices in urban learning communities. *Human Development, 45*(4), 312–321.

Gutiérrez, K. (2004a). *Rethinking education policy for English learners.* Washington, DC: Aspen Institute.

Gutiérrez, K. (2004b). Literacy as laminated activity: Rethinking literacy for English learners. In C.M. Fairbanks, J. Worthy, B. Maloch, J.V. Hoffman, & D.L. Schallert (Eds.), *National Reading Conference yearbook* (pp. 101–114). Chicago, IL: National Reading Conference.

Gutiérrez, K. (in press). White innocence: A framework and methodology for rethinking educational discourse. *International Journal of Learning.*

Gutiérrez, K., Asato, J., Pacheco, M., Moll, L., Olson, K., Horng, E. et al. (2002). "Sounding American": The consequences of new reforms on English language learners. *Reading Research Quarterly, 37*(3), 328–343.

Gutiérrez, K., Asato, J., Santos, M., & Gotanda, N. (2002). Backlash pedagogy: Language and culture and the politics of reform. *The Review of Education, Pedagogy, and Cultural Studies, 24*(4), 335–351.

Gutiérrez, K., Asato, J., Zavala, M., Pacheco, M., & Olson, K. (2004). *Nationalizing and institutionalizing reform: The effects of educational policies on teachers and English learners.* Paper presented at the annual meeting of the American Educational Research Association, San Diego, California.

Gutiérrez, K., Baquedano-Lopez, P., & Asato, J. (2001). English for the children: The new literacy of the old world order. *Bilingual Review Journal, 24*(1&2), 87–112.

Gutmann, A. (1996). Responding to racial injustice. In K.A. Appiah & A. Gutmann (Eds.), *Color conscious: The political morality of race* (pp. 106–163). Princeton, NJ: Princeton University Press.

Kluger, R. (1975). *Simple justice.* New York: Vintage Books.

Ladson-Billings, G. (2004). Landing on the wrong note: The price we paid for *Brown. Educational Researcher, 33*(7), 3–13.

Lau v. Nichols, 414 U.S. 563. (1974).

Lawrence, C. (1995). The id, the ego, and equal protection: Reckoning with unconscious racism. In K. Crenshaw, N. Gotanda, G. Peller, & K. Thomas (Eds.), *Critical race theory* (pp. 25–256). New York: The New Press.

Paige, R. (2002). *Remarks by U.S. Secretary of Education Rod Paige to the* Brown v. Board of Education *50th Anniversary Commission, Howard University School of Law.* Retrieved December 12, 2005, from http://www.ed.gov/news/speeches/2002/11/11132002.html

Plessy v. Ferguson, 163 U.S. 537. (1896).

Reed, D. (2001). *On equal terms.* Princeton, NJ: Princeton University Press.

Reid, T.R. (2005, December 9). Spanish at school translates to suspension. *The Washington Post*, p. A03.

Santos, M. (1992, October). *Demystifying affirmative action.* Paper presented at the annual meeting of the American Association of Schools, Colleges, and Universities, Pomona, CA.

Street, P. (2004, May 27). Educational apartheid. Why we are in no mood for a Brown v. Board birthday bash. *The Black Commentator, 92.* Retrieved January 3, 2006 from http://www.blackcommentator.com/92/92_Brown.html

Unz, R., & Tuchman, G. (1997). *English language education for children in public schools.* Retrieved March 31, 2000, from http://www.onenation.org/fulltext.html

Welner, K., & Oakes, J. (1996). Liability grouping. *Harvard Educational Review, 66*(3), 451–470.

Williams v. State of California, *supra,* 34 Cal.3d at 26–28. (2004).

CHAPTER 10

A Multivoiced Response to the Call for an Equity-Based Framework

YOLANDA J. MAJORS AND SANA ANSARI

Yes, the miners' canary, as Gutiérrez and Jaramillo remind us, is a warning of approaching dangers (this volume, pp. 173–189). Cloaked in yellow, it lifts its voice in protest and critique, a warning that perhaps also signals resistance to impending dangers that lurk ahead. . . . As we write this piece, it is the end of the Fall term. "The Hawk" (how many Chicagoans refer to winter's wind) has arrived with familiar ferocity and chill. Within and beyond the slightly ajar university classroom door we recently shared, it is quiet, except for a few lingering footsteps in the distance of Eddie, our service engineer. . . .

(*Yolanda*) Eddie reminds me so much of my uncle Joe though they look nothing alike. Perhaps it is less the embodiment of my uncle and more my imaginings of him in his current job as the day-shift doorman of a high-rise nestled within the downtown skyline that I am reminded of. My uncle had worked over 35 years (after returning from Vietnam with a Purple Heart), supporting a wife and two daughters as a state postal service employee. Shortly after retirement, however, he found it necessary to return to work "in order to make ends meet." Though according to him, the pay "does what it does," my uncle makes the most of his new position, and like Eddie, I imagine, he does so in quiet, masked dignity. His life, to me, illuminates a lived tension in the lives of many minority faculty who grapple with negotiating culture, class, and race across the life span.

Yolanda Majors is an Assistant Professor of Curriculum and Instruction at the University of Illinois at Chicago.

Sana Ansari is a graduate student in Curriculum and Instruction at the University of Illinois at Chicago.

Equity-Based Framework: What Are Its Implications for Teacher Education?

(*Yolanda and Sana*) It has been one of those semesters where the demand to engage in critical meaning making and the urgency to instill a transformative[1] (Banks, 1998), equity-based framework and pedagogy seem to have collided in our predominantly white preservice classroom. Part and parcel of this equity-based framework is the focus on critical self-reflection in which students examine issues from various perspectives. In an attempt to enact the stated college mission, this approach encourages future teachers to confront their own cultural spaces as sites of ideological development and, more importantly, their privileged positions. Using culture and language as a starting point to discuss literacy and learning was met with a marked lack of engagement, and as a result, the university classroom had become a site of conflict, resistance, and silence. Inherent in this conflict is a collision of ideologies, which brings to bear the problems and inconsistencies of instilling a transformative framework to future urban educators. Now, in the stillness interrupted by Eddie's whistles, I have come to the page where I may perhaps disentangle the impact.

The urban classroom, be it located at the university or the high school, provides a unique context to explore the hierarchical nature of race relations. Unfortunately, there is a "color-blind" discourse that does not nurture any exploration of this phenomenon. We would like to argue that exploring these complicated and nuanced issues of culture, class, and racial identity are essential to understanding literacy and learning, and thus an essential component of teacher education. This imperative becomes increasingly clear as the racial divide grows between teacher and student in the urban classroom; *not* attending to this discourse has significant implications for both future teachers and their future students. First and foremost, ignoring the hierarchy serves to calcify it even further, and second, in not paying attention to difference, teachers do a disservice to the students they teach in that they privilege their own cultural and intellectual practices. All of this is further complicated by the cultural and racial disconnections, connections, matches, and mismatches that often emerge in classrooms between teachers and students (Milner, 2005).

Though much has been written about black teachers, their teaching experiences, and the nature of urban black classrooms prior to and since the *Brown* (1954) ruling (Foster, 1990; Irvine & Irvine, 1983; Ladson-Billings, 2000; Siddle-Walker, 2000), much of this work is situated in predominantly black settings (Milner, 2005). Another layer of complexity that remains unaddressed is the impact of cross-racial education, that is, the ways in which larger sociopolitical relations of class and race shape the unique relationship of black teacher and white student. As this chapter will argue, the *Brown* legacy, although important, "retains a limited function in ratifying "progressive" and "equity minded" school reform in the long term" (Gutiérrez & Jaramillo, this volume, p. 177), and while Gutiérrez & Jaramillo explore this in the preceding chapter, we extend the argument to the context of teacher education. As the cultural divide between urban educators and the student population grows, it becomes ever more urgent to address particular concerns of culture and the social construct of race with future urban educators. The projected enrollment of students of color in major cities, particularly African American and Latino, is likely to increase, while the teacher population remains majority white middle class females. This apparent cultural divide needs to be addressed through changes in the university teacher education curriculum. In order to address such limitations further work is warranted, so as to explore, for example: (1) the impact of an equity-based framework as a curriculum design principle in university and high school classroom contexts; (2) the social relations based on race within the classroom and the educational system writ large that lay "dormant" but still affect the dynamics of education, most importantly the ways in which these dynamics reify dominancy of particular classes and groups; and (3) teacher preparation as it deals with the issues of urban education.

Such work (both theoretical and practical), like the miners' canary, could unveil the silenced and unaddressed ideological and historical factors that inhibit and complicate our abilities to create and sustain rich, transformative, learning communities. Furthermore, the implementation of an equity-based curriculum design that attempts to denormalize the dominant group experience against the backdrop of the experiences of those from underserved "diverse" populations extends the challenge of how educators respond to the call for "race conscious practices that go beyond the limitations of legal remedies and their monitoring apparatus" (Gutiérrez & Jaramillo, this volume, p. 174).

There are several sites for this particular exploration into equity-based change, for example, the urban classroom, school administration, educational policy, and teacher education, to name a few. The site that will be explored here is the urban university preservice classroom. There are various reasons that make this site especially relevant and, consequently, entail a sense of urgency. One reason, we argue, is that preservice teacher education provides the most significant opportunity for exploring issues of implementation within the context of urban education; that is, are teachers using the notion of equity to drive their teaching practices? Furthermore, urban teacher preparation is a critical setting for developing an equity-minded teaching force. Educating future teachers to be conversant with an increasingly diverse population of children is of vital importance in taking a step toward the initial promise of *Brown v. Board*. This step, hopefully, creates a population of teachers who can model the equity-based framework in their own classrooms and communities. Moreover, as significant forces in teacher education, the university classroom and university policies that state a commitment to urban populations ground the movement in praxis.

Taking on this responsibility calls attention to the complexities of teaching and learning, specifically as they relate to privilege. This setting provides insight into how "White innocence" (Gutiérrez, in press) is manifest in everyday interactions and conversation, and, furthermore, how the subtext of White innocence in these environments limits the opportunities of all people and not just the marginalized. The larger consequence of maintaining this innocence ensures that the state of affairs of urban education will not change; in fact, it will serve to further solidify the current systemic inequities. Last, examining the university classroom calls attention to how race and racism enter into our subjectivities and ideological stances. Hence, the classroom and the ensuing curriculum serve as a catalyst for the manifestation of underlying and sometimes repressed assumptions (as may be illustrated through silence rather than overt conflict).

While the *Brown* decision was a landmark decision in that it addressed, through the legal system, the ways in which systemic and institutional racism informed the state of education, it was merely the first step toward creating equity for students of color. We are now in a historical moment where we can examine the *Brown* decision and its inability to propel any extensive reforms. This mindfulness toward equity-based education and reform leads us to the arena of higher education, where there is still much work to be done. In examining the university structure, this chapter will raise questions as to how institutional protocols can and should be put in place that will ensure that the commitment to urban education is being met, specifically in teacher preparation.

In responding to Gutiérrez and Jaramillo, we will be doing two things. First, we will attempt to characterize the atmosphere of our classroom and the inherent and varying attitudes of the students. Second, in discussing the conflict and tension in the classroom, we examine these questions: What were the emerging understandings of literacy of the content area preservice teachers? Were the students able to take a critical stance in their attitude toward education and literacy? In trying to defuse tension in the classroom, there was a precarious balance struck between simultaneously considering the learning opportunities and developmental needs (psychological, emotional, etc.) of the students and their emerging understandings. These various tensions (which created destructive silences) is the space from which we may begin to examine how university institutions can reexamine policies and create some netting that will allow for constructive conversations and student development.

Negotiating Difficult Discourse

(*Yolanda*) The stillness surrounding my university classroom (where I am an African American professor in the context of a predominantly white classroom) represents the intersection where *the old* (prior attempts to achieve educational equity through classroom design) meets *the new* (redesign as an extension of critical reflection). My own position as a scholar of color, as well as being in a position of power, creates a unique dynamic between the students and myself. From the moment I walk into class, the canary perches itself onto the windowsill, and there is an implicit assumption that any position I take on race is one that is personally invested and propelled by both a personal and political agenda. Many scholars of color face this issue when they bring up issues of race in the classroom (Ahlquist, 1991; Ladson-Billings, 2000; Tatum, 1994). Any discourse on race is seen as politically and socially biased, while my white students' "color-blind" attitude is perceived as neutral. In throwing a wrench into this myth, my students are faced with the idea of difference, which they are often unwilling or unable to digest. Implicit in this discomfort is a normalization of their own cultural experiences and backgrounds. They are not different . . . I am.

The students in the course were upperclassmen in their last semester of course work before their student teaching assignments. The course I was teaching focused on literacy and content area teaching; not methods so much as shifting the sensibility of teaching and learning. Part of this ideological shift was an examination of cultural, social, and linguistic contexts as the broader framework for literacy. Because it was a content area course, at least half of the class was made up of math and science majors, while the other half was in history. Of the 15 students in the class, 10 were Caucasian, three were Asian American, and two were Latino American. The majority of the students were white middle-class women. This class was a requirement for all secondary teachers, and it was generally a course that was taken before student teaching. It was also the only literacy class requirement for students, so their only exposure to potential ideas of cultural context and its connection to teaching and learning was a one semester, three credit hour course—one obvious reflection of the institutional obstacles toward equity-based change.

A marked sensibility in the class was the attitude toward urban and suburban schools. Even though the college's stated mission is to serve the urban population and to develop teachers to work in urban schools, many of the students, upon graduation, openly stated that they wanted to teach in suburban schools. Additionally, the students enrolled in the class were offered the opportunity to observe me teach at a high school in the city (where I am also a language arts instructor); however, many in the class did not see it as an opportunity as much as an obligation. There was a distinct lack of interest in taking this up as a learning opportunity. Many of the students were concerned about going into the high school's neighborhood by themselves. One student expressed surprise upon arriving at the school, commenting that it was not at all what she had "expected."

In this stillness, I am pausing with my collaborator, coauthor, and graduate student, Sana, to take stock of both the *said* and the *unsaid* in preservice classroom discourse regarding the interconnections between language, literacy, and culture. Thinking back to when I first took note of the canary's cry (which I will get to in a moment) I think of those students who "got it," who made that reflective leap instantiated through a curriculum "infused with multiple views and perspectives" (Milner, 2005), designed to teach students to think critically and to develop the skills to formulate, document, and justify their conclusions and generalizations (Banks, 1998, p. 32).

Most of all, at this intersection, I am thinking of my students who did *not* get it but, rather, deflected their ownership of learning to my responsibility to teach to the normalized tradition that does not speak of race. What was apparent in the silencing of racial talk or consideration is the reluctance of many preservice teachers to reflect on their own experiences as part of larger social and economic contexts, thus stunting their ability to understand culture as part of literacy and learning. Thus, I wonder about our disparate readings of the canary's call, as well as the role I play and value in helping students negotiate the ways in which to heed warnings of danger, real and imagined. This is a particularly difficult task to undertake, especially when those in danger see the canary's call as an annoyance, and it is further complicated by the sheer lack of institutional structures that will ensure development in the area of cultural awareness.

As I begin to survey the outcomes, I also have the honor and challenge of extending the conversation initiated by Gutiérrez and Jaramillo. It is the landmark 1954 *Brown* decision which frames this chapter and whose tenets these authors have eloquently laid out for us, arguing that "the *Brown* decision addressed the issue of segregation in educational settings, but was never intended as a means for re-mediating general and more fundamental educational disparities and other legal racial segregations" (this volume, p. 174). Central to Gutiérrez and Jaramillo, and elaborated on here, is the distinction between an equity-minded agenda in education (where moral, ethical, and equity issues take center stage) and an agenda that considers equal opportunity to be the single organizing principle of reform. I take up this "organizing principle" in my examination of the preservice teachers. As noted, helping teachers think about equity, ethics, and equal opportunity necessitates a shifting of sensibilities, namely in the area of literacy.

As this chapter will illustrate, in the absence of an equity-minded agenda, there is (in addition to the preservation of "White innocence") an overwhelming lack of critical reflection and resistance to institutionalized notions of self—a concept that is marked by a lack of reflexivity and the adoption of a one-size-fits-all approach to learning and teaching (Majors, 1998). Thus, in not naming "self" as a part of the larger contexts that shape it, there is a profound lack of understanding subjectivity and power. White innocence functions most effectively through its silence. We focus here as well on the effects of systematic, race-based, institutional practices instituted via local and mandatory policies. We further argue that an equity framework when practiced in a classroom as a site of critical resistance can provide robust learning practices that are simultaneously race-conscious and equity-oriented, but there are challenges for teaching and learning.

Teacher Education: Creating Change or Instantiating Privilege?

(*Yolanda and Sana*) The landmark 1954 *Brown* decision addressed the issue of segregation in educational settings. As Gutiérrez & Jaramillo point out, the decision of the Court:

imparted a notion of educational equity that dealt with the underlying pathology of the forced separation of children on the basis of race . . . [a] decision [that] signaled a telling and unprecedented shift in legal doctrines, as *Brown* mandated a set of race-conscious remedies intended to reverse an era of court-approved race-conscious segregation legalized by *Plessy* and continues to serve for many in this country as a foundational building block toward establishing an "interracial democracy." (p. 175, 176)

Decades ago, this landmark decision was shepherded by lawyers acting in the "public interest" and driven by "the commitment to integration as the appropriate solution to black children's educational needs" (Delgado & Stefancic, 2000, p. 46). Today that commitment is mirrored by many in the education community who strive to achieve educational equity and equality through the institutionalization of race-conscious educational policies that focus on "gross demographic shifts," such as increased proportions of diverse student enrollments for purposes of integration of learning environments, university classrooms among them (Gutiérrez, in press).

As Gutiérrez and Jaramillo explain, it is the *Brown* decision upon which many of the hopes and assumptions for integration rest as a mediational tool for "cross-cultural relations, perceptions, and historical inequities" (this volume, p. 175). However, "the problem was that the lawyers' commitment to integration often flew in the face of what was best for the African American communities they legally represented, or what those communities themselves desired" (Bell, 1995, p. 37). Missing from consideration was an interrogation of the underlying racial ideology, "both historical and functional," that informed the U.S. cultural model and the legal approaches that led to the segregation of school children. In looking at the history of law as an institution and its investment in self-interest, one has to ask: How are the practices of self-interest manifest in other institutions, namely higher education? It is at this point of crisis that universities need to reassess how their policies for teacher education impact (or do not) future educators. "Soft" legal approaches that do not really locate the cause of segregated educational practices (i.e., economics, racism, etc.) but rather attempt to modify the symptoms (i.e., segregation in schools) really serve to further institutionalize race-based practices in schooling.

Nested within the implications of the Court's decision are legal approaches instantiated in local educational reform efforts. Taking its cue from the Court, many higher educational institutions, in their efforts to represent the interest of the public (through the soft legal approaches embodied in local policies and doctrines), equate quality education with quantifiable increases in student enrollment. Absent from this view, however, is the consideration of the existent dominant ideological practices and social structure of the classroom context, one that is dominated by a predominantly white student body and professorate within which both nondominant students and teachers "carry perspectives that have been historically silenced and marginalized" (Milner, 2005). According to Milner (2005):

in colleges of education, and particularly preservice and in-service education programs, the programs are largely tailored to meet the needs of White female teachers (Gay, 2000), and Black teachers, along with other teachers of color (male and female), are left out of the discussion. Where curricular materials were concerned in her study, Agee (2004) explained that "the teacher education texts used in the course made recommendations for using diverse texts or teaching diverse students based on the assumption that preservice teachers are White." (p. 749)

In this post-*Brown* era, failure to account for the historical and existent nature of the classroom context constitutes an "interest convergence" (Bell, 2004), whereas the urban classroom objective would appear to advance the interests of white elites, with minority students and faculty left with little incentive (or support) to eradicate (challenge) it.

As noted by Gutiérrez and Jaramillo, others (Street, 2004) have argued that an interracial democracy is difficult to achieve without directly confronting white supremacist ideologies that were not overturned by the hard legal mandates of *Brown*. Although *Brown's* intent was to dismantle dual school settings to ensure equal educational opportunity for nondominant students, the rulings' framers and supporters did not adequately account for the degree to which "White supremacy and racism were instantiated in the U.S. cultural model" (Ladson-Billings, 2000). By not accounting for the existence of the noxious gases that permeate our culture, we omit notions of self in relation to the Other, which serve to reify institutionalized approaches that perpetuate a white supremacist hierarchy. Hence, this lack of self-reflection normalizes the position of those in power and highlights the difference inherent in the Other.

The Necessity of Naming Race: Are Educational Institutions Color-blind?

(*Yolanda*) Having been bussed to an all-white elementary school, decades after the *Brown* decision, I was to get my first canary's warning of the dangers that approached. 1970s television had given me a glimpse of what life was like for the people who lived beyond the west side of Chicago. At Bell Elementary School on the largely white north side, where I was bussed, all the kids in my class were white and the teacher never messed with me. In fact, she never said anything to me at all. No one said anything. Except once, when a classmate's father got on our bus with a gun and told the bus supervisor that if she brought any more "Niggers" back to the school he would blow her head off (Majors, 1998). I repeated the experience to my mother along with the request that she call the "bus lady" and ask her not to bring any more Niggers back to school so that we would not get in any more trouble. Instead, my mother spoke to the teacher, who finally began to speak to me. In fact, she moved my seat from the back of the class to the front. This spatial distraction did not change the peripheral nature of my presence in class, however. As I sometimes reflect on that experience of not long enough ago, I strain to see lessons found beneath the pain of learning through my integration. I think about the damage silence causes.

Although decades have passed between the *Brown* decision and my entry into Bell School, such counter-stories attest to how the decision enabled the court to absolve itself of the history, steeped in racism, leading up to and beyond their ruling, and the implications of that oversight. At the time of the *Brown* decision, the U.S. Supreme Court argued that its decision to overturn previous cases allowing segregation was based on scientific evidence previously unknown to the court. This "who knew?" moment absolved historical discriminatory practices and beliefs; provided the context for a redemptive move by the court; pre-served "White innocence" and the status quo; and, as a result of all of these, required no fundamental structural change in the legacy of cul-tural, social, and institutional racism in the United States (Santos, 1992). Furthermore, this explanation, presented as progressive, was a denial of all that was old news to the children who shared my bus and their parents and grandparents, who caught whiff of the awful stenches outside and inside the classroom for generations.

By framing the decision around what it perceived to be "new research studies that demonstrated the negative psychosocial stigmas experienced by segregated Black youth" (Gutiérrez, in press), the court absolved itself of the legacy of racism and of inhumanity and stayed secure behind "White innocence." This innocence is not a phenome-non restricted to institutions, but also to individuals who deny their complicity in a larger system steeped in racism and racist practices.

Furthermore, in preserving this innocence, there are no structural protocols for long-term reform efforts. Such security enables dominant class stakeholders to account for the surface structural change initiated by the *Brown* ruling without addressing the weaknesses in the foundation, at little or no added cost to themselves.

Developing New Models

(*Yolanda and Sana*) As Gutiérrez and Jaramillo ask, if legal precedent was indeed set by the *Brown* ruling, in what ways has it contributed to school reform in the United States? We would like to respond to this question by first drawing a distinction between what might be considered *hard* and *soft* legal precedents. "Judicial intervention is now considered one of the main mechanisms for transforming K-12 schooling, as well as institutions of higher learning . . . For example, in the realm of affirmative action, school funding, and more recently, the implementation of equal opportunity to learn standards . . . the law has demonstrated its capacity to redefine access and to redistribute resources" (Gutiérrez & Jaramillo, this volume, p. 176–177). The capacity to redefine and redistribute marks legal precedents as hard in that, structurally, the implications are perhaps grounded in far-reaching (long-term) egalitarian objectives. In contrast, soft legal precedents might be considered as loosely established—less far-reaching and less well-defined sets of objectives whose aims are to demonstrate the existence of some capacity to redefine access without doing away with established social norms. Soft legal precedents prevail in the realm of some local curriculum contributions or additive reform efforts (Banks, 1998), institutional mission statements that promote diverse climates, and reform efforts that aim to increase student enrollment by quantifiable percentages and margins.

Although where they differ is in the depth of their structural impact, fundamentally, what these two share is that they are both partial to extant systems of economic and racial hierarchies. Neither hard nor soft precedents take into consideration the underlying narratives and historical agents left to enact or react to the enacted policies. In fact, both retain a limited function in ratifying progressive and equity minded school reform. Not unlike the Court, university structures and systems that ground themselves in soft approaches and whose endpoints are "gross demographics" absolve themselves of accounting for the historical and ideological undercurrents that maintain the status quo. Such systems, in their attempts to call attention to equity-minded policies and approaches in the absence of true attempts at reform, reify "White innocence" as proposed by Gutiérrez (in press):

Utilizing a *White innocence* analytic framework is one step towards a critical analysis of the consequences of our empirical work on those we "study." ... I think this is particularly important because it has become commonplace to study cultural communities even when we know very little about the community, its history, its shared and varied practices, and to carry out our work without the accompanied examination of the assumptions we hold vis-à-vis these communities. Such analyses requires moving from gross demographics as the endpoint of educational research to disaggregating the categories conceptually, analytically and ideologically, to understand the significant variance across individuals and communities and their practices. For example, statements such as "the classroom has a large proportion of 'diverse' students" attribute difference to one side of the contrast. In referring to students from educationally underserved populations as diverse both implies that the others are standard and thus normalizes the dominant group (Gutiérrez & Rogoff, 2003). (Gutiérrez, in press)

Such a distinction between hard and soft legal precedents enables us to consider the legacy of the *Brown* decision in relation to the communities and community voices and in relation to the local institution and its position vis-à-vis the *Brown* decision, and in terms of the framing discourses which present "uncomplicated understandings" of the practices of nondominant youth without embedding them as part of larger toolkits and more complex landscapes.

A Second to the Call for a New Analysis

(*Yolanda*) Earlier in this chapter I shared the story of my early experiences attending Bell School decades after *Brown*. My story has been shared before, most recently this past semester with our preservice students at the university where we teach. Although this institution sits in the heart of a major city, with all the characteristics of a major city, the majority of our education students are white and female. Less than 3 miles up the road, at the urban high school where I also teach, the students are African American. The demographic, historical, and ideological contrasts between these two contexts are alarmingly sharp, even as one population prepares to service the other.

These university students are content area, preservice teachers who are interested not necessarily in literacy, but in gathering the tools with which to teach their subject matter effectively. Therefore, there is a substantial ideological leap that needs to be made in order for students to understand the inevitable roles that literacy *and* culture play in teaching and learning. There is an immediate resistance to many ideas that are presented in a literacy course because, as a rule of thumb, this course is the first encounter many of the students have in examining the cultural and social nature of learning.

This dilemma is echoed by many professional organizations. For example, according to the International Reading Association, "Historically, some secondary teachers in the content areas have resisted the idea that helping students with literacy skills is part of their jobs, according to Jim Rubillo, executive director of NCTAA. This attitude must change, said Rubillo and other representatives of the content area associations who were present, if older students are to achieve their full potential" (International Reading Association, 2005). Thus, our challenge is to bridge the ideological gap between university preservice students and secondary language arts students, starting with nurturing self-reflexivity and race-consciousness within my preservice teachers. In not addressing the complications of race, there is an inherent normalizing and thus privileging of a particular intellectual and cultural practice. Jerome Bruner (2005), in his address to the National Academy of Education, posed a question that brings to the forefront the issues of overcoming ideological roadblocks: "How do you teach in order that students will grasp the possibility of what's on the other side?"

Even as I sit and reflect now, I can recall the day, midsemester, when the canary finally cried from its perch. I am sure that the call was loud and clear as I remember feeling a jolt and looking up and outside toward the downtown skyline. However, for each of us in the room that day, that call heeded different warnings. The call came as I distributed a reading for the following week to the class. Although it had not been announced previously that they would be reading one of my published articles, I believed that it was important that these students gain a level of self-knowledge and awareness as they attempted to understand others (Milner, 2005), and to facilitate that process, I attempted to connect my students' own experiences with new ones, beginning with my own, that I believed could enlighten them about issues of race, culture, and education. As I walked around the class distributing the reading, I overheard one white female student say to another (loud enough for me to hear), "She's published? Wow, must be a low ranking journal." This comment, to say the least, caught me by surprise, but not as much as the comment to follow: "It must be about race." One of the most damaging and inherent dangers of talking about race as a *minority problem* is that it deflects responsibility and, more importantly, assumes that it is not really a problem that the white majority needs to consider; in other words, it is not a "real" problem. Despite the fact that there had been no announcement as to the scope and content of the article (this was to be the first of two articles distributed over the course of the semester which would even allude to race), my student concluded that my attempts to exemplify and foster self-reflection were below-standard and narrowly appropriated to the limited sphere of the context of race relations.

Undergirding this lapse in communication were the assumptions of preservice teachers concerning the nature of literacy in relation to race and their fears of the urban community that had gone unaddressed. Then there were my readings as a black teacher in a classroom of white students, where I picked up on these assumptions and attempted to address them by invoking a transformative approach (Banks, 1998) while the preservice teachers enacted "White innocence." What was striking in the conversations that ensued was the silence that surrounded any notion of difference. In fact, there was an insistence on teaching and viewing all students in the same way.

The Enactment of "White Innocence" in the Preservice Classroom

(*Sana*) I co-taught the course with my professor and mentor Dr. Yolanda Majors. As an East Indian-American, my position was slightly different than hers and added a more layered and complicated dynamic to the dichotomized nature of race in the classroom. One of the reasons for constructing a multivoiced narrative of this particular experience is that it creates a more complex picture of things that transpired. We shared this course and our experiences were both shared and individualized. What is important to note is that because of the nature of the subject matter in the classroom, any discussion of culture in the classroom was further complicated by our position as women of color. Consequently, any discussion of systemic racism was perceived and documented by many in the classroom as accusatory and agenda-driven.

There were several instances throughout the semester when students tried to enact a color-blind ideology within the classroom by claiming that race was not a relevant issue to teaching and learning. In fact, one student asked, "Why do we always talk about race?" Interestingly, the word "race" itself did not come up that often, and the focus of the course was on literacy and its mediating factors, namely, culture and language. Many students voiced the belief that race was not a significant factor in socialization and was a nominal factor in considering academic success or failure. Inherent in this attitude is the notion that culture, race, and language are neutral and any reference to cultural difference is somehow a specialized discourse. In fact, the examination of *specific* cultural and linguistic backgrounds of students, that is, students of color, was a deviation from the normal discourse on literacy learning and teaching, and thus, not necessarily relevant to teacher practice and curriculum development. Ironically, although students insisted that they utilized "color-blind" practices, resistance to discussions of race further highlighted difference.

While *Brown* eradicated de jure segregation, de facto segregation and its byproduct was, and still is, a force to contend with, especially as manifested in the attitudes of the students in the classroom. There was a vast difference between the sensibilities of the students of color and the white students in the classroom, and this dynamic contributed to classroom silences (as will be discussed later in the chapter). Segregation can be typified in individuals' inability or unwillingness to be conversant with other cultural groups and it also plays a large role in creating the phenomenon of White innocence. The ideological conflict was further complicated by the many layers of difference, along racial, ethnic, and class lines, that were present in the classroom.

As an initial exercise in stretching students' understanding of race, education, and systemic imbalances, I distributed an article by Danny Martin, an African American math educator, that discussed the math socialization of African American students. One of the strongest and most immediate responses that I received, which was echoed by other students in the class, was that all students are socialized in math in a very similar fashion, and race is not a factor that needs to be considered. In fact, the student also questioned the nature of "racism" that was being addressed in the article, saying, "These are just the perspectives of some individuals, not necessarily a reflection of what really happened." For me, the canary's call was loud and clear and quite alarming. For the students, with the exception of the few minority students, this comment was merely matter of fact, expressing reality. As the discussion progressed, I encouraged students to consider how systemic and institutional influences inform individual lives, namely, by asking students to consider how institutional obstacles may affect teaching and learning. I also asked students to consider the inequities inherent within the educational system and how they might impact intellectual and academic development. Students were asked to think about the various factors that affect academic success. However, the response, over and over, focused on the role of individual motivation as a significant contributing factor to academic success. Literacy provided access to social mobility, and the individual drive to succeed provided access to literacy.

Despite the fact that systemic inequities exist within school systems, there was a conscious refusal by the students to see how larger forces shaped individuals. Individual effort and motivation were perceived as the most important factors for academic success. In the absence of an equity-minded agenda, there was (in addition to a preservation of "White innocence") an overwhelming lack of critical reflection and resistance to *institutionalized notions of* self—a concept that is marked by a lack of reflexivity and the adoption of a one-size-fits-all approach to learning and teaching. If race is the miner's canary, where in the context of this classroom was the danger?

There were some students, two Latino students in particular, who resisted this notion of literacy and who emphasized the role of encouragement as the determining factor of success. These two students continually problematized the state of education, pointing out the inherent assumptions about students, especially students of color, that many teachers bring into their classrooms, and sharing their own stories. However, I noticed that whenever these students spoke up in class there was very little response, almost as if their experiences and perspectives were not valid. Many of the students were not willing, or maybe not ready, to think about racism as a very tangible reality, a reality that continues to affect many people. So the question becomes: Why are some stories heard and not others? And why were narratives of racial oppression not perceived as valid entry points or data?

While much of what I said was met with puzzled looks and furrowed brows, I did notice some appreciative nods and signs of agreement from my Latino students. But as the semester progressed, these two students stopped speaking up and gradually fell silent. While their divergent opinions had added a constructive and critical element to the discourse in the classroom, by the end of the semester, there was a monochromatic tinge to discussions. As soon as there was mention of race, students would opt out of the discussion, and as classroom talk moved away from language and culture, there was a sense of relief. In trying not to privilege my own voice, I tried on many occasions to step out of the discussion, only interjecting to clarify or ask questions. This did not help; for all practical purposes, difference did not exist, in that it was willfully ignored.

While there were numerous attempts made to encourage students to talk about race, it was a topic that was rarely broached by the students themselves. Students were told that the classroom was a safe space to discuss their ideas and honesty would be the only way to create constructive and meaningful models for learning. We were forthright in our assurance that, while race was an uncomfortable topic, this uneasiness was normal and expected. What we hoped for was that students would move past their initial discomfort. The silence was pervasive.

Hull and Schultz (2002) discuss the issue of silence and the enactment of color-blind discourse, describing how "White students in their single-race groups enacted this silence by avoiding talk about difficult topics and by reaching agreement quickly, masking dissenting opinions. In several of the all-White and mixed-race focus groups, students claimed to be color-blind and participated in talk that erased their differences, working toward common ground. However, students speaking candidly in the single race groups of African-American students did not claim to be color-blind" (p. 131). The white students in our class were wary of laying claim to the discourse of race, and while the causes for this cannot be determined outright, the implications are heavy.

Conclusion

An equity-based framework, when practiced in a classroom as a site of critical resistance, can provide robust learning practices that are simultaneously race-conscious and equity-oriented, but there are challenges for teaching and learning. First and foremost is the challenge of creating a safe space to dialogue about race and racial assumptions. Many students may not be willing to talk about their ideas as part of their execution of privilege and willful ignorance. The challenge is to unpack assumptions but, at the same time, create the opportunity for transformative conversations. This is part of the socialization process of students in preservice classrooms, and an area of research that needs further exploration. Second, an important step toward recognition of historical and political racial injury is disentangling white privilege. Part and parcel of unpacking privilege is an understanding of how culture, history, and social economy inform individual lives. Because economic and racial privilege allow for and create a sensibility of individual will and the importance of self-motivation, it is a particular challenge to get students to think about individuality within context.

While there is an existing dialogue in preservice education, it is limited in its scope and function. Much of this discourse focuses on paying lip service to teaching all students and taking into consideration their cultural contexts, but there is no ensuing critique of the ways in which the school system and teachers reify racist pedagogy. We believe that not only must we continue the dialogue, but that dialogue must be critical and include within it historical and ideological issues along with the socializing structures that sustain such ideologies as normative. The challenge here is for the institution and the teacher to work to create a useful frame that honors students' development yet challenges their norms.

An attempt to achieve educational equity through classroom practices in preservice teacher education via an equity-based framework contains an activist dimension. It not only identifies our traditional context of teaching and learning as persistently inequitable and supremacist, but seeks to change it, setting out not only to ascertain how the classroom organizes itself along racial lines and hierarchies but also how to transform it for the better (Delgado & Stefancic, 2000). An important and determining factor in activating this goal is to create a curriculum for preservice educators that allows students to interrogate the inherencies and difficulties of an inequitable educational system and, further, to recognize institutional and cultural privileges that sustain their own power. Naming whiteness as a race *denormalizes* the cultural practices and epistemologies that have come to be standard in educational curriculum and pedagogy. The danger of not naming race (including whiteness) only serves to maintain white power and privilege.

As a form of oppositional work, an equity-based framework actively challenges the universality of white experience and judgment as the authoritative standard that binds people of color and normatively measures, directs, controls, and regulates the terms of proper thought, expression, presentment, and behavior. The task of this approach is to identify values and norms that have been disguised and subordinated in the law (Delgado & Stefancic, 2000). In order to train more caring teachers, we need to develop a body of teachers who are racially aware.

The intersection where our students and our own experiences meet serves as a microcosm of society where ideological and historical factors hit the fan. Hence, it is a space where this framework can be productive, creating conversation, generating tools, and extending voice. This is a goal that needs to be aggressively addressed, as student populations grow diverse and their teachers do not.

NOTES

1. According to Banks (1998, 2001, 2003), the aims of the transformative approach to multicultural education are to teach students to think critically and to develop the skills to formulate, document, and justify their conclusions. Such an approach affords students opportunities to engage in critical thinking and to develop more reflective perspectives about what they are learning. The approach pushes students to look with the head and the heart as they critically examine issues both inside and outside the classroom.

REFERENCES

Agee, J. (2004). Negotiating a teaching identity: An African American teacher's struggle to teach in test-driven contexts. *Teachers College Record, 106*(4), 747–774.

Ahlquist, R. (1991). Power and imposition: Power relations in a multicultural foundations class. *The Journal of Negro Education, 60,* 158–169.

Banks, J.A. (1998). Curriculum transformation. In J.A. Banks (Ed.), *An introduction to multicultural education* (2nd ed., pp. 21–34). Boston: Allyn & Bacon.

Banks, J.A. (2001). Citizenship education and diversity: Implications for teacher education. *Journal of Teacher Education, 52,* 5–16.

Banks, J.A. (2003). Teaching literacy for social justice and global citizenship. *Language Arts, 81,* 18–19.

Bell, D. (1995). *Brown v. Board of Education* and the interest convergence dilemma. In K. Crenshaw, N. Gotanda, G. Peller, & K. Thomas (Eds.), *Critical race theory: The key writings that formed the movement* (pp. 20–29). New York: The New Press.

Bell, D. (2004). Silent covenants: *Brown v. Board of Education* and the unfulfilled hopes for racial reform. New York: Oxford University Press.

Brown v. Board of Education, 347 U.S. 483 (1954).

Bruner, J. (2005, October 21). *Teaching the hypothetical.* Address delivered at the National Academy of Education annual meeting, New York, NY.

Delgado, R., & Stefancic, J. (Eds.). (2000). *Critical race theory: the cutting edge* (2nd ed.). Philadelphia, PA: Temple University Press.

Foster, M. (1990). The politics of race: Through the eyes of African-American teachers. *Journal of Education, 172*(3), 123–141.

Gay, G. (2000). *Culturally responsive teaching: Theory, research, and practice.* New York: Teachers College Press.

Gutiérrez, K. (in press). White innocence: A framework and methodology for rethinking educational discourse. *International Journal of Learning.*

Gutiérrez, K.D., & Jaramillo, N.E. (2006). Looking for educational equity: The consequences of relying on *Brown.* In A. Ball (Ed.), *With more deliberate speed: Achieving equity and excellence in education—Realizing the full potential of* Brown v. Board of Education. *The 105th yearbook of the National Society for the Study of Education*, Part II (pp. 173–189). Malden, MA: Blackwell.

Gutiérrez, K.D., & Rogoff, B. (2003). Cultural ways of learning: Individual styles or repertoires of practice. *Educational Researcher, 32*(5), 19–25.

Hull, G. & Schultz, K. (Eds.). (2002). *School's out!: Bridging out-of-school literacies with classroom practice.* New York: Teachers College Press.

International Reading Association. (2005). IRA, others develop middle, high school literacy coaching standards. *Reading Today, 23*(3), 1. Retrieved December 13, 2005, from http://www.reading.org/publications/reading_today/samples/RTY-0512-coaching.html

Irvine, R.W., & Irvine, J.J. (1983). The impact of the desegregation process on the education of black students: Key variables. *Journal of Negro Education, 52*(4), 410–422.

Ladson-Billings, G. (2000). Fighting for our lives: Preparing teachers to teach African American students. *Journal of Teacher Education, 51*(3), 206–213.

Majors, Y. (1998). Finding the multi-voiced self: A narrative. *Journal of Adolescent and Adult Literacy, 42*(2), 76–83.

Milner, H.R. (2005). Developing a multicultural curriculum in a predominantly white teaching context: Lessons from an African American teacher in a suburban English classroom. *Curriculum Inquiry, 35*(4), 391–427.

Santos, M. (1992, October). *Demystifying affirmative action.* Paper presented at the annual meeting of the American Association of Schools, Colleges, and Universities, Pomona, CA.

Siddle-Walker, V. (2000). Valued segregated schools for African American children in the South, 1935–1969: A review of common themes and characteristics. *Review of Educational Research, 70,* 253–286.

Street, P. (2004, May 27). Educational apartheid. Why we are in no mood for a *Brown v. Board* birthday bash. *The Black Commentator, 92.* Retrieved February 12, 2006 from http://www.blackcommentator.com/92/92_Brown.html

Tatum, B.D. (1994). Teaching white students about racism: The search for white allies and the restoration of hope. *Teachers College Record, 95,* 462–476.

Part Three
Comparative Reflections on *Brown v. Board of Education*

CHAPTER 11

The Ties That Bind: Race and Restitution in Education Law and Policy in South Africa and the United States of America[1]

JONATHAN D. JANSEN

> I, speaking now as a judge, have no hesitation in saying that as far as I am concerned, the greatest legal decision of the 20th century was *Brown*.

Albie Sachs, constitutional court judge, South Africa, April 22, 2004

The parallels between South Africa and the United States run deep (Frederickson, 1981; Magubane, 1987; Marx, 1998). Both countries were occupied by European settlers. Both were at various points governed by ideologies of white supremacy. Both have slave histories. Both institutionalized social discrimination based on race. Both operated segregated education systems, superior for whites and inferior for blacks. Both faced intense struggles against racial domination and unequal schooling. And both eventually established new laws and policies that made racial discrimination illegal and legitimized the quest for equal educational opportunities. For the United States, that moment of transition, at least as far as education is concerned, was the

---

Jonathan D. Jansen serves as Dean of Education at the University of Pretoria and as Vice President of the Academy of Science of South Africa. His received his doctorate from Stanford University and his MS in science education from Cornell University.

211

landmark ruling of 1954, described in the shorthand, *Brown v. Board of Education*; for South Africa, that moment came 40 years later when every citizen could, for the first time, vote on a nonracial basis under the legal frame provided by a new constitution.

There are, of course, important differences between the two countries that partly explain their different historical trajectories of oppression and struggle. The numbers were radically different, with black people in the United States constituting a numerical minority and black South Africans a demographic majority. Black people originally came to the United States, against their will, as slaves from mainly West Africa; black South Africans were the indigenous inhabitants of the Southern African landscape. The civil rights struggle of African Americans was for recognition and inclusion against the claims of the American Constitution; the anti-apartheid struggle of black South Africans was for national liberation and the establishment of a new social order and, by implication, a new constitution. Whereas African Americans as a declining demographic minority have limited options in radically altering the entrenched patterns of unequal education in the face of a powerful white electorate, black South Africans brought to power an essentially black nationalist government with a decisive electoral mandate for pursuing social and educational change.

Ties of Oppression and Solidarity

Despite these differences, the long relationship between the two countries reveals often unacknowledged ties of racial oppression as well as strong bonds of racial solidarity in the struggle for freedom. Early South African colonial masters and their education officers, such as C.T. Loram and M.S. Davis, among many others, visited the South of the United States in the early part of the 20th century to study models of black education such as Tuskegee University that could be transplanted into South Africa. The historian R.H. Davis, Jr. (1990) observed that Native Commissioner C.T. Loram "found in the United States educational theories and practices that provided guidance for developing schools which could inculcate African subservience to and acceptance of white authority" (p. 109). American institutions such as Teachers College, Columbia University trained both the early and later black leadership of South Africa—including a future president of the African National Congress (Dunton, 2003)—while at the same time providing the ideological training grounds for a generation of segregationist leaders in successive governments of the same country (Fleisch, 1995).

American foundations and corporations further cemented the racialised links between white/black South Africa and white/black America in the field of education. The Carnegie Corporation, for example, funded libraries and exchange visits by mainly white South African librarians so that "Ideas gathered from library services offered to African Americans were adopted and adapted for Blacks in South Africa" (Rochester, 1999, p. 28). This of course had little to do with liberating the intellectual faculties of black South Africans, for "the provision of library services for Blacks was supported officially and by White liberals only when libraries had become part of a system of social control" (p. 31).

At the very time that the U.S. government was flirting with apartheid South Africa through morally bankrupt policies such as "constructive engagement,"[2] the streets of Washington, New York, San Francisco, and many other cities were filled with protestors calling for stronger action from the U.S. Congress against the white regime in Pretoria. As Malcolm X invited comparison with Steve Biko among street-level activists in South Africa, and Martin Luther King Jr. offered intellectual and spiritual sustenance to a new generation of church rebels like Alan Boesak and Frank Chikane, Nelson Mandela became a symbol of resistance for black struggles in the United States. Even as American companies joined their local counterparts in the exploitation of black workers in the mines and factories of South Africa, American campuses were boiling over with student protests insisting on university divestments from firms doing business with apartheid. The ties, indeed, run deep.

Against this historical backdrop of collusion and cooperation, academics and researchers from the two countries gathered in Pretoria, South Africa, in April 2004 to reflect on the meanings of the 50th anniversary of *Brown* and the 10th anniversary of South Africa's transition to democracy. This historic conference brought together the foremost legal (and specifically education law) scholars in the United States and South Africa, and a few comparative scholars from Europe and the United Nations, to ask fundamental questions such as: How far have we come since 1954 and 1994, respectively? And what lessons should be drawn across these two contexts that could inspire action and instruct thought in the ongoing struggle for equal educational opportunities in the United States and South Africa?

What I wish to do is offer my response to these questions through a bifocal lens: first, the lens of my experiences *doing change* as an academic leader, researcher, teacher, and policy analyst in South Africa; and second, the lens offered by my own research on *thinking change* with respect to educational opportunities in South Africa and the United States; in this respect, I will be drawing on South African and American scholars' presentations from the Pretoria conference (later collected in book form) that dealt with *Brown*, postapartheid society, and educational opportunities.

Reexamining Scholarship on *Brown* and the Postapartheid Period

I find the metaphor of the bifocal lens very useful because on the one hand I want to see far (the United States) and near (South Africa), and move easily between what is familiar to me in my domestic experience and between what is perhaps less familiar to me in the international context; although I must confess that part of my enjoyment in thinking comparatively comes from spending much time in learning and activism in American universities as a graduate student. But the bifocal lens analogy also reflects my intention to move between the everyday, empirical experience of change and continuity, and the broader quest for theorizing across these two exciting national contexts; to move between theory and practice, hopefully shaping both.

Thinking Comparatively About Education Law and Policy

De Groof and Lauwers (2005), although writing mainly from a comparative European perspective, offer important insights for young scholars and the uninitiated. They first propose what it means to think comparatively with respect to education and education law:

More than using comparative law as a reservoir of solutions from which the best practise will have to be chosen, comparative education law can become an effective contribution to some convergency or harmonization of law. (p. 43)

I agree, recognizing of course that there are other forces in this highly networked global community that further collude to "harmonise" policy regimes across nation-states so that it is now possible to speak about policy as a transnational phenomenon (see Jansen, 2005a).

Education policy students frequently pose the question about how to think of or conceive the relationship between education law and education policy. Here de Groof and Lauwers (2005) offer important starting points for such conceptualization, worth quoting at length:

Unavoidably, each comparative approach needs to discuss the relation between educational law and policy in more detail. Educational legislation has strong instrumental aspects because it serves certain *policy goals*. Therefore educational legislation can be regarded as "purposive law." But if educational law is regarded merely as an instrument of educational policy, the comparison will focus on policy goals, and little or no attention will be paid to legal principles and values. A critical approach to comparative educational law will have to involve a critical reflection on policy, as well as revealing any contradictions between law and reality (emphasis in the original). (p. 43)

With these brief pointers for a comparative reading of education law, I now wish to shift the focus to a policy and political perspective on education legislation using, as indicated, a bifocal lens.

The Symbolic Functions of Education Law and Policy

The problem with much academic writing and indeed public consumption of governmental policy and law is that it subscribes to a literal reading of policy as official intentions, and then "reads off" such pronouncements a set of well-minded and good-hearted commitments to changing the status quo. There is very little consideration of, first, the possibility that the *primary* motivation for a new legal or policy order might be its symbolic functions (Jansen, 2002) rather than its practical consequences; and there is even less deliberation, second, on the enormous implementation hurdles that radical or even small shifts in constitutions, laws, or policies must scale in order to show desired effects in schools and classrooms. South Africans have been particularly susceptible to assumptions about the redemptive powers of legal and political instruments—perhaps a consequence of three centuries of domination in which the oppressive force of establishment law so effectively penetrated every aspect of black lives and experiences.

It does not surprise, therefore, that education law scholars frequently point out that *rights on paper* is not the same thing as *rights in practice*. Nieuwenhuis (2005), writing from South Africa, goes even further to insist that state decrees amount to "metaphysical, romantic delusion" and that "Social equality will be gained only in the hearts of men [sic], not from the laws of state" (p. 195). It was Daniel (2005) who recognized—citing the famous civil rights lawyer, Derrick Bell—that "the appearance of justice" (p. 161) serves an important function in pacifying dominant (read white) groups while at the same time holding forth the illusion of justice for the disadvantaged. I sense the frustration of U.S. colleagues, black and white, in the face of 50 years of struggle to see *Brown* more forcefully enacted within education practice rather than only celebrated in education law. Russo and Perkins (2005) go further and blame "judicial indifference" (p. 120) for the lack of progress under *Brown*. It would be instructive to juxtapose their concept of "judicial indifference" with Thro's (2005) thesis that "judicial restraint" (p. 139) explains the unequal outcomes of schooling.

Education Law, Policy, and the Matter of School Discipline

Another way of comparing the perspectives on education law and educational opportunity is through the lens of studies on school discipline. Speaking from the U.S. context, Cambron-McCabe and McCarthy (2005) demonstrate that disciplinary regimes in American schools (such as zero-tolerance) work to disproportionately marginalize black youth in the search for order and stability. Speaking from the South African context, Joubert, de Waal, and Rossouw (2005) simply document legal and policy provisions on discipline, drawing on recent case law. Whereas the first contribution shows the racially unequal consequences of discipline, the second relays the purposes of discipline. What is absent in both contributions is a critical discussion on why we are speaking about discipline in the first place, what its political functions were and are in both societies, and how discipline came to assume normative reality in race-determined societies. Here the works of Michel Foucault and critical sociologists on the institutionalization of punishment offer an important lens on discipline and its historical functions. It is not clear to me, in education law writings generally and especially in the Joubert et al. (2005) paper, what the purpose of simply reciting what appears in court documents or in school experiences might be, without a deeper theoretical inquiry into what such events mean.

Brown *Reassessed*

Nevertheless, the critical assessments of *Brown* and its consequences (or nonconsequences) could in some quarters be dismissed as too cynical given the political significance of progressive policy signaling. Here Sachs (2005, p. 5) is unequivocal:

However much disappointment there has been that the promise of *Brown* has not been fulfilled . . . It set a marker in terms of creativity, in terms of resonance, in terms of integrity, philosophical and legal integrity, for the whole world. . . . The Justices were saying that there are certain forms of conduct that are just not sustainable, that just cannot be tolerated, in a society with pretensions to justice.

But *Brown* was also positive in its practical consequences, as Harvard's Charles Willie (2005) argues: "The overall conclusion we derive from this analysis," insists Willie, is that "the *Brown* decision enhanced the education of black people in the United States and did not harm the education of white people. Actually, the 'justice as fairness' doctrine helped everyone" (p. 84).

It should be said, though, that the majority of American conference participants/authors were very critical of the impact and legacy of *Brown*. Such negative assessments could be attributed to the continuing white domination of a minority that is, demographically, not even the most important minority in American society as that nation heads into the 21st century. But a radical position then raises the uncomfortable question: Why is it that South Africa, with a black majority government and population, with all the international goodwill in the world, with a reasonably stable and progressive economy, with a highly regarded policy infrastructure, and with what is frequently lauded as one of the most progressive constitutions in the world—seems to be heading, according to research and experience, in the same direction, viz., that despite 10 years of intense policymaking and planning, white schools remain markedly privileged and protected while black schools, urban and rural, remain marginalized in both resources and performance?

The Politics of *Brown* and Postapartheid Education Laws

It seems to me that a large part of the answer resides in political explanations rather than in what Nieuwenhuis (2005, p. 195) calls "the empirical arrangement"—that is, within the legal and policy domain. Analyses of the political represent a weakness in writings on *Brown*—a lack of a sustained analysis of *power* in explaining the limits and proclivities of the state, whether in South Africa or the United States, to effect the kinds of changes signaled in law and policy. It is instructive to recall that unlike many other African states, South Africa did not gain democracy through military conquest but through negotiated settlement. Furthermore, the relative scale and health of the national economy made investor confidence a crucial variable in policy signaling in the post-Cold War period. And the white community was well established and going nowhere, as in the classical exodus of whites from former colonies to the metropole. In fact, South Africa—as in the case of the United States—could hardly describe its white citizens in terms of the classical language of colonies and settlers; these are Africans (though black nationalists are ambivalent if not angry about such a designation) with a sizeable share and contribution to this modern economy, albeit a standing that results from racialised accumulation under apartheid.

The economic and (relative) demographic strength of the white minority, coupled with the reality of a negotiated settlement, immediately placed the new government under some constraint with respect to the scale and ambition of social and educational reforms. I say "some" constraint because this factor—the constraining conditions of negotiated settlement—is often overstated in the post-independence literature. For what explains the difference between a theory of change and a theory of constraints is politics. What disabled change in South Africa was the demobilization of (anti-apartheid) social movements that could press for and insist on change in the political arena once formal democracy was achieved.[3] The obvious and powerful counterexample is the Treatment Action Campaign (TAC), which continues to win important legal and political battles that ensure that basic drugs are widely available to black and women patients suffering with HIV/AIDS. There were no similar movements in education after 1994 to insist that *the light of rights* illuminate the continuing problems of access to quality education for those most marginalized in postapartheid schools, such as rural children.

This is of course not a case against the formal declaration of progressive policies or the establishment of more humane laws. Indeed, as de Groof and Lauwers (2005), in their magisterial review of education law in the European Union, and Singh (2005) in his fine-grained analysis of legal instruments under the United Nations, demonstrate, the existence of such laws and policies not only set the standard for acceptable behaviour of the commonwealth of nations, it also enables action against or support for those who fail to advance access and equity for disadvantaged groups, such as women, ethnic minorities, and the disabled. Singh reminds us that the subject in international law is not simply educational opportunities, but identifying and redressing the barriers, such as racial discrimination, that prevent such opportunities from being taken up. He points to a very important paragraph in the Programme of Action that came out of the World Conference against Racism, Racial Discrimination, Xenophophia and Related Intolerance held in Durban, South Africa in 2001. In the section on "Access to Education Without Discrimination," governments are alerted

to ensure equal access to education for all in law and in practice, and to refrain from any legal or any other measures leading to imposed racial segregation in any form in access to schooling. (p. 55)

The Crooked Line Between Policy and Legal Intentions and Educational Practice

Yet in both South African and American studies on educational opportunity, like those discussed in this chapter, there is a refusal to draw a simple implementation line between education law/policy and education practice. Scholars seek to demonstrate the complexities in design and implementation of reforms in law and policy on the basis of some of the most well-described case studies (Sayed & Jansen, 2001; Thro, 2005) and reflections on the subject in both countries. In his impressive account of the relationship between accountability and quality under the Bush Administration, Daniel (2005) demonstrates that in the attempt to hold schools accountable for student achievement, education legislation actually further distanced disadvantaged students from educational opportunity and social integration.

It is a complex argument put forward by Daniel (2005), but one worth pursuing. In short, parents could take their children out of public schools that underperform and place them in alternative institutions called charter schools. Charter schools are public schools with special exemptions from standard state regulations. The only problem is that these schools not only overrepresent black (and Hispanic) students relative to other race groups, but there is little evidence of achievement gains in these schools relative to their public counterparts. What Daniel then demonstrates is that in the zeal for raising test scores, "equality finds itself trumped by quality" with official blessing: "the courts have accepted the provision of a return to one-race schools due to choices of domicile causing self-segregation" (p. 161).

In a similar vein, Beckmann and Prinsloo (2005) demonstrate the complexities of accountability-based reforms in South Africa and the consequences for equal educational opportunities. Their work shifts the interrogation to the state itself, and asks: "what has the state taken for its account . . .?" (p. 270). This is a very different focus from the literature in both contexts where the accountability focus remains the ability (or incapacity) of those down the policy implementation line, such as practitioners. This of course places accountability squarely in the political domain, and shifts the gaze of performance to the state. In any event, the conclusion reached by Beckmann and Prinsloo is a radical one: "if invoking accountability does not produce anticipated or intended results it does not serve any purpose" (p. 270). One could go further, of course, and ask about the desirability of the intended results— whether this was worth achieving in the first place. But I digress.

Continued Segregation in South Africa

The problem in South Africa with respect to equal educational opportunities is that complex shifts have taken place in the first decade of democracy that could not have been completely predicted.

First, an upper class of white schools remained largely if not exclusively white using two main instruments: school fees and language policy. After 1994, the elite white schools dramatically increased their school fees on the grounds that the state's decision to reduce the number of teachers under its rationalization programme threatened the quality of education in these schools. By raising the school fees, these schools could generate the kind of revenue from parents that allowed them to employ their own teachers under so-called governing body posts, and thereby keep the learner/teacher ratio relatively small. In blunt terms, for these schools class size was a proxy for education quality. The obvious effect of this quadrupling (in many cases) of school fees was that the only students of colour who could access these schools were the children of the national and international elite, for example, the children of the small but growing new black elite in South Africa, the children of embassy staff, and a limited number of children granted bursaries by the school itself.

This scenario more or less describes the typical white English school. In the process of generating such substantial revenue from parental income, these schools effectively blurred the line between public and private institutions. In fact, in many schools there were more teachers employed by the school governing body than by the relevant state authority (in South Africa, the provincial government).

Here is the first political dilemma. The government is reluctant to intervene on this front for the following reasons. In performance terms, these schools have always offered a high quality of education— measured in conventional terms—and any governmental intrusion could in fact undermine their capacity to continue doing so. In political terms, there is also the real risk that by heavy-handed intervention in these schools, middle-class white parents could in fact flee the public school system altogether, thereby creating serious problems of legitimacy for the otherwise mediocre government-controlled (public) schools. In financial terms, these schools actually relieve the state of an added financial burden by raising private funds within the public sector to maintain schools and pay teachers. Under increasing fiscal duress, departments of education are reluctant to intervene where they in fact do not have to fund such schools. In theory, limited state funding could be diverted to underdeveloped schools rather than to shore up the elite public schools.

Second, another group of elite white schools effectively wielded language policy as the determining basis for access to schools; this scenario typically applies to white Afrikaans schools. In these schools, an Afrikaans requirement[4] effectively excluded black students for whom English or one of the other nine official languages was more likely to be the language of access to school. The argument as to whether such schools consciously or deliberately used the Afrikaans language to exclude black students is a moot point; the consequences are the same, viz., that there sits around the country a visible number of exclusive or near-exclusive white, Afrikaans schools that are well-resourced and effectively off-limits to black students.

Here is the second political dilemma: these schools resist integration on grounds of a powerful constitutional argument—the protection of minorities and minority languages, a issue taken up by both Kroes (2005) and Malherbe (2005) in the South African context. Malherbe takes a position that calls for balance between "the constitutional values of dignity, equality and freedom when pursuing equal educational opportunities" and cites the example of "the unrelenting pressure on Afrikaans medium schools to become parallel or dual medium institutions" (p. 106). The problem with these kinds of arguments is their lack of graciousness, and their singular lack of acknowledgment of history and politics in analyses that far too often betray an underlying logic of racial self-protection under the guise of minority rights.

The fact is that Afrikaans was one of only two official languages for at least half of the previous century—at the expense of other African languages; that Afrikaans might have been a language spoken by a demographic minority (white Afrikaners), but it was also the language of officialdom of a political majority (white South Africans); that Afrikaans still holds powerful negative memories of its role as the ideological vehicle for suppressing black nationalist aspirations that climaxed in the 1976 Soweto Student Uprising; and that Afrikaans still carries the heavy burden of white nationalist ambition within post-apartheid society. I have attended far too many parent meetings, university assemblies, and quasi-political gatherings of Afrikaners to be dissuaded that there are not powerful groups that seek to reestablish the link between white separatism and a race-exclusive ownership of the Afrikaans language, and the ideal place to continue harbouring such ambitions in a democratic state are schools and churches. It is for this reason that language policy and religious policy have become the major areas of policy and legal contestation after 10 years of democracy.

The Consequences of Indifference, Resistance, and Complexity

There are negative consequences for students: Their isolation in white, Afrikaans-exclusive schools for 12 years seriously disables them from social integration in the broader South African community. As a black dean and academic leader at a former all-white, Afrikaans-exclusive university, I witness daily the extreme difficulties young people from such schools encounter in an integrated higher education community (see Jansen, 2005b for an extended discussion). The only way in which to achieve Malherbe's (2005) "balance" is to have schools with dual or, better still, multilingual practices on the same school grounds: you learn in and through the medium of Afrikaans, and you learn with and among children from diverse linguistic, cultural, religious, and social backgrounds. This is the only way in which to both affirm Afrikaans as one of 11 official languages and to break the underlying white nationalist ambition that undermines both Afrikaans and white Afrikaans-speaking students.

At root, such behaviour constitutes a threat to the very constitution of a fragile democracy such as South Africa. As Charles Willie (2005) concludes about the American experience:

The continued existence of a democratic nation-state is jeopardized when its citizens believe that they have to obey the law only if they like it. This is precisely what many white people believed. Those who did not like the court order on desegregation decided not to obey the law. This was a serious challenge to the continued existence of our democratic nation. There is no democracy if the people obey the law only when they like it. (p. 83)

The Place of Religion

The related (to language) concern, religious education, is taken up by Wanda (2005), who reviews recent South African government policy and law with respect to the practice and place of religion in educational institutions. Public education institutions cannot be used as sites to promulgate a particular religious view; the routine compulsory school assemblies conducted as Christian church services fly in the face of the spirit of government policy for a broader and more accommodating school environment. Yet voluntary religious observation and participation are encouraged but "they are not to be regarded as forming part of the official educational function of the public school," argues Wanda (p. 33).

Here I think the position of the South African government is sensible. But tackling the same topic in American public education, Mawdsley and Russo (2005, p. 205) throw the proverbial spanner in the works with two riveting questions that deserve deliberation:

If public schools must excise all religious symbols or practices that might be perceived as endorsed by the schools, at what point does such elimination go beyond neutrality and demonstrate hostility to religion?

How can public schools be expected to teach tolerance for the religious beliefs of its students when every effort is made to eliminate religious content from the schools?

The answers to these questions are not important; the complexity of pursuing laws and policies on religious education is what should be appreciated in the way these questions posed the problem. I do not think South Africa has gone this far, and maybe it should, for many public schools are still adorned as Christian institutions even when there are growing numbers of students from other faiths. As I have written elsewhere (Jansen, 2004a), the South African government made a crucial error at an earlier moment in the way it promoted a values-in-education policy that backfired badly in the public domain. By removing religion and faith from the consideration of values, and replacing this with completely bland and neutral content, there was a revolt from black and white fundamentalist Christians, who found coincidence of purpose in a highly religious country. Faith is important, and important in nations like South Africa and the United States. The challenge remains to find ways of representing faith that do not encourage dominance—the unyielding aspiration of fundamentalists—and demonisation of others, but advance tolerance, even the embrace, of persons irrespective of their religious beliefs. This is challenging enough in times of peace; as the U.S. experience has shown, war can inflame the worst kinds of religious zealotry and misguided patriotism that no law or policy can begin to dissipate.

But I wish to return to what I earlier referred to as a blurring of the lines between public and private education in South Africa, as there are major contestations on the subject of what arena (public or private) offers greater opportunities for disadvantaged students. I find Brown's (2005) work to offer a sophisticated and nuanced account of privatization and educational opportunities. His argument is in essence that it depends on resources, not school classification: "Rich children attend wealthy public schools, middle class parents send their children to moderately funded schools and the poor send their children to less well funded schools" (p. 164). He then goes on to explain how parents, teachers, and politicians use their power to channel students towards, and limit access to, the most well-funded schools.

This is a crucial issue, for as local scholars have observed, there is a definite trend towards a deracialised middle class in South Africa's elite public schools. As a result, other kinds of inequalities begin to surface, based on class status rather than racial designation. The fairly common misconception that private education automatically implies quality education for all is exactly that—a misconception. Again, the issue is power. As Brown (2005) reiterates,

Even if Americans were not divided along racial and social class lines, politics would still play a significant role in the allocation of school resources for the simple reason education is the largest component of local and state budgets. (p. 176)

There is an unfortunate omission in many of the assessments on education law, policy, and the quest for equality—and that is the vexing issue of school governance in South Africa. Intellectually, this question of who should control our schools is one of the most complex and intriguing sites of contestation between government and schools in South Africa; politically, it is one of the most frustrating.

The Problems and Possibilities in the Quest for Democratic Participation

The education struggle against apartheid was premised on the notion that democratic participation in school governance was fundamental to the transformation of schools. Black parents and students were long denied full participation in governance by the apartheid state which would, from time to time, place control directly under the rule of its heavy-handed white bureaucracies or hand over administration to illegitimate black functionaries of the state who enjoyed very little, if any, respect in the surrounding school community (for a fuller discussion, see Jansen, 2004b). In this fiery context, democratic participation became a core commitment of the ideals of struggle.

What could *not* have been anticipated in the 1970s and 1980s was that these very ideals, codified in the South African Schools Act (No. 84 of 1996, Department of Education, 1996), would be invoked by conservative schools to wield exclusionary ethnic and racial politics. There is evidence that in rural black communities, for example, schools would refuse to appoint governors on the basis of their political affiliations or personal connections to powerful school interests. There is also abundant evidence that conservative white schools would use a range of tactics to keep governing bodies (and therefore authority over teacher appointments and admission policies) predominantly or exclusively white—even when there was a growing black student presence in the school.

These kinds of observations lay partly behind the motivation of the Minister of Education to institute a Ministerial Committee on school governance, whose 2003 brief was telling:

identifying any patterns or trends in relation to race, class, gender and disability . . . capacity and representation. . . . for possible changes of legislation or policy that will serve to strengthen democratic school governance. (Department of Education, 2003, p. 1)

What was made clear was that the concept of participation after apartheid required urgent deconstruction, and that participation's multiple meanings and invocations in unequal societies could thwart the very democratic impulses and ideals that gave birth to this important notion.

But values such as participation not only lose their democratic sting by virtue of how they are used among ordinary people; they could also be cancelled out by the pursuit of conflicting constitutional values. Here Thro (2005), who is the State Solicitor General of the state of Virginia, in the United States, offers one of the most sophisticated analyses of education law and finance available in the literature, setting himself the task of explaining "how two American constitutional values, judicial restraint and decentralization, work together to prevent adequate funding for another constitutional value, equality of education for all" (p. 139).

Judicial restraint means that the courts are reluctant to intervene or review judgments. At the same time, the individual states (not the federal government) are empowered to make wide-ranging decisions on governance, textbooks, curriculum, etc., so that "the constitutional value of decentralization precludes [the courts] from fully vindicating the constitutional value of free public education" (Thro, 2005, p. 144). Thro then shows how the financing of education—a state or decentralized function—under these constraining conditions means, in effect, that "whether a child receives a quality education will be, in large part, the result of an accident of geography" (p. 145).

Thro's (2005) work must be read in conjunction with that of Davies (2005), who reflects on the attempts of the South African government to decentralize school education functions to nine provinces and to achieve "inter-provincial functional equity" (p. 126) given historical inequalities among different regions of the country. But given the scale of need across 29,000 schools, the deep legacies of inequality, vastly different provincial capacities to implement national mandates, and the racially skewed distribution of income, the results are the same in the sense that which school a student attends in which province will determine the quality of education they receive.

What is to be done? It seems to me that the first thing worth doing is a broad-based education campaign that informs ordinary citizens about their own power and authority to claim their rights against the constitution of democratic societies within which they live. Albie Sachs (2005), constitutional court judge in South Africa, recalls that when the South African Constitution was being drafted, the American experience with *Brown* and associated legislation made a lasting impact on and influenced the spirit and the substance of the African deliberations. Indeed, there still seem to be strong bonds of friendship and professional exchange between American and South African jurors on constitutional matters, including education.

Sachs (2005) recalls that the struggle to achieve the rights proclaimed in *Brown* and enshrined in the South African Constitution came at great personal cost. Sachs, for example, lost one of his limbs and scarred his face as a result of an apartheid bomb targeting him during his years in exile. The telling of his story humanizes the myriad of laws and policies, in both countries, and the need for rights to be claimed in order for them to be acknowledged in contexts where power and privilege are unequally distributed.

Whether rights are claimed and exercised in the courts or the streets, in schools or homes, in prisons or hospitals, the effort has to be advanced by ordinary people against the odds. If there is one thing that *Brown* teaches South Africa, it is that the struggle for equal educational opportunities will be a long one, and that successes as well as reversals are inevitable. If there is one thing that South Africa teaches the United States, it is that the passion and hope of ordinary people can inspire judicial activity and stir judicial conscience by relentlessly exposing "the contradictions between law and reality" (de Groof & Lauwers, 2005).

This is what recent scholarship on *Brown* and South Africa achieves—it reminds us of the ties that bind South Africa and the United States . . . not always noble or progressive, but always intimate and intense. I am happy to leave the final word to Albie Sachs (2005) who describes "these connections [as] very personal," and concludes:

We enter into a dialogue as equals. It is a matter of pride that our Court's decision abolishing capital punishment in South Africa is read in many jurisdictions by many lawyers in the United States. In our judgment we drew on Blackmun . . . Brenner . . . Thurgood Marshall . . . The spirit of *Brown* might be wavering a little bit in the United States of America . . . But I have no hesitation in saying that the spirit of *Brown* in alive and well on the Constitutional Court of South Africa. (p.18)

NOTES

1. This chapter is an edited version of a review of papers prepared by South African and international scholars, mainly from the United States, comparing experiences since the 1954 *Brown* decision (United States) and after 10 years of democracy in education in South Africa. These papers, and the fuller version of this chapter, appear in Russo, Beckmann, and Jansen (2005). Also, the title of this chapter is similar to that of Bernard Magubane's (1987) book on the same subject, and I wish to acknowledge that fact. I would like to thank Drs. Mokubung Nkomo, Charlie Russo, and Neil Roos for their excellent comments on an earlier draft of this chapter.

2. This policy, largely shaped by the politics of the Cold War in Southern Africa, was crafted by Chester Crocker who went on to become U.S. Assistant Secretary of State for Africa under President Ronald Reagan, and whose administration adopted "constructive engagement" (as opposed to *direct confrontation*) in its dealings with South Africa.

3. The main mechanism for this demobilization of the anti-apartheid nongovernmental organisations, for example, was that their external or overseas funding was not directed to the coffers of the democratic government as a legitimate development actor; while this was understood, such a migration of funds effectively meant that non-governmental organisations could not play as strong a developmental and democratic role in post-apartheid society.

4. Afrikaans was one of two official languages under apartheid South Africa, and by far the dominant language of government, policing, bureaucracy, and oppression. The perceived decline in Afrikaans in schools and universities has led to a resurgent Afrikaner nationalism on the one hand, and a broader cultural concern among mostly white Afrikaners about the future of the language on the other hand. By invoking Afrikaans-only schools, the inevitable charge from black parents and communities is that this is not simply a means of language protection or promotion, but an effective tool to limit racial access to these privileged schools to black students, most of whom are not competent in the Afrikaans language.

REFERENCES

Beckmann, J., & Prinsloo, J. (2005). Towards an analytical framework for accountability regarding equal educational opportunities. In C. Russo, J. Beckmann, & J. Jansen (Eds.), *Equal educational opportunities: Comparative perspectives in education law.* Brown v. Board of Education *at 50 and democratic South Africa at 10* (pp. 258–275). Pretoria, South Africa: Van Schaiks Publishers.

Brown, F. (2005). Privatization of elementary and secondary education in America. In C. Russo, J. Beckmann, & J. Jansen (Eds.), *Equal educational opportunities: Comparative perspectives in education law.* Brown v. Board of Education *at 50 and democratic South Africa at 10* (pp. 164–181). Pretoria, South Africa: Van Schaiks Publishers.

Cambron-McCabe, N., & McCarthy, M. (2005). Student discipline and equal educational opportunities in the United States. In C. Russo, J. Beckmann, & J. Jansen (Eds.), *Equal educational opportunities: Comparative perspectives in education law.* Brown v. Board of Education *at 50 and democratic South Africa at 10* (pp. 222–235). Pretoria, South Africa: Van Schaiks Publishers.

Daniel, P.T.K. (2005). A critical analysis of school choice, educator accountability and the new desegregation in American public schools. In C. Russo, J. Beckmann, & J. Jansen (Eds.), *Equal educational opportunities: Comparative perspectives in education law.* Brown v. Board of Education *at 50 and democratic South Africa at 10* (pp. 148–163). Pretoria, South Africa: Van Schaiks Publishers.

Davies, H. (2005). Some aspects of equity in the funding of public schooling in South Africa. In C. Russo, J. Beckmann, & J. Jansen (Eds.), *Equal educational opportunities: Comparative perspectives in education law.* Brown v. Board of Education *at 50 and democratic South Africa at 10* (pp. 122–136). Pretoria, South Africa: Van Schaiks Publishers.

Davis R.H., Jr. (1990). Charles T. Loram and the American model for African education in South Africa. In P. Kallaway (Ed.), *Apartheid and education: The education of Black South Africans* (pp. 108–126). Johannesburg, South Africa: Ravan Press.

de Groof, J., & Lauwers, G. (2005). Increasing access to education throughout European society. In C. Russo, J. Beckmann, & J. Jansen (Eds.), *Equal educational opportunities: Comparative perspectives in education law.* Brown v. Board of Education *at 50 and democratic South Africa at 10* (pp. 35–54). Pretoria, South Africa: Van Schaiks Publishers.

Department of Education. (1996). *South African Schools Act (No. 84 of 1996).* Pretoria, South Africa.

Department of Education. (2003). *Brief to the Ministerial Committee on School Governance.* Pretoria, South Africa.

Dunton, C. (2003). Pixley Kaisaka Seme and the African Renaissance debate. *African Affairs, 102,* 555–573.

Fleisch, B. (1995). *The Teachers College club: American education discourse and the origins of Bantu education, 1914–1951.* Ph.D. dissertation, Columbia University.

Frederickson, G.M. (1981). *White supremacy: A comparative study in American and South African history.* Oxford, UK: Oxford University Press.

Jansen, J.D. (2002). Policy as political craft: Explaining non-reform in South African education, 1994–2000. *Journal of Education Policy, 17*(2), 199–215.

Jansen, J.D. (2004a). The politics of salvation and the school curriculum. *Verbum et Ecclesia, 25*(2), 784–806.

Jansen, J.D. (2004b). The regulation of teacher accountability and autonomy in South Africa. *Research Papers in Education, 19*(1), 51–66.

Jansen, J.D. (2005a). Targeting education: The politics of performance and the prospects of education for all. *International Journal of Educational Development, 25*(4), 368–380.

Jansen, J.D. (2005b). Black dean: Race, reconciliation and the emotions of deanship. *Harvard Educational Review, 75*(3), 306–325.

Joubert, R., de Waal, E., & Rossouw, J.P. (2005). A South African perspective on the impact of discipline on access to equal educational opportunities. In C. Russo, J. Beckmann, & J. Jansen (Eds.), *Equal educational opportunities: Comparative perspectives in education law*. Brown v. Board of Education *at 50 and democratic South Africa at 10* (pp. 208–221). Pretoria, South Africa: Van Schaiks Publishers.

Kroes, H. (2005). The language perspective. In C. Russo, J. Beckmann, & J. Jansen (Eds.), *Equal educational opportunities: Comparative perspectives in education law*. Brown v. Board of Education *at 50 and democratic South Africa at 10* (pp. 236–257). Pretoria, South Africa: Van Schaiks Publishers.

Magubane, B. (1987). *The ties that bind: African American consciousness of Africa*. Trenton, NJ: Africa World Free Press.

Malherbe, R. (2005). The Constitution and equal educational opportunities. In C. Russo, J. Beckmann, & J. Jansen (Eds.), *Equal educational opportunities: Comparative perspectives in education law*. Brown v. Board of Education *at 50 and democratic South Africa at 10* (pp. 110–122). Pretoria, South Africa: Van Schaiks Publishers.

Marx, A.W. (1998). *Making race and nation: A comparison of the United States, South Africa and Brazil*. Cambridge, UK: Cambridge University Press.

Mawdsley, R., & Russo, C. (2005). Religion and American public education: An overview. In C. Russo, J. Beckmann, & J. Jansen (Eds.), *Equal educational opportunities: Comparative perspectives in education law*. Brown v. Board of Education *at 50 and democratic South Africa at 10* (pp. 198–207). Pretoria, South Africa: Van Schaiks Publishers.

Nieuwenhuis, J. (2005). From equality of opportunity to equality of treatment as a value-based concern in education. In C. Russo, J. Beckmann, & J. Jansen (Eds.), *Equal educational opportunities: Comparative perspectives in education law*. Brown v. Board of Education *at 50 and democratic South Africa at 10* (pp. 182–197). Pretoria, South Africa: Van Schaiks Publishers.

Rochester, M. (1999). The Carnegie Corporation and South Africa: Non-European library services. *Libraries and Culture, 34*(1), 27–51.

Russo, C., Beckmann, J., & Jansen, J. (2005). *Equal educational opportunities: Comparative perspectives in education law*. Brown v. Board of Education *at 50 and democratic South Africa at 10*. Pretoria, South Africa: Van Schaiks Publishers.

Russo, C., & Perkins, B.K. (2005). Equal educational opportunities: An American point of view. In C. Russo, J. Beckmann, & J. Jansen (Eds.), *Equal educational opportunities: Comparative perspectives in education law*. Brown v. Board of Education *at 50 and democratic South Africa at 10* (pp. 110–121). Pretoria, South Africa: Van Schaiks Publishers.

Sachs, A. (2005). Equal educational opportunities and the Constitutional Court. In C. Russo, J. Beckmann, & J. Jansen (Eds.), *Equal educational opportunities: Comparative perspectives in education law*. Brown v. Board of Education *at 50 and democratic South Africa at 10* (pp. 3–18). Pretoria, South Africa: Van Schaiks Publishers.

Sayed, Y., & Jansen, J. (Eds.). (2001). *Education policy implementation: The South African case*. Cape Town, South Africa: University of Cape Town Press.

Singh, K. (2005). Non-discrimination and equal educational opportunities: UNESCO's normative action. In C. Russo, J. Beckmann, & J. Jansen (Eds.), *Equal educational opportunities: Comparative perspectives in education law*. Brown v. Board of Education *at 50 and democratic South Africa at 10* (pp. 55–76). Pretoria, South Africa: Van Schaiks Publishers.

Thro, W.E. (2005). The American paradox: How constitutional values inhibit the achievement of quality education. In C. Russo, J. Beckmann, & J. Jansen (Eds.), *Equal educational opportunities: Comparative perspectives in education law*. Brown v. Board of Education *at 50 and democratic South Africa at 10* (pp. 137–147). Pretoria, South Africa: Van Schaiks Publishers.

Wanda, B. (2005). Religion in public schools: Some observations on the South African national policy on religion and education. In C. Russo, J. Beckmann, & J. Jansen

(Eds.), *Equal educational opportunities: Comparative perspectives in education law*. Brown v. Board of Education *at 50 and democratic South Africa at 10* (pp. 19–34). Pretoria, South Africa: Van Schaiks Publishers.

Willie, C.V. (2005). *Brown v. Board of Education*: A restoration of equity in public education. In C. Russo, J. Beckmann, & J. Jansen (Eds.), *Equal educational opportunities: Comparative perspectives in education law*. Brown v. Board of Education *at 50 and democratic South Africa at 10* (pp. 77–88). Pretoria, South Africa: Van Schaiks Publishers.

CHAPTER 12

The Ties That Bind: A Response to Jonathan Jansen

CHIKA TREVOR SEHOOLE

In his critique of academic writing about and public consumption of government policy and law, Jonathan Jansen warns against a tendency to subscribe to a literal reading of policy as official intention. He makes the case that the intentions and functions of some of these policies or laws might be *symbolic*; therefore, skepticism and caution should play a role in examining any of them. Jansen uses his argument of the symbolic functions of education law and education policy as a basis for explaining the lack of progress in achieving equity and justice under *Brown v. Board of Education* (1954) in the United States and the lack of progress in achieving social goals after 12 years of freedom in South Africa.

In his chapter, Jansen (this volume, pp. 211–230) presents an account of unpredictable and complex shifts that took place in the first decade of democracy in South Africa, and he argues that these shifts, often accomplished through law or policy, account for the lack of change. For example, elements of democratic decision making in the legislation, intended to empower parents, were used by parents at some schools to ensure that they remained exclusively white, using expensive school fees and language policy to maintain their exclusivity (Vally & Dalamba, 1999). He also highlights the political dilemmas these kind of exclusionary practices posed for the state, demonstrating the extent to which policies and laws could be used to perpetuate and maintain the status quo. What this shows is that the policies and laws are, in and of themselves, insufficient to effect change when social, political, and economic factors are so influential. Despite 12 years of intense policy-making and planning in South Africa, there are still white schools that remain markedly privileged and protected, while urban and rural black schools remain marginalized in terms of both resources and perfor-

---

Chika Trevor Sehoole is a senior lecturer on the Faculty of Education at the University of Pretoria in Tshwane, South Africa.

mance—this despite numerous policy statements that commit government to redress, equity, and quality in education.

The situation described above is best summarized by a quote Jansen cites: "The continued existence of a democratic nation-state is jeopardized when its citizens believe that they have to obey the law only if they like it" (Willie, 2005, p. 83), along with the understanding that law can be subverted not only in a covert way, as Willie suggests, but in an overt way as well. The fact that the law cannot be "enforced" in such situations highlights the legal fragility or pliability of the notion of equality. In reflecting on the 50 years since *Brown*, Smith (2004) points out that the end result is a heightened awareness that equal opportunity does not just evolve with changes in people's hearts, but must be achieved through direct, affirmative efforts by social and political institutions. Orfield (2004) alludes to the conditions under which enactment of a law or issuance of a regulation actually produces the intended change: clear legal authority, clear policy goals, firm enforcement, measurement of and accountability for results, and a combination of incentive, persuasion, and consistency to produce results, especially on controversial issues requiring difficult change. When powerful forces oppose a policy, a legal change permitting reversal is more likely to be relatively self-executing than a change that helps minorities. So, if this is the case, what is then the purpose of the law? Despite the legal ruling to desegregate schools in the United States with the *Brown* decision, a decision that was delivered more than 50 years ago, we now see discussion of "re-segregation" appearing more frequently in research and commentary in the United States (Kozol, 2005; Orfield & Lee, 2006).

My purpose for this chapter is two-fold: to build on Jansen's work so as to develop further an examination of both the U.S. and South African black education experiences with respect to (1) the curriculum taught in schools and (2) the experiences of students and educators in desegregated schools. This chapter argues that the efficacy of education policies and laws aimed at redressing racial discrimination and attainment of equity and social justice should be judged not only on the merits of the law or policy but on what happens, literally, within the desegregated schools in a given school system.

In this regard, the conduct of parents, teachers, administrators, and students serves as a basis to judge the efficacy of these policies and legal judgments. For example, teachers filter policy through their own lens and in particular through their cultural lenses, which in racialised societies will undoubtedly be coloured by racial undertones. Policy is interpreted and enacted through these lenses by educators and administrators in schools. Power relations are also at play, especially as the curriculum could be delivered from a particular perspective, and this ultimately impacts issues of equity in educational delivery. In terms of school administration, in desegregated schools you may find that school culture, as expressed through norms, values, and codes of conduct, is left intact or modified to hide overt exclusionary practices. This would very much reflect the history of the school during the segregation era. In instances where they have been modified, they have been difficult to detect and oppose. In this case, minority or nontraditional students coming into such schools may find that it is expected that they change and assimilate into a racist institutional culture despite the advent of educational laws and policies that direct school systems to eradicate segregation. In developing this argument, lessons are drawn from both the United States and South Africa in terms of their experiences with implementing desegregation policies.

Recent History and Parallels

Jansen's chapter begins by drawing powerful historical parallels between the United States and South Africa, including the facts that both countries operated segregated educational systems that were superior for whites and inferior for blacks, and both countries ultimately outlawed racial segregation through their legal systems. Jansen presents further powerful parallels and contrasts between the two countries in legal, educational, political, and organisational spheres and highlights the ties that bind them to this day.

The dawn of democracy in South Africa was preceded by an attempt to preserve white privilege by privatizing some of the white schools. This took the form of transferring the control of these schools into the hands of School Governing Bodies (SGBs) and the school principal. Different "models" were created that allowed parents in white schools to vote as to whether to desegregate or not, a vote that was affected by ideology, the decline in white population and the change in suburban populations, and the option of opening new schools designed to preserve white teachers' positions in the face of declining white school population. In April 1992, the Minister of Education for whites in the apartheid parliament House of Assembly announced that all white schools would be converted into "Model C" schools. In other words, they would become state-aided schools run by the management committee/SGB and the principal. Under this arrangement, a set number of scholastic expenses were paid by the state while the rest of the costs were borne by parents. The management committee had the power to appoint teachers, decide on the admission and language policy, deal with curriculum developments, and impose fees.

The move to Model C was actually an attempt to cut state costs by shifting the financing and control of white schools to parents. It could also be argued that it had the effect of "protecting" these schools against rapid changes that could be imposed by the envisaged new government, which was to take office in May 1994 and which for the first time in the history of South Africa would constitute a black majority. This government inherited an education system that was characterized by inequalities, including the subsidization of expenses for white school children at 107%, Indians at 97%, coloured at 78%, and Africans at 56%, and up to 39% for the Transkei[1] (Sehoole, 2005). Translated into figures in "The Values in Education Report" (Working Group on Education, 2000), it was shown that in 1994

the pre-democratic era government was still spending R5 403 ($900) per white learner, compared, for example, to R1 053 ($153) for every black African learner in the Transkei. The cumulative consequence of this unequal system was a desperately under-educated black African population. (p. 4)

What flowed from the designation of Model C schools was the exclusion of black students from enrollment, largely because of the high fees. Many other black pupils were turned away after failing the selection measures, admission tests, and other so-called meritocratic criteria that masked explicit institutional and societal racism (Vally & Dalamba, 1999). Even in the postapartheid period, there is evidence that some of these schools continue to practice such exclusionary tactics.

The American Experience

For the U.S. context, Orfield and Eaton (1996) argue that a decade after the *Brown* decision, 98% of black students in the United States remained in completely segregated schools. They contend that there was only a very serious national effort to eliminate segregation for a brief period in the 1960s and 1970s. The expansion of desegregation was halted, however, when more conservative judges were appointed to the Supreme Court in 1974, ruling in *Milliken v. Bradley* that interdistrict remedies could not be used between a city (in this case, Detroit) and the surrounding suburbs to force integration of city schools. In the 1990s what was now the most conservative Supreme Court in years issued a series of decisions leading to the termination of many deseg-regation orders and the rise of resegregation (Orfield & Eaton). Orfield (2004) observes that the desegregation movement in the United States, which began with a court decision and became a basic objective of a large social movement, faces significant obstacles. There is a great deal of evidence showing that crucial elements to move schools towards real integration were rarely fully realized and that the country has been moving backward, in many cases resegregating public schools, since the 1980s.

As an example, Arias (2005), in her study of the impact of *Brown* on a Latino school district, discusses the *Diaz v. San Jose Unified School District* (SJUSD) decision, in which the Ninth Circuit Court of Appeals found that the district acted with segregationist intent in maintaining racially identifiable schools. The circuit court found that the SJUSD failed to comply with state desegregation guidelines, disregarded racial balance in planning sites for new schools, and used racial criteria inap-propriately in the assignment of faculty and staff and in its policies concerning the busing of students for purposes other than desegrega-tion. The burden of desegregation ultimately fell on the students and their families, through a busing remedy, and it took years for additional remedies, more closely tailored to the needs of the community, to be implemented, largely as a result of unwavering pressure on the part of those affected.

The South African Experience

Just as the *Brown* decision ended legal segregation in education in the United States, the new postapartheid government in South Africa passed laws that outlawed desegregation and racism in schools. Key legislation included the Constitution and the Bill of Rights (Act 108 of 1996) that provided mechanisms whereby specific denials of equality arising from discrimination may be challenged. In addition, Section 29 of the Bill of Rights deals with issues such as the right to education, redressing past discriminatory practices, and language in education. Besides the Constitution, the South African Schools Act (1996) has had a pivotal impact on the desegregation of schools. It repealed all apart-heid laws pertaining to schools, and it provides a framework for a unified school system. The key features of the act are:

1. The proclamation of two categories of schools: public schools (98% of schools) and independent (formerly private) schools.

2. The establishment of school governing bodies at all schools, empowered to determine the admissions, language, and religious policies of the school within national norms and provincial frameworks.

3. The levying of school fees determined at an annual meeting of parents of the school implemented by the school governing body (as will be discussed, what was intended as empowerment measures for parents resulted in a subversion of the original intent and was used to undermine government desegregation policy).

What Progress Has Been Made to Achieve Some of the Policy Goals?

The proceedings of a colloquium on school integration held at the University of Pretoria in October 2003 presented some of the changes in some of the schools in the Gauteng Province (the economic hub and richest province in South Africa) in the years after apartheid ended. A study by Sujee (2004) showed a shift of African students from formerly black education departments to formerly white education departments between 1996 and 2002. The greatest movement was among Indian and coloured students who had moved from their respective schools to former white and independent schools. The majority of white students (86%) remained in their former white schools, but this number had decreased from 1996 as some students moved into independent schools. The percentage of white students in independent schools increased from 8% to 13.5% percent (in 2002), prompted, possibly, by some middle-class white parents withdrawing their children from formerly white public schools as the latter started experiencing an increase of black students (Orfield [2004] shows a similar pattern of the decrease in the percentage of white students in U.S. schools attended by black students, from 36% in the 1980s to 31% in 2000). The effect of this is racial and cultural misalignments that are bedeviling antiracism and equity efforts in these schools.

The preceding sections have provided *some* evidence of desegregation, although not satisfactory evidence. While the figures might tell us something about how some schools might have moved from apartheid-style segregation (while some have remained the same) they tell us nothing about the linguistic, cultural, and national diversity of the learners and teachers. I argue that it is equally important to focus on what happens in schools *once nontraditional students have been admitted*, rather than relying on (and being complacent about) statistics on the changing colour of students in previously segregated schools.

The Extent of Integration in Schools

Given that these students come from different backgrounds characterized by racial prejudice, what is the extent of racial integration in
these schools? Getting black students into better white schools is not
enough; measures that will lead to the success of these students in these
schools are also necessary. A conducive environment created by the
school will take into account school procedures and discipline, teacher
conduct and attitude, school curriculum, and the general conduct and
attitudes of other students in the school. As the Values in Education
Report (2000) argues, this approach should be anchored by the values
of tolerance—not simply "putting up with people," but a deeper and
more meaningful effort towards mutual understanding, reciprocal altru-
ism, and the active appreciation of the value of human difference. To
reach that state of human consciousness requires not only a truthfulness
about the failures and successes of the human past but the active and
deliberate incorporation of differences in the moral traditions, arts,
culture, religions, and sporting activities in the ethos and life of the
school (Working Group on Values in Education, 2000, pp. 21–22); in
essence, a culture of critical multiculturalism in which students' different identities are recognized and used as the basis for developing antiracist pedagogical practices in these new desegregated schools. As
Jackman and Hardiman (1981) highlight

A multicultural organization reflects the contributions and interests of diverse
cultural and social groups in its mission, operations, and . . . service of delivery;
acts on a commitment to eradicate social oppression in all forms within the
organization; includes the members of diverse cultural and social groups as full
participants, especially in the decisions that shape the organization; and follows
through on the broader social responsibilities, including support of efforts to
eliminate all forms of social oppression and to educate others in multicultural
perspectives (as cited in Pope, 1993, p. 203)

Integration is used in this chapter to refer to a process whereby one
interrogates the quality of contact not only in the personal attitudes of
teachers but also in the institutional arrangements, policies, and ethos
of the school (Sayed, 2001, p. 154), rather than focusing on physical
proximity and headcounts. One study by Vandeyar and Killen (2006)
explored the state of desegregation and integration in South African
schools 11 years after the demise of apartheid. The study found that
desegregation as assimilation is occurring in these schools, but institutionalized racism, often justified via the institutional ethos, is still per-

vasive. Manifestations of this at the classroom level included negative stereotyping of black students, selective empathy, discriminatory seating arrangements, devolution of authority to students on a racial basis, and aversion to the use of indigenous African languages. Under these conditions, black students were discriminated against and denied a fair chance to feel at home and succeed in their studies. The study shows the limitations of desegregation policies without accompanying integration measures, and underscores teachers as key to the success of integration.

Fennimore (2005) captures this succinctly by sharing the response of a New York school board president to her criticism of unfairness in the way a program for gifted children was constructed. His reply to Fennimore was "I don't care! What is fair does not concern me" (p. 1966). Such a response shows the insensitivities of some officials to policy measures aimed at redressing the obvious inequalities in unequal societies such as the United States.

Curriculum Issues, Scholarship, and the Representation of Blacks

One of the critical issues associated with curriculum studies has to do with the extent to which curriculum is used as an instrument for social control. This includes the representation (or nonrepresentation) of minority or oppressed groups in curriculum content. In societies characterized by inequalities, curriculum can exclude the history of oppressed and less dominant groups. Jansen's chapter does not address the exclusion in so many curriculums of the progressive history of struggle by African Americans as well as the liberation struggle in South Africa and the broader African continent.

In the South African context, the little history that did filter into the curriculum was written from a white person's perspective and very often represented a distorted view that sought to perpetuate the existing stereotypes about blacks in general and black South Africans in particular. During the last years of apartheid, curriculum and textbooks unsuccessfully tried to provide less overtly racist perspectives; racialised content still dominated the ideological perspectives of the education system. This must be understood in the light of apartheid philosophy that was meant to present everything white as a model, or an ideal to be pursued and emulated by blacks. In the heyday of apartheid in the 1970s and 1980s, black South Africans were cut off from the outside world and were not supposed to be exposed to any philosophy or influence other than that which promoted apartheid or portrayed whiteness as an ideal. The struggles of African Americans in the United States paralleled those of South Africans. The writings of Steve Biko[2] of South Africa and Malcolm X in the United States raised concerns about issues affecting black people on both sides of the Atlantic. However, there was a deliberate attempt by the apartheid state to make sure that these experiences were not shared so that they could feed off each other. In fact, a movie about Steve Biko, his life and philosophy, and the circumstances of his death was outlawed by the apartheid government and only shown after the formal end of apartheid policy.

With respect to apartheid policies, the marginalisation of black history involved not only African Americans in the United States but the liberation struggle and postindependence African history of the rest of the African continent. The rare African history content in the school syllabus featured African leaders who were used as puppets by their former colonial masters or who were in collusion with the apartheid regime in furthering those aims. For instance, in studying Zaire (now Democratic Republic of the Congo), students would learn about Mobuto Seseko, a collaborationist, but nothing about popular opposition leader Patrick Lobumba. In South African history, they would be taught about men such as Mangope, Matanzima, and Mphephu rather than liberation movement leaders such as Nelson Mandela and other current and past African National Congress (ANC), Pan Africanist Congress, and Black Consciousness Movement (BCM) leaders.

In apartheid schools, the content presented was primarily Eurocentric and Western in nature. The limited references made to black South Africans were stereotypical in nature and often portrayed black people in a negative way. For example, the South African history taught in primary and secondary schools begins with arrival of white people in South Africa in 1652. Despite the white colonialists having come from Europe with nothing but their five ships, they are generally portrayed in the history books as rich farmers with large tracts of land and herds of cattle. Black people who tried to repossess the cattle taken from them by the whites are portrayed as thieves. The history of the expansion of whites from the coast into the interior (called the Great Trek) presents white Afrikaner leaders as men of courage and perseverance who boldly crossed frontiers, while African leaders were portrayed as devious and uncivilized. All too often, Afrikaners were given credit for achievements that were not theirs and portrayed as civilizers of South Africa, while native (and black) South Africans were portrayed as barbarians (Schoor et al., 1981).

By the end of secondary school, black pupils' memories are of white heroics juxtaposed against black savages and their backwardness and uncivilized conduct. Reinforced by the state's electronic and print media, which portrayed liberation fighters such as Nelson Mandela as "terrorists" and the apartheid army as "security forces," the South African history taught in the schools had minimal positive depictions of black people. In addition, the state further reinforced its disdain for both black history and the use of texts authored by blacks by banning many of the texts that sought to challenge the apartheid regime. Some teachers were able to counter all this by using texts to "invert" their portrayals, so at least sometimes the stream of intended racial consciousness was sabotaged, using state-approved materials.

The representation of blacks in South African history to school children has parallels with Mamdani's (1998) characterisation of their representation in South African universities and colleges. He points out that the history is presented in most cases in a racialised way through the eyes and experiences of whites. In his critique of the content and structure of an African studies course taught at the University of Cape Town, he pointed out that historically

African Studies developed outside Africa, not within it. It is a study of Africa, but not by Africans. The context of this development was colonialism, the Cold War and apartheid. This period shaped the organisation of social science studies in the Western Academy. The key division was between the disciplines and area studies. The disciplines studied white experiences as universal, human experiences; area studies studied the experience of the people of color as ethnic experiences. (p. 1)

Mamdani's (1998) description of African studies also holds true for the history taught in South African schools. The divisions he outlines are common to South Africa's curriculum content, with its prescribed texts that address African history and the experiences of black people from a white perspective presented as universal truth. The focus of South African history and culture was on African ethnic differences and the "backwardness" of the latter, while the "white Christian civilization" was extolled. The negative portrayal of blacks and the celebration of whites in classrooms became a point of protest in a lecture hall at the University of Zululand[3] (South Africa) in the 1960s when one student vented his anger and frustration at the distortions in history taught there. The student complained, "We are tired of spending months tracing the origins of apartheid to the English to justify biases of Afri-

kaner lecturers; we want to learn about achievements of Africans"
(Nkomo, 1984, p. 74).

Celebrating Resistance

While the history of black people was excluded from the formal
curriculum or portrayed in a negative light when it was included, there
were extracurricular activities at black university campuses and schools
that aimed at undermining the apartheid system. The student movement in universities and schools served as important sources of political
education and was often more interesting than the dull content taught
in the lecture halls.

In the 1970s, South African students at primary and secondary
schools were organized under the auspices of the South African Student
Movement (SASM) and at university under the banner of the South
African Student Organisation (SASO) (Badat, 1999). These were all
aligned to the BCM led by Steven Biko and became one of the avenues
for resistance to the apartheid system in general, as well as an affirmation and celebration of black struggles and heroics. When the liberation
movement in Mozambique (northeast of South Africa) triumphed over
Portuguese colonialists in 1974, SASO at the University of the North
organized rallies to celebrate the attainment of freedom by the people
of Mozambique. The students saw this victory as an affirmation, in
political terms, of black consciousness and the confirmation of black
identity in the continent of their birth. The fact that these students were
able to identify with the victory of other Africans defeated the very
purpose—isolation—for which historically Black universities were created, as part of the divide and rule strategy of apartheid (known as
separate development) that was meant to foster allegiance to varied
racial and ethnic groups rather than promote solidarity across groups.
As another example of the effectiveness of the student movement,
secondary school students in Soweto, led by SASM, are credited with
having laid the foundation for the demise of apartheid when they led a
1976 march of over 10,000 students to protest the use of Afrikaans as
the compulsory language of instruction in schools.[4]

Afrikaans was seen as the language of the oppressor, and even
though there were other grievances against the apartheid system, the
move by the apartheid government to force this upon students sparked
violent protests throughout the country. The crisis of the 1976 uprisings
and the subsequent school boycotts of the 1980s focused attention on
youth and demonstrated the extent to which educational institutions
had become sites of struggle. As Kallaway (1984) argues, the very

institutions designed to propagate "education for domestication" turned out to be Trojan horses. He notes, "The upsurge of student power, probably without historical precedent, linked to heightened community consciousness and worker organization, accompanied by a new wave of armed incursions from the liberation movement, marked the beginning of a new era of resistance to apartheid" (p. 20). The government later retreated on its plans to force the use of Afrikaans as a medium of instruction. However, seeds of protests were already laid and the decade of the 1980s was characterized by school boycotts throughout the country, which later led to the unbanning of the liberation movement and the release of Nelson Mandela and other political prisoners in 1990.

Many African countries also played an important role in the struggle against apartheid. Countries like Tanzania not only donated land to house South Africans in exile, but also allowed for the establishment of schooling facilities for South African children in exile. Zambia housed the headquarters of ANC in its capital, Lusaka, and further made land available for the establishment of training camps for the liberation armies to fight the apartheid system. This is an important chapter in the history of education in South Africa *and* Africa that reflects both the role of African countries in shaping South Africa's history and our connectedness as African people, and it was not included in the curriculum of South African students.

Struggling With the Past Today

There is currently a concerted effort by the Department of Education to redress the imbalances of the past and to provide students with a holistic picture of the events of the past. The Outcomes Based Education paradigm is designed and presented as a pedagogical approach that will allow teachers and students to be creative and form their own opinions about the materials they have to deal with, rather than assume the role of passive learners as in the past. An attempt has been made to provide an unbiased view to students and to draw on the students' value system, while presenting the history in context.

The Values in Education Initiative (Working Group on Values in Education, 2000) was begun by the Department of Education to investigate appropriate values for South Africa to embrace in its primary and secondary educational institutions. Its findings and recommendations go a long way towards the redress of some of the distortions of the past. In its report entitled "Values, Education and Democracy," the working group makes a case for the use of the teaching of history and the presentation of the truth about human failures and achievements in schools to correct some of the distortions of the past. The recommendations seek to encourage openness, an understanding of our diverse histories, and a mutual grasp of and respect for cultural origin. The working group argues that more than any other discipline, put to good use and taught by imaginative teachers, history can promote reconciliation and reciprocal respect of a meaningful kind, because it encourages knowledge of the other, the unknown, and the different (p. 23). The Department of Education provides a broad list of prescribed learning materials that schools can select from. A panel of experts has been established to formulate this list, which is checked against a set of criteria based on the tenets outlined in the Constitution of the country, that is, race, gender bias, and equity.

But just as there are loopholes in the interpretation of policy, there are loopholes here as well. For example, some historically white schools still utilize a mathematics book featuring chapters written only by authors with a Eurocentric perspective, potentially creating the perception that the domain of mathematics resides in the Western world only. Many texts still retain the Eurocentric context in translation from English to African languages. The Department needs to look more closely at continuing imbalances and set conditions in which prescribed texts are more reflective and sensitive to race, avoiding unintended messages to students.

The redress of distortions of the past also finds expression through some new teacher education programmes that deal with issues of diversity and a more expanded range of materials and authors for classrooms. The Post Graduate Certificate in Education at the University of Pretoria is one example. One of its modules adopts an approach that is a move away from celebratory and assimilating approaches to one that interrogates power relations; that moves from a colourblind approach to one that validates the identity of each student. The class methodology is one of simulation and experiential learning. This approach provides students with experiences that reflect and validate their existence and provide them with an opportunity to learn about other cultures. The impact of these initiatives remains to be seen or tested on the ground.

So while Jansen's chapter correctly highlights the often unspoken ties of racial oppression as well as the strong bonds of racial solidarity in the struggle for freedom between the United States and South Africa, it would do well to recognize the deliberate strategy to undermine the struggle for freedom and self-determination by blacks in both countries, especially in the 1960s, and the potential power these ties would have had in being used to challenge the status quo. At the same time, resistance to systems of segregation and oppression on both sides of the Atlantic, leading to abolition of the system and subsequent reform initiatives, also need to be highlighted.

Indeed, in the late 1980s, South African civic organisations drew some lessons from the Civil Rights Movement in the United States in embarking on a campaign of civil disobedience that targeted segregated facilities such as trains, buses, churches, and beaches that were designated for whites only. There were also peaceful mass protests in various cities against the apartheid system and a call for the release of political prisoners and the unbanning of the liberation movement in the late 1980s. Acts of civil disobedience by black people in attending white churches, riding on trains designated for white people, and swimming on beaches reserved for whites were reported in the media during that period.

Opening the Box: Are the Goals of Desegregation Policies Realized in Schools?

This section argues that any response to education policies and laws aimed at redressing racial segregation and discrimination and fostering the attainment of equity and social justice should be based on what happens *within* desegregated schools. In this regard, the conduct of teachers and administrators and their responses to policy serve as a basis to judge the efficacy of these policies and judgments. In essence, educational policies and laws are put into action on the ground, inside local schools; therefore, the process of policy implementation in schools must be fully examined to determine the true impact.

Jim Crow and the Brown *Decision*

Jim Crow laws in the United States were designed, implemented, and upheld by local and state governments between the end of the Civil War and the 1950s. Since the *Brown* decision, however, laws, court rulings, and official policies of government—along with many heroic efforts by citizens—have eliminated the formal legal architecture of educational discrimination. In South Africa, racial discrimination in education was formalized in the schooling system with the passing of the Bantu Education Act in 1953. Thus when the *Brown* decision dismissed the notion of "separate and equal" in education, South Africa went in the opposite direction by embracing this principle. It was after four decades that South Africa, through the election of a new government in 1994, effectively abolished the principle of separate and unequal education by outlawing racial segregation in schooling.

Since the ending of legal racial segregation in education, both countries have embarked on various desegregation initiatives that are worth exploring in order to highlight common trends and differences. In the United States, desegregation took place through a combination of policy measures, including various court orders such as those mandating the busing of children from segregated schools and minority communities to white areas and schools. In South Africa, racial discrimination was outlawed in the new Constitution of 1996.

Given the statutory racism that has characterized these societies, racism that determined the residential areas people lived in and the kinds of facilities they could use, the end of legal discrimination did not result in an end to the practice of racial discrimination or segregation. In both societies, these practices were and continue to be perpetuated despite the written laws that suggest the contrary. However, since the laws that outlawed segregation, schools have now been desegregated. Students have been provided with the opportunity to be in close proximity to each other, but South African schools have not yet reached *integration* in terms of the qualitative changes in the ethos of the school and change in the curriculum, assessment practices, and school culture.

Experiences in desegregated schooling systems show that policies, laws, and court orders are not enough to achieve the intended goals of desegregation. Human agency is key, whether it results in either the realisation or the undermining of policy goals. In both societies, there is evidence of measures that are deliberately undertaken to undermine policy, and some of these take place within the schools. Fennimore (2005), for example, shows how racially discriminatory practices by school boards in some U.S. districts generate de facto resegregation. These practices include drawing school boundaries in ways that maximize racial homogeneity in schools; locating new schools in white suburbs rather than midway between black and white communities; permitting greater numbers of advanced placement courses to be offered in middle-class white schools; and allowing better qualified teachers unfettered freedom to move to schools with less challenging middle-class students.

Fennimore (2005) also analyzed emergent issues of discrimination, false meritocracy, and persistent inequity, arguing that classism combined with racism enabled school districts and privileged parents in two school districts in the United States to defend inequitable opportunities when they combined with the appearance of parental choice. She asserts that the development of selective choice programs, as opposed to efforts to enhance equity, allow for continued resistance to equal educational opportunity. Taking a historical perspective, she argues that it was only after *Brown I* and *II* (1955) and subsequent state legislation that educators and others were able to more fully identify and understand the subtle workings and interplay of prejudice, discrimination, and false meritocracy that fueled unequal treatment of students in school. This understanding came about because of the ways in which schools ultimately responded over time to the mandates of *Brown II* in 1955, which mandated that school districts proceed to implement school desegregation with "all deliberate speed."

As Fennimore (2005) shows, over time, many school districts took advantage of the vague language of desegregation orders and policies to resist implementation, in the process recreating stratification in new forms. The districts that resisted the implementation of equitable programs were often responding to demands of socially prominent citizens. She concluded that any racial differences in outcomes that can be traced to resegregation—differential access to better teachers, safer schools, and more rigorous academic climates—are evidence of racial discrimination by a school system.

The same forms of resistance through the distortion of policy were also displayed in South Africa with the manipulation of the South African Schools Act (1996), which gave powers to parents on school governing bodies to determine school policies. As Jansen notes in his chapter, the use of language policies and school fees resulted in the exclusion of blacks and poor people and contributed to the continued existence of exclusively white schools. In this context, multi-tiered school systems come to be seen as viable. Former Model C schools normally had powerful SGBs, enjoying professionals (lawyers, accountants, etc.) as members as well as enhanced financial resources.

What is of additional concern is that, in capitalist societies like South Africa and the United States, leaving the system (e.g., moving children to private schools) is an option that is only available to rich and influential people, not to the poor. The influence of powerful sectors of society in determining what is just is also revealed in the reluctance of the courts to intervene in cases where laws are being disobeyed, which tends to be explained in terms of "judicial restraint." Judicial restraint is often exercised in instances where the interests of dominant classes are not the interests being threatened.

The fact that schools are desegregated, or assumed to be, does not necessarily turn everyone into a nonracist or make them more capable of dealing with issues of diversity. There are often deeply entrenched racial stereotypes, symbolism, and practices that are displayed and perpetuated within the school. One good example is a case that made news in South Africa in late 2005. A white blond female student had braided her hair and come to school, and she was ordered by the school authorities to undo the hair. She was told that the school policy did not allow braiding, even though black pupils were allowed to braid their hair. In a similar case in a school in Pretoria, a white immigrant school girl from Ethiopia protested about discrimination when she, too, was not allowed to come to school with braided hair; again, black students in this school seemed exempt from such a rule. She inquired why the black pupils were not asked to remove the braids. The teacher answered, "Because they are Black and you are White." Inquiring further whether there were different school rules for white and black students, she was told, "Unfortunately you happen to be in South Africa . . . Blacks are Blacks and Whites are Whites. They will always be treated differently because they are different" (Phatlane, forthcoming).

This crude racialisation of student treatment obviously goes against the intended policy of desegregation and nonracialism. What it reveals is that racism is not something that one is born with; it is a social construct. In this case the internal workings of the school are such that they foster perceptions and social dispositions that promote racism. Sadly, the result is that a child could conceivably enter school without harbouring any racial stereotypes and leave the school having learnt them. What is evident is that despite the "formal" ending of racial discrimination in education, racial disparities still continue, regardless of the educational laws and policies that have been established to eradicate racism and oppression in school systems.

Conclusion

Jansen's chapter makes an important contribution to the body of literature on educational law and policy in highlighting the inadequacies of such interventions in addressing redress and social justice issues in education. It further makes an important contribution in encouraging writings in education and law to use or apply theory that might draw from the legal, social, political, or economic domains to offer explanations of why laws are not implemented as they ought to be or as they were intended to be. This critique was intended to highlight some strengths and weaknesses of Jansen's chapter with respect to aspects of education policy and law.

Indeed, there are ties that have historically bound the United States and South Africa together and still continue to do so today. This chapter has highlighted some of these ties—especially in terms of the patterns of resistance to segregationist school policies in the two systems.

What is the way forward? Should there continue to be different rules for the poor and the rich in societies where there is supposed to one law for everybody? Should there continue to be a dual system of education in both countries? It is worth reminding governments in both countries—governments which espouse democracy and the rule of law that promise social justice, equity, and equality during elections—that these promises need to be followed through in practice during the tenure in office. It is not impossible for some of these policies to be enforced.

As Orfield (2004) shows, following a decade of slow progress in the implementation of the *Brown* rule, especially with respect to desegregation, a concerted effort of the newly elected U.S. Congress in 1964 led to rapid change in the implementation of the *Brown* decision. The Southern states went from virtual apartheid to becoming one of the most integrated areas in the United States—in terms of schools—in just five years. In paying tribute to these changes, Orfield argues that it is clear that government determination can make a difference even in basic institutions in rigidly stratified societies with hostile leadership. The will to change is a critical component in making sure that laws are not only written and passed, but are truly instruments of justice as intended.

NOTES

1. Trankei is one of the areas proclaimed as an "independent homeland" to which Xhosa-speaking people in South Africa were restricted. There were four such homelands, part of the divide-and-conquer strategy of the apartheid government, in South Africa, the others being Bophutswana for Batswana, Venda for VaVhenda, and Ciskei for Xhosas. Note that the Xhosas were further divided among themselves into two "homelands."

2. Steve Biko was a BCM leader in South Africa who died in prison while being detained by the apartheid government.

3. This is one of the three black universities that were established following the passing of the Extension of University Education Act of 1959, which introduced racial segregation in higher education in South Africa.

4. In the South African context, ethnicity was a subdivision of race and was based on language group, for example, the University of Zululand (UNIZUL) was created for the Zulus; the University of the North (UNIN) for the Sotho, Venda, and Tsonga; and Fort Hare for the Xhosas. Between them they seek to promote ethnic distinction and pride.

REFERENCES

Arias, M.B. (2005). The impact of *Brown* on Latinos: A study of transformation of policy intentions. *Teachers College Record, 107*(9), 1974–1998.

Badat, S. (1999). *Black student politics, higher education and apartheid: From SASO to SANSCO, 1968–1999*. Pretoria, South Africa: Human Sciences Research Council.

Brown v. Board of Education, 347 U.S. 483. (1954).

Brown v. Board of Education, 349 U.S. 294. (1955).

Constitution of the Republic of South Africa Act, 1996. (1996). No. 108 of 1996.

Diaz v. San Jose Unified School District, 471 U.S. 1065. (1985).

Fennimore, B.S. (2005). *Brown* and the failure of civic responsibility. *Teachers College Record, 107*(9), 1905–1932.

Jansen, J.D. (2006). The ties that bind: Race and restitution in education law and policy in South Africa and the United States of America. In A. Ball (Ed.), *With more deliberate speed: Achieving equity and excellence in education—Realizing the full potential of* Brown v. Board of Education. *The 105th yearbook of the National Society for the Study of Education*, Part II (pp. 211–230). Malden, MA: Blackwell.

Kallaway, P. (1984). *Apartheid and education*. Johannesburg, South Africa: Ravan Press.

Kozol, J. (2005). *The shame of the nation: The restoration of apartheid schooling in America*. New York: Random House.

Mamdani, M. (1998). Teaching Africa at the post-apartheid University of Cape Town: A critical view of the "Introduction to Africa" core course in the Social Science and Humanities Faculty's foundation semester 1998. *Social Dynamics, 24*(2), 1–32.

Milliken v. Bradley, 418 U.S. 717. (1974).

Nkomo, M. (1984). *Student culture and activism in black South African universities: The roots of resistance*. Westport: Greenwood Press.

Orfield, G. (2004). The American experience: Desegregation, integration, resegregation. In M. Nkomo, C. McKinney, & L. Chisholm (Eds.), *Reflections on school integration* (pp. 95–124). Pretoria, South Africa: Human Sciences Research Council.

Orfield, G., & Eaton, S.E. (1996). *Dismantling desegregation: The quiet reversal of Brown v. Board of Education*. New York: New Press.

Orfield, G., & Lee, C. (2006). *Racial transformation and the changing nature of segregation*. Cambridge, MA: The Civil Rights Project, Harvard University.

Phatlane, R. (forthcoming). *The experience of diversity in desegregated schools in South Africa*. Doctoral dissertation in progress, University of Pretoria.

Pope, R.L. (1993). Multicultural-organization development in student affairs. *Journal of College Student Development, 34*(3), 201–205.

Sayed, Y. (2001). Post-apartheid educational transformation: Policy concerns and approaches. In Y. Sayed & J.D. Jansen (Eds.), *Implementing education policies: The South African experience*. Cape Town: University of Cape Town Press.

Schoor, M.C.E., Coetsee, A.G., Lambrechts, H.A., Oberhoster J.J., & Pienaar, K.J. (1981). *Senior History for South African Schools, Standard 9*. Goodwood: Nassou Limited.

Sehoole, M.T.C. (2005). *Democratizing higher education: Constraints of reform in post apartheid South Africa*. New York: Routledge.

Smith, A.N. (2004). *Separate is not equal: Brown v. Board of Education: A guide for study and discussion*. Smithsonian National Museum of American History. Retrieved March 13, 2006, from: http://americanhistory.si.edu/Brown/resources/pdfs/projectessay.pdf

South African Schools Act, 1996. (1996). No. 84 of 1996.

Sujee, M. (2004). Deracialisation of Gauteng schools: A quantitative analysis. In M. Nkomo, C. McKinney, & L. Chisholm (Eds.), *Reflections on school integration* (pp. 43–60). Pretoria, South Africa: Human Sciences Research Council.

Vally, S., & Dalamba, Y. (1999). *Racism, "racial integration," and desegregation in South African public secondary: A report on a study by the South African Human Rights Commission*. Johannesburg, South Africa: SAHRC.

Vandeyar, S., & Killen, R. (2006). Teacher-student interactions in desegregated class-rooms in South Africa. *International Journal of Educational Development*, *26*(4), 382–393.

Willie, C.V. (2005). *Brown v. Board of Education*: A restoration of equity in public education. In C. Russo, J. Beckmann, & J. Jansen (Eds.), *Equal educational opportu-nities: Comparative perspectives in education law*. Brown v. Board of Education *at 50 and democratic South Africa at 10* (pp. 77–88). Pretoria, South Africa: Van Schaiks Publishers.

Working Group on Values in Education. (2000). *Values, education and democracy—Report of the Working Group on Values in Education*. South African Government Information (May 9, 2000). Retrieved January 12, 2006, from http://www.info.gov.za/otherdocs/2000/education.htm

CHAPTER 13

Brown v. Board of Education: *A South African Perspective*

NEVILLE ALEXANDER

> State actions were highly consequential in shaping the template of
> modern race relations. Where and when states enacted formal rules
> of domination according to racial distinctions, racism was re-enforced.
> . . . Where racial domination was not encoded by the state, issues and
> conflicts over race were diluted. . . . (Marx, 1998, p. 267)

Although I knew very little about the details of *Brown v. Board of
Education* as a legal matter when I read about it as a young second-year
student at the University of Cape Town in 1954, the Court's verdict had
a direct influence on my political perspectives and on my aspirations as
a would-be teacher for the rest of my life. With rare exceptions, any
black university student in South Africa in the 1950s was a highly
conscious political being. In one way or another, s/he was inevitably
involved in what was ultimately the political struggle of resistance
against the racist policies and practices of the ever more self-confident
and aggressive apartheid ideologues and bureaucrats of that period.[1]

In 1953, I had joined the Teachers' League of South Africa (TLSA)
as a 17-year-old student associate. I was to receive my introduction to
the politics of the liberation movement by dint of participating in the
meetings and discussions and, above all, reading with great care the
literature of that unique organisation of dedicated professionals who,
in their own minds, constituted "the vanguard of the struggle."

The TLSA, as far as its specific political and professional concerns
went, was, like so many organisations in colonial and neocolonial con-

---

Neville Alexander is director of the PRAESA Project for the Study of Alternative
Education in South Africa at the University of Cape Town.
Portions of this chapter are based on an occasional paper published by PRAESA in
2004.

texts, lamentably parochial. However, it was led for some three decades by men and women—some of whom had studied in Europe for short periods—who, because of their paranoically masked Marxist, indeed Trotskyist, leanings, were intent on being all the more visibly "internationalist," that is, cosmopolitan. As a consequence, its members were regularly regaled with copious references to international, especially European, events and literature. This had a magical impact on the readership and membership of the organisation, as it projected onto our unschooled minds a kind of Vygotskyan zone of proximal development, an aspirational space, which was electrifying as a source of motivation. In any event, it was in this context that I read about and came to discuss the implications of the famous case. The killing off by judicial fiat of the myth of "separate but equal," which was, rhetorically, the raison d'être of the policy of apartheid, was for black South Africans (we called ourselves "Non-Europeans" in those days) akin to a ritual of profound emotional and spiritual significance.

Coming as it did at the very moment when the notorious Bantu Education Act[2] was first being implemented, the judgement in *Brown* armed the opponents of this legislation with additional weaponry, that, derived as it was from the leader of the "free world," was all the more potent. South African liberals had a field day in attacking the evidently stone-deaf neo-Nazi apartheid regime from the position of the moral high ground. Left-wing opponents of the regime, such as the members of the TLSA, had a more ambivalent position since in their view, slanted by both a class struggle as well as an anti-Western angle of vision, it was always advisable to examine carefully any gifts borne by the ruling class of the United States. Even though we were stridently anti-Stalinist and consistently critical of the authoritarian and tyrannical rule of the Communist Party of the Soviet Union, we were even more ardently and implacably opposed to the enticements of what to us was the imperialism of the West. In reflecting on the dynamics of that period, I find that we were decidedly myopic in not making much more of the political propaganda value of the Court's judgement. However, living as we did in one of the most oppressive and racist states in the world at the time, I understand why we were not, as it were, overwhelmed by what to us was the obvious. In the throes of a life-and-death struggle, mere constitutionalism or legalism, useful and necessary as it is, is certainly not enough. Twenty years after the Court's ruling, a pseudonymous writer in *The Educational Journal*, the organ of the TLSA, lauded *Brown's* historic significance and summed up our evaluation of the Court's judgement as follows:

It is seldom appreciated or recognised that *Brown* came out of a particularly structured society at a particular time; it came from a Supreme Court which, like the schools it made a decision about, was and is an inseparable part of that society, reflecting and interpreting its changing needs and policies and Administrations. To start with an illusion that the U.S. Supreme Court could fundamentally alter the U.S. school system, because of an ikon [sic] called the Bill of Rights, is to end up with a delusion that it can eliminate the vested economic, political and social inequalities in American society generally. (Titus, 1974, p. 7)

From Brown *to* Bakke

So much for what are, I hope, relevant reminiscences. Four years after the above-mentioned celebratory but critical article appeared, the same author penned a piece under the title I use above as a subheading. Its import is obvious to those who have followed the attempts in the United States to work out in practical terms the implications of the *Brown* decision. Titus (1978) reminds us sarcastically that with reference to the Court's injunction that the Board of Education of Topeka and, by extension, all other segregationist school authorities had to "make a prompt and reasonable start toward full compliance ... (and to proceed) with all deliberate speed" to admit children to school on a nondiscriminatory basis, the phrase "with all deliberate speed" had come to be equated with "any perceptive[3] movement" (p. 6). The resultant frustration and disillusionment among black people and other minorities in the United States were among the elements that later fuelled the dissatisfaction and the militancy that flared up in the form of the Civil Rights Movement and its various spin-offs. Titus correctly demonstrates how President John F. Kennedy's administration proactively introduced the first affirmative action measures with a view, among other things, to heading off precisely this militancy.[4]

In this chapter I am not, however, going to discuss the dynamics of affirmative action in the United States, or even go into the debates concerning this agonising issue in any detail (see Cose, 1998, for the most readable discussion). My focus is unerringly on recent developments in South Africa, where we are in certain respects going through a replay of what happened in the United States from the 1950s to the 1980s. Specifically, I pose the question: how optimistic can we be that

[though] ... minor disturbances had broken out at schools across the country, when contrasted with America's decades-long struggle for desegregation that spilled blood in cities across the nation, South Africa's experiment with equality in the schools was proceeding swimmingly. (Cose, p. 69)

And I go on to consider the deeper implications for the shaping of social identities and for the cohesion of the society inherent in the implementation of an affirmative action strategy under the social and historical conditions obtaining in post-apartheid South Africa.

The argument of this chapter rests on two theoretical propositions and is driven by a specific political objective. I take it as my point of departure to be a fact that despite the tenacity of social identities, they are historical phenomena and, thus, changeable, always changing, and at bottom fluid. I also take it for granted that prejudice and discrimination, viewed as collective behaviour, can only be changed fundamentally if social policy is approached in a holistic manner, that is, if the material bases on which they thrive are considered to be necessary components of that which has to be changed. Ultimately, it is my view that in the South African context, the promotion or entrenchment of racial identities for the supposed purpose of redress holds within it the danger of genocidal conflict.

Limits of Comparative Studies

South Africans, of course, have learned from the experience of the United States. However, some of the trajectories we are being made to follow are eerily similar to those which the people of America have, in the best cases, already left behind or, in the worst cases, appear to have got stuck in. I am particularly concerned about the unproblematic manner in which the discourse of affirmative action in the United States is replicated in the completely different historical and social context of what we sometimes call the New South Africa. For while it is perfectly true to maintain that "the uniqueness of a political culture can only be understood in comparison with similar situations elsewhere" (Adam, Slabbert, & Moodley, 1997, p. 8), it does not follow at all that the conceptual and discursive tools one uses to draw the comparison are totally symmetrical. Or to put it differently, what is unique is by definition not comparable. In the present case, apart from the different historical trajectories, there is one fundamental point of difference which gives rise to two completely different social dynamics in the respective countries. While it may be a trite observation, it seems to me essential that we bear in mind that in the case of the United States, we are dealing with a situation in which black people are a minority in both the numerical and the social senses of the term, whereas in South Africa, we have a newly enfranchised black majority imbued, generally speaking, with a historically evolved ethos of humanistic tolerance ("ubuntu") and a keen desire for inclusive national, indeed continental, unity. This difference is, as I have said, vitally important precisely because of the fact that the state has what I call the paradigmatic prerogative to establish and impose the "template" which Marx (1998) refers to in the epigraph to this chapter. The fact that the current South African government is exercising this prerogative in a manner that I believe could easily boomerang on the next generations is a matter of grave concern.

Let us dwell on this difference between the national templates for a few more sentences. In the United States, after the assimilationist melting pot discourse made way for the pluralist or multicultural discourse of the mosaic or salad bowl, roughly during the 1960s, a distinctive ethnic paradigm has systematically and decisively informed all decisions pertaining to intergroup relations. While it is a fact that African Americans never even made it into the melting pot (as James Baldwin acidly observed), on the surface, in the current hegemonic discourse of hyphenated citizenship, all appear to be equal and operating on the proverbial level playing field because race and ethnicity have been conflated. I must confess that the taken-for-grantedness of this ethnic frame of reference never ceases to amaze and at the same time alienate me. This is undoubtedly the consequence of the undiminished radical fervour with which I believe that racial identities can and should be deconstructed. Our South African experience warns me that a social construct based on supposed biological, and for most people intellectual, difference, is more dangerous than any other marker of social difference. And, unsurprisingly, many U.S. intellectuals share the same sense of unease at the thought that "race" and racial prejudice may be with us forever. Ellis Cose (1998), for example, writes:

(Racial) color-blindness is a fantasy, something that exists only in the unreal world of the imagination. . . . [Certainly] at this moment, one would be hard pressed to dispute the point. Yet the goal of race neutrality is one we cannot afford to abandon—not if we believe that America can achieve its potential, not if we wish to keep alive faith in the triumph of good ideas over bad. (p. 244)

In every society tainted by racist policies and practices, the approaches to eliminating racism will necessarily be different. That much is indisputable. Comparative studies help us to identify those areas that require special care and attention and also to anticipate problems and avoid unnecessary dilemmas (Frederickson, 2001).

Because of the general character of this proposition, it is essential that I point to the equation of "race" and gender as biologically based markers of difference. I believe that this is a discussion that is still in its infancy but will not canvass it here. Suffice it to say that the actual dynamics of race—as opposed to gender-related struggles against oppression and exploitation—are very different in pivotal respects. Consequently, it is a mistake to mechanically read off tactics and strategy deriving from one domain of struggle for purposes of applying them to the other.

The experience of the United States since the *Brown* decision 50 years ago represents an entire archive from which postapartheid South Africa can learn a great deal if we study it carefully. However, we can also choose to ignore or, worse, misread these lessons, and as a result find ourselves repeating history and wasting another two generations as we did, perforce, during the 45 years of apartheid rule.

The Role of the State in the Evolution of Racial Identities

From among the host of relevant issues, I shall foreground for discussion only three matters of paramount concern, especially to the current and the next generation of South Africans. These are: the role of the state in the formation of racial identities; the best approaches to redressing the imbalances inherited from the apartheid-colonial past; and the modalities of the realisation of a nonracial educational system.

I begin by taking it as a given that in the first decade of the 21st century any lingering belief in "race" as a valid biological entity is anachronistic. Similarly, there ought to be no reason to debate the social reality of "race." These are matters on which scholarly consensus can be said to have been reached even though there are many different theories about why these propositions are valid.[5]

The bibliography on the formation of racial identities, viewed as a subset of social identities, is a very long one (see, e.g., Balibar & Wallerstein, 1991; Hamilton et al., 2001; Marx, 1998; Reisigl & Wodak, 2000). However, the crucial issue I want to focus on is the fact that in modern times, it is the state that possesses the paradigmatic prerogative, in that social identities are inscribed, as it were, in the hegemonic discourse of those who wield economic, political, military, and symbolic power. This is not to deny the equally demonstrated fact that the subaltern groups codetermine the set of social or collective identities that eventually come to characterise the particular social formation. They do so by contesting, rejecting, or assuming (accepting) the "prescribed" identities.[6] Often, they also initiate such identities through self-labeling. Such labels, in turn, are sometimes "accepted" and per-petuated by the dominant strata, if they are deemed to reinforce the promotion of the vested or perceived interests of these strata. In the final analysis, it is the state, by virtue of its monopoly on the deployment of legitimate force, that imposes or reinforces the identities that crystallise over time.

The modalities and technology of racial classification by the state are demonstrated most clearly in the early history of apartheid. One of the few scholars who has made a detailed study of these processes concludes that

> The architects of apartheid racial classification policies recognized explicitly that racial categories were constructs, rather than descriptions of essences. (Posel, 2001a, p. 109)

She teases out the almost caricatural irony: that precisely because of the life-and-death seriousness with which the apartheid strategists and ideologues viewed the issue of "race," their attention to detail brought them face-to-face with the anomalies and idiosyncrasies of racial identities. She also traces the real trajectories by which these nefarious and totally fantasised notions became internalised to a large extent among the vast majority of the people of the country.

> If constructs, these categories were powerfully rooted in the materiality of everyday life. The ubiquity of the state's racial designations, and the extent to which they meshed with lived hierarchies of class and status, meant that apartheid's racial grid was strongly imprinted in the subjective experience of race. . . . [It] would be difficult to deny the extent to which the demarcation of South African society into whites, Indians, coloureds, and Africans has been normalized—for many a "fact" of life. (Posel, 2001a, p. 109)

Given that social identities are historical, not primordial, phenomena, the proposition that the state or, less globally, the ruling elites, have the power to create the "template" from which such identities are derived and shaped over time devolves a heavy responsibility on those who are placed in charge of overseeing the evolution of a new historical community in a distinctively transitional and, indeed, transformational period. To take the attitude that the question of social identities is best left alone or, worse, that the inherited identities should be allowed to perpetuate themselves, is to abdicate the responsibility of leadership and to commit oneself to maintaining the old order in all but name.

The Cuban Experience

Social revolutions are by definition periods of radical transformation in all or most aspects of a society. A glance at what happened in

Cuba after the 1959 revolution should, therefore, give us useful pointers to what is possible, on the assumption that one of the most fundamental objectives of the revolutionary leadership was the eradication of
racism and racist attitudes and behaviour. Cuba has a special significance for South Africans and Namibians because of the unwavering
support the revolutionary government gave to their respective struggles for national and social liberation. Despite foreign policy differences, there continues to be a special relationship between the African
National Congress (ANC)-led government of South Africa and the
government of Cuba.

With reference to the role of the state in the pre-1959 republican
period of modern Cuban history, de la Fuente (2001), in his authoritative and exhaustive study of this question, states that

[more] often than not . . . it is the failure of the government to act that has
contributed the most to the continuing significance of race in Cuban society.
The state's limited intervention in "private" social spaces has meant that
racism has been allowed to operate virtually unhindered in this sphere.
(p. 336)

After 1959, there was a concerted effort "to socialize younger generations in a new egalitarian and color-blind social ethic" (p. 337). De la
Fuente provides an account of the advances the Cuban revolution made
in this respect and, in his own words, concludes that "(the) impact of
this radical program of social engineering should not be underesti-
mated" (p. 337).

On the other hand, he points to the "paradoxes" that emerged in
the process. In particular, he is critical of the way in which the colour-
blind ethos invisibilised "race" and thereby rendered it difficult and
even impossible to track positive (or negative) change or to launch
serious public discussions of the issue.

Thus the ultimate irony is that the same government that did the most to
eliminate racism also did the most to silence discussion about its persistence.
(de la Fuente, 2001, p. 338)

Despite its antidiscriminatory position and egalitarian social policies, the revolutionary government failed to create the color-blind society it envisioned in
the early 1960s (de la Fuente, 2001, p. 322)

These conclusions have a salutary ring for even the most starry-
eyed South African optimist with regard to strategies calculated to

eliminate racism and racial prejudice. For, if in a society that had undergone such a profound social transformation as postrevolutionary Cuba, racial prejudice has not been eliminated after 45 years; and, worse still, if under conditions of the remarketisation of large sectors of the post-Wall Cuban economy even exploitative racist labour practices are becoming "normal" again, it is self-evident that in postapartheid South Africa, where no such social revolution has taken place, we are faced with an inordinately more complex and difficult challenge.

That the attenuation and eventually the elimination of racial prejudice and discrimination will take many decades is almost self-evident. However, what the Cuban experience underlines is that the state has ample room for creating conditions in which the salience of "race" and the rigidity of racially defined identities can be reduced and gradually changed in a more positive direction. It also raises the very difficult question, in the context of postapartheid South Africa, of how "formerly excluded communities [can] be recognised without perpetuating apartheid categorisations" (Abebe, 2001, p. 2). Franklin (1993) reminds us of the real challenge we face on the ground. With reference to the United States, he writes that

African-American biological features, when associated with class and cultural differences, are more indissoluble than ethnic differences in the absence of biological ones. Race ideology as it applies to African-Americans . . . is ever-present and "helps insiders make sense of the things they do and see—ritually, repetitively—on a daily basis" . . . Race thinking and interpretations of events, even when incorrect, provide coherence to both whites and blacks, albeit for different reasons. . . . *Breaking away from the perennial patterns of activity is a necessary precondition to eliminating the ideological categories that explain and justify the animosities embedded in everyday practices.* (p. xxiii, emphasis added)

I shall address this issue in the final paragraphs of this chapter. For the moment, however, it is necessary to underline two related questions that I believe require of us an unequivocal commitment, especially in South Africa where a new historical community is coming into being. The first of these is the fact that social identities, again, are inherently unstable and malleable within definite but generally unknown limits. Today, in the social laboratory of postapartheid South Africa, we are able to observe firsthand the remaking of apparently immutable social identities. Fascinating debates are being conducted in the media, in learned journals, in lecture halls, in churches, and among families and communities about what it means to be an "African" or an "Afrikaner," among others. These debates are, of course, the result of the peculiarities of South African history; they are nonetheless of universal relevance. When the lyrical words of the then deputy-president of the country in a speech that began "I am an African" gave rise to a wave of euphoria in a country that until that moment in 1996 had been divided along lines of "race," we can be sure that we are witnessing a shift to a totally different conceptual universe from the previous racially defined one. Conversely, the unraveling of the supposedly immutable identity of the "Afrikaner" can be followed in the courageous prose of the historian, Hermann Giliomee (2003), in the last chapter of his "biography" of his people. Both of these examples demonstrate the real possibility of moving away from a racial and ethnic social grid towards a more inclusive and continuous, multicultural understanding of difference and variation.

There is, to put it differently, no barrier in principle to any attempt to create conditions in a conscious and planned manner that will facilitate the strengthening of certain kinds of social categories rather than others. This obviously raises a range of ethical questions connected with the notion of social engineering. In my view, all governments are involved in social engineering to some degree or another at all times. The real issue is to ensure that through open, democratic debate in the media and in other civil society forums, an authoritarian political culture does not become the norm. The second issue, also touched on earlier, is whether or not a raceless society is possible or even desirable. Cose (1998) puts the crucial question in the following terms:

> whether it is possible to divorce any system of racial classification from the practice of racial discrimination, whether a nation splintered along racial lines—a nation that feels compelled to rank people on the basis of race (aesthetically; professionally; socially; and, most insistently, intellectually)—is capable of changing that propensity any time soon. (p. 26)

In the South African debate, the one side of the argument is put very clearly and firmly by, among others, Abebe (2001; see also Greenstein, 1993, and O'Malley, 1994), who argues that the majority of South Africans place much greater weight on their "primary" identity, determined by "race" or "ethnic group," than on the national (South African) identity:

> To deny this is to repeat the common mistake, especially on the part of the Left, to underestimate the ontological commitments to racial and ethnic identities and their role in shaping historical struggles. (p.14)

As against this, on the side of the so-called Left, we have to record increasing ambivalence. As the ANC-led government's vulnerability to a social paradigm that incorporates the continuation of the notion of racial identities takes ever firmer hold on the consciousness of the population, reinforced by the cynical, profit-oriented, and consumerist practices of the establishment media, ever fewer people are willing to speak up for the possibility of that different world: the raceless and, let it not be forgotten, the *classless*, society that was the lodestar of the liberation struggle. However, it is important to remember that South Africans are, in this respect, as in most others, no different from people throughout the rest of the world. People act and interact with one another in terms of the primacy of whatever subnational identities seem relevant to them, for the simple reason that, with very few exceptions (in the case of the countries of the economic South of the globe), they never have occasion to contrast their "national" identities. Despite mass tourism, it remains true that only a very small percentage of people actually interact on a regular basis with foreigners. Exceptions occur on a large scale in the sphere of mass competitive sports codes (such as football) where national chauvinism of a more or less dangerous kind rules supreme. The post-World War II migrant-worker phenomenon, prevalent mainly in the economic north of the globe, is another sphere in which the worst side of "national" identities become manifest.

Despite the practical complexities involved in the analysis of social or collective identities, I continue to take as my compass the views elaborated by Balibar and Wallerstein (1991) in their seminal study, in which they assert that all social identities are "historical constructs" that are "perpetually undergoing reconstruction." In recent years, because of the hegemony of "race thinking" in the "new" South Africa, I have become more conscious of the significance of the caveat they added at the time:

That is not to say they are not solid or meaningful or that we think them ephemeral. Far from it! But these values, loyalties, identities are never primordial and, that being the case, any historical description of their structure or their development through the centuries is necessarily primarily a reflection of present-day ideology. (p. 228)

The Affirmative Action Conundrum

The strategies of the postapartheid governments to achieve "historical redress," variously referred to as affirmative action, levelling the playing fields, redressing the imbalances of the past, corrective action, and other such elegant variations, are restricted by as many material as ideological constraints. The dilemma of the South African government, which was placed in office as the result of a decade of recurring waves of mass mobilisation for fundamental social transformation during the 1980s, derives from the fact that there was no *social* revolution. The political revolution or "regime change" that took place means that constitutional and peaceful processes to effect a gradual transfer of power to, and a redistribution of resources in favour of, "the people" it represents must be initiated. Power is instantiated in many different guises in any given society. However, in a modern industrial state, control of the armed forces and the capacity to create employment and wealth are the critical loci of such power. In the compromise that gave birth to the new South Africa, one of the crucial elements was the agreement to integrate the armed units of the previous regime and of the liberation organisations. This latter process has been taking place in a manner that can only be described as the *absorption* of the former guerrilla combatants by the standing army of the apartheid regime, despite all the outward trappings of a different entity. The relevance of this observation is to be found in the fact that it is this new South African National Defence Force that is the ultimate custodian of the Constitution, as much devoted to upholding the continuity of the capitalist state, stripped of its apartheid trappings, as it is, for symbolic purposes, to highlighting from time to time the discontinuity between the postapartheid and the apartheid dispensations. The cohesion of the state and the society as well as the guarantee of normality that comes from a working economic system are the essential elements that have to be defended by the integrated Defence Force.

Symbolic power, it can be said, is almost completely under the control of the leadership of the ANC and its allies. Those who control military and economic power have, by and large, come to terms with this fact. In the present context, it is pertinent to point out that the very same individuals who were financing the divisive "multinational," that is, racist, policies of the Afrikaner National Party are today financing the "nonracial," nation-building strategy of the ANC!

In the context of the "negotiated revolution" or of a "regime change," it is obvious that if there were to be any sudden or rapid redistribution of economic resources (wealth), the confidence of property owners and especially of investors in the stability and sustainability of the new dispensation would vanish overnight. The consequences of such a development are, in the hackneyed phrase eternalised by John

Vorster, too ghastly to contemplate. For this reason, affirmative action programmes similar to those undertaken in the United States have come to be the preferred mode of "leveling the playing field." With the exception of a fringe group of irredentist Afrikaner ("Boer") racists, there is not much disagreement among most South Africans that historical redress is essential if peace and progress are to prevail. How, and how rapidly this process should happen, remains a national bone of contention.

Four anchor laws have been passed in order to effect gradual change in favour of those who have been incongruously labeled "the *previously* disadvantaged.*" These are the Employment Equity Bill (1997), the Public Service Laws Amendment Act of 1997, the Skills Development Act (1998), and the Skills Development Levy Act (1999).[7] In a nutshell, these laws are calculated to make all workplaces and all state or state-aided institutions representative of the "demographics" of the country, that is, to ensure racial proportionality. The relevant "races" are exactly the same four categories entrenched during the 40 lost years of apartheid, namely, so-called Africans, whites, coloureds, and Indians. The rationale for this approach is, quite simply, that we must use the same categories that once fostered differential treatment in order to both determine the quanta of preference that will incrementally reduce the supposed handicaps (or head starts) of the different groups and at the same time also enable us to "measure" the fact and the rate of change that it is assumed will be effected by these means. In Posel's (2001b) elegant turn of phrase: "(previously) the locus of privilege, now race has become the site of redress" (p. 17).

This is not the place to discuss the effectiveness or even the overall desirability of the specific strategy adopted by the ANC-led government to ensure the redistribution and the augmentation of economic resources, knowledge, and skills. Suffice it to say that this discussion is the very stuff of parliamentary politics in South Africa today and although it is my opinion that we have here the typical emission of much sound and even more fury—both of which signify nothing—it is precisely these theatricals that ought to convince us that South Africa has become what I have dubbed "an ordinary country" (Alexander, 2002). My concern is rather with the formation and entrenchment of racialised identities in a situation and in a period where this eventuality might be avoided. Posel (2001a, 2001b) and Maré (2001), among others,[8] have spelled out in some detail the paradoxes and the possible unintended consequences inherent in the application of this particular approach to historical redress.

The issues that arise are obvious to all but those who will not see. Let us, by way of example, consider the (deliberate?) confusion emanating from one of the most high-profile government bureaucrats and ANC leaders. In an article written in the context of a debate on whether South Africa's "transition to democracy" can be said to have come to an end after only 10 years, Morobe (2004) comes down firmly on the side of an indefinite process of change for the better. With regard to the question of identity, he opines, in a revealing mixture of metaphors, pathos, and bathos, that

The legacy of apartheid is deeply embedded in everybody's subconscious, and we must draw it out, bring it out of the closet, deprive it of its subliminal abodes. Here I hasten to make a distinction between racial awareness (and embracing of difference) and racism (the use of racial categories as a basis for discrimination). I recognise the need for and urgency of a variety of interventions—quotas, empowerment targets and affirmative action. But these are much easier to achieve than undermining the psycho-social manifestations of racial typecasting. . . . Those born since the birth of true democracy in this country must be saved from the racist psychosis in which apartheid justifies all manner of self-interest. . . . [It] is not our generation that will enjoy a truly non-racial society.

This apparent unawareness of the implications of continuing the racial typecasting of apartheid's grey men in order to eliminate "racism" is reminiscent of the cavalier approach to the AIDS pandemic displayed by some of the leaders of the ANC. For, from the point of view of the civil service (and even of large civil-society organisations), the question "Who does the racial identification?" obtrudes itself. As Posel (2001b) points out,

Implementing the Employment Equity Act, along with other more informal strategies of redress informed by the same racial logic, presupposes the capacity to distinguish, once again, between "Africans," "Indians," "Coloureds," and "whites." (p. 18)

And Maré (2001) describes the Orwellian universe of mundane but nonetheless humiliating procedures that universities, among other parastatal institutions, are compelled to follow in order to discover whether they are approaching the optimal "demographic" proportions with respect to their student, academic, and service staff complements. As one who has refused to submit to such legally required racial self-identification and stereotyping, I know exactly what Maré means when he refers to the banality of the fact that

To meet with the requirements of the Employment Equity Act, to gain admission or be refused permission to Universities, to claim travel allowances, to play in sports teams . . . each requires a statement of race belonging. There is no opportunity in these forms to avoid the issue. At every level there is an official, from the government minister . . . to the company personnel officer or employment equity manager, to monitor adherence or compliance or progress. No provision is made for alternatives to the basic "four races"[9] of apartheid South Africa, or to reject such classification . . . Where race is "legally" . . . required and it has not been provided, citizens are allocated to a category by line managers or human resources personnel. (p. 17)

This unthinking (?) continuation of apartheid-style racial categorisation, allegedly to get beyond apartheid and even beyond racism, is all the more reprehensible in the context of "postapartheid" South Africa, because there are very obvious and completely feasible alternatives. What is required is attention to detail in specific domains of life and a national commitment to redress all disadvantage at all levels of the society, regardless of colour, creed, or gender. This would mean, for example, a principled decision to problematise all racial categories and prioritising class as a measure of disadvantage.[10] There are many ways of doing so but a simple example will suffice.

On the assumption that there is an actual reason for doing so, anyone who would have been older than 16 years in 1994 could be required to say how s/he was classified racially under the apartheid system. Anyone younger than that could be asked to indicate, if s/he knew, how one or the other of her/his parents had been classified at the time. Or, to take another obvious example: In the civil service or in any relevant private-sector situation where knowledge of an African language is already or will become an increasingly important skill, by virtue of the coincidence of home language and apartheid racial classification, more emphasis on linguistic skills would provide an organic self-correcting mechanism. This would, moreover, provide the incentive to Afrikaans- and English-speaking South Africans themselves to learn and to encourage their children to learn one of the indigenous African languages. This materially based practice of prioritising multilingualism, in turn, would constitute one of the main pillars on which cultural and symbolic unity will be based in the future.

A further issue of principle, certainly for the next decade or so, would require a clear commitment to prioritising a massive training programme as opposed to a token "representivity." Of course, we should not underestimate the importance of changing managerial and administrative frontline staff in terms of the genuinely inspiring dimension of social transformation. However, this should never become a practice of merely "putting black faces in white places." Frontline people should not simply represent African masks worn by unreconstructed apartheid apparatchiki. The very jobs will have to be reconceptualised in terms of a more authentic African clientele and an African reality, at the beginning of the 21st century, that takes into consideration, for instance, the primacy of oral media. This must happen without letting up on the expansion and deepening of literacy, especially in the African languages themselves; a multilingual as opposed to a monolingual habitus, cooperative forms of action as opposed to the universally assumed instinct towards individual aggrandizement and gratification, and so forth. But, as long as jobs continue to be formulated only in terms of the inherited qualities and functions, it is axiomatic that the most likely people to fit the profile are English- and/or Afrikaans-speaking males. To move away from this, clusters of jobs should be advertised such that, for example, a trainer is appointed together with two juniors or apprentices and part of his/her job description would be the requirement that s/he train the other members of the team over a 3- to 5-year period to become fully competent in the job.

Back to School Integration

In a recent radio panel on the subject of school integration after "10 years of democracy," one of the panelists appealed to South Africans to stop believing that "education can carry the entire burden of transformation," a point that brings us back to where we started and to the implications of *Brown*.

At the important National Conference on Racial Integration and Racism in Schools, convened in Randburg, Gauteng province, on March 4–6, 1999, a formal statement that summarised the report of a research team appointed by South Africa's Human Rights Commission to investigate the state of racial inequity in the schools was issued. The report was extremely critical of the performance of the central as well as of the provincial departments of education. Among other things, the research team slated the department(s) for their

failure to understand the complex manifestations of racism [which] has resulted in the absence of a systematic programme of transformation of the learning and teaching spaces and the elimination of all forms of racism and racial discrimination. (Vally & Dalamba, 2002, p. 53)

Coming as it did, only 5 years after the formal introduction of the new system, this was unquestionably a harsh judgement. Space does not permit analysis of the contradictions, tensions, ineptitude, and down-right sabotage with which the Department of Education was confronted in the first few years of attempting to establish a formally integrated system of school and higher education. A complicating issue was the fact that in the first years of the new dispensation, very few analysts made the distinction between "desegregation" and "integration." While the repeal of racially discriminatory legislation and official practices was, if not straightforward, overtly obvious and verifiable, getting school communities (parents, teachers, and students) to implement the evolving new curriculum consensually—which is what "integration" translates into on the ground and especially at the chalk face—was and remains a very different order of challenge.[11]

Five years later, on the eve of the celebration of "10 years of democracy," Salim Vally of the Education Policy Unit of the University of the Witwatersrand in Johannesburg, one of the authors of this report, told the *Sunday Independent* newspaper in an interview that

the country is as divided as before. . . . He . . . [said] racism is as rife at an individual level and heavily entrenched in democratic South Africa at an institutional level. Schools and tertiary education providers had done little to promote integration, although they had become desegregated. (Naidu, 2003, p. 7)

Vally went on to lambaste government for not even attempting to implement some of the central "concrete, low-cost initiatives" recommended by the conference five years earlier and referred to the relevant legislation and regulations as "fairy-tale laws." While conceding that some units in the Department of Education were making ad hoc attempts to deal with the question of racial prejudice in schools, he insisted that there was an absence of any systematic, long-term approach and that

eliminating racism requires restructuring power relationships in the economic, political and cultural institutions of society and creating new conditions for interpersonal interactions. (Naidu, 2003, p. 7)

What could "integration" mean in the South African context? In my view, quite apart from any generic meaning the term might have, the demographic reality of the country is such that deracialisation of public institutions must imply and make possible the attainment of equity in all domains, that is, the possibility of comparable life chances. "Race" or colour, like gender or disability, is only one of a range of markers of difference on which discrimination and marginalisation can be, and usually is, based. This is another way of saying that deracialisation under the prevalent conditions is not primarily concerned with "integration" or even "assimilation," whatever that might mean. These are questions that have to be left to the organic processes of social evolution which, let it be said, include contestation and conflict. In this connection, it is useful to refer to the bitter experience of the United States where people have learned, after 5 decades of "integration," that

desegregation is not the same as integration; . . . black students don't necessarily achieve more in integrated environments than in largely black environments; . . . [and] the mixing of black children and white children, in and of itself, does not automatically reduce prejudice or black students' sense of academic and social inferiority. (Cose, 1998, p. 72)

By way of a final statement on this central question of school integration, I want to state simply and clearly that in South Africa, the centuries of colonialism and segregation capped by the 45 years of formal apartheid have culminated in a racial-caste system at the socio-cultural level of analysis. This system, regardless of the underlying economic system and power relations, will take decades—if we are to be optimistic in our prognostications—to dismantle and even longer to be displaced by a system of social relations in which "race" will no longer be significant in any social domain. In the educational domain, there are certain technical moves that will facilitate these developments in the short to medium term. One of the most important of these, whatever our professional reservations and critique may be, has already been instituted. I refer to the new curriculum,[12] which, theoretically and as far as the administrative capacity of the Department of Education can guarantee, is consistently nonracial.

The Colour-Coding of Wealth

In conclusion, in respect to the central question of this chapter, that is, the making and unmaking of racial identities, there is a ray of hope that has begun to light up a sky that otherwise seems only to be full of foreboding.[13] In an ironic twist, what I refer to as the colour-coding of wealth by working-class people in the townships of South Africa may be heralding the end of racial identities in the usual biological sense there. This is the opposite of the well-established practice of referring to certain types of work as "black," regardless of the colour of the person so occupied. The "social blackness" of prostitution or of drug dealing as an occupation, for example, is embedded in the subconscious of most people in South Africa.

I have myself observed and often hear others confirm that it is becoming customary to refer to wealthy middle-class black people, especially those who move around in flashy motor cars, as "umlungu"[14] or some other variant of the word that means "white man" or "white woman." This could, and probably does, mean that biologically based racial identities are viewed as rooted in a past where only "white" people were wealthy. This transposition of "class" onto "race" on the ground, as it were, is the final, if paradoxical, vindication of those of us who, like Posel (1983), believe that both class- and race-reductionism are analytical dead-ends and that

what is fundamental and distinctive about the South African case is the *unity* of class and race as the source of structural differentiation in the society. (p. 62)

"Nonracialism" is the founding myth of the new South Africa. This chapter, I hope, has demonstrated that, speaking generally, the political class has not yet begun to understand all the implications of this slogan. Those who have done so but continue to act in a manner calculated to perpetuate racial identities are, clearly, manipulating the popular mind by using the term to signify no more than a "myth" in the usual meaning of the term. As a consequence, and because of the genocidal potential of a social grid based on the perpetuation of racial and competitive, reified ethnic identities, antiracist leadership in government and in civil society have to be clear that the struggle continues and that the next historic task that faces us is the final eradication of racial thinking, the most deadly of viruses, from the body politic. In order to do this, we have to undertake the necessary preventive measures in the economic base and in the cultural assumptions and practices of the society so that the virus cannot thrive. In a globalising world where soon even Martians will no longer be aliens but in all likelihood U.S. citizens, and where there are virtually no barriers to the free flow of ideas, goods, capital, and, under increasingly paranoid conditions, even of people, it is high time that we plan for a second Copernican revolution. This is a revolution of the conceptual universe that will populate the heads of the coming generations, no longer cluttered with superstitions such as "race," caste, and reified "ethnicity."

It is a task, the initiation of which many people inside and outside South Africa optimistically believe to be possible for those who brought about the "miracle" of the new South Africa. But miracles are in fact terribly mundane phenomena once one begins to look into their genesis, and it might be more realistic to take the view that in spite of very favourable historical conditions, the jury of history will remain out for many a long year before even the glimmer of a verdict will become possible.

NOTES

1. The Afrikaner National Party had been in power for only six years in 1954.

2. This refers to the racially segregated educational system that was formally imposed by the (Afrikaner) National Party as one of the main pillars of the apartheid system. It perpetuated and intensified the system under which the education of "non-Europeans," that is, black South Africans, prepared them for life in a subordinate society where, according to Dr Henrik Verwoerd (1954), one of the architects of the system, they could not "rise above certain levels of (unskilled or semi-skilled) labour."

3. Probably intended to read "perceptible" (N.A.).

4. In retrospect, it is not surprising, of course, that a court ruling that granted equality of treatment in respect of education had to eventuate in some kind of affirmative action strategy, as it inevitably drew attention to the fact that the "playing fields" were far from being level! The passing of the Civil Rights Act 10 years after *Brown*, especially its Title VII nondiscrimination provisions, represent the formal acknowledgement of this trajectory.

5. Recent developments in the study of the human genome all point in the same direction. For a well-considered analysis with respect to the genetic argument, see James (2004).

6. In the South African context, recent examples of such contestation are the labels "Bantu," "Coloured," and, at the time of writing, "Afrikaner."

7. For the purposes of this chapter, I do not consider the recent preoccupation with so-called (Black Economic) Empowerment Charters in major economic sectors, as these affect, generally speaking, only a tiny layer of upwardly mobile black middle-class individuals. It is a sphere of the formal economy in which, at best, a small group of satellite black capitalists are being given opportunities to enrich themselves and to deploy whatever entrepreneurial energies they have.

8. The History Workshop of the University of the Witwatersrand and the Wits Institute for Social and Economic Research fashioned a timely forum for many of the country's intellectuals and activists to discuss these and related issues in a high-profile conference under the umbrella title "The Burden of Race?" 'Whiteness' and 'Blackness' in Modern South Africa" (July 5–8, 2001).

9. The equivalent forms of the University of Cape Town originally made provision for a racial category that was labeled "Unknown." As the result of vigorous protest and passive resistance by many staff members, these forms have been revised to provide space for, among others, a category entitled "Not declared."

10. At the level of detailed implementation, of course, all such suggestions throw up countless problems. Cose (1998), in the U.S. context, shows that this approach is not necessarily the panacea that many people believe it to be. He summarises his own position as follows:

> A system that intelligently tried to take the totality of one's experience into account and to select and nurture those who are truly most deserving would not eliminate

questions of race from the admissions process, for race is a fact of life and, for some people, a component of the barriers they have had to overcome. It would, however, mean that race is not inappropriately taken into consideration, that Latino or black is not, ipso facto, taken as a surrogate for deprived. (pp. 121–124)

In my view, we are able, in the South African context, to approach the matter somewhat differently because of the balance of power on which the new dispensation rests. In fact, as I demonstrate, we can use affirmative action to problematise and undermine racial identities, instead of entrenching them.

11. In the 1999 report (published officially only in 2002) of the research team appointed by the SAHRC to investigate racism, "racial integration," and desegregation in South African public secondary schools, the authors tend to stress mutual social acceptability and tolerance as indices of "integration." However, they arrive at the damning conclusion

If we understand integration to mean fundamental changes not only in the personal attitudes of learners and educators but also in the institutional arrangements, policies and ethos of the school then this is absent from almost all of the schools studied. (Vally & Dalamba, 2002, p. 24)

This study remains the most authoritative of its kind yet undertaken in postapartheid South Africa.

12. "The curriculum" is, naturally, never the same for any two students and certainly not for students who come from more, or less, advantaged strata of any social formation.

13. Cose (1998) refers to the racism as "one of the most Byzantine—not to mention sensitive—issues of the current age, and one made all the more difficult by the fact that there is no conceivable solution that will not leave some group feeling resentful and betrayed" (p. 132). One of George Bush's "lasting" contributions to world history may turn out to be the fact that his crusade against "global terror" has led to the displacement of "race" by "religion," specifically Islam, as the most ominous marker of difference in the modern world.

14. The singular form in isiXhosa of a generic Nguni word. Chinua Achebe (1966), in his clairvoyant novel, *A Man of the People*, already referred to this class as "the black white-men of Africa 40 years ago."

272   A   SOUTH   AFRICAN   PERSPECTIVE

REFERENCES

Abebe, Z. (2001). Imposed ethnicity. In Z. Abebe (Ed.), *Social identities in the new South Africa*, Vol. 1 (pp. 1–23). Social Identities Series. Cape Town, South Africa: Kwela Books and SA History Online.

Achebe, C. (1966). *A man of the people*. New York: The John Day Company.

Adam, H., Slabbert, F., & Moodley, K. (1997). *Comrades in business: Post-liberation politics in South Africa*. Cape Town, South Africa: Tafelberg.

Alexander, N. (2002). *An ordinary country: Issues in the transition from apartheid to democracy*. Pietermaritzburg, South Africa: University of Natal Press.

Balibar, E., & Wallerstein, I. (1991). *Race, nation, class: Ambiguous identities*. London: Verso.

Brown v. Board of Education, 347 U.S. 483 (1954).

Cose, E. (1998). *Color-blind: Seeing beyond race in a race-obsessed world*. New York: Harper-Perennial.

de la Fuente, C. (2001). *A nation for all: Race, inequality and politics in twentieth-century Cuba*. Chapel Hill and London: University of North Carolina Press.

Employment Equity Bill of 1997. (1997). 1 December. *Government Gazette*, *390*(18481).

Franklin, R. (1993). *Shadows of race and class*. Minneapolis: University of Minnesota Press.

Frederickson, G. (2001). Race and racism in historical perspective: Comparing the United States, South Africa and Brazil. In C.V. Hamilton, L. Huntley, N. Alexander, A. Guimaraes & W. James (Eds.), *Race and inequality in Brazil, South Africa and the United States* (pp. 1–26). Boulder, CO: Lynne Reinner.

Giliomee, H. (2003). *The Afrikaners: Biography of a people*. Charlottesville: University of Virginia Press.

Greenstein, R. (1993). Racial formation: Towards a comparative study of collective identities in South Africa and the United States. *Social Dynamics*, *19*(2), 1–29.

Hamilton, C.V., Huntley, L., Alexander, N., Guimaraes, A., & James, W. (Eds.). (2001). *Beyond racism: Race and inequality in Brazil, South Africa and the United States*. Boulder, CO: Lynne Rienner.

James, W. (2004). *The colour of our skins*, July 1. Retrieved September 17, 2005, from http://www.africagenome.co.za/pdf/presentation_skin_colour.pdf

Maré, J. (2001). *Race counts in contemporary South Africa: Classification, categorisation and filling in forms*. Paper prepared for the conference on "The Burden of Race? 'Whiteness' and 'Blackness' in Modern South Africa," Johannesburg, South Africa. University of the Witwatersrand, Unpublished Mimeo.

Marx, A. (1998). *Making race and nation: A comparison of the United States, South Africa and Brazil*. Cambridge, UK: Cambridge University Press.

Morobe, M. (2004, January 16). A dash of realism. *Mail & Guardian Online*. Retrieved October 14, 2005, from http://www.mg.co.za/articledirect.aspx?area=%2finsight%2finsight_comment_and_analysis&articleid=40675

Naidu, E. (2003, December 21). Inequality makes rights for all a "fairytale façade." *Sunday Independent*.

O'Malley, K. (1994). A neglected dimension of nation-building in South Africa: The ethnic factor. In N. Rhoodie & I. Liebenberg (Eds.), *Democratic nation-building in South Africa*. Pretoria: Human Sciences Research Council Publishers,

Posel, D. (1983). Rethinking the "race-class debate" in South African historiography. *Social Dynamics*, *9*(1), 50–66.

Posel, D. (2001a). Race as common sense: Racial classification in twentieth-century South Africa. *African Studies Review*, *44*(1), 87–113.

Posel, D. (2001b). *What's in a name? Racial categorisations under apartheid and their after life*. Paper prepared for the conference on "The Burden of Race? 'Whiteness' and 'Blackness' in Modern South Africa," Johannesburg, South Africa. University of the Witwatersrand, Unpublished Mimeo.

Public Service Laws Amendment Act of 1997. (1997). Act 47 of 1997, 13 October 1997. *Government Gazette*, *388*(18366).

Reisigl, M., & Wodak, R. (Eds.). (2000). *The semiotics of racism: Approaches in critical discourse analysis*. Vienna: Passagen Verlag.

Republic of South Africa. (1998). *The Skills Development Act No. 97 of 1998*. Department of Labour. Pretoria: Government Printer.

Republic of South Africa. (1999). *The Skills Development Levies Act No. 9 of 1999*. Department of Labour. Pretoria: Government Printer.

Titus, A. (1974). Twenty years after *Brown v. Board of Education*: U.S. school segregation then and now. *The Educational Journal*, *(June)*, 5–7.

Titus, A. (1978). From *Brown* to *Bakke*: "Race" and equality in United States education. *The Educational Journal*, *(July–August)*, 4–9.

Vally, S., & Dalamba, Y. (2002). *Racism, "racial integration" and desegregation in South African public secondary schools*. A Report on a Study by the South African Human Rights Commission (SAHRC). Cape Town, South Africa: SAHRC.

Verwoerd, H. (1954). *Bantu education: Policy for the immediate future*. Statement in the Senate of the Parliament of the Union of South Africa, 7 June 1954. Pretoria, South Africa: Department of Native Affairs.

CHAPTER 14

Brown v. Board: *With All Deliberate Speed?*

MONICA HENDRICKS

This chapter argues that a detailed, grounded understanding of classroom literacy practices as well as of learners' writing is crucial to begin to change the ongoing and patently unequal educational outcomes that schools often produce. It is impossible to intervene realistically and effectively in an evidential vacuum. The 1955 *Brown v. Board of Education* judgement called for "all deliberate speed" in desegregating education in the United States. Yet, rather than signalling speed or urgency, that formulation was actually a multipurpose compromise that allowed pro-segregationist southern states to decide their own timeframes for desegregation. The wording also avoided the court issuing a ruling it could not enforce and preserved the unanimity of the judges (Patterson, 2001). Half a century after the *Brown* judgement, racial discrimination in education persists in the United States, as evidenced by the continuing case of *Williams v. State of California.*[1]

Williams represents yet another attempt to redress enduring educational inequality in the United States through a legal challenge. There is a long history of American courts being used as a vehicle to pursue black civil rights. The legal route, however, is generally a technical, expensive, and individualised way of making political gains. By comparison, in South Africa, mass-based popular organisation (including trade unionism) was the dominant expression of political and civil rights struggle throughout the 20th century. The formation in 1912 of the African Native National Congress (now known as the African National Congress, or ANC) was the start of urban nontribal black civil and

Monica Hendricks works as a research officer at the Institute for the Study of English in Africa at Rhodes University. She was awarded a Spencer Fellowship in 2001 for doctoral studies in the School of Education, University of the Witwatersrand, which she successfully completed in 2006.

political rights organisation. Other political organisations also engaged in political struggle, challenging the power and influence of the ANC at various times. Among the most significant of these were the Industrial and Commercial Workers' Union (1920s), the All African Convention (1930s), the Non-European Unity Movement (1940s), the Pan-African Congress (1960s), and the Black Consciousness Movement in the 1970s—all examples of popular mass-based organisations as visible manifestations of the struggle for human rights.

This chapter problematises both Alexander's discussion of social identity and contemporary South African state policies meant to redress inherited historic imbalances that remain in present-day South Africa. In his broad-ranging discussion Alexander explores

the deeper implications for the shaping of social identities and for the cohesion of the society inherent in the implementation of an affirmative action strategy under the social and historical conditions obtaining in post-apartheid South Africa. (this volume, p. 254)

He provides mainly anecdotal evidence to support his antiracist position. Political advocacy supported by piecemeal evidence, however, lacks the history and detail that systematic empirical analysis can bring to understanding the changing particularities of discrimination. Social identity is a complex interplay of physical and social elements, some of which can change and others which cannot. Identity is not only a construct of mind that is endlessly fluid, as Alexander (this volume, p. 254) suggests. While social elements of identity such as accent and class can change, identity is also a construct based on personal experience. Outward appearance, including immutable physical characteristics, such as shape of head or skin colour, profoundly shapes the manner in which others position people.

By way of detailed empirical evidence, this chapter is concerned with the quality of South African schooling and children's writing ability in English. It is common knowledge that education was an integral component of the apartheid system and was therefore structured in profoundly unequal and racist ways. I consider the extent of integration and access in postapartheid schools, as education has the potential not only to reproduce the status quo, but also to interrupt its smooth reproduction. Even though English is the home language of less than 10% of the population in South Africa (Statistics SA, 2003), it is the most widely used language of instruction and assessment, and is therefore important for learners' academic success.

Social Identities and Historic Imbalances

In assessing the significance of *Brown* for a postapartheid South Africa, Alexander contends, "the promotion or entrenchment of racial identities . . . holds within it the danger of genocidal conflict." (this volume, p. 254) With this dire warning as a central issue informing his discussion, Alexander considers the role of the state in the formation of racial identities and also the best approaches to redressing the imbalances inherited from the apartheid-colonial past.

In writing about the limits of comparisons, Alexander notes not only that South Africa and the United States differ in that South African blacks are in the majority, but also that this "newly enfranchised black majority [is] imbued, generally speaking, with . . . a keen desire for inclusive national, indeed continental, unity" (this volume, pp. 254–255). While this may well be the case at the level of rhetoric, with then-Deputy President Mbeki's lyrical "I am an African" speech of 1996 being probably the most famous example, there is little evidence for Alexander's claim of a general inclusive nationalism or pan-Africanism on the ground. As a matter of fact, a regrettable xenophobia extends to fellow Africans; attacks on African foreigners in South Africa are, unfortunately, regularly committed both by criminal elements[2] and by the police.[3] While xenophobic assaults on African foreigners are reported often, foreigners from elsewhere (e.g., Europe, Asia, or the United States) are seldom targeted.

A reason for the persistence of racism is doubtless that, after more than a decade of democracy in South Africa, a plethora of policy enacted by the democratic government has failed to change the extremely unequal socioeconomic conditions inherited from apartheid. We are far from transforming the societal and material conditions that underpin racist and discriminatory attitudes, which Alexander (2002) rightly insists are a precondition for the eradication of prejudice. South Africa's gini coefficient (a measure of income inequality commonly used by economists) of 0.64 in 2003 (Tempest, 2004) suggests deep-seated problems of inequality. The black middle class may have doubled in size (Southall, 2004), but it remains numerically small, and the unemployment rate of 41.8% nationally (Tempest) and difficulty in finding work (Lucas, 2003) affects mainly black South Africans. In short, colour and class continue to be closely associated. Given these conditions, general scientific agreement (see Cashmore, 1996; Dubow, 1995) that there is no biological basis for the idea of different human races has had little impact on the reality that blackness continues to function as a somatic marker of social inequality and disadvantage.

The state policy of affirmative action is a current that necessarily recognises racial classification. Alexander is critical of affirmative action both because it categorises people racially and because it requires, as a matter of policy, that people classify themselves racially. Yet, ironically, proponents of affirmative action argue that the purpose of such a racially based policy is precisely to redress grossly unequal societal and material conditions that underpin racist and discriminatory attitudes (Alexander's point). Alexander's claim that there are "very obvious and completely feasible alternatives" (this volume, p. 265) is not entirely convincing. His proposal that people should indicate what their apartheid classification (or their parents') had been is no real alternative, because it merely repeats long-standing racialised categories.

Racially based classification predates apartheid and has its origins in 19th century British and Afrikaner settler policies (Khalfani & Zuberi, 2003).[4] Resistance to racially based categories also has a long history. Different organisations devised a variety of inclusive terms in the struggle to build a unified opposition among politically oppressed and disenfranchised South Africans of all colours. Designations such as "African," "Non-European," and "black" have been used numerous times to transcend racialised divisions. Despite being (a central) part of the anti-apartheid struggle, the majority ANC government prefers apartheid-style categories to drive its official policy of affirmative action.

Alexander's second suggestion, of using *class* as a way of acknowledging historic disadvantage, comes up against the complexities of operationalising such a concept, along with the question of whether a person's historic or contemporary class position is what counts. The third proposal, using language knowledge and proficiency as a means of classifying people, is the one option that is feasible. It would have the added advantage of increasing the currency of indigenous languages, if proficiency in an indigenous African language became a prerequisite for a permanent job in the civil service, for instance. Although indigenous languages have been official since 1996, socially powerful mother-tongue speakers seldom use African languages in prestigious formal domains. Nor has official status acted as an impetus for Afrikaans- or English-speakers to learn an indigenous language. Yet, it is important that Afrikaans- and English-speaking children learn African languages for the purposes of nation building and for ensuring that previous racist divisions do not persist. As Mamdani (1996) notes, apartheid produced a dual identity: race solidarity among its beneficiaries, and an ethnic particularism [based largely on linguistic differences] among its victims. . . . The legacy of apartheid is summed up in not one, but two sets of identities: racial and ethnic. (p. 4)

At issue is whether the *purpose* of a racially based policy like affirmative action can contribute to building national unity or whether it creates, at worst, a token black representivity or, at best, a black elite.

The Extent of Integration in Postapartheid Schools

Few would disagree with Alexander that desegregation of schools is not the same as integration, which he defines as the "deracialisation of public institutions [which] must imply and make possible the attainment of equity in all domains, that is, the possibility of comparable life chances" (this volume, p. 267). Among the battery of laws and policies enacted post-1994 to reform South Africa's racist education system, the 1996 South African Schools Act (No. 84 of 1996) and an outcomes-based curriculum (National Department of Education, 1997, 2002) stand out as especially important.

The goal of the South African Schools Act was to decentralise decision making and expand parents' democratic participation in schools through participation on a School Governing Body (SGB). Yet, what the Schools Act demonstrates more than anything else is the decisive impact of middle-class interests on education policy and schooling. The Act requires parents, through SGBs, to play an active role in the appointment of teachers, disciplinary matters, and decisions about school language policy, as well as maintain oversight of the school's financial management and budget. Fulfilling these functions requires from parents time and, more importantly, high levels of literacy and numeracy. Generally, it is mothers more than fathers who play an active and supportive role in their children's schooling. In rural South Africa this is especially true, as the remnants of the long-standing migrant labour system mean that many households are headed by women. A survey in three rural provinces found disturbingly low literacy levels, especially among women. Overall, 36% of female household heads in KwaZulu-Natal, 25% in the Eastern Cape, and 23% in Limpopo had had no formal schooling at all (Nelson Mandela Foundation, 2005, p. 28). The levels of schooling of the remainder of the women were low, mostly too low to enable them to play the sort of role envisaged in the Schools Act. Soudien (2004) argues:

The Act projected parental identity around a restrictive middle class notion of who the parents were and how they functioned. . . . [The] upshot of the practice was that in black schools, SGBs continued to be dominated by their principals or their teachers. In formerly white schools [the better-resourced schools which black middle class children are now attending], middle class [mainly white] parents dominated. (p. 108)

Given the limited success of policy in producing integrated parental involvement in school governance, what is the nature of integration among learners? Summarising two large-scale studies that examined learner migration in Gauteng province, Soudien (2004) shows that "the movement from formerly black schools to Indian and coloured schools has been as strong as, if not stronger than, that of black people into formerly white schools" (p. 99). However, the migration has been one way; there has been no parallel movement of nonblack learners into formerly black schools. Because "almost 75% of [South African] schools are formerly designated as black" (p. 97), one can judge the limited impact of educational desegregation and the unchanged racialised demographics of, in particular, rural schooling, which serves half of South Africa's learners (Macfarlane, 2005). It is only better-resourced schools that have become more linguistically and culturally diverse in terms of learners, while poorly resourced township and rural schools remain almost exclusively black. By necessity, fees at such poorly resourced schools are low, so schools cannot afford to buy equipment and resources, and are completely dependent for support on the Education Department, which for the past 10 years has only allocated about 10% of its budget to material resources; the remainder goes to pay salaries. Better-resourced schools charge higher fees, effectively excluding poor children, and these higher fees allow such schools to pay for extra teachers, smaller classes, and the resources that the Department does not supply. Fiske and Ladd (2004) make the point that:

although formerly white schools are now racially integrated [!], most African and coloured students continue to attend schools that are essentially all black. . . . racial integration will never play more than a minor role in determining the quality of the educational opportunities available to black students. . . . the main determinant of educational opportunities and outcomes for black students will be the quality of the schools formerly designed to serve African and coloured students. (p. 99)

The implications for South African youths' identity construction, given that the majority of schools remain under-resourced and exclusively black, are summed up by Fine, Burns, Payne, and Torres (2004), who argue that because schools are "intimate places where youths construct identities, build a sense of self, read how society views them. . . . Buildings in disrepair are not, therefore, merely a distraction; they are identity producing and self-defining" (p. 2198). The social impact on poor, mainly black children who attend rundown schools that are short of up-to-date textbooks and have poorly qualified teachers must surely be an educational reproduction of black poverty.

To support and complexify this stark judgement of the effect of education in poorly resourced schools, the quality of education is considered further. However, before moving on to issues of educational quality, it is worth reviewing research findings about the social identities of children at desegregated high schools (Grades 8–12) that are mistakenly regarded as "racially integrated."

Contested Social Identities at Desegregated High Schools

In a study of a desegregated Durban high school, one of Dolby's (2001) main structuring questions was "How do youth, who find themselves involuntarily at the forefront of desegregation, think about and live with difference?" (p. 111). She argues that, "part of the job of educational research is to unpack how race functions as a set of practices within schools" (p. 112), and she concluded that a racialised identity construction was flourishing at the school she studied. On the one hand, a school identity of *whiteness* was reflected largely through school administrators, who employed measures such as recruiting white students and mandating school uniforms in an attempt to bolster standards. Dolby claims that standards were associated with whether or not students wore the full school uniform, as opposed to their actual academic performance, because black students typically outshined whites academically (p. 36); in addition, the full uniform was more affordable for white than black students. Sport was also manipulated—rugby, a particular marker of whiteness in KwaZulu-Natal, is compulsory for male students, while basketball (a sport most male students prefer) is not, and gets less funding. And good basketball results do not get the same acclaim as good rugby results. Establishing *blackness*, on the other hand, was the work of teachers who "try to fix students' selves in the ethnic practices of Zuluness" (p. 54), rather than recognise these students' cultural understandings and practices as modern and dynamic.

Klaas's (2004) study of racial integration in two single-sex (boys' and girls'), formerly whites-only boarding schools in the Eastern Cape highlights the importance of understanding teacher attitudes, even when the purpose of the study is examining integration among learners. Klaas found that sport in the boys' school acted as a vehicle for integration among students, while at the girls' school sports fostered division. Whereas the girls' school "allowed and justified racial polarization in sport and racialised separate residences" (p. 241), the boys' school "seemed to hold the multiracial structure together through regimentation of sport as the dominant symbol of masculinity" (p. 242).

Although in interviews teachers claimed to be colour-blind in their classrooms, Klaas (2004) found that teachers' attitudes and actions demonstrated "[t]he contradictions between their allegedly colour-blind approach and their claiming that African and Coloured students were different [particularly in the girls' school]"(p. 238). Teachers' own limitations with regard to issues of integration at school were compounded by "[b]oth schools' unwillingness to transform a traditional curriculum [which] made it extremely difficult to use pedagogy as an instrument to enhance more possibilities of racial integration" (p. 239). Comparable observations have been made (e.g., Harley & Wedekind, 2004) about other "desegregated" schools' responses to the pedagogical challenges of the new curriculum with its inclusive non-racist and non-sexist values.

Although Klaas (2004) argues that teacher–student social relations at both schools were more fraught than student–student relations, he found that student relations were also shot through with racialised tensions and stereotyping, with black and coloured girls, more than black boys, experiencing difficulties. Similar gendered differences around students' integration in schools have also been found in British research (Phoenix, 2001).

Quotes from student study participants (Klaas, 2004) bear testimony to the prevalence of racialised stereotyping:

There are very few Coloured here. So you don't really have a choice . . . you have to be nice to everybody. . . . People have this thing that we are Coloureds and we stick together, it's just rubbish. . . . People who speak to me, they expect me to be loud, and to gossip a lot, and to be sneaky. We expect Coloureds to drink a lot. (Marina, p. 166)

Like if something happens people would say "You Coloureds you gonna drink this weekend" and I ask "Why do I have to go and drink?" "All Coloured drink" so next week he comes and sees that I have not drunk . . . you don't have to change but you have to prove them wrong. (Stuart, p. 226)

In brief, the point must be reiterated that the "almost 75% of [South African] schools . . . formerly designated as black" (Soudien, 2004, p.

97) continue to be attended almost exclusively by black students. Studies into the culture and inclusivity of the minority of schools that have
become desegregated (Dolby, 2001; Klaas, 2004) find that these schools
still foster the notion that whiteness is an unproblematic good.

Equally important, can good quality education that encompasses
knowledge outcomes as well as intellectual and affective spheres of
learners' development (Valdes, 2004, p. 4) be achieved in such schools?
While these schools may be desegregated, they are certainly not
integrated, and they fall short of giving all learners "the possibility of
comparable life chances" (Alexander, this volume, p. 267), the hallmark
of an integrated education system.

The Nature of Access and the Quality of Education

Social justice with regard to education has two elements: equality
of access to educational facilities without regard to gender, race, class,
religion, nationality, or place of origin; and equality of opportunity to
learn, with a comparable quality of teaching and material resources
across the country. With regard to access, parents' ability to pay school
fees decides whether or not children go to school at all and what schools
children can attend. So we have an immediate problem in South Africa
with regard to equality of access to schools.

Despite school fees, in 2002, South Africa was one of the top 10
countries in the world as far as primary school enrollment was concerned (Ericsson & Cronje, 2004). However, there is a serious dropout
rate that develops from primary school to high school. Out of a student
population of 13.8 million (aged 5–19 years) in 2000, 11,598,701 (84%)
were enrolled in school. More detail about the differential impact of
the poor retention rate can be seen in the official Assessment Report
on the UNESCO Education for All programme, which found that in
rural areas 19.1% of children between the ages of 6–14 had dropped
out, compared to 11.4% in urban areas (Beard & Shindler, 2001, p. 137).
The dropout rate of children older than 14 in the final 4 years of high
school rises steeply to above 40% nationally. According to a 2003
Treasury Report, "on average, for 100 children in Grade 1 there were
52 in Grade 12 [the final year of school]" (Govender, 2005, p. 1).

Curriculum policy intends equal opportunity to learn for all South
African children, as the new curriculum (Department of Education,
2002) claims "to create a lifelong learner who is confident and independent, literate, numerate, multi-skilled, compassionate, with a respect for
the environment and the ability to participate in society as a critical and

active citizen" (p. 3). These broad principles are specified in learning outcomes and assessment standards for the different content areas of the curriculum.[5] Although curriculum policy may intend equal opportunity to learn for all, large-scale national testing in the period 1998–2002 shows that students "are performing far below the international benchmarks for their age and grade cohorts" (Taylor, Muller, & Vinjevold, 2003, p. 47). The challenge is to understand *why* it is that South African students underperform on international tests and to measure the extent to which national curriculum aims are, or are not, being met. The concept of opportunity to learn is a useful research tool, because its emphasis on "classroom processes that translate school resources such as teachers and instructional materials into effective teaching and learning" (McDonnell, 1995, p. 312) avoids the validity problems inherent in testing and measures whether or not a school delivers to students the opportunity to learn the material specified in the curriculum.

To illustrate the varying opportunities to learn, I discuss part of my own doctoral research on language policy and practice with regard to classroom writing in four schools with different language learner profiles and human and material resources. Because actual learning achieved in school is a surer measure of knowledge than testing, I relied on the regular everyday classroom writing produced during Grade 7 "learners of English as an additional language" classes as the main evidence of written competence. Children's writing ability in English is important for their academic success, as English is the most widely used language of instruction, assessment, and higher education. Moreover, writing underpins the broader educational outcome of literacy.

Language and Schools

To ensure social justice in terms of language, the South African education system needs to develop learners' proficiency and literacy in English as an additional language without also contributing to the dominance of English and the consequent marginalisation of African languages. Although children can learn additional languages in natural multilingual contexts, bilingualism is often not reciprocal. Generally, the less powerful learn the language of the more powerful; locally this means that the African languages of the largely poor majority are seldom valued or learned by the mainly better-off minority of Afrikaans- and English-speakers. Given the growing inequality between the few "haves" (largely but not entirely English-speaking) and the many "have-nots" (mainly African language speakers) in contemporary South Africa, it is especially important that schooling deliver on the language curriculum intentions of using and maintaining children's home language *and* developing proficiency in English. For the majority of poor children this could be achieved through additive multilingualism: African language-based education, at least for the initial phases of schooling, serving as the basis for developing literacy in English.

Schools have become increasingly complex language learning environments as students' migrating and teachers' redeployment overlay the racialised pattern of material inequality inherited from apartheid. Table 1 indicates the degree of differentiation among the four studied schools and (if fees are taken as a proxy for social class) of the societal differences in wealth and poverty. These four schools[6] represent a range of different contexts that continue to bear the traces of apartheid social and educational engineering. Enoch Sontonga, a formerly Africans-only school, and John Bishop, a formerly coloureds-only school, are historically disadvantaged state schools. Sea View, a formerly whites-only state school, and St. Katherine's, an independent school that has admitted students regardless of colour since 1982, are well resourced. In fact, St. Katherine's, as the fees would suggest, caters mainly to the children of wealthy parents, a small multilingual cosmopolitan elite.[7]

The availability of reading materials, which have particular significance for children's literacy and writing development, is further evidence of school differences. The distribution of these cognitive resources reflects the persistent divide between the rich and the poor. Like the schools cited in *Williams* (Oakes & Saunders, 2004), Enoch Sontonga and John Bishop had too few textbooks for each student to have his or her own copy, and there were also no school libraries. Sea View and St. Katherine's, on the other hand, have school libraries, sufficient textbooks for each student, and the capacity to print worksheets regularly.

Township schools such as Enoch Sontonga have remained exclusively black, and the isiXhosa-speaking learners, who have little con-

TABLE 1
ANNUAL SCHOOL FEES

School	Annual Fees 2003
Enoch Sontonga	R50
John Bishop	R100
Sea View	R2,750
St. Katherine's	R22,380

tact with English home language speakers or print material, are
learning English as a second language (L2) and use English as the
medium of instruction and assessment. Some desegregated schools,
such as John Bishop and Sea View, have become Afrikaans/English
dual-medium and offer English and Afrikaans as L1 and L2, respectively, to different learners in the same class taught by the same
teacher, while African languages are taught as L3, and are accorded
less curriculum time than a foreign language[8] or not taught at all (De
Klerk, 2000). The results are that: (1) many African-language speakers do not learn their home language at school and (2) a child's home
language cannot be assumed from the language he or she studies as
L1 at school. Both of these outcomes are completely contrary to the
additive multilingual aims of language-in-education policy. Thus far,
research about how language teachers at dual-medium schools, like
John Bishop and Sea View, negotiate between L1 and L2 in the same
class, and the actual level of language taught and learned in the complex linguistic environment of these Afrikaans and English classrooms, is scarce. St. Katherine's is an independent school where
English is taught as L1 and Afrikaans and isiXhosa as L2. Although
the majority of learners are English-speakers, Afrikaans, English, and
isiXhosa are all additional languages for the particular student whose
writing was analysed in this study, as she is a seTswana home language speaker.

  I analysed the amount and variety of children's written work in their
English lessons for the first semester of Grade 7 (19 weeks of teaching
time, excluding a short Easter break and the midyear examination). I
was also interested in examining whether and why contemporary South
African children's classroom writing in their additional languages is
"alive with possibility"[9] or routinised and dull. In analysing children's
classroom writing, I categorised the quantity of writing and indicated
the sort of support children had during the process of writing. Support
for writing is an important measure of whether or not children's
autonomy as writers is being developed through classroom writing.
Research in Britain indicates that bilingual children who became competent English L2 writers took "a controlling interest in writing . . .
[and] made choices about best topics" (Datta, 2000, p. 123). The writing
of the children at all four schools was a combination of grammar
exercises (of various sorts) and extended texts. In addition to these two
categories, I categorised comprehension exercises separately in a third
category because of their significance as a widespread, uniquely educational genre that links reading and writing.

Raison and Rivalland (1997, p. 15) describe four ways of writing: modelled, shared, guided, and individual. However, these terms have certain shortcomings: first, the terms "shared" and "guided" do not specify whether a text was produced jointly by a teacher and learners, or independently of the teacher by a group of learners collaboratively, or individually with the guidance of a writing "frame"; second, none of the terms takes into account whether or not learners had any choice about topics for their writing. I therefore adapted Raison and Rivalland's terms: instead of referring to "modelled" texts, I use the term "copied" (coded as copied), as it is common for South African learners to copy a model text from the board, without the text serving as a model of a genre for learners' own subsequent writing of the same genre. I introduce the term "controlled" (coded as contr) for grammar exercises in which children fill in a missing word or choose the correct word from a pair. "Guided" writing (coded as guided) includes grammar exercises in which children transform a sentence or text (e.g., direct to indirect speech), as well as genre writing where children write longer texts for which the teacher provides a frame. I use the term "independent" (coded as indep) for texts that learners produce without a frame.

Examining Children's Writing

The most striking feature of Tables 2, 3, 4, and 5 is that the bulk of children's writing consists of word and sentence-length decontextualised grammar tasks, mostly controlled or guided. The anomalous result is that learners are guided in the easier grammar tasks, while they write the more cognitively demanding comprehension exercises and extended texts largely independently. Only at St. Katherine's (poetry) and John Bishop (fact-based personal description/information) were learners guided in particular genres. At John Bishop and Sea View, state schools that have become linguistically diverse, learners wrote fairly similar amounts in total—three comprehension exercises at both schools, for example. At these two schools, learners also wrote summaries, an important language-based reading and writing skill and particularly necessary for learning content in other subject areas. Their differences lie in the balance of grammar exercises and extended texts and the nature of support for this writing. John Bishop learners wrote nine extended texts (two of which were copied) compared to Sea View's five, whereas Sea View learners did many more grammar exercises than the John Bishop learners, especially whole-sentence rather than single-word tasks. At St. Katherine's, learners did double the number of comprehension exercises that learners at Sea View or John Bishop had done,

TABLE 2
AMOUNT AND KIND OF ENGLISH WRITING AT ENOCH SONTONGA, JANUARY–JUNE 2003

	Learners' names and favourite fruit	Spelling tests	Vocabulary from Compr. 1	Punctuation, capital letters	Dictation	Vocabulary from Compr. 2	Filling in verbs and prepositions	Forming antonyms from prefixes	Vocabulary
Grammar exercises	3 words (contr)	5, 10, 19, 10 words (contr)	10 words (contr)	3 sentences (contr)	5 sent's (contr)	8 sentences (contr)	8 words (contr)	10 words (contr)	10 sentences (indep)
Comprehension exercises		Comprehension 1 from a READ book 15 sentences (indep)		Comprehension 2 from a READ book 8 sentences (indep)					
Extended texts		Poem on coal, done by six learners (indep)		Ad/poster about coal (group project) (indep)		Template of a friendly letter (copied)			

Note: READ (Read, Educate, and Develop Trust) is a nongovernmental organization that works to improve the quality of education and reduce illiteracy in South Africa.

TABLE 3
AMOUNT AND KIND OF ENGLISH WRITING AT JOHN BISHOP, JANUARY–JUNE 2003

	Identify nouns	Match adjective to body parts	Word puzzle	Word search	Arranging words in alphabetical order	Vocabulary, explanatory sentences of new words	Punctuation, capital letters	
Grammar exercises	22 words (contr)	14 words (contr)	22 words (contr)		24 words (contr)	6 sentences (indep)	10 sentences (contr)	
Comprehension exercises	Comprehension 1: Artero Argosy (teacher written) 13 sentences (indep)		Comprehension 2: from a READ book 5 sentences (indep) 7 words (contr)		Comprehension 3: from a READ book 3 sentences (indep) 7 sentences (contr)			
Extended texts	Factual description 11 sentences (indep)	Friendly letter (copied)	Factual info 7 sentences (guided)	Diary 5 sentences (guided)	Feelings, family and locality (indep)	2 poems and 1 prayer (copied)	Summary of READ stories, varied number (indep)	Grade 7B only Recount (indep) Dialogue (guided)

TABLE 4
Amount and Kind of English Writing at Sea View, January–June 2003

	Punctuation of direct speech	Direct to reported speech	Vocabulary words to replace 'said'	Negation	Spelling tests	Punctuation, capital letters	Punctuation, commas	Vocabulary plurals and meanings	Dictation, homily
Grammar exercises	12, 3, 9 sentences (contr)	8, 7, 4, 8, 8, 5, 22, 14, 8, 22, 7, 6, 6 sentences (guided)	11 sentences (contr)	6 sent's (contr)	10, 15, 15, 15, 20 words (contr)	21 words, 4, 9, 3 sentences (contr)	6, 6, 3, 14, 14 sentences (contr)	18 words (contr)	5 lines (contr)
Comprehension exercises	Comprehension 1: 8 sentences (indep)		Comprehension 2: 7 sentences (indep)		Comprehension 3: 15 sentences (indep)				
Extended texts	Autobiography (indep)	How I feel when . . . (indep)	Diary (one week) (indep)	Poem, Respect (indep)	Summary (indep)				

TABLE 5

AMOUNT AND KIND OF ENGLISH WRITING AT ST. KATHERINE'S, JANUARY–JUNE 2003

	Vocabulary	Vocabulary	Vocabulary, synonyms for 'happiness'	Vocabulary, replace 'got' and 'nice'	Vocabulary, dictionary extract	Vocabulary, replace 'go'	Punctuation (exclamation marks)	Vocabulary replacing nonsense words in Jabberwocky	Simile and metaphor
Grammar exercises	22 words (contr)	35 words (contr)	24 words (indep)	5 words (contr)	7 sentences (contr)	14 sentences (contr)	11 sentences (contr)	13 words (indep)	2 sentences (guided)
Comprehension exercises	Compr. 1 (Romeo + Juliet)	Compr. 2 (Punctuation)	Compr. 3 (Monsoon)	Compr. 4 (Mafutu + the snake)	Compr. 5 (2 ways of seeing)	Compr. 6 (The king) 4 sentences			
	12 sentences (indep)	4 sentences (indep)	8 sentences 4 words (indep)	10 sentences (indep)	10 sentences (indep)	11 words (indep)			
Extended texts	Response to photo	Poem on colour	Love poem	Autobio	Poem on lion				
	11 sentences (indep)	5 lines (guided)	9 lines (guided)	17 sentences (indep)	11 lines (indep)				

and six compared to Enoch Sontonga learners' two. In every respect, learners at Enoch Sontonga wrote much less than any other learner. Most disturbingly, none of the learners, besides six who wrote a poem, did any independent, individual extended writing at all. Most wrote their first extended text on their own as part of the mid-year examination.

The development of *quality* in writing critically depends on the quantity written. Together with regular opportunities to write individually and independently, children also need to receive constructive feedback about the structure and coherence of their texts. L2 learners in particular require explicit teaching of the linguistic and structural features of different genres as well as follow-up grammar lessons to remediate the grammatical errors in their own writing. It is all but unavoidable that grammar tasks will have a tenuous connection to children's own writing, with limited prospects to develop the quality of writing, when learners do no independent individual writing, as was the case at Enoch Sontonga.

The second noticeable trend is that children's extended texts are very similar—self-descriptive and autobiographical. These genres are repeated in the other languages children learn in school (details of their Afrikaans and isiXhosa writing are beyond the scope of this chapter), to the point where assignments must be boring for learners to write and monotonous for teachers to mark. It is possible that autobiographical writing is such a common choice for Grade 7 learners because "located at the interface between orality and writing, autobiography . . . appears as a tool to trace a difficult personal voyage from popular culture to scholarly culture" (Lusebrink, 2003, p. 8). There is little evidence of writing for the wide range of purposes envisaged in the new curriculum. Instead, personal expressive writing predominates, and learners seldom have a say in topic choice. In view of Datta's (2000) research, as well as the curriculum imperative to develop learners' critical, evaluative, and problem-solving abilities, their limited role in topic choice is problematic. There is only one example of a factual impersonal genre, the recount by John Bishop learners. According to Kress (1994), writing impersonal genres frees learners from considering the needs of the reader and enables them to foreground the subject matter, which sets the basis for the development of abstract, cognitively demanding academic writing. As these Grade 7 learners are at the start of the senior phase of their schooling, it is especially important for them to develop a level of literacy that will give them access to the abstract disciplinary forms of knowledge taught at high school and university.

While content-based cognitively demanding writing is vital to academic success, learners' literacy levels are widely regarded as an important measure of educational quality primarily because they are crucial to learners' intellectual and affective development. In excellent high-quality classroom literacy practices, writing is used to link personal introspective forms of self-knowledge and learning with abstract content-rich meta-cognitive understanding. A writing teacher like Kamler (2001) seeks to "disrupt the binary division between personal and factual writing" (p. 83), arguing that to improve a writer's writing a teacher needs to work with the genre and linguistic features of text as well as the writer's subjectivity. Kamler relates how she taught a failing student to develop her writing of argument through employing the subtleties of modality, conditional clauses, and impersonal formulations. Most empoweringly, she taught her student

the various motivations for using nominalization, for example, to make information more concise and highlight abstract ideas rather than people and actions . . . [and that] there are also ideological reasons for omitting agency and hence causality and responsibility. (p. 106)

Kamler's expertise may not be standard practice, even in Australia (where she works). Certainly it provides a stark contrast to what prevails in the language lessons of the four teachers in this sample and, I would argue, in most South African language classrooms, where teachers privilege grammar exercises and personal, expressive extended writing. Despite language curriculum reform that includes critical language awareness and advocates a genre approach, there is no sign that writing practices have been influenced by more recent curriculum and pedagogical developments.

The Limits of the "New Curriculum"

It is clear that the new curriculum is making little difference with the systematic variation in the quality of learners' written outcomes at differently resourced schools. On the one hand, in the sector of state schools that has diversified linguistically and culturally (like John Bishop and Sea View), the new curriculum has gone some way in terms of equalising the amount that learners write. There remains, however, a deep divide between the small elite at very privileged schools and the majority of learners at materially deprived state schools. Learners at a poorly resourced school like Enoch Sontonga write too little in total to have a chance to develop cognitive academic language abilities. Yet, even in an optimally resourced school like St. Katherine's, where children did the most independent writing, there were few factual, impersonal, cognitively demanding genres, which are the basis of abstract, disciplinary-based academic writing. The perception that access to quality education has become the preserve of a South African middle class that includes increasing numbers of people of colour is common (e.g., Soudien, 2004); however, my research findings echo many other studies (reviewed in Taylor et al., 2003) that question such assumptions about the quality of education even in well-resourced schools. All learner achievement studies conducted within the last eight years in South Africa find that learners' scores "are far below what is expected at all levels of the schooling system, both in relation to other countries, including other developing countries, and to the expectations of the new South African curriculum" (Taylor et al., p. 41). The inescapable reality is that critical questions need to be asked about the *quality* of education, systemically, in South Africa. The presence of an enlarged black middle class has had no apparent impact on the quality of education for the majority of children whose parents are working class or unemployed.

Actualising the Potential of Curriculum Reform

Ten years after democratic change in South Africa, schooling remains deeply inequitable. Race is still the determining marker of inequality in education, with class coming a distant second in replacing colour as the primary basis of division. As in the United States, more than half a century after the landmark case of *Brown*, South Africa, more than a decade after democracy, is far from the goal of equality of access or comparable quality of teaching and resources in our schools. There are serious, complex barriers to overcome before the education system in either country can begin to give children comparable life chances. As noted by Alexander, even in Cuba, which has achieved remarkable levels of educational equality,[10] de la Fuente (2001) finds that vestiges of racism persist. The reason for *Brown* was that racism in the United States could (and did) sanction educational inequality; the Cuban experience shows that an exceptional degree of educational equality per se does not guarantee the end of racism.

What needs to happen before the passing of another 50 years (or 10, in the South African case) to realise the full potential of *Brown*? In both the United States and South Africa, it is difficult to know whom to hold accountable when schools fail to give children the basics, like adequate numbers of up-to-date textbooks. Timar's (2004) observation of the American system of schooling is equally true of South Africa: "[t]he diffusion of responsibility among various state actors and the lack of coordination among them make oversight both everyone's and no one's responsibility" (p. 2076).

This chapter argues that a detailed, grounded understanding of classroom literacy practices as well as of learners' writing is crucial to begin to change ongoing and patently unequal educational outcomes. It is impossible to intervene realistically and effectively in an evidential vacuum. It is even more important that the political will to enact equitable educational policy, informed by research, extends to the provision of good quality schooling for all children. The discourse around the 2004 case of *Williams* refers to adequacy as well as equity in education (e.g., Timar, 2004, p. 2058). The differences between the two concepts are unclear. If adequacy is taken as a basic, common minimum level of educational resource, does this signify a dilution of the original *Brown* expectation of educational equality towards something more realistic and achievable?

NOTES

1. *Williams v. State of California*, filed in 2000, is a class action suit which charged that "schools that have the fewest qualified teachers, least adequate curriculum materials, and poorest facilities of all schools in the state . . . [serve] primarily low-income children, immigrant children, and children of color" (Oakes, 2004, pp. 1889–1890).

2. Newspaper reports that foreign African nationals and asylum seekers are attacked, robbed, and killed in South Africa are common (e.g., Bro, 2005).

3. An investigative television programme, *Special Assignment*, highlighted a bloody police assault on a Congolese woman in Johannesburg ("Kwere-kwere," 2005).

4. Khalfani and Zuberi (2003) trace the present four-way categorisation of African, Indian, Coloured, and White from the 1911 Census, when the population was divided into three categories: Bantu, Mixed and other coloured, and European/White. A fourth category, corresponding to "Indian," was introduced in the 1918 Census as "Asiatic."

5. The Revised National Curriculum Statement (RNCS) for Languages (Department of Education, 2002) has three learning outcomes related to written competence. They are: outcome four, that "the learner will be able to write different kinds of factual and imaginative texts for a wide range of purposes"; outcome five, that "the learner will be able to use language to think and reason, as well as access, process, and use information for learning"; and outcome six, that "the learner will know and be able to use the sounds, words, and grammar of the language to create and interpret texts."

6. All school names are pseudonyms.

7. The independent school sector caters to "only 2.1% of learners overall" (Hofmeyr & Lee, 2004, p. 143).

8. Kaplan and Baldauf (1997) claim that, "Most foreign language education around the world at the present time is structured to be delivered in classes of 50 to 75 at a rate of three 50-minute periods each week" (p. 129).

9. A popular advertising jingle claims that present-day South Africa is "alive with possibility," in contrast, presumably, to the former political dispensation in which the aspirations of the majority of the population were denied.

10. The 2001 Annual Report of the United Nations Development Programme, Chapter IV (b) articles 64 and 65, makes special mention of Cuba's 97.4% school enrolment rate being uniform throughout the country and by sex.

REFERENCES

Alexander, N. (2002). *An ordinary country.* Pietermaritzburg: University of Natal Press.

Alexander, N. (2006). *Brown v. Board of Education*: A South African perspective. In A. Ball (Ed.), *With more deliberate speed: Achieving equity and excellence in education— Realizing the full potential of* Brown v. Board of Education. *The 105th yearbook of the National Society for the Study of Education*, Part II (pp. 251–273). Malden, MA: Blackwell.

Beard, S., & Shindler, J. (2001). A statistical overview of education in South Africa. In K. Fieldgate & M. Henning (Ed.), *Education Africa Forum* (pp. 134–148). Pinegowrie: Education Africa.

Bro, T. (2005, August 4). East London unsafe say Somalis. *Dispatch Online.* Retrieved February 8, 2006, from http://www.dispatch.co.za/2005/08/04/Easterncape/asomal.html

Brown v. Board of Education, 349 U.S. 295 (1955).

Cashmore, E. (1996). *Dictionary of race and ethnic relations* (4th ed.). London and New York: Routledge.

Datta, M. (2000). aami ekta bhooteir golpo likhba. In M. Datta (Ed.), *Bilinguality and literacy: Principles and practice* (pp. 93–135). London: Continuum.

De Klerk, V. (2000). Language shift in Grahamstown: A case study of selected Xhosa-speakers. *International Journal of the Sociology of Language, 146,* 87–110.

de la Fuente, C. (2001). *A nation for all: Race, inequality and politics in twentieth-century Cuba.* Chapel Hill and London: University of North Carolina Press.

Department of Education. (2002). *Revised national curriculum statement for grades R–9: Languages.* Pretoria: Government Printer.

Dolby, N. (2001). *Constructing race: Youth, identity and popular culture in South Africa.* Albany, NY: SUNY Press.

Dubow, S. (1995). *Illicit union: Scientific racism in modern South Africa.* Johannesburg: Witatersrand University Press.

Ericsson, N., & Cronje, F. (2004). Education. In J. Tempest (Ed.), *South Africa survey 2003/2004* (pp. 238–250). Johannesburg: South African Institute of Race Relations.

Fine, M., Burns, A., Payne, Y.A., & Torres, M.E. (2004). Civic lessons: The color and class of betrayal. *Teachers College Record, 106*(11), 2193–2223.

Fiske, E.B., & Ladd, H.F. (2004). *Elusive equity.* Washington, DC: Brookings Institution Press.

Govender, P. (2005, September 18). School dropouts set off alarm bells. *The Sunday Times,* p. 1.

Harley, K., & Wedekind, V. (2004). Political change, curriculum change and social formation, 1990–2002. In L. Chisholm (Ed.), *Changing class: Educational and social change in post-apartheid South Africa* (pp. 195–220). Cape Town: HSRC Press.

Hofmeyr, J., & Lee, S. (2004). The new face of private schooling. In L. Chisholm (Ed.), *Changing class: Educational and social change in post-apartheid South Africa* (pp. 143–174). Cape Town: HSRC Press.

Kamler, B. (2001). *Relocating the personal.* Albany, NY: SUNY Press.

Kaplan, R. B., & Baldauf, R. (1997). *Language planning: From practice to theory.* Clevedon: Multilingual Matters.

Khalfani, A.K., & Zuberi, T. (2003). Racial classification and the modern census in South Africa, 1911–1996. *Race and Society, 4*(2), 161–176.

Klaas, J.J. (2004). *Racial integration in South African education: An ethnographic study of race relations in two historically white secondary schools.* Unpublished Ph.D. thesis, Faculty of Education, Cambridge University, UK.

Kress, G.R. (1994). *Learning to write.* London: Routledge and Kegan Paul.

Kwere-kwere. (2005, September 13). SABC 3 TV. *Special Assignment*. Retrieved February 8, 2006 from http://www.sabcnews.co.za/specialassignment/kwere.html

Lucas, P. (2003). Job market welcomes graduates, but historical hurdles remain. *HSRC Review*. Retrieved February 10, 2006 from http://www.hsrc.ac.za/about/HSRCReview/Vol1No3/HSRCReview.pdf

Lusebrink, H. (2003). The dynamics of autobiography: From anthropological anchorage to the intercultural horizons. *Mots Pluriels* No 23. Retrieved May 6, 2004, from http://www.arts.uwa.edu.au/MotsPluriels/MP2303hjl.html

Macfarlane, D. (2005, May 27–June 2). Treat rural schools as special case, report urges. *Mail and Guardian*, p. 4.

Mamdani, M. (1996). Reconciliation without justice. *South African Review of Books, 46*, 3–5.

McDonnell, L.M. (1995). Opportunity to learn as a research concept and a policy instrument. *Educational Evaluation and Policy Analysis, 17*(3), 305–322.

National Department of Education. (1997). *Foundation phase policy document. Intermediate phase policy document. Senior phase policy document*. Pretoria: Government Printer.

Nelson Mandela Foundation. (2005). *Emerging voices*. Cape Town: HSRC Press.

Oakes, J. (2004). Investigating the claims in *Williams v. State of California*: An unconstitutional denial of education's basic tools? *Teachers College Record, 106*(10), 1889–1906.

Oakes, J., & Saunders, M. (2004). Education's most basic tools: Access to textbooks and instructional materials in California's public schools. *Teachers College Record, 106*(10), 1967–1988.

Patterson, J.T. (2001). Brown v. Board of Education: *A civil rights milestone and its troubled legacy*. New York: Oxford University Press.

Phoenix, A. (2001). Racialization and gendering in the (re)production of education inequalities. In B. Francis & C. Skelton (Eds.), *Investigating gender: Contemporary perspectives in education*. Buckingham: Open University Press.

Raison, G., & Rivalland, J. (1997). *First steps: Writing developmental continuum*. Melbourne: Heinemann Rigby.

Soudien, C. (2004). "Constituting the class": An analysis of the process of "integration" in South African schools. In L. Chisholm (Ed.), *Changing class: Educational and social change in post-apartheid South Africa* (pp. 89–114). Cape Town: HSRC Press.

South African Schools Act (No. 84 of 1996). Pretoria, South Africa.

Southall, R. (2004). South Africa's emerging black middle class. *HSRC Review, 2*(3), 12–13.

Statistics South Africa. (2003). *Census 2001: Census in brief*. Pretoria, South Africa: Author.

Taylor, N., Muller, J., & Vinjevold, P. (2003). Lessons from learner assessment. In N. Taylor, J. Muller, & P. Vinjevold (Eds.), *Getting schools working* (pp. 34–47). Cape Town: Maskew Miller Longman.

Tempest, J. (Ed.). (2004). *South Africa Survey 2003/2004*. Johannesburg: South African Institute of Race Relations.

Timar, T.B. (2004). School governance and oversight in California: Shaping the landscape of equity and adequacy. *Teachers College Record, 106*(11), 2057–2080.

Valdes, H. (2004). Quality and equity in education: Present challenges and perspectives in modern societies. Keynote address at the Eleventh International Literacy and Education Research Network Conference on Learning, Havana, Cuba, June 2004.

Part Four
Looking Forward: Pressing Challenges That Lie Ahead

CHAPTER 15

The Meaning of Brown . . . *for Now*

GLORIA LADSON-BILLINGS

Louisiana, Louisiana, they're trying to wash us away . . . they're trying to wash us away.

Lyrics by Randy Newman, sung by Aaron Neville (1991)

I am completing this chapter at the same time that my television, radio, and newspapers are filled with images of the horror that is Hurricane Katrina. These images are the starkest indications that America is sharply divided along race and class lines. Tens of thousands of poor people are displaced and penniless. Their homes, jobs, possessions, and hope have washed away in the putrid, toxic waters of Lake Pontchartrain and the Gulf of Mexico. Hundreds, perhaps thousands, have died. Americans outside of the area have had to transition from the military assault known as "shock and awe" to a federal disaster response that has been called "shockingly awful."

Watching hour after hour of around-the-clock coverage of the aftermath of the hurricane has reminded me how tenuous the hold large segments of our society have on the promise of America. It has both saddened and sickened me, not because the images showed me something I did not know, but rather because they underscored the brutality

---

Gloria Ladson-Billings is Kellner Family chair in urban education and a professor of curriculum and instruction and educational policy studies at the University of Wisconsin, Madison.

and high cost of poverty. Like many academics, I have gone to the city of New Orleans many times. It is a relatively inexpensive city in which to hold a conference or meeting. It is a city especially organized to host lots of celebrations. From the Sugar Bowl on January 1 to Mardi Gras in February to the steady stream of conferences, conventions, and concerts, New Orleans is a party city. But any visitors who have bothered to wander a few blocks beyond Canal Street and the French Quarter could not help but see abject poverty staring them in the face.

I opened the chapter with some lyrics from the song, "Louisiana-1927" (Newman, 1991), sung by New Orleans native Aaron Neville. In the haunting refrain, Neville sings, "They're trying to wash us away. They're trying to wash us away." The lyrics invoke more than the hurricane and flood conditions of 1927, or even 2005; they also evoke the powerlessness and futility of struggling against white supremacy, particularly when that supremacy is undergirded by all of the social, cultural, economic, and political institutions. *The Wall Street Journal* staff reporter, Christopher Cooper (2005), reports that the wealthy white families of New Orleans escaped much of the tragedy. Their homes were not flooded, they called in private security to protect them and their property, and they flew in provisions to stay comfortable. But it is not merely how they survived the hurricane and flooding, but their plans for rebuilding the city that bears examination. According to Cooper:

The power elite of New Orleans—whether they are still in the city or have moved temporarily to enclaves such as Destin, Florida, and Vail, Colorado— insist the remade city won't simply restore the old order. . . . The new city must be something very different, Mr. Reiss says, with better services and fewer poor people. "Those who want to see this city rebuilt want to see it done in a completely different way: demographically, geographically, and politically," he says. "I'm not just speaking for myself here. The way we've been living is not going to happen again, or we're out." (p. A-1)

Celebrating *Brown*

The last few years (2004–05) have been filled with commemoration, reflection, and scholarship around the landmark Supreme Court decision, *Brown v. Board of Education* (1954). It was right and proper to take a 50-year retrospective at one of the more significant court rulings of the 20th century. It was also important to look at the decision in relationship to the current conditions of U.S. public schools and to ask what meaning *Brown* has for contemporary schooling. In this chapter I use the theoretical lens of Critical Race Theory (CRT) to interrogate the *Brown* decisions (both 1954 and 1955) to consider what they mean for education today. I look at three scenarios that respond to the question of whether or not *Brown* could be decided in the same manner today as it was decided in 1954. The first scenario is proposed by what I call the "racial optimists."[1] These are people who not only believe that *Brown* would be decided the same way today as it was in 1954, but that the decision reflects the inherent equality and fairness of the United States. The second scenario is that of "racial liberals." They believe that *Brown* would be decided the same way, but see it as an unfinished project that can only be completed through American jurisprudence and incremental social changes. Racial liberals believe that such changes should occur at no cost or sacrifice to them (Kidder, 2004). The third scenario is that of the "racial realists." They contend that *Brown* was never solely about righting past racial wrongs and in the long run it may not have served black people as well as it should and could have. Racial realists challenge the notion that the nation will willingly do anything that primarily benefits people of color.

A Note on CRT

Although a number of education scholars are using CRT as an analytical lens through which to explain education inequities, often those outside of the CRT paradigm are confused about what it means and how it can serve as a useful rubric for education research and theorizing. In this section of the chapter I provide a brief summary of CRT and explain its use in education theorizing.[2]

CRT, according to Delgado (1995), "sprang up in the mid-1970s with the early work of Derrick Bell and Alan Freeman, both of whom were deeply distressed over the slow pace of racial reform in the United States" (p. xiii). They argued that the traditional approaches of filing amicus briefs, conducting protest marches, and appealing to the moral sensibilities of decent citizens produced smaller and fewer gains than in previous times (i.e., during the 1960s and 1970s).

CRT is both an outgrowth of and a separate entity from an earlier legal scholarship movement called critical legal studies (CLS). CLS is a leftist legal movement that challenged the traditional legal scholarship that focused on doctrinal and policy analysis (Gordon, 1990) in favor of a form of law that spoke to the specificity of individuals and groups in social and cultural contexts. CLS scholars also challenged the notion that "the civil rights struggle represents a long, steady, march toward social transformation" (Crenshaw, 1988, p. 1334).

Crenshaw (1988) further argues that, "Critical [legal] scholars have attempted to analyze legal ideology and discourse as a social artifact which operates to recreate and legitimate American society"(p. 1334). Scholars in the CLS movement decipher legal doctrine to expose both its internal and external inconsistencies and reveal the ways that "legal ideology has helped create, support, and legitimate America's present class structure" (p. 1350). The contribution of CLS to legal discourse is in its analysis of legitimating structures in the society. Much of the CLS ideology derives from the work of Gramsci (1971) and depends on the Gramscian notion of "hegemony" to describe the continued legitimacy of oppressive structures in American society. However, CLS fails to provide pragmatic strategies for material social transformation. Cornel West (1993) asserts that:

critical legal theorists fundamentally question the dominant liberal paradigms prevalent and pervasive in American culture and society. This thorough questioning is not primarily a constructive attempt to put forward a conception of a new legal and social order. Rather, it is a pronounced disclosure of inconsistencies, incoherences, silences, and blindness of legal formalists, legal positivists, and legal realists in the liberal tradition. CLS is more a concerted attack and assault on the legitimacy and authority of pedagogical strategies in law school than a comprehensive announcement of what a credible and realizable new society and legal system would look like. (p. 196)

CLS scholars critique mainstream legal ideology for its portrayal of U.S. society as a meritocracy but failed to include racism in its critique. Thus, CRT became a logical response for the discontent of legal scholars of color.

CRT begins with the notion that racism is "normal, not aberrant, in American society" (Delgado, 1995, p. xiv), and, because it is so enmeshed in the fabric of our social order, it appears both normal and natural to people in this culture. Indeed, Derrick Bell's (1992) major premise in *Faces in the Bottom of the Well* is that racism is a permanent feature of American life.

Second, CRT departs from mainstream legal scholarship (and even CLS) by sometimes employing storytelling to "analyze myths, presuppositions, and received wisdoms that make up the common culture about race and that invariably render blacks and other minorities onedown" (Delgado, 1995, p. xiv). According to Barnes (1990), "Critical race theorists . . . integrate their experiential knowledge, drawn from a shared history as 'other,' with their ongoing struggles to transform a world deteriorating under the albatross of racial hegemony" (pp. 1864–

1865). Thus, the experience of oppressions such as racism or sexism has important aspects for developing a CRT analytical standpoint. To the extent that whites (or in the case of sexism, men) experience forms of racial (or gender) oppression, they may develop such a standpoint. For example, the historical figure John Brown suffered aspects of racism by aligning himself closely with the cause of African American liberation. CRT scholars use stories or narratives because they add necessary contextual contours to the seeming "objectivity" of positivist perspectives.

Third, CRT insists on a critique of liberalism. Crenshaw (1988) argues that the liberal perspective of the "civil rights crusade as a long, slow, but always upward pull" (p. 1334) is flawed because it fails to understand the limits of current legal paradigms to serve as catalysts for social change and because of its emphasis on incrementalism. CRT argues that racism requires sweeping changes, but liberalism has no mechanisms for such change. Rather, liberal legal practices support the painstakingly slow process of arguing legal precedence to gain citizen rights for people of color.

Fourth (and related to the liberal perspective), is the argument posed by CRT that whites have been the primary beneficiaries of civil rights legislation. CRT points out that civil right laws and policies like affirmative action, school desegregation, and equal opportunity hiring all benefit whites even more than people of color. For example, more white people received jobs as a result of affirmative action (i.e., white women who, in general, live with other white people—spouses, partners, children—are the major beneficiaries of affirmative action. White parents and students were often given inducements to attend schools with black children, such as magnet programs and special extracurricular enticements).

In the following section of this essay I construct scenarios that represent composites of positions on school desegregation that come from actual post-*Brown* events and perspectives. The actual details of the events are less significant than the positions they represent. By creating categorical notions of the perspectives, we can move away from seeing them as idiosyncratic and recognize them as ideological positions that shape and color the way we understand *Brown* as a legal decision.

Racial Optimists and the Promise of America

I use the term *racial optimists* to describe those who endorse a notion of "color-blindness" (Crenshaw, 1988) regarding the racial condition of the society. Current neoconservative rhetoric espouses this position.

This position looks at the racial history of the United States and sees a steady line of progress where people have gone from chattel slavery to full citizenship in a relatively "short" 400 or so years. Public figures such as Supreme Court Justice Clarence Thomas, former University of California regent Ward Connelly, and Hoover Institution Scholar Shelby Steele are contemporary examples of racial optimists. They argue that race is an incidental, not constituent, aspect of who they are and should not be taken into consideration when making public policy decisions. For the racial optimist, *Brown* broke down a barrier that helped us move away from race as a social dividing line.

The racial optimist sees *Brown* as a correctly decided decision that reaffirmed the basic principles of the nation and granted full legal and social citizenship to blacks and other citizens of color. Racial optimists latch on to 13 words from the slain civil rights leader Martin Luther King's famous "I have a dream" speech and use them to legitimate their argument that groups' rights need not be protected because individual rights already are (Dyson, 2000). Thus the words, "judged by the content of their character, not the color of their skin" have been turned on their heads to obviate their full impact in the context of a speech that was designed to call the federal government into question for failing to make good on a promissory note to black people.

For the racial optimist, the very idea of *Brown* proves that race is of declining significance (Wilson, 1978) and that race relations are on a course of steady progress. The litmus test of racial progress for racial optimists is the growth of the black middle class, the presence of more blacks in positions of leadership, and the civil and social rights that have emerged from both legislation and court decisions.

The perspective of the racial optimist is plausible if one indeed subscribes to a grade school textbook-like reading of the United States. At its base, we are describing a "good" nation, motivated by the best in human intentions and a desire to be a beacon of freedom and a lighthouse of liberty. Thus, renderings of U.S. history such as those of Howard Zinn (1997), Patricia Limerick (1987), or Ron Takaki (1993) are seen as either distortions or outright lies.

For the racial optimist, problems of school equity were *solved* by *Brown*, and the academic failure of large numbers of black and brown children reflect personal and moral failings. They do not do well in school because their parents are not supportive. They do not do well because their peers thwart their academic ambitions (McWhorter, 2000; Ogbu, 2003). They do not do well in school because they do not want to do well.

The racial optimist views *Brown* as an end point, not a beginning. Crenshaw (1988) identifies "restrictive" and "expansive" views of anti-discrimination law and it would be safe to say that racial optimists endorse the restrictive view:

[The restrictive vision] . . . treats equality as a process, downplaying the significance of actual outcomes. The primary objective of antidiscrimination law, according to this vision, is to prevent future wrongdoings rather than to redress present manifestations of past injustice. "Wrongdoing," moreover, is seen primarily as isolated actions against individuals rather than as a social policy against an entire group. Nor does the restrictive view contemplate the courts' playing a role in redressing harms from America's racist past, as opposed to merely policing society in order to eliminate a narrow set of proscribed discriminatory practices. (p. 1333)

Racial optimists see *Brown* as a "front end" agreement to level the racial playing field by providing access to previously exclusive arenas. They do not believe that the decision needs or requires equality of outcomes. Racial optimists feel that allowing equal access is the primary obligation of the state and that outcomes are a function of individual effort and ability, not state responsibility. Because of their reliance on "present-ism" racial optimists typically ignore the history of past wrongs. Their focus is on current conditions and they do not entertain arguments on the cumulative effect of past injustices and inequities (Robinson, 2000).

Racial optimism is compatible with the narrative of the United States that suggests that individuals have the ability to rise above their circumstances and experience success based on their own efforts and abilities. *Brown* is seen in retrospect by racial optimists as evidence of the national promise available to all citizens. The paradox of racial optimists' current support of *Brown* (in theory) is their actual opposition to *Brown* at the actual moment of its implementation. Many of the people who now celebrate *Brown* as a uniquely American decision formerly decried this same decision as an intrusion of the federal government into the purview of the state and local governments.

The typical racial optimist also is a free market capitalist who believes that race relations are better resolved without government intervention. She believes that the less visible the federal government is in the lives of its citizens, the better. For racial optimists *Brown* is less about mandates and implementation than it is about reconstructing a principle of equality—moving from separate and equal to separate as inherently unequal.

Below I offer a vignette that characterizes a racial optimist's perspective:[3]

Southtown was a midsize community that was known for its racial strife. When the Brown v. Board of Education *decision was rendered, Southtown was clear that it would not comply. Schools in Southtown were strictly segregated by race. White students attended school on the west side of town; black students attended school on the east side. West side schools had the most up to date textbooks, materials, and supplies. Its teachers had graduated from the local teachers college and were members of the local churches, civic groups, and clubs. East side schools received their textbooks from the west side schools' castoffs. The physical facilities on the east side were deplorable—drafty buildings, small classrooms, faulty wiring—and the classrooms were overcrowded. All of the east side teachers were African Americans who had attended the state's Historically Black College.*

A decade passed before Southtown did anything to implement the Brown *decision. Finally, under the threat of loss of federal funds, the schools of Southtown were forced to desegregate. Once the desegregation plan was developed, some interesting things began to happen. A significant number of white parents organized and opened private schools. Once the desegregation order was put in place, a number of the segregated African American schools were closed and this resulted in the firing of a large number of the African American teachers.*

Once the African American students began attending the newly desegregated schools they experienced a variety of forms of racism—overt and covert. Some students were quickly placed in low-level learning tracks segregated by race, while a few were placed in classrooms with white children, but were regularly ignored by both the teacher and their white classmates. Over time, student achievement among the black and white students varied widely. Black students' achievement lagged behind that of whites, and they were three times more likely to drop out of school and five times more likely to be suspended from school than white students.

Racial optimists believe that the achievement gap that resulted between blacks and whites in Southtown is a manifestation of the failure of the individual black students, their families, and their community. They did not see that the schools had any responsibility for ensuring that equality of access was translated into equality of achievement.

Racial Liberals

The second scenario involves what I term the *racial liberals*. People in this category are by far the most visible and vocal in the school desegregation discourse. They believe, like racial optimists, that *Brown* was a correctly decided case that represents the best of American jurisprudence. Unlike racial optimists, racial liberals feel that *Brown* has fallen short—not because it was the wrong decision, but because it was not fully implemented. One of the challenges for racial liberals is their conflation of notions of desegregation and integration. For the purposes of this discussion I am defining desegregation as the physical act of placing students from racial ethnic groups in a school setting with another racial group where one group has previously been disadvantaged by a variety of structural and symbolic barriers and the other group has historically and consistently benefited from this arrangement. The typical arrangement involved placing black and white or brown and white students together. This does not imply the placing of two marginalized groups together, for example, placing black and brown students in the same school.

School integration, as I am using it in this discussion, is a more planned and deliberate activity that involves taking students from the physical state of being placed in the school with a different racial group to being fully incorporated into the life of a school. Integrated schools have subordinated group members as full participants in every strata of the school—classes, extracurricular activities, and community presence. Unfortunately, the more common model is the desegregation model where, for example, black students are in the school with white students, but rarely are a part of the entire school. What one observes in this setting is that although the school is desegregated in the aggregate, it is resegregated in the particular. White students dominate higher-level classes and high status activities (e.g., the orchestra, the honor society) while black and brown students fill lower level and basic classes and low status programs (e.g., remedial classes, vocational tracks).

One of the models of school desegregation is the magnet school. The premise of this design is to create some specialty program at a school that allows it to attract students from a variety of parts of a geographic region, giving priority to those students from a racial/ethnic group that is underrepresented. However, at some magnet schools, we observe the formation of two schools within the same building (Goldring & Smrekar, 2000). In a performing arts magnet in a western state we saw that the top floors of a high school building housed the magnet and the lower floors housed the "regular" school. What was more evident was those top floors were all white while the bottom levels were all Latina/o. This school might be designated as a desegregated school; it would meet the overall criterion for desegregation. Latina/o students are less than 40% of the total school, but they are wholly concentrated in the program outside of the magnet school.

Because racial liberals may confuse desegregation with integration, they tend to see the success of *Brown* through mathematical lenses. The important aspect of desegregation for racial liberals is that it (desegregation) is put into place. Racial liberals are aware of the unequal academic outcomes that continue to exist between black and white students. They also believe that schools have some responsibility for mitigating the disparities. However, their assumption is that *Brown* remedies continue to be the appropriate ones for coping with issues of school inequity. Racial liberals refer to *Brown* as unfulfilled, implying that persistence on this course will (or should) lead to the hoped-for equality of outcomes. Unspoken among racial liberals are the ways that their own self-interests are a necessary component of their support of school desegregation. Below is a vignette from a racial liberal perspective:

Northtown is a bustling city that had not given much thought to school desegregation immediately following the Brown *decision. Almost two decades later, its history of residential, de facto segregation created very unequal schooling experiences for black and white children. After a series of lawsuits, black parents in Northtown secured a consent decree that required compliance with the law. The Northtown School District designed a desegregation plan based on a magnet school model. Primarily, students from white communities would be enticed to attend schools in black communities because of the special programs and incentives that would be offered.*

Northtown's magnet schools included programs in performing arts, science, technology, engineering, mathematics, world languages, humanities, and fine arts. Its incentives included free after-school programs and free extracurricular opportunities such as camping and skiing trips. After several years the school district declared the desegregation efforts of Northtown a success. Their indicators for this success were the ability to retain white families, the absence of overt white resistance to the desegregation plan, and the popularity of the incentives (as evidenced by the number of white students taking advantage of them). Despite these claims of success, the data showed that African-American (and Latino) students lagged well behind their white counterparts on academic and behavioral measures (i.e., rates of suspension, expulsion, assignment to special education for "behavior disorders"). However, few people raised any questions about how success was being measured. Northtown's majority citizens bragged openly about the success of desegregation in their town. They insisted that their provisions for equal opportunity ensured that all students were treated "fairly," yet they admitted that they "still needed to work on" improv-

*ing the academic performance of their black and Latino students. More impor-
tant, Northtown's white families raved about how important it was for their
white children to "have the opportunity" to attend school with "diverse others."*

Racial Realists

The final category is that of *racial realists*. They are a small but
emerging voice in the *Brown* discourse. On the one hand they understand the value of *Brown* at its particular historical moment, but are less
sanguine about its benefits. Racial realists argue that the Supreme Court
justices were less motivated, in the *Brown* decision, by a belief that black
children were entitled to equal education than by the growing concern
for limiting Cold War propaganda that the Soviet Union was spreading
(Dudziak, 1995). Indeed, the consent decree (*Brown II*) with its "all
deliberate speed" provision virtually insured that the original decision
would be severely curtailed. Racial realists consider the costs of *Brown*
(Ladson-Billings, 2004) and challenge the notion that the decision was
universally beneficial to black students.

Racial realists look at *Brown* in the context of ultimate benefit to
black students. Thus, questions of equal educational outcomes are first
and foremost in their evaluation of *Brown's* effectiveness. They are less
focused on the number of black children who have the "opportunity"
to attend schools with white children than the number of black children
whose opportunities manifest as improved school performance. Racial
realists place more emphasis on raising black children's academic
achievement than on merely insuring that the numbers meet federal
compliance (Tate, Ladson-Billings, & Grant, 1993).

*The school board of Midtown had worked tirelessly to achieve school
desegregation targets. However, with each passing year, more of its white
citizens elected to leave the town's public schools. A significant number of the
white citizens moved outside of the city limits into suburban school districts
while another group was wealthy enough to send their children to private
schools in Midtown. Many of the remaining white families continued to put
pressure on the school board to curtail busing for racial integration. In the
midst of this continued upheaval over school desegregation a group of black
parents came up with a plan of their own. Instead of trying to find ways to
make school desegregation work, these parents proposed a plan to create an
excellent all black school district. "We can't force white people to go to school
with us," argued one of the black parents. "If they want to go, then let them
go. We just want to know why our schools have to deteriorate because they
leave."*

The group's plan was to create an all black school district with a curriculum designed to address the specific needs of black children. Its course offerings would include African and African American history and culture, African American Literature, and other courses that included African, Afro-Caribbean, Afro-Brazilian, and African American art forms. Because of the crisis situation among African American boys, the group proposed two single-sex schools that black parents could select. Unfortunately, one of the first challenges the group faced was a lawsuit from women's groups who claimed that their proposal violated Title IX.

The black parents' group spent several years in court defending their position. In the interim more white families migrated to the suburbs or sent their children to private schools. Finally, the courts rendered a decision. The Midtown black parents group lost the case. They could not establish a separate black school district with two single-sex schools. Ironically, the number of white students had so drastically dwindled that Midtown had become a virtually all black school district, but an all black school district without the power to institute the curriculum changes that the parents' group wanted. As one parent commented, "we tried to secede from the district and all the while white people were seceding from us—and taking all the resources with them."

In their attempt to regroup, some of the black parents' group decided that it was time to join forces with Midtown's more conservative forces and push for voucher programs that would allow their children to attend better schools. Others rejected this strategy and considered other legal tactics for improving black children's achievement. The splintering of their efforts meant that small pockets of black children did get better educational opportunities, but the majority of Midtown's black students continued to go to substandard city schools where their academic performance continued to suffer. When asked by a reporter covering a story on the 50th anniversary of Brown *what the decision meant for the schoolchildren of Midtown, the president of the black parents' group replied succinctly, "Absolutely nothing!"*

New Narrative Possibilities for *Brown*

The cynics among us may believe that *Brown* has become a failed effort on the road to equal opportunity via school desegregation. My own inclination is to concern myself with what *Brown* has not accomplished and what its costs have been (Ladson-Billings, 2004). *Brown* does still offer some hope but that hope is grounded in a perspective of the decision not as an ending point, but as a starting point. One of the major challenges for the lay public in understanding legal decisions is in recognizing that the law sans enforcement cannot produce change.

Jonathan Kozol (2005) points out that the nation's public schools are actually more segregated today than they were before the *Brown* decision. The issue is not merely the failure of school desegregation to place black and white and brown and white students in the same classroom. More important, students in these separate classrooms (and schools) experience incredibly unequal circumstances.

Discussions of *Brown* often neglect the series of legal decisions that effectively rolled back *Brown's* intent. The Nixon administration worked hard to ensure that school desegregation would be a short-lived phenomenon. Decisions such as *Milliken v. Bradley* (1974), *San Antonio School District v. Rodriguez* (1973), *Board of Education of Oklahoma v. Dowell (1991)*, and *Freeman v. Pitts* (1992) each made it possible for states and localities to render *Brown* ineffective. *Milliken* closed off opportunities for racially isolated communities of color to include students from white suburbs to foster school desegregation; *Rodriguez* said that children had no constitutional right to equal school expenditures; *Dowell* and *Pitts* permitted school districts that were formerly desegregated to return to neighborhood schools because they were considered "unitary"—that is, there was no separate school district set up for children of color. All of these cases effectively diluted the power of *Brown*, making it little more than symbolic in most major urban school districts.

My stance as a racial realist makes me sound both cynical and hopeless. The promise of *Brown* seems to have evaporated in that small moment of civil rights activity in the 1960s. However, I am not without hope. It is just that my hope has moved away from waiting on justice to prevail in the courts and for a conscience to be awakened in white middle-income communities. I have learned the limits of liberalism when whites believe that it is possible to have justice without having to give up anything. My hope now resides in parents and community organizers who believe that they have a right and responsibility to demand excellent education.

Despite the challenges of recent federal legislation (i.e., reauthorization of Title I, known as No Child Left Behind), a number of community groups of color are developing strategies to ensure that their children receive quality education. In Chicago, the Black Star Project (http://www.blackstarproject.org/wp/) is promoting community action by reporting on the achievement gap and helping parents develop strategies for supporting their children. At the beginning of the 2005 school year Black Star promoted a "Million Fathers Back to School" event where hundreds of parents escorted their elementary-aged students back to school. Still other parents are looking for ways to leverage new regulations regarding charter schools. Although these efforts are small and do not address the systemic problems that plague public schools in the nation's poorest communities, they do represent a level of agency that mainstream America is largely unaware of.

Another strategy that is starting to gain momentum is a legal one. To date, several communities in New York, South Carolina, and North Carolina have charged that their states have failed to live up to the state constitutional guarantees of "adequate basic education" for all citizens. In almost every case the state has resisted the notion that school ineq-uities are tied to race. Instead, the plaintiffs in these cases have had to make an argument based on socioeconomic status, knowing that race and class covary and that underserved poor children in urban areas are much more likely to be underserved poor children of color.

One of the challenges of using *Brown* as the cornerstone of educational equality comes out of the way the case was argued. The attorneys for the plaintiffs built their case on a foundation of black inferiority. As Prendergast (2003) states, "the arguments of psycholog-ical harm, as construed in *Brown I*, provided grounds for overturning separate but equal without challenging White supremacy" (p. 24). The experts for the plaintiffs argued that black inferiority was exacer-bated by segregation and that was the primary reason to overturn the separate but equal principle. By pathologizing the plaintiff instead of addressing the underlying pathology of the defendant—white supremacy—the ruling and its implementation were limited. Instead of seeing the ruling as something the nation was doing to live up to its own promise, it ultimately became something whites were doing for blacks. Thus, the failure of blacks to achieve in school is read as their inability to take advantage of the opportunity benevolent whites provided them.

My argument is that *Brown* is not an ending point, but rather a starting point, even more than 50 years later. It is a first step in exposing ongoing inequities in the nation's schools. At a minimum, schools must provide students with adequate resources to learn and participate fully in the knowledge economy. The promise of *Brown* was that desegre-gated schooling would help close the achievement gap that exists between black and white and brown and white students. Hindsight tells us that such a hope was naïve at best. As Anyon (2005) has demon-strated, the challenges of urban education go far beyond the school-house doors. They extend to federal and state policies that make it almost impossible for some groups to earn a living wage and participate fully in society. These policy decisions sustain an underclass and guarantee that their children will stay trapped in the lowest social rungs.

Brown can only be successful if communities of color mobilize to develop strategies that confront the ongoing structural concerns that decades of neglect have produced. What *Brown* means for now is wholly dependent on one's ideology. For the conventional, *Brown* remains iconic—a great decision widely celebrated as a symbol of American values of democracy, equality, and justice. For others, *Brown* is a failed project—another example of the U.S. failure to truly serve all of its citizens. And for still others, *Brown* is a starting point—an example of how Bell's (1980) notion of interest convergence is enacted. The whites supported it because it was an exemplar of America's exceptionality (Appleby, 1992). Blacks hailed it as one of the first real opportunities to receive quality education. Unfortunately, *Brown's* full promise has not been realized for either group.

Historian James Patterson (2001) reports that Justice Thurgood Marshall's former aide, Robert Carter, wrote in 1994, "for most black children, *Brown's* constitutional guarantee of equal educational opportunity has been an arid abstraction, having no effect whatsoever on the educational offerings black children are given or the deteriorating schools they attend" (p. 210).

Brown is a significant piece of U.S. history and jurisprudence. Along with cases like *Marbury v. Madison (1803)*, *Dred Scott v. Sanford* (1857), *Plessy v. Ferguson* (1896), *and Roe v. Wade* (1973), it represents part of the official knowledge (Apple, 2000) that all U.S. schoolchildren should study. But studying requires more than memorizing names, dates, and events. It means interrogating the underlying history and ideologies that make such decisions possible. Students studying *Brown* in segregated settings must be prompted to ask what, if anything, has changed in our society to reflect the ruling.

The one ray of hope in *Brown* is that it was crafted in what is a relatively young nation that had endured 250 years of chattel slavery and another 100 years of socially sanctioned apartheid. The works of courageous people like Rosa Parks, Septima Clark, Myles Horton, Martin Luther King, Jr., Medgar Evers, Malcolm X, Stokely Carmichael, and countless others show us that there is something redemptive in struggle. Systems of oppression can be challenged and people can be both liberated and transformed. But, whether *Brown* is the vehicle that makes such transformation possible is an unanswered question. My best guess is that *Brown* will remain an important symbol with limited success.

Notes

1. I am introducing the notions of "racial optimists," "racial liberals," and "racial realists" to describe a range of explanations of inequality I have observed.

2. Portions of this section are summarized from an earlier publication (Ladson-Billings, 1998).

3. Each of these vignettes represents actual events that have emerged in the history of school desegregation. I have fictionalized and compressed them for the purpose of this discussion.

REFERENCES

Anyon, J. (2005). *Radical possibilities: Public policy, urban education, and a new social movement.* New York: Teachers College Press.

Apple, M.W. (2000). *Official knowledge: Democratic knowledge in a conservative age.* New York: Routledge.

Appleby, J. (1992). Rediscovering America's historic diversity: Beyond exceptionalism. *The Journal of American History, 79*, 419–431.

Barnes, R. (1990). Race consciousness: The thematic content of racial discrimination in critical race scholarship. *Harvard Educational Review, 103*, 1864–1871.

Bell, D. (1980). *Brown* and the interest convergence dilemma. In D. Bell (Ed.), *Shades of Brown: New perspectives on school desegregation* (pp. 90–106). New York: Teachers College Press.

Bell, D. (1992). *Faces in the bottom of the well.* New York: Basic Books.

Cooper, C. (2005, September 8). Old line families escape worst of flood and plot the future. *The Wall Street Journal*, p. A–91.

Crenshaw, K. (1988). Race, reform, and retrenchment: Transformation and legitimation in antidiscrimination law. *Harvard Law Review, 101*, 1331–1387.

Delgado, R. (Ed.). (1995). *Critical race theory: The cutting edge.* Philadelphia: Temple University Press.

Dred Scott v. Sandford 60 U.S. 393 (1857).

Dudziak, M. (1995). Desegregation as a cold war imperative. In R. Delgado (Ed.), *Critical race theory: The cutting edge* (pp. 110–121). Philadelphia: Temple University Press.

Dyson, M.E. (2000). *I may not get there with you: The true Martin Luther King, Jr.* New York: The Free Press.

Goldring, E., & Smrekar, C. (2000). Magnet schools and the pursuit of racial balance. *Education & Urban Society, 33*(1), 17–35.

Gordon, R. W. (1990). New developments in legal theory. In D. Kairys (Ed.), *The politics of law: A progressive critique* (pp. 413–425). New York: Pantheon Books.

Gramsci, A. (1971). *Selections from the prison notebooks.* New York: International Publishers.

Kidder, T. (2004). *Mountains beyond mountains.* New York: Random House.

Kozol, J. (2005). *The shame of the nation: The restoration of apartheid schooling in America.* New York: Crown Publishers.

Ladson-Billings, G. (1998). What is critical race theory and what is it doing in a nice field like education? *International Journal of Qualitative Studies in Education, 11*(1), 7–24.

Ladson-Billings, G. (2004). Landing on the wrong note: The price we paid for *Brown*. *Educational Researcher, 33*(7), 3–13.

Limerick, P. (1987). *The legacy of conquest: The unbroken past of the American West.* New York: W.W. Norton.

Marbury v. Madison 5 US 137 (1803).

McWhorter, J. (2000). *Losing the race: Self-sabotage in Black America.* New York: The Free Press.

Newman, R. (1991). "Louisiana-1927" [Recorded by Aaron Neville]. On *Warm your heart* [CD]. New York, A& M Records.

Ogbu, J. (2003). *Black American students in an affluent suburb: A story of academic engagement.* Mahwah, NJ: Lawrence Erlbaum Associates.

Patterson, J. (2001). Brown v. Board of Education: *A civil rights milestone and its troubled legacy.* New York: Oxford University Press.

Plessy v. Ferguson, 163 U.S. 537 (1896).

Prendergast, C. (2003). *Literacy and racial justice: The politics of learning after* Brown v. Board of Education. Carbondale: Southern Illinois University Press.

Robinson, R. (2000). *The debt: What America owes Blacks.* New York: E.P. Dutton.

Roe v. Wade, 410 U.S. 113 (1973).

Takaki, R. (1993). *A different mirror: A history of multicultural America*. Boston: Little
    Brown Co.
Tate, W.F., Ladson-Billings, G., & Grant, C.A. (1993). The *Brown* decision revisited:
    Mathematizing social problems. *Educational Policy, 7*, 255–275.
West, C. (1993). *Keeping faith: Philosophy and race in America*. New York: Routledge.
Wilson, W.J. (1978). *The declining significance of race: Blacks and changing American institu-
    tions*. Chicago: University of Chicago Press.
Zinn, H. (1997). *A people's history of the United States*. New York: New Press.

CHAPTER 16

The Premise of Black Inferiority:
An Enduring Obstacle Fifty Years Post-Brown

CARLA O'CONNOR

Gloria Ladson-Billings explains in her chapter that, in part, the promise of *Brown v. Board of Education* has not been realized because it was premised on black inferiority. She elaborates that "instead of addressing the underlying pathology of the defendant—White supremacy"—the evidence, case, and accordant ruling "pathologiz[ed] the plaintiff" (this volume, p. 311). Although the premise of black inferiority predates *Brown*, 50 years post-*Brown* we are no closer to eradicating this premise from the imagination of the U.S. public. We continue to confront it in academic, popular, and professional discourse on black academic achievement. It is articulated implicitly via the differential focus on and treatment of the black–white achievement gap. It pervades some of our more prominent explanations of why blacks underperform in school. It is echoed in popular renderings (as captured in the media and via the perspective of public figures) of why blacks compete less favorably than whites on a variety of academic measures. It is articulated in the hearts and minds of teachers charged with educating black youth.

As conveyed by Ladson-Billings, the premise of black inferiority is one of those "myths, presuppositions, and received wisdoms that make up the common culture about race and that invariably render blacks and other minorities one down" (Delgado, 1995, p. xiv, cited this volume, p. 301). In this response chapter, my analysis begins by elucidating how the premise of black inferiority was articulated in the written opinion of *Brown*. I then discuss some of the ways this premise haunts contemporary academic and popular discourse on black achievement.

Carla O'Connor is Associate Professor of Education, University of Michigan. Her areas of study are the sociology of education, urban education, and cultural studies and her research focuses on the racial identity, schooling experience, and educational resilience of African Americans.

The findings reported herein were supported by grants from the Spencer Foundation and the William T. Grant Foundation.

I begin by analyzing educational researchers' differential focus on
and treatment of the black–white achievement gap in comparison to
other documented gaps in achievement. I then turn my attention to one
of the most prominent explanations of black underachievement—the
notion that blacks disengage from school out of fear of (being accused
of) "acting white." I report on the extent to which the "acting white
hypothesis" is prominently featured in print media and other outlets
for popular consumption, and subsequently draw upon empirical data
to show how teachers employ both the premise of black inferiority and
the acting white hypothesis in their effort to make sense of the achievement gaps they confront everyday in school.

I denote how these academic and public discourses and these teacher
perspectives pathologize black people, and conclude by discussing how
academic, popular, and professional interest in black pathology compromises contemporary efforts to make sense of why blacks perform in
school as they do, and impinges, in turn, on the promise that *Brown*
would deliver educational equity.

The Written Opinion

In *Brown* the justices concluded that it was "the *policy* of separating
the races" that "is usually interpreted as denoting the inferiority of the
Negro group" (author's emphasis). In echoing the findings of the social
science evidence provided to them, Chief Justice Earl Warren, in pen-
ning the opinion, conveyed the belief that psychological harm already
had been done as a consequence of this policy; that is, black children
had already internalized this inferiority which had retarded, in turn,
their educational and mental development. He wrote:

To separate [black children] from others of similar age and qualification generates a feeling of inferiority as to their status in the community that may affect
their hearts and minds in a way unlikely to be undone . . . the policy of separating the races is usually interpreted as denoting the inferiority of the Negro
group. A sense of inferiority affects the motivation of a child to learn. Segregation with the sanction of law, therefore, has a tendency to [retard] the educational and mental development of Negro children and to deprive them of some
of the benefits they would receive in a racial[ly] integrated school system.
(*Brown*, 1954)

The logic and content of the written opinion conveyed that the
effect of segregation on black educational outcomes was *indirect* as it
operated via its influence on black students' perceived inferiority (or

negative esteem). In doing so, the effect of segregation was reduced to a social psychological reaction, as opposed to an institutionalized or material force that was internalized and which then systematically compromised black students' educational outcomes. Black people's sense of inferiority was consequently positioned as the most proximate explanation for black students' depressed educational outcomes. This foregrounding of *deficiencies* (in this case, psychological failings), while institutionalized inequities faded to the background (or in some cases remained unnamed), is not anomalous to this written opinion and the specific social science evidence upon which it drew.

Educational research has often highlighted the influence of those deficiencies that presumably characterize what it means to be black. Some of this research has been aimed at documenting psychological deficiencies among African Americans; for example, psychological research was often conducted under the presumption that "African Americans lacked certain personality traits deemed necessary for achievement strivings" (Graham, 1994, p. 55). Graham points out that within the field of motivation research, the study of the relationship between black students' motivation and their educational outcomes "has been guided less by general theoretical principles than by the relationship of particular constructs to socioeconomic status, the ease with which comparisons could be made, and the availability of explanations to account for *presumed* motivational deficits in Blacks" (author's emphasis) (p. 56). However, in analyzing the findings from this literature, Graham found that research findings generally contradicted the presumption that motivational deficits (e.g., low self-esteem, learned helplessness, hopelessness, low expectations) would account for why blacks performed poorly in school. On the contrary, blacks demonstrated little evidence that they had low expectations, felt hopeless, marginalized the importance of individual effort, gave up in the face of failure, and experienced low self-esteem. Their outcomes on several measures (e.g., self-concept, expectations) regularly exceeded that of the whites who often served as the comparative group (e.g., Friend & Neale, 1972; Hare, 1980; Kugle, Clements, & Powell, 1983; Whitehead & Smith, 1990).

When not focused on psychological deficiencies, educational researchers have denoted black inferiority in other ways. In some instances, as is the case with the treatment of the black–white achievement gap, the exact nature of the inferiority went unnamed, but the logic and content of the analyses nevertheless communicated this presumption. As I will discuss below, this more subtle insinuation of black inferiority is realized, in part, as a consequence of how educational researchers have named and emphasized the achievement differentials between blacks and whites in ways that do not parallel the study and naming of other achievement differentials.

In other instances researchers have focused less subtle attention on either the presumed genetic or cultural deficiency of blacks (e.g., Deutsch, 1967; Jensen, 1969). Although the suggestion of genetic inferiority is less rampant now than in the periods preceding and immediately following the *Brown* decision, recent work conveys that this perspective has not fallen completely out of favor (e.g., Herrnstein & Murray, 1994). References (often implicit) to black cultural deficiencies are still a common part of the U.S. landscape (Bonilla Silva 2001; Darity, 2002). The contemporary infatuation with the acting white hypothesis offers the most palatable evidence that teachers, academics, and the general public can be swept up by notions that signal black inferiority. The privileging of the black–white achievement gap and the contemporary love affair with the acting white hypothesis lock blacks and whites into a superior–inferior binary. I begin by discussing how that binary is articulated via the discourse around black–white achievement differentials.

"The" Achievement Gap

During the fall of 2004, I was invited to participate on a panel in a session entitled "Indicators of Inequity and Inequality: The Persistence of the Achievement Gap." I began my talk by drawing the audience's attention to the title of the session and the fact that in the absence of more specific identifiers we all knew that the subject of the panel was none other than the black–white achievement gap. The study of this gap has so dominated the educational discourse on achievement differentials that any reference to "the" achievement gap has become the recognized shorthand for the "black–white" achievement gap.

On the one hand, the extensive focus on the black–white achievement gap can be productive. The study of the black–white achievement gap provides one reference for marking and subsequently exploring racial inequities. We can use these demarcations to advance policies and reforms aimed at producing equity, provided that we also challenge, complicate, and extend the oversimplified conceptualizations of those phenomena that are said to lie at the heart of "the gap." On the other hand, our differential treatment of the black–white achievement gap relative to other achievement differentials compromises our ability to interpret precisely and respond effectively to how and why blacks perform in school as they do.

Although educational researchers do not restrict their study of achievement differentials to those between blacks and whites, these other differentials are rarely reduced to simple binaries. Even when binaries are evident empirically it is not commonplace for these differentials to be discursively designated as "gaps." For example, researchers have documented the extent to which girls have outperformed boys on a wide variety of educational indices including grade point average, high school graduation, and college matriculation and completion (Mickelson, 1989). They have alternatively documented how boys outpace girls in light of the underrepresentation of women in advanced math and science courses in high school and in math and science majors in college (Cavanagh, 2005; National Council for Research on Women, 2001). In discussing and documenting such achievement differentials between men and women researchers do not rely on binary classifications that parallel that of the black–white achievement gap; that is, although researchers make reference to and rely upon the concept of "gender gaps," these gaps are not typically reduced to or discursively categorized as "male–female" or a "boy–girl" achievement gaps.

Alternatively, it is well known that, on average, children of middle-class origins academically outperform children of poor and working class origins. Researchers have consistently documented that socio-economic status (measured by a host of indices including parents' education, parents' occupation, wealth, qualification for free or reduced lunch) is positively correlated with a host of educational outcomes (i.e., test scores, high school graduation rates, college matriculation and completion, summer learning) (Burkham, Ready, Lee, & LoGerfo, 2004; Coleman, 1990; Goldrick-Rab, 2006; Jencks, 1973). Yet we have not defined these gaps using nomenclature that parallels that of the black–white achievement gap. There is no reference to a "rich–poor" gap or a "middle class–working class" gap. Detractors might argue that researchers commonly rely on measures of parents' education and occupation when defining students' social class statuses and these measures do not translate into simple binaries. But how then should we account for the regular reliance on crude and dichotomous indices of social class (i.e., "qualifies for free or reduced lunch" versus "does not qualify for free or reduced lunch")? There is no recognized educational nomenclature that captures such binaries.

Additionally, racial gaps in achievement do not exist exclusively between blacks and whites, yet we do not extend nomenclature for these other racial gaps. There is no proffered classification for the achievement gaps that exist between minority groups or gaps that exist between whites and nonblack minority groups. The most telling unnamed racial gap is that which has been documented between Asian Americans and whites.

The academic underperformance of whites relative to Asian Americans often goes unnoted and if noted, regularly remains unanalyzed. Why are researchers inclined to ignore or conflate the academic performance of whites and Asian Americans, even though Asian Americans have been shown to outpace white Americans on a number of academic indices (e.g., educational attainment, overrepresentation in institutions of higher education, performance on standardized tests, enrollment rates in advanced math and science courses) (Hirschmann & Morrison, 1986; Wong, 1990)? The study of the black–white achievement gap conveys that "gaps" are worthy of empirical study, yet certain gaps are either deemed unworthy of substantive exploration or receive inadequate empirical attention. What prompts researchers to become preoccupied with some gaps while they lend little empirical or conceptual attention to others?

Lee (2006, p. xi), commenting on the effort to counter the notion that blacks are genetically inferior to whites (e.g., Jencks & Phillips, 1998), asks: "Why are investigations of this sort considered necessary— or even valid?" She continues:

To my knowledge, there are no comparable studies examining the potential genetic basis for the differences in test score achievement between white and Asian and white and Asian-American students. If test score data can serve as an adequate and reliable basis for evaluating potential genetic differences in populations, then perhaps we should undertake empirical studies to determine whether there is a genetic basis for why Asian and Asian American students typically outperform their white counterparts, particularly in the areas of mathematics and science. The very question is absurd, however; and no scholar, to my knowledge, takes it as a topic worthy of empirical investigation.

Although Lee focuses on academic deliberations regarding genetic inferiority, I would add that researchers find it equally absurd to explore whether or not cultural differences (and by implication cultural deficits on the part of white Americans) explain why Asian American students outperform whites on a variety of academic measures. That is, they do not explore what it is about whites or whiteness that explains their underperformance vis-à-vis Asian Americans. Instead the study of the relationship between Asian American culture and Asian American academic success is either articulated in the absence of a comparative group or in relation to other minority groups (see Slaughter-Defoe, Nakagawa, Takanishi, & Johnson, 1990, for a review of some of this literature). Consequently, whites are never situated in ways that would position them as inferior to some other racial group. My intent is not to simplify the educational variation that exists among Asian Americans or to stereotype them as a "model minority," but to direct us to reevaluate why and how racial groups are positioned as they are in the discourse on differential achievement.

The emphasis on the black–white achievement gap not only eschews the examination of the variety of achievement gaps that exists between racial groups, but it also inadvertently homogenizes the experiences of both black and white people. The white–black comparison paints both racial groups with broad strokes and causes us to lose sight of the variation in achievement that exists within each group. The fact that some black students are successful in school and perform comparably and/or exceed the performance of whites receives insufficient attention. And while some researchers have documented the underperformance of poor and working class whites, with few exceptions (e.g., Heath, 1983), the import of social class and how it is articulated in relation to white (as opposed to black) underperformance is rarely studied in its own right or treated as a cultural phenomenon.

As a consequence of marginalizing within and across racial group variation in achievement, the heightened focus on the black–white achievement gap locks whites into a position of superiority vis-à-vis the inferior position of blacks. This binary implicitly situates whites as the normative referent for interpreting how black students perform in school. When whites are positioned in this way, we are inadvertently oriented toward examining what it may be about blacks or blackness that produces underachievement. The contributions of other factors, such as the culture and structure of schools and society and the attitudes and perspectives of whites (including schooling agents) fade to the background.

Ready parallels can be drawn between the U.S. emphasis on the black–white achievement gap and the prominence of the acting white hypothesis. In ways similar to the conclusions I draw in the paragraph above, America's infatuation with this hypothesis, often referenced in efforts aimed at explaining the black–white achievement gap, diverts attention away from the enduring structural constraints that shape black people's ability to succeed in school and in society more broadly and redirects attention toward alleged "problems" within black students, families, and communities. My discussion of the acting white hypothesis begins with a summary of its logic and origins. I subsequently discuss its influence in academia and its coverage in the popular press, and then examine how teachers in one high school exploit this hypothesis and other deficit explanations to account for black underperformance in school.

The Infatuation With the Acting White Hypothesis[1]

The acting white hypothesis, which was highlighted in Fordham's (1996) study of black high school students in Washington, District of Columbia, was first forwarded in Fordham and Ogbu (1986). As a consequence of this article and more elaborate enumerations of the hypothesis in Ogbu's and Fordham's single authored publications (Fordham, 1988, 1991, 1996; Ogbu, 1987), academia, the general public, and schoolteachers became familiar with the notion that black students extend limited effort in school because of a collective and oppositional orientation toward acting white.

Grounded in Ogbu's (1974, 1987, 1991, 2003) cultural ecological theory (CET), the acting white hypothesis is premised upon CET's distinction between voluntary (e.g., Asian Americans) and involuntary (e.g., African Americans, Native Americans, Puerto Ricans, Mexican Americans, etc.) minorities. According to CET, involuntary minorities, having been incorporated into the United States by force and having been historically disadvantaged in the competition for educational, social, and economic rewards, develop a distinct cultural frame of reference that produces maladaptive educational consequences. Their frame of reference does not afford them the opportunity to imagine their oppression in the United States as: (1) escapable (they have no homeland to go back to if things become unbearable); (2) temporary (they have elaborate historical evidence of the enduring nature of their subjugation); (3) justifiable (because they are not "guests" in a "foreign" land they are less able to rationalize the discrimination they experience); or (4) relatively positive (they have no compatriots "back home" who face a worse situation than that which they encounter in the United States) (Ogbu, 2003).

Given this frame of reference, involuntary minorities conclude "that they are far worse off than they ought to be because of white treatment" (Ogbu, 1987, p. 331) and develop an oppositional stance and identity vis-à-vis white Americans and what they see as indices of white culture. In turn, they "equate following the standard practices and related activities of the school that enhance academic success with 'acting white'" (p. 330). Faced with the burden of risking their own racial identity or affiliation with other blacks (particularly their black peers who impose social sanctions against acting white), black students opt to extend limited effort in school.

Treatment in the Popular Press

Sometimes inappropriately conflated with CET, the acting white hypothesis has been cited in or has been the focus of a bevy of articles in academic journals (O'Connor, Horvat, & Lewis, 2006; Ogbu, 2004). It has been the focus of panels at regional and national academic conferences and the subject of sole authored and edited volumes, and has been taken up by emerging scholars in their dissertation research (see Ogbu, 2004 for more information on these activities). Although much of this intellectual effort has been directed toward refuting the credibility or generalizability of the hypothesis, the attention to the hypothesis in a wide variety of academic outlets, for whatever purpose, attests to its influence (Horvat & O'Connor, 2006).

The extent to which the hypothesis has been chronicled in the popular press and articulated by public figures is especially telling. Since the publication of the *Urban Review* article, which introduced the acting white hypothesis (Fordham & Ogbu, 1986), as many as 158 popular press articles (including editorials) have made reference to the acting white hypothesis. Moreover, since the first popular press mention of the premise in 1987, the number of print media references to acting white has grown aggressively (see O'Connor et al., 2006, for a complete review of this growth in coverage).

During the first year of popular coverage, most references to the fear of acting white or being accused of acting white in relation to black school performance were closely aligned with Fordham's and/or Ogbu's interest in having us understand how this fear developed in response to black people's historical and contemporary experience with racial oppression and with U.S. society's differential reward and opportunity structure (e.g., Fordham & Ogbu, 1986; Ogbu, 1987). As early as 1988, however, all references to these structural antecedents were for the most part excluded from print media coverage and few articles attributed the hypothesis to the work of either Fordham or Ogbu. Additionally, most references to the relationship between the fear of acting white and black underachievement presented the phenomenon not as an academic hypothesis, but rather as a foregone conclusion, a taken-for-granted reality (O'Connor et al., 2006). Diane Ravitch cautioned "way too much has been made of the purported unwillingness of black students to study for fear of 'acting white'" ("The Answer," 1997).

As O'Connor et al. (2006) document, the acting white hypothesis has been taken up by a wide cast of characters. Teachers incorporate it into articles and editorials about their experiences in predominantly white and predominantly black high schools. Parents mention it in letters they write to newspaper editors about their own experiences, or those of their children, or their friends' children. Celebrities (e.g., Spike Lee), columnists, and public intellectuals (sometimes one and the same; e.g., D'Nish D'Souza, John McWhorter, Henry Louis Gates, William Raspberry, Thomas Sowell), and the leadership of national black organizations (e.g. the NAACP and the National Urban League) refer to it in efforts to analyze crises in the black community.

The print media's extensive reference to the acting white hypothesis pales in comparison, however, to the prime time television coverage it received during the 2004 Democratic National Convention. Barak Obama, state senator from Illinois, offered the following remarks in his keynote address to convention delegates:

Go into any inner-city neighborhood, and folks will tell you that government alone can't teach kids to learn. They know that parents have to parent, that children can't achieve unless we raise their expectations and turn off the television and eradicate the slander that says a black youth with a book is acting white.

Over time, the acting white hypothesis was increasingly invoked to convey how black culture, rather than racism or other structured inequities (e.g., low teacher expectations, poor curriculum, inadequate school funding), was responsible for (or at the very least *more* responsible for) the low achievement of black youth (O'Connor et al., 2006). Importantly, many of the articles that marginalized or were inattentive to structural factors were written in response to the Supreme Court's decision (*Grutter v. Bollinger*, 2003) to uphold affirmative action in university admissions. In these instances most references to the acting white hypothesis were offered in the effort to report on the perspectives of those who criticized the Court's decision (O'Connor et al., 2006). One such article quoted a member of the Center for Equal Opportunity who claimed:

The question underlying the University of Michigan cases is why are so few African-American 17 and 18-year-olds academically competitive with white and Asian 17 and 18-year-olds. . . . The answer to that question is not discrimination. . . . The answer is extremely high illegitimacy rates, poor public schools, and a culture that too often views studying hard as "acting white." (Richey, 2003, p. 1)

As early as 2002, Fordham was reported as "fear[ing] that the acting-white idea had been distorted into blaming the victim" (Lee, 2002, p. 3).

The cumulative result of the media's simplification of the acting white hypothesis and its near-total silence regarding the structural factors CET identifies was a public investment in the belief that the culture of African Americans was the source of the achievement gap. This, in turn, made it easier for conservative activists to orient public sentiment toward policies and practices that would further circumscribe the already inadequate gains that have been made since *Brown*.

The promulgation of the acting white hypothesis continues to occur every day in schools. Below I document how teachers in one comprehensive high school invoke the acting white hypothesis alongside other indices of black cultural deficiencies to explain local gaps in black and white academic achievement. As with what occurs on the macropolitical stage, their analyses divert attention away from institutionalized practices that impinge upon black achievement.

The Everyday Perspectives of Teachers

What follows is a report of how teachers at Hillside High School sought to explain the underrepresentation of black students in the most rigorous academic courses in their school. Hillside is a large comprehensive high school situated in a small affluent city that is home to a prestigious university.

Hillside's enrollment approaches 2,700 students. Nearly three quarters of the Hillside student body is white, and black students make up about 15% of the student body. Asian American students, at about 6% of the student body, represent the next largest minority group, followed by Hispanic students who hover around 3% of the population. Middle Eastern, Native American, and multiethnic students combined constitute 3% of the student body. During the period in which data were collected for this phase of the project (2003–04) Hillside High had 144 classroom teachers (including long-term substitutes) of whom 11 were identified as African American.

As is commonly the case in comprehensive high schools, the curriculum at Hillside was hierarchically organized. The bottom of the hierarchy featured remedial and vocational courses while the top featured Advanced Placement (AP) and accelerated (AC) courses. Researchers have repeatedly documented the extent to which a highly stratified academic system educationally disadvantages those who find themselves at the bottom of the hierarchy. In comparison to their peers who are at the top, students at the bottom experience less time on task and more impoverished curriculum and pedagogy (Oakes, 1985). Ultimately, they learn less than their peers in more rigorous courses (Hallinan, 2000; Oakes, 1985). Because Hillside's academic hierarchy was also racially stratified (a common occurrence for comprehensive high schools serving a diverse population; see Oakes, 1990, 1994), black students were disproportionately represented at the bottom of the academic hierarchy and, therefore, disproportionately placed at academic risk in light of curricular and pedagogical inequities.

Although black students constituted 15% of the student body, my visits to AP and accelerated classes revealed that when black students were present in these classes (and often they were not), their number was usually limited to one and occasionally two students in the classroom (or 3–8% of the class). College prep courses that were neither AP nor AC usually had between two and four black students. In contrast, my visits to remedial math and vocational classes revealed that black students made up 20–40% of those enrolled.

In the course of pursuing an ethnographic examination of how black students in this racially stratified academic system negotiated the relationship between racial identity and high achievement performance, I asked the 24 teachers who taught academic (as opposed to vocational, fine arts, and physical education) subjects to the black students in the study why so few were enrolled in the most rigorous courses in the high school. In most instances these teachers shied away from answering the question directly. Instead of explaining why so few black students were in these classes, they opted to list the qualities that characterized the black "exceptions."

They explained that the few black students enrolled in these rigorous courses came from "good families." They had parents who not only acted "as [good role] models" but who "value[d] education and imagine[d] that it [was] the number one way to advance in the world." According to these teachers, these parents "supported" and "pushed" their children academically and "encouraged a good work ethic." In some cases teachers commented that the students' fathers were "present" or were "strong." Nearly all of the teachers conveyed "it's about what influence the parents have."[2]

If teachers forwarded these descriptors in the effort to explain the presence of the one or two black students in the accelerated and advanced courses, by implication these same teachers believed that the majority of black students—those who were not enrolled in these courses—did *not* come from good two-parent families in which parents were effectual, valued education, pushed and supported academic success, and instilled a good work ethic. Most teachers' implicit characterization of black cultural deficiencies, however, extended beyond the insinuation of inferior parenting. More than half of the teachers offered perspectives that were consistent with the acting white hypothesis. For example, having asked a teacher of a college prep Humanities seminar why so few black students were enrolled in her course, she first noted, "I think the answer is very complicated." Yet she followed with a reductionist account of the acting white hypothesis. She explained:

[This course] is perceived as a high-powered course [and] within the black student body there is the sense that being academically successful is being white. This course is seen as a home for the academically successful.

She, however, added:

And then our curriculum is designed to be on Western Civilization which is sometimes perceived as exclusive. I think that that has been overemphasized in a way that does damage. Along the same note when [black students] see African-American images in the art they get excited and become engaged. So I make a point of bringing that in as much as possible.

This teacher acknowledges, in part, how an Eurocentric curriculum and the absence of African American "images" might quell the academic enthusiasm of black students. She also reports on her efforts to include artwork that features black images, as she recognizes how excited and engaged black students become when they see themselves in the art included in the art history segment of this interdisciplinary seminar. Nevertheless, she maintains that the perception that a focus on Western Civilization is exclusive has been inappropriately stressed and is detrimental. Thus, while she is inclined to qualify the extent to which an Eurocentric curricular emphasis may thwart black academic engagement, she offers no qualifications when she extends her belief that black students associate being academically successful with being white and therefore opt not to enroll in her class because it is the "home" for the academically successful.

In response to the same question about black representation in the most rigorous courses in the school, a Calculus teacher conveyed his disgust with what he referred to as the "attitude" of black students. He explained:

I'm so sick of the attitude that you can't play the white man's game. Their own peer group telling them they can't take the class—own peer group won't allow it. I've been here since 1993–1994 and it's always a fight to get black students to excel. It's not about ability. This doesn't apply [to one of the respondents in your study]. But too many of the black kids fall into that trap. [The respondent in your study] is too strong for that. Here black kids get pressure if they excel. Black students don't even think of [the respondent in your study] as Black. It's the rare student like [this same student] who has the strength to say no. Or they have the rare parent.

Like the Humanities teacher, the Calculus teacher imagined that black students were ensnared in some kind of cultural "trap"—one that was set and monitored via peer relations and sanctions. In the case of the Calculus teacher this trap was reflected in the black attitude that schooling was a white man's game and that black adolescents colluded (sometimes ineffectively in the case of the exceptionally strong student who had the rare black parent) in efforts to ensure that other black students would not play the game.

Often, teachers' unreflexive acceptance of the premises of the acting white hypothesis were situated in less elaborate commentary. For example, one teacher, after commenting on the importance of good parenting, added, "Then there's the peer pressure not to do well. But some [black] students have not succumbed to that pressure. They are doing well in school and are very popular, too." Consistent with the acting white hypothesis, Hillside teachers expressed time and time again that black peer relations were maladaptive and impinged on black achievement.

Importantly, these teachers' emphasis on negative black peer pressure and the acting white hypothesis was not echoed by the black students interviewed for the research project. Only a handful of the nearly 50 students interviewed indicated that accusations of acting white were wielded in response to black students' making strong academic efforts or excelling in school. The disjuncture between teacher and student perspectives regarding the salience of the acting white hypothesis is not an isolated finding. Carter (2005) found that while black and Latino students associated acting white with cultural styles and tastes that were manifested via speech, dress, and acquaintances, it was not associated with academic excellence. More pointedly, Tough (2004, p. 52), citing the findings from Tyson, Darity, & Castellino's (2005) multi-school study, reported:

The one school where [Tyson and Darity] did find anxiety about "acting white" was the one in which black students were drastically underrepresented in the gifted-and-talented classes. And significantly, at this particular school, the notion of the burden of "acting white" was most pervasive not among the black students interviewed by the researchers, but among their teachers and administrators, who told researchers that blacks are "averse to success" and "don't place a high value on education."

Some teachers did not state in explicit terms that they believed that black students were averse to academic success. They nevertheless conveyed that a black racial identity (especially if heightened) was incompatible with academic excellence. This stance was communicated circuitously by a Chemistry teacher who had been teaching at Hillside since the 1960s. In response to my inquiry about black students' enrollment in classes in the upper end of the academic hierarchy, he began by stating that back in the 1960s "there was a lot of racial tension" in the school: "You could cut the tension with a knife. Students were afraid. Teachers were afraid." He noted, however, that "it was not all about race." He mentioned students "walk[ing] out" in pursuit of the right to smoke on school grounds, and then mentioned the one black kid on the swim team:

there was a black kid on the swim team and we had some kids from the south—some kids who were really racist. And yet Deven [the black kid] didn't have a hard time. I asked [the other members of the swim team] why. They said, "Well Deven is not Black."

The teacher then lamented, "I don't see that anymore. So many of these [black] kids wear race on their sleeves." Taking a less than direct route in his effort to answer my question, this teacher ultimately associated the underrepresentation of black students in high-level courses with what he saw as black students' tendency to wear "race on their sleeves." This contemporary cultural orientation was contrasted with a bygone era, when a black student like Deven was not even read as black by some of the most racist students in the school.

Ultimately each of these teachers concluded that blacks were primarily, if not exclusively, responsible for their underrepresentation in

Hillside's more competitive academic courses. They referenced a variety of culturally laden explanations that highlighted deficits in black parenting, family values, peer relations, racial identities, and racialized beliefs about academic success.

Out of the 24 academic teachers I formally interviewed, only two departed from perspectives like those featured above. One of these teachers, Ms. Ramirez, was Latina. The second, Ms. Davis, was a white woman who had received her M.A. in a certification program that emphasized social justice and prepared teachers to work in urban settings. A third teacher, Ms. Allen, a white woman who I would later learn was gay, caught me in the hall after overhearing my interview with the math teacher, who explained that he was "sick of the [black] attitude that you can't play the white man's game." She began by saying "If you have some time, I would like to offer you a *different* perspective" (original emphasis). As we walked down the hall and came to a stop outside her classroom, she explained to me that she had been teaching in the 9th grade remedial math program for several years and every year she had black students, usually male, who should not have been placed in her class and should have been enrolled in Algebra 1-2. She continued, "By the time I recognize that they have been misplaced it's too late to transition them into the higher level math course. They've already missed too much. They can't catch up." She then sighed, "While the white students are given the benefit of the doubt when it comes to placement, black students aren't."

Ms. Ramirez, who taught Spanish, echoed these last sentiments, and also offered some insight into why Ms. Allen might have felt that "catching up" was not feasible. Ms. Ramirez was also distressed by how many black students were placed in courses below their skill level, commenting, "It's a shame. It's disgraceful. Drives me crazy." She too was concerned that "by the time [I] recognize their misplacement so much time has passed." She often worked to get the misplaced students up to speed so that they could transfer into the higher-level course and not be lost, explaining:

I used to meet with these students during their lunch hour, or before, or after school. I would tutor them over the summer. But then the union said, "You can't do that." So now I tell them to call me [with a lowered voice, as if to mimic the way she needed to communicate this offer to the students].

Finally, Ms. Davis explained to me: "We don't make African American students feel as if they're welcome in these courses. The students know that teachers doubt their ability to compete in these courses. That stuff just hangs in the air. And it is heavy—real heavy."

Out of the 25 teachers I spoke with regarding Hillside's racially stratified academic hierarchy, only these three conveyed that institutional practices and school culture contributed in substantive ways to the inequitable distribution of black students across the academic hierarchy. Although they did not name the precise source of these inequities, their perspectives suggested that something had gone awry institutionally, particularly in regards to the regular relegation of black students to courses that were below their aptitude. In the case of Ms. Davis, she indicated that teachers' low expectations of black students so pervaded the culture of Hillside High that it hung heavy in the air and impinged on the likelihood that black students would eagerly enroll in the school's most competitive academic courses.

In another venue it would be important to explore the fact that these "different" perspectives all came from women, two of whom represented other marginalized identities and a third who had participated in a nontraditional teacher certification program. For the purposes of this chapter, however, my interests rest with the fact that the 22 other teachers I spoke with were singularly focused on black cultural deficits in their efforts to explain why black students underperformed in school (save the exception of the teacher who made a qualified reference to how a Eurocentric curriculum might work against black academic engagement).

The Struggle for Educational Equity Continues

It wasn't that we wanted our children to go to school with white children. That was not the gist of it at all. We wanted our children to have a better and equal education, which we knew that they were not getting. (Vivian Scales, cited in Anderson, 2001)

Fifty years post-*Brown*, black people are still wanting for a better and an equal education. However, their wants have suffered under the weight of the premise of black inferiority. As elucidated in this chapter, the presupposition of black inferiority pervades not only academic and popular discourse on black achievement, but teacher interpretations of why blacks underperform in school. These discourses and interpretations privilege black–white binaries. Sometimes they do so empirically (as in the case of the emphasis on the black–white achievement gap as compared to gaps involving other groups). Other times they do so conceptually (as in the case of the prominence of the acting white hypothesis, which pits black and white racial identity in opposition).

These binaries situate whites as the normative referent for interpreting black educational outcomes and experiences. Whites are consequently locked into a position of superiority vis-à-vis the inferior position of blacks, and so, we are directed to focus our attention on what it must be "about" black people or blackness that causes them to lag behind in school.

By honing in on presumed deficiencies in the black community, researchers and the public run the risk of inadequately recognizing and analyzing how institutionalized inequities (e.g., racial discrimination, low teacher expectations, inequitable tracking and grouping, systematically poor instruction, inadequate school funding) depress black educational outcomes (O'Connor & Fernandez, forthcoming). In the absence of such attention, affirmative action and other policies aimed at redressing continued inequities are delegitimized and retain a shadow of their former influence. Moreover, we compromise research and policy efforts aimed at reforming the culture and practices of schools in ways that would allow us to realize the *promise* of *Brown*—the promise that black children would finally get what they were not getting: a better and equal education.

NOTES

1. This section of the chapter is largely taken from O'Connor et al. (2006).

2. The terms found within quotation marks represent verbatim phrases and statements from the teachers who were interviewed.

REFERENCES

Anderson, J. (2001). Introduction to part three, 1950–1980: Separate and unequal. In S. Mondale & S.B. Patton (Eds.), *School: The story of American public education* (pp. 123–130). Boston: Beacon Press.

Bonilla Silva, E. (2001). *White supremacy and racism in the post-civil rights era.* Boulder, CO: Lynne Rienner.

Brown v. Board of Education 347 U.S. 483–496 (1954).

Burkham, D.T., Ready, D.D., Lee, V.E., & LoGerfo, L.F. (2004). Social class differences in summer learning between kindergarten and first grade: Model specification and estimation. *Sociology of Education, 77*(1), 1–31.

Carter, P. (2005). *Keepin' it real: School success beyond Black and White.* New York: Oxford University Press.

Cavanagh, S. (2005). Educators revisit girls' loss of math, science interest. *Education Week, 24*(34), 6.

Coleman, J. (1990). *Equality and achievement in education.* Boulder, CO: Westview Press.

Darity, W.A. (2002). *Intergroup disparity: Why culture is irrelevant.* Unpublished manuscript, Chapel Hill, NC.

Deutsch, M. (1967). *The disadvantaged child.* New York: Basic Books.

Fordham, S. (1988). Racelessness as a factor in Black students' school success: Pragmatic strategy or pyrrhic victory. *Harvard Educational Review, 58*(1), 54–84.

Fordham, S. (1991). Racelessness in private schools: Should we deconstruct the racial and cultural identity of African-American adolescents? *Teachers College Record, 92*(3), 470–484.

Fordham, S. (1996). *Blacked out: Dilemmas of race, identity, and success at capital high.* Chicago: University of Chicago Press.

Fordham, S., & Ogbu, J.U. (1986). Black students' school success: Coping with the "burden of 'acting White.'" *The Urban Review, 18*(3), 176–206.

Friend, R., & Neale, J. (1972). Children's perceptions of success and failure: An attributional analysis of the effects of race and social class. *Developmental Psychology, 7,* 124–128.

Goldrick-Rab, S. (2006). Following their every move: An investigation of social-class differences in college pathways. *Sociology of Education, 79*(1), 61–80.

Graham, S. (1994). Motivation in African Americans. *Review of Education Research, 64*(1), 55–118.

Grutter v. Bollinger (02–241), 539 U.S. 306 (2003), aff'd, 288 F.3d.

Hallinan, M.T. (2000). *Ability group effects on learning in high school.* Paper presented at the annual meeting of the American Sociological Association, Washington, DC.

Hare, B. (1980). Self-perception of academic achievement variations in a desegregated setting. *American Journal of Psychiatry, 137,* 683–689.

Heath, S.B. (1983). *Ways with words: Language, life, and work in communities and classrooms.* New York: Cambridge University Press.

Herrnstein, R.J., & Murray, C. (1994). *The bell curve: Intelligence and class structure in American life.* New York: Free Press.

Hirschman, C., & Morrison, W. (1986). The extraordinary educational attainment of Asian-Americans: A search for historical evidence and explanations. *Social Forces, 65,* 1–27.

Horvat, E.M., & O'Connor, C. (2006). *Beyond acting White: Reframing the debate on Black student achievement.* Lanham, MD: Rowman & Littlefield.

Jencks, C. (1973). *Inequality: A reassessment of the effect of family and schooling in America.* New York: Harper & Row.

Jencks, C., & Phillips, M. (1998). *The Black–White test score gap.* Washington, DC: Brookings Institution Press.

Jensen, A.R. (1969). How much can we boost IQ and scholastic achievement? *Harvard Educational Review*, *39*(1), 1–90.

Kugle, C., Clements, R., & Powell, P. (1983). Level and stability of self-esteem in relation to academic behavior of second graders. *Journal of Personality and Social Psychology*, *44*, 201–207.

Ladson-Billings, G. (2006). The meaning of *Brown* . . . for now. In A. Ball (Ed.), *With more deliberate speed: Achieving equity and excellence in education—Realizing the full potential of* Brown v. Board of Education. *The 105th yearbook of the National Society for the Study of Education*, Part II (pp. 298–315). Malden, MA: Blackwell.

Lee, C. (2006). Forword. In E.M. Horvat & C. O'Connor (Eds.), *Beyond acting White: Reframing the study of Black academic achievement* (pp. ix–xiii). Lanham, MD: Roman & Littlefield.

Lee, F. (2002, November 29). Why are black students lagging? *The New York Times*, Section B, p. 9.

Mickelson, R.A. (1989). Why does Jane read and write so well? The anomaly of women's achievement. *Sociology of Education*, *62*, 47–63.

National Council for Research on Women. (2001). *Balancing the equation: Why are women and girls in science, engineering, and technology?* New York: NCRW.

Oakes, J. (1985). *Keeping track: How schools structure inequality*. New Haven: Yale University Press.

Oakes, J. (1990). *Multiplying inequalities: The effects of race, social class, and tracking on opportunities to learn mathematics and science*. Santa Monica, CA: RAND.

Oakes, J. (1994). More than misapplied technology: A normative and political response to Hallinan on tracking. *Sociology of Education*, *67*, 84–88.

Ogbu, J.U. (1974). *The next generation: An ethnography of education in an urban neighborhood*. New York: Academic Press.

Ogbu, J.U. (1987). Variability in minority school performance: A problem in search of an explanation. *Anthropology and Education Quarterly*, *18*, 312–334.

Ogbu, J.U. (1991). Immigrant and involuntary minorities in comparative perspective. In J.U. Ogbu & M. Gibson (Eds.), *Minority status and schooling: A comparative study of immigrant and involuntary minorities* (pp. 3–33). New York: Garland.

Ogbu, J.U. (2003). *Black American students in an affluent suburb: A study of academic disengagement*. Mahwah, NJ: Lawrence Erlbaum Associates.

Ogbu, J.U. (2004). Collective identity and the burden of "acting white" in Black history, community, and education. *The Urban Review*, *36*(1), 1–35.

O'Connor, C., & Fernandez, S.D. (forthcoming). Race, class, and disproportionality: Reevaluating the relationship between poverty and special education placement. Special Volume on the disproportionate representation of minority students in special education. *Educational Researcher*.

O'Connor, C., Horvat, E.M., & Lewis, A. (2006). Framing the field: Past and future research on the historic underachievement of Black students. In E.M. Horvat & C. O'Connor (Eds.), *Beyond acting White: Reframing the study of Black academic achievement* (pp. 1–24). Lanham, MD: Rowman & Littlefield.

Richey, W. (2003, March 28). Affirmative action evolution. *Christian Science Monitor*, p. 1.

Slaughter-Defoe, D.T., Nakagawa, K., Takanishi, R., & Johnson, D.J. (1990). Toward cultural/ecological perspectives on schooling and achievement in African- and Asian-American children. *Child Development*, *61*(2), 363–383.

The answer to racial discrimination cannot be more discrimination. (1997, December 14). *Louis Post-Dispatch*, p. B3.

Tough, P. (2004, December 12). "Acting White" myth. *New York Times Magazine*, Section 6, p. 52.

Tyson, K., Darity, W., & Castellino, D.R. (2005). It's not "a Black thing": Understanding the burden of acting white and other dilemmas of high achievement. *American Sociological Review*, *70*(4), 582–634.

Whitehead, G., & Smith, S. (1990). Causal attributions by Black and Whites. *Journal of Social Psychology, 130*, 401–402.

Wong, M.G. (1990). The education of white, Chinese, Filipino, and Japanese students: A look at "high school and beyond." *Sociological Perspectives, 33*(3), 355–374.

CHAPTER 17

"If Justice Is Our Objective": Diaspora Literacy, Heritage Knowledge, and the Praxis of Critical Studyin' for Human Freedom[1]

JOYCE E. KING

The capacities of men [and women] were constantly leaping out of the confinements of the system. (C.L.R. James, 1970)

The visionary social struggle that resulted in the 1954 *Brown v. Board of Education* decision did not take into account the ways ideologically distorted knowledge sustains societal injustice, particularly academic and school knowledge about black history and culture. This delimited vision of equal justice raises a number of questions of concern to this chapter: "Is equal access to a faulty curriculum justice" (King, 1992)? What pedagogical alternatives are available, if academic scholarship and school knowledge are flawed by the ideology of white supremacy racism? If racial division is learned, does our vocation as educators call for the critical moral agency to realize the unfulfilled hopes of *Brown*? In other words, "if justice is our objective," how can we educate for true human freedom? This chapter presents a morally engaged pedagogical approach that has evolved from my teaching and research on race, ideology, and education: the praxis of Critical Studyin,' which addresses these questions (King, 1995a, 1995b, 1997). Four key points delineate the logic of this pedagogical praxis and the conceptual tools—Diaspora Literacy (culturally informed knowledge) and Heritage Knowledge (group memory)—that define it.

The first key point is that African people's humanity has been totally denied. As a result, the next generation is alienated from their identity and heritage and unprepared to participate in the struggle for justice. Second, the cost of this dehumanization, alienation, and

Joyce E. King is the Benjamin E. Mays Chair for Urban Teaching, Learning, and Leadership and Professor of Educational Policy Studies in the College of Education at Georgia State University.

Black people's assigned alter-ego role as the penultimate "other" to whiteness—as slaves, second-class citizens or the post-*Brown* jobless, miseducated, criminalized underclass—is the attenuation of white people's humanity as well (Jensen, 2005; King, 2005; Wynter, 2006). Third, within this cultural framework in which to be white is to be more intelligent and more civilized, thus more human, a mode of black thought exists that is alternative to these "rationalizations" of Western thought and the white "monopoly" on humanity (Wynter, 2006, p. 162). Finally, educators have a moral obligation to counter-act alienating ideological knowledge that obstructs the right to be literate in one's own heritage and denies people the rights of "cultural citizenship." Such literacy does nothing to detract from being an American, but is fundamental for the "promotion of the well-being and preservation of particular groups" (Aoishima Research Institute, 2005) and genuine participation in a true democracy (Flores & Benmayor, 1997). The praxis of Critical Studyin' demonstrated in this chapter makes the traditions of black thought and ways of being, normally negated by ideological distortion and denial of black humanity, available to support human freedom.

Critical Studyin' takes its name from the thinking/theorizing of enslaved African Americans who, when they were "contemplating their enslaved existence and how to be free," stated they were "studyin' freedom." S.E. Anderson suggests the term Critical Studyin' to update the context of culturally grounded "practical-critical activity" (Kilminster, 1979), or praxis, that nurtures human freedom (Anderson, 1995, personal communication, July 16, 2003). This means becoming cognitively and emotionally free of ideological constraints on knowledge, thought, and morally engaged action or pedagogy. Studyin' (pronounced *stud*-un) in African American Home Language or Ebonics can mean acquiring knowledge or thinking autonomously or giving consideration to someone or something. Roediger (1998) uses a similar "Black vernacular English" (BVE) definition of "study," (i.e., "academic study and hard thought undertaken in much less formal contexts") to situate a collection of essays by Black writers writing on "what it means to be white" within the tradition of black thought (p. xii). This chapter demonstrates liberating knowledge for human freedom gained through Critical Studyin' in classroom and community contexts from within a Black Studies theoretical perspective. By deciphering the implications of ideological conceptions of "Blackness" (and socially constructed "whiteness"), Critical Studyin' offers a pedagogical alternative to alienating knowledge that rationalizes injustice, corrupts scientific reasoning, and obstructs critical moral agency.

Pedagogical Implications of the Ideology of Racial Reasoning

You have really educated me today. I didn't know any other people had been slaves except Black people. (California teacher, 1992 Textbook Adoption Committee)

As a form of knowledge, ideology bears a relationship to power and agency for domination or for human freedom. Following Karl Marx's "critique of ideology," and as further developed by Karl Mannheim, Jurgen Habermas, Paul Ricouer, and Anthony Giddens, I understand the antithesis of dominating ideological knowledge, which alienates people from themselves and their own best interests, to be *liberating* knowledge (King, 1992, 1995b). Before *Brown* challenged the legal infrastructure of the ideology of white supremacy racism (without eradicating it), the national mythology of black inferiority, a legacy of slavery, was normalized in history, religion, politics, science, aesthetics, and ethics—all academic disciplines. This ideology was institutionalized in every aspect of society, from inequitable educational practice and anti-literacy laws to the 1896 U.S. Supreme Court's *Plessy v. Ferguson* decision. *Plessy* upheld as national policy the Jim Crow system of racial apartheid that gave legal sanction to the fiction of "separate-but-equal" public institutions and facilities. The nation still needs to be liberated from ideological myths, masquerading as objective scientific or academic knowledge, that rationalize and obscure dominating power relations.

The National Mythology of Black Inferiority

The mythology of inherent black inferiority that justified African enslavement still has relevance today. How else could *The Bell Curve*, a book arguing that Black people are genetically inferior to white people, "remain on the *New York Times* best seller list for 15 weeks and sell a million copies within the first 18 months of its publication" (Banks, 2006, p. 148)? How else could the general population remain silent about the massive incarceration of Black people in the U.S. since the *Brown* "victory"? This myth is an expression of the belief structure of race that has long contaminated knowledge of Africa, black experience, and the meaning of "civilization" (Munford, 2001). An essay published in the *North American Review* (a journal of "literature and culture") defended slavery to its readers as late as 1896. Entitled "A Southerner on the Negro Question," the passage below presents the gist of the essay's argument that slavery was beneficial to African people and was, therefore, morally just:

> The Negro has not progressed, not because he was a slave, but because he does not possess the faculties to raise himself above slavery. . . . Where the Negro has thriven it has invariably been under the influence and by the assistance of a stronger race. These wanting, he has inevitably and visibly reverted toward the original type. . . . Slavery, whatever its demerits, was not in its time the unmitigated evil it is fancied to have been . . . to the Negro it was salvation. It found him savage and in two hundred years gave seven million of his race a civilization, the only civilization it has had since the dawn of history. (Mays, 1967, p. 342)

This racial reasoning made centuries of kidnapping and enslavement and decades of lynching seem morally justified and perfectly normal in the South and the North. That such dysconsciousness (King, 1990) or impaired thinking hinders the critical thought that moral agency requires becomes clear when the "Southern viewpoint" (abetted by Northern complicity) is compared to the empirical record and the experiences of those who were enslaved (Farrow, Lang, & Frank, 2005; Lester, 2005). According to theologian James H. Cone (1972), slavery meant:

> being snatched from your homeland and sailing to an unknown land in a stinking ship . . . [it] meant being regarded as property, like horses, cows, and household goods. For blacks the auction block was one potent symbol of their subhuman status. . . . Slavery meant working fifteen to twenty hours a day and being beaten for showing fatigue. It meant being driven into the field three weeks after delivering a baby. It meant having the cost of replacing you calculated against the value of your labor during a peak season, so that your owner could decide whether to work you to death. It meant being whipped for crying over a fellow slave who had been killed while trying to escape. (p. 21)

The belief structure of race, discussed in greater detail below, blocks understanding of the costs of this racial reasoning for all people, that is, for Western "civilization." Critical Studyin' affirms this understanding of human freedom, which the ideology of white supremacy racism negates.

Slavery, Ideology, and Pedagogy

One of the most damaging, ideologically biased narratives of the black experience in academic scholarship and school knowledge concerns slavery. The trauma Black students experience when the subject comes up in schools is a continuing legacy not only of slavery but also of the culture-systemic belief structure of race, which *Brown's* emphasis on legal equality did not dislodge. As I have noted (King, 1992):

Educators and parents are painfully aware that many Black students are traumatized and humiliated when reading about slavery. They often report that Black students do not want to discuss slavery or be identified with Africa and many admit that they lack the conceptual tools to intervene in this dangerous dynamic. Moreover, there is a generalized silence about it in the disciplines and fields of pedagogical inquiry that might otherwise be of help to them. (p. 328)

Historian Peter H. Wood (2003) also concludes that, after decades of scholarship:

the heart of the enslavement experience and its deepest moral and social implications still seem to elude us. This is especially true in the classroom, where even our best books and articles, lectures, and films too often continue to fall short of the mark. (p. 20)

In the absence of scholarly support for a clear pedagogical consensus, state and local politicians are attempting to legislate how slavery and the black experience are taught. In Philadelphia, for instance, a new required course in African American history has been installed. New York's legislature established the "Amistad Committee" to make recommendations to the legislators and the governor for curriculum and textbook changes. This committee will "examine whether slavery and the 'physical and psychological terrorism' against African-Americans in the slave trade is adequately taught in schools and textbooks" (Gormley, 2005).

What Is Wrong With Our Education?

The degradation of men [sic] costs something to both the degraded and those who degrade. (W.E.B. Du Bois, 1909/2001)

In the early 1990s a group of Sylvia Wynter's students at Stanford University organized themselves as the Institute N.H.I., or "No Humans Involved," the code the Los Angeles police reportedly used when answering a call involving Black or Latino youth. In a "Knowledge for the 21st Century" reader and workshops the students posed this question: "What is wrong with our education?" (King, 2006). A controversial textbook adoption process was occurring in California during this time, and many examples of conceptual flaws in knowledge came to light. Examples such as those below demonstrate all too clearly "what is wrong":

- *"Our" human origins in Africa.* The 6th grade narrative of "our early human origins" opens with a description of "naked, dark-skinned" proto-humans on the plains of East Africa millions of years ago eating the "marrow oozing from a bloody bone." The Teacher's Edition of the text directed the teachers to say that a cave-dwelling European Cro-Magnon Man with a "larger brain" (than that of the proto-humans in Africa) in one text's illustration "looked just like us."

- *The first immigrants.* American Indians, described in the texts as "the first immigrants" who "came" to the Americas across the Bering Strait, questioned the presentation of this Western scientific theory as fact. Ignoring the wide range of scholarship (and indigenous knowledge traditions) about the origins of indigenous people in early America fundamentally denies their humanity.

- *Human sacrifice.* A Chicana (Mexican American) teacher tearfully confided to me her reservations about presenting the chapter on the Aztecs of ancient Mexico to her Mexican American students because the text mentioned their religious practice of "human sacrifice" without discussing the indigenous cultural viewpoint.

- *Africans selling their own people into slavery.* African enslavement was represented as a story of how "forced immigrants came" to America: their greedy local rulers participated in the Transatlantic slave trade in order to buy "luxury" items from the Europeans. Not examined was the long tradition of slavery in Europe, the very different nature of lineage-based domestic bondage and indentured servitude among indigenous "African" peoples, or the cultural logic that permitted the Catholic Church to approve so-called "Just Wars" that Europeans then instigated among rival rulers to sustain a constant flow of captives for this "trade" and secure the profits this global enterprise produced.

These examples illustrate conceptual flaws in history textbooks that a diverse array of parents, other educators, and I opposed when the California State Curriculum Commission (on which I served) considered them for adoption (King, 1992). Despite opposition from concerned parents in a number of communities, many teachers who reviewed the textbooks were eager to have them adopted and made available to the schools for purchase. Although the textbooks were eventually approved with some minor revisions, teachers who supported the adoption chose to ignore the ideological perspective bias the above examples demonstrate. These teachers defended the normative monocultural (white) point of view in the textbooks as "multicultural." State officials and the corporate media deceptively reframed community opposition to the texts as an "us versus them" ethnic conflict. Somewhat cynically, official spokespersons asked: "Can't a White author write accurately and with sensitivity about the experiences of other groups?"

This question artfully dodges issues of ideology and the social interests any author's (or educator's) perspective can represent. In my experience, teachers who are constrained by the mindset of "whiteness" often do not consider that there is anything wrong with the United States or with their own education. For example, the mostly white pre-service teachers I taught in California for 12 years generally accepted the myth of the United States as a white nation that was just *becoming* more diverse. Upon entering the credential program, they also believed that their mission as teachers was to help these diverse "others" to be like them (King, 1997). These student teachers struggled with the realization that white supremacy racism not only denies equitable education to the poor and students of color, but also that miseducation for domination denies white teachers and students opportunities to realize their full humanity (Woodson, 1933).

Many white teachers (and scholars) who equate "equality" with assimilation and "color-blindness" dismiss the idea that Black (and Latino) students can benefit from educational experiences that connect them with their African heritage and identity. Nor do those holding this view, including some Black teachers, understand how U.S. society might benefit from Black people's development along these lines. A teacher in an "urban education" master's degree program dismissed a presentation I made recently on the subject this way: "Why should I talk to my Black students about their African heritage when some of them don't even know who their daddies are?" One reason is that research and practice show positive benefits of such identity development for Black student achievement (Glenn, 2003; King, 2005). The way Africa and black experience and culture are normally taught institutionalizes a dangerously incomplete conception of what it means to be African and what it means to be human, which obstructs Black students' opportunities to identify with their heritage. Others are denied opportunities to grasp fully the implications of the degradation of blackness for society and their own well being.

Critical Studyin' from Practice-to-Theory

The problem here is that few Americans know who and what they really are . . . most American whites are culturally part Negro American without even realizing it. (Ralph Ellison, 1986)

Critical Studyin' from practice-to-theory is inspired by the organizing-as-pedagogy tradition and education theory of activist educators like Myles Horton (Horton, 1990), Septima Clark (Brown, 1968), Ella Baker (Ransby, 2003), and Paulo Freire (1971). Learning for consciousness transformation is common to the educational practice Horton developed at Highlander Folk School, in the Citizenship Schools that Clark developed as Highlander's Education Director, in her earlier adult education pedagogy, and in the Freedom Schools that Baker's Student Nonviolent Coordinating Committee protégés organized (Payne, 2000). In addition, Freire's *Pedagogy of the Oppressed* and Wynter's (1992) "deciphering praxis" of Black Studies are important theoretical influences on the praxis of Critical Studyin'.

"Practice-to-theory" refers to remembering or theorizing how to reconnect the dismembered existential reality of African descent people. The goal is to recover historical consciousness, identity, and collective memory from ideologically biased narratives of significant historical-cultural junctures in black experience and culture. At these junctures in the "making of America," the knowledge, labor, and spirituality—in essence, the culture of African descent people—has been "stolen" or rendered invisible or inaccessible for Black people's group benefit and society's moral and ethical development. A Black Studies theoretical lens, Diaspora Literacy, makes it possible to decipher these "codifications" to foster what Freire describes as an "encounter with the world," but from an alternative vantage point of Black Heritage Knowledge. This praxis of teaching *through* culture contrasts with pedagogical approaches that emphasize "cultural knowledge," that is, what teachers can be expected to know *about* students (King, 2004), or with forms of "critical pedagogy." This approach adapted Freire's methods to the U.S. context; however, it cultivates the "critical consciousness" of individuals and subsumes matters of race and culture within a class analysis (Leonardo, 2002).

Diaspora Literacy

Busia (1989) borrows the concept of "diaspora literacy" from Vévé Clark's (1991) definition: "the ability to comprehend the literature of Africa, Afro-America, and the Caribbean from an informed, indigenous perspective" (p. 42; King, 1992, p. 318, n. 2). My use of the concept refers to reading the "word and the world" for the benefit of humanity through various cultural signs in the lived experiences of Africa's people here and there in the world. Diaspora Literacy means decoding "concrete situations of alienation" or "coded existential situations" (Freire, 1971) in "the culture of everyday" black life (Ransby, 2003) from a culturally informed perspective. Critical Studyin' focused on these significant historical junctures (situations) can develop Heritage Knowledge that permits African descent people to make connections with the African family and with larger issues of social justice in the world. Others develop more complete historical knowledge, critical thinking skills, and self-knowledge.

Heritage Knowledge

Heritage Knowledge is a cultural birthright of every human being. Equating heritage with a group's memory of their collective history, Clarke (1994) explains that unless a people "take pride in its own history and loves its own memories, it can never fulfill itself completely," adding that the "ultimate purpose of heritage and heritage teaching" (or Heritage Knowledge) is liberation "from the old ties of bondage" (p. 86). Clarke uses a poignant metaphor for this way of teaching/knowing: "A person's relationship to his heritage, after all, is the same as the relationship of a child to his mother." Also, Heritage Knowledge permits "a people to develop an awareness and pride in themselves so that they themselves can achieve good relationships with other people" (p. 86). Good relationships are possible by overcoming the constraining effects of the ideology of white supremacy racism on our collective memories, historical consciousness, and on knowledge.

Theorizing Black Experience: Alterity and Identity

At this level of Otherness the "negro" was not even considered, since he was not imagined to have languages worth studying, nor to partake in culture, so total was his mode of Nigger Chaos. (Sylvia Wynter, 1984)

bell hooks (1998) equates "theorizing black experience" with seeking to "uncover, restore as well as to deconstruct our history and our culture" so that "new paths" can lead to "complete self-realization" (pp. 46–47). However, these paths are blocked by academic and corporate media misrepresentations that connect African descent people to all manner of imagined "Nigger Chaos" (Wynter, 1984). So, it is not surprising to hear African American students declare, "I ain't no

African." Robinson (2000) situates group self-realization within a cogent analysis of the black problem with blackness:

Far too many Americans of African descent believe their history starts in America with bondage and struggles forward from there to today's second-class citizenship. The cost of this obstructed view of ourselves, of our history, is incalculable. How can we be collectively successful if we have no idea or, worse, the wrong idea of who we were and, therefore, are? We are history's amnesiacs fitted with the memories of others. Our minds can be trained for individual career success but our group morale, the very soul of us, has been devastated by the assumption that what has not been told about ourselves does not exist to be told. (p. 7)

The praxis of Critical Studyin' locates the black struggle for group "self-realization" and equal justice within the project of advancing human freedom (Wynter, 2006). Baldwin (1996), in a "Talk to Teachers," written 40 years ago but still relevant, explains the white problem with whiteness, and why white teachers need to be liberated from its myths and privileges:

The paradox of education is precisely this—that as one begins to become conscious one begins to examine the society in which he is being educated . . . and a price is demanded to liberate all those white children—some of them near forty—who have never grown up, and who will never grow up because they have no sense of their identity. What passes for identity in America is a series of myths about one's heroic ancestors. (pp. 219, 224–225)

Indeed, the dominant conception of "our national identity" is one of the most potent myths that constrain the moral agency of teachers, that is, their ability to identify with social justice as a legitimate part of their vocation (King, 1990). Missing in the scholarship and in the broader understanding of the unfinished business of *Brown* is a focus on the pedagogical implications and the conceptual tools needed to address this obstacle, which prevents individual and collective success for African descent people and also distorts white identity.

A Way Out: The Perspective Advantage of Alterity

White supremacy racism idealizes "human beingness" as a white, middle-class "mode of being." Black people (and others) who are subordinated to this dominant "paradigm of value and authority" experience a "psychic disorder and cultural malaise" that results from the sense of "nihilated identity" this (racial) subordination produces

(Wynter, 1989, p. 639). Derived from the French words "néant" or "néantisé," "nihilated" means the total denial of one's identity (as a human being). Negating conceptions of blackness (e.g., black and evil, black-hearted, blacklist, black sheep of the family, blackballed, etc.) are commonplace in English and in the languages and metaphors of other societies as well. In Brazil, for example, I was given a list of terms for conceptual blackness in Portuguese that included "Dia do Branco": Monday is a "White Day"—a "day of work"—because (it is believed that) Blacks don't (want to) work. Another example demonstrates the underlying biological conception of blackness as genetically defective. A self-described "racial realist," a white professor in an Australian university, wrote to a local paper warning that the settlement of Sudanese refugees in Sydney would lead to "a surge in crime and violence." The university administrators repudiated the professor's claims that "sub-Saharans" with "lower IQs and high levels of serum testosterone" enhanced the "risk of all these problems," and canceled his classes ("Australian Professor," 2005).

Wynter argues that within the cultural framework that these examples illustrate, any "sign of blackness" (or N.H.I.) denotes an "ontological lack," the total "absence of true (human) beingness" (Wynter, 1984, 1997, 2006). The willingness of so many to believe the widespread (but false) reports of Black people engaging in savagery (e.g., raping babies) in New Orleans in the aftermath of Hurricane Katrina exemplifies the "rules" that govern behavior and perception with regard to "conceptual blackness" and "conceptual whiteness" (King, 2006; Wynter, 1992). Paradoxically, this imposed liminal status of alterity gives Black people a particular "perspective advantage" that is akin to W.E.B. Du Bois's concept of double consciousness or Black people's "second sight" behind the "veil" of oppression (Wynter, 1997).

The perspective advantage of alterity can also be seen in the geopolitical controversy that erupted between Mexico and the United States when Mexico's "beloved" Black child comic book character, "Memin Pinguin," was immortalized in a series of commemorative postage stamps in 2006. An international racial hullabaloo erupted and charges of racial stereotyping as demonstrated by Memin Penguin's "exaggerated" features were lobbed at Mexico and its leaders. President Vicente Fox and his government "flatly rejected" complaints from prominent U.S. Black leaders and the White House. Quite surprisingly, an organization that represents some 50,000 Black Mexicans living on the Pacific coast, the Asociacion Mexico Negro, injected their (alterity) perspective and black identity into the debate. In a letter to Fox, the

Black Mexicans stated that Memin Pinguin is indeed stereotypical and racist. Lacking the perspective advantage of the Black Mexican experience of racism, other non-Black Mexicans stressed the "innocence" and "artistic value" of this cartoon ("Sixto Valencia Burgos," 2005). (Note: This is not to argue that no Black Mexican would see things from this dominant perspective.)

The Will to Blackness

It had something to do with his blackness, I think—he was very black—with his blackness and his beauty, and with the fact that he knew that he was black but did not know that he was beautiful. (James Baldwin, 1955)

The remainder of this chapter presents various examples of the knowledge and insights Critical Studyin' can generate. It would seem that 50 years after *Brown* and after Baldwin wrote the above lines, a focus on the "beauty" of blackness would be unnecessary. However, the examples of liberating knowledge in this chapter are intended to illustrate the alterity perspective that recovers and reclaims blackness, as well as black thought, social explanation, and theorizing, from ongoing ideological distortion and omission. The knowledge tradition and alternative vision of society that Dispora Literacy reveals as Heritage Knowledge can be "read" in black experience and cultural practice, in Black Studies theorizing, and in black creative expression. For example, coded meanings and cultural signs are found in black music (the spirituals, the blues and hip-hop), folk humor (e.g., Langston Hughes's Jesse B. Semple character) and folklore, minstrelsy, theater, film, and today's Spoken Word Movement (Fisher, 2003). Woods (1998), for example, has this to say about the blues as a form of popular black working class theorizing: "Emerging out of the rich tradition of African song-centered orature, and under conditions of intense censorship, secular and sacred songs became fountainheads of cultural transmission and *social explanation*" (p. 56, emphasis added).

"The Boondocks" comic strip, created by the young Black cartoonist, Aaron McGruder, shows the educational potential of the younger generation's vision and thought. Though not without controversy, this comic strip appears in over 250 syndicated newspapers (with over 30 million readers) and is now televised. The radical educators of Rethinking Schools (2001/2002) recommend it as a teaching resource: "The Boondocks comic strip has been critical and profound during a period when much of American popular culture seems cowed by conformist pro-war pressures. Excellent to use with students." Several Boondocks strips discussed below demonstrate not just a nonconformist critique, but a black alterity perspective in which a satirical critique of the nation's leaders is embedded in black cultural signs.

In the July 4, 2003 strip, Caesar reminds his best friend, Huey Freeman, the precocious Black-militant child-scholar, that July is "Black English Month." The July 17 strip is an exaggerated account of President George W. Bush delivering his widely publicized (and criticized) "Bring 'em on!" speech in Ebonics. An unseen television reporter's commentary delivered in standard English sets the context for this portrayal of the president "acting black" (King, 1995b): "After more U.S. soldiers were killed and wounded in Baghdad, President Bush taunted the Iraqi insurgents, saying he was thus far 'unimpressed' with the casualty figures." In the next panel, using language of the "street" the way urban Black youth might challenge each other to a fight, the president says to the Iraqi "Guerilla Fighters": "Is that the best you can do? A few dead? A few injured? Big Whup! Y'all shoot like my blind one-armed grandmother!" In the last panel, the television reporter speaks in Ebonics and his "finger snap" in the final caption is another clearly recognizable "sign of blackness": "The president then informed the Guerilla Fighters that 'they had betta bring it like it ain't neva been brought!' and *snapped his fingers twice*" (emphasis added).

This black speech mode is also associated with the braggadocio and ritualized aggressive style of some forms of hip-hop music and rap performance. Many urban Black youth and the acting black White "wannabes" who emulate them adopt this loud, loquacious, exaggerated performance style. This bravado recalls earlier flamboyant Black male personalities and performers who (unlike Bush) were masters of the spoken word, such as Little Richard (a rambunctious, style-setting singer) and Cassius Clay (Muhammad Ali, the poetic world champion boxer). The highly visual metaphor ("like my blind one-armed grandmother") is another "cultural sign" of blackness or everyday black language that is a staple element of the "Dozens," an indirect form of playful ritual "insult" perfected to a high art by consummate BVE speakers (Smitherman, 1986). Portraying the president "acting black" perhaps satirizes or "signifies" on his lack of actual combat experience. The "finger snap," the way Black females may punctuate their speech, introduces an indirect critique of the president's "manliness." While ostensibly a critique of the war, this panel actually reveals the hypocrisy of the (white) power structure: society's criminalization of young Black males associates *them* with ever-present violence and aggression. However, the subtext of this comic strip presents the Commander-in-Chief of the world's most powerful nation as having the attitude and demeanor of a petulant, volatile, to-be-feared urban street combatant. This is minstrelsy without masking (blackface). Understood from a culturally informed point of view, the (implied) swaggering braggadocio also hints there may be more talk than substance in the taunt: "Bring 'em on!"

In another Boondocks strip that encodes a black alterity perspective in black language and cultural signs, (then National Security Advisor) Condoleeza Rice's authenticity as a Black person is questioned (see Figure 1). Caesar, Huey's young friend who identifies totally with urban "street" subculture, asks Huey a question about Rice—a question that implies that Rice might not be *culturally* black. "Girl talk" among the "Sistahs" (Black women who are close friends) serves as a metaphor that signifies autonomous black critical thought and authentic (chosen) blackness. Caesar reasons that if Rice doesn't talk *with* other Black women the way black women usually talk among themselves, as (real) Black people do, maybe she is disconnected from Black people's ways of being (and from a black alterity perspective).

"Reading" these comic strips from a culturally informed perspective can serve an educative function. They also convey an important under-standing about blackness from a black alterity perspective: the "*will* to blackness" (Dubey, 1994) or chosen blackness is an alternative to nihi-lated identity. Staying "culturally black" is an achievement that Critical Studyin' can facilitate. The first of the "Ten Vital Principles for Black Education and Socialization" delineated by the American Educational Research Association's Commission on Research in Black Education is relevant: "We exist as African people, an ethnic family. Our perspective

FIGURE 1

THE BOONDOCKS, JULY 18, 2003

must be centered in that reality" (King, 2005, p. 20). If such socialization is the primary responsibility of parents and communities, teachers
can nevertheless learn how to recognize and counter alienating school
knowledge that negates the choice to identify with blackness.

Rewriting Knowledge/Rethinking Education for Human Freedom

But can you expect teachers to revolutionize the social order for the good of
the community? Indeed, we must expect this very thing. The educational system
of a country is worthless unless it accomplishes this very task. (Carter G.
Woodson, 1933)

Historians acknowledge that how history is written influences both
the way history is taught (or not taught) and historical understanding
(Fitzpatrick, 2002; Loewen, 2005; Weinburg, 1991). I teach and write
about such matters, not as a historian but as a sociologist interested in
the "sociology of knowledge that functions as ideology" (King, 1992).
What follows are six examples of Heritage Knowledge that Critical
Studyin' generates through a Diaspora Literacy "reading" of significant
historical-cultural junctures in the black experience. These examples
demonstrate: (1) indigenous perspectives on African people's cultural
practice before the Holocaust of enslavement; (2) how indigenous
knowledge, including the oral tradition, enables the recovery of the
existential reality of African descent people from negative stereotypes
like Aunt Jemima; (3) the stolen knowledge, stolen labor, and stolen
culture of Black people; and (4) a significant "generative theme" of
Critical Studyin': rewriting knowledge for human freedom.

Pre-Holocaust African Beginnings

To interrogate the black experience before the Holocaust of enslavement that Europeans institutionalized and globalized, Critical Studyin'
acknowledges humanity's origins in Africa (White et al., 2003) and uses
African language, Songhoy-senni, to examine indigenous cultural practices before the arrival of Europeans. (Songhoy, Songhay, and Sonrai
refer to "the people"; "senni" means language.) The Songhoy Empire
is known for the universities that were developed in ancient Mali and
for the manuscripts of the fabled libraries of Timbuktu written by
indigenous African scholars in Arabic, Songhoy-senni, and other local
languages. African languages bring the indigenous perspective to bear
on the examination of one of the most alienating and divisive narratives
about the black experience: "Africans sold their own people into

slavery" (King, 1992). Songhoy-senni, which conveys the worldview of the Songhoy people, is used to decode the concept of "slave" and the meaning of lineage from the African point of view.

Academic scholarship and textbooks fail to give adequate attention to the significance of "lineage" in the African context when explaining how European enslavement of Africans came about. Also excluded is adequate discussion of the indigenous systems of indentured and domestic servitude on the continent that preceded European and Arab slavery. Usually, it is acknowledged that African peoples engaged in various forms of bondage, servitude, and enslavement that differed significantly from the European system of chattel slavery-for-life (Bailey, 2005; Carney, 2001). However, as Davidson (1961) has suggested, greater inquiry into both "the mind of the European and the conditions in Africa" (King, 1992, p. 329) is required. The significance of lineage is evident in the meaning of the word "slave" (*barnya*) in Songhoy-senni: "someone who doesn't even have a mother" (H. Maiga, personal communication, June 1, 2003). That is, freeborn men and women who were captured in war were no longer protected by their lineage—their mother's clan. These "lineage-less" persons were never regarded as less than human and could also recover their freedom. They sometimes even rose to prominence among their captors. Hearing this explanation in community workshops, African Americans immediately connect this information with the lamentation our enslaved ancestors expressed in the "sorrow song": "Sometimes I feel like a motherless child, a l-o-n-g w-a-y-y-y from home" (Drake, 1977, p. 12). Through African language study, a neglected resource that offers educators unique access to the indigenous African worldview, teachers can learn to make connections to enable Black students "to recognize and affirm their collective identification" with African people (King, 1994, p. 24).

Aunt Jemima: Oral Tradition and African Spirituality

A counternarrative of the Aunt Jemima stereotype represents another example of Heritage Knowledge that Critical Studyin' generates. As opposed to the hurtful taunt, "Aunt Jemima, Ain't yo' mama black?" the oral tradition identifies "Jemima women" as caring, commanding spiritual community mothers who descended from Ifa priestesses of the Yoruba people of West Africa. In various locations, these women (Orixá) are called Yemaya, Yemanya, or Iemoja. According to the oral tradition, once these priestesses learned the truth about what was happening to those who were captured and sold into slavery, they voluntarily allowed themselves to be captured and sold so they could come to the Americas to look after and protect their people. In Brazil Yemanya is the Yoruba (African) deity associated with motherhood and rivers and thus with the Middle Passage—and slavery. "Re-membering" African women as spiritually empowered *protectors* and *responsible leaders* in this way evokes healing, cathartic emotions, and memories. Perhaps this narrative is so evocative because the "psychic malaise" many Black people experience is the absence of a sense of "belonging" and care. This personification of African womanhood negates the distortions of Black women reified in fiction, film, and the fantasy world of commercial advertisement. Compared to the "half true," partial narrative of greedy African kings who betrayed and sold "their own people" into slavery for European luxury goods, this potent symbol valorizes African spirituality and leadership.

Carolina Gold: The Making of America

The rice grown and processed by enslaved Africans and the foundation of one of the wealthiest of America's colonial economies is known as "Carolina Gold" (Carney, 2001). African women's sophisticated indigenous system of knowledge made Carolina and Georgia rice cultivation and processing possible and extremely profitable. To recover this heritage from ideological distortions of African womanhood and academic narratives of Africans who supposedly "arrived" here empty-headed and empty-handed requires knowledge of cultural signs (Diaspora Literacy) that pertain to centuries of indigenous rice cultivation in West Africa (Wood, 2003). Carney documents in *Black Rice: The African Origins of Rice Cultivation in the Americas* how Europeans *falsely took credit* for this fundamental African knowledge and complex technical know-how:

The knowledge and the expertise to adapt cultivation of a preferred [African] dietary staple to New World conditions proved among the scant "possessions" remaining to slaves pressed into slavery from rice-growing regions. . . . Key aspects of rice culture embodied specialized knowledge systems, often the domain of African women. (pp. 97, 107)

"Carolina Gold" is one of innumerable examples of stolen knowledge, stolen labor, and stolen culture, the "love and theft" (Lott, 1993) dynamic in the "making of America." In his essay "What Would America Be Without Blacks?" Ellison (1986) notes that Americans (and American popular culture) are culturally "part Negro." Critical Studyin' questions such as these have allowed the many students, teachers, and

community educators I have taught for 25 years to see the need to
rewrite knowledge and to rethink their own education: "What would
the United States be like today if African people were just arriving?"
and "What can Black Americans be proud of?" The most illuminating
responses acknowledge the hidden achievements of African people as
well as whites like John Brown, Mother Jones, and many others who
struggled for justice.

Elvis: Acting Black

The pattern of appropriating and mimicking black culture, including white artists "acting black," offers other historical-cultural junctures in which Diaspora Literacy develops consciousness transforming
Heritage Knowledge. For example, Critical Studyin' deciphers the
identity marketing of Elvis Presley as a white black singer ("The
King of Rock 'n Roll") without recognition of his apprenticeship to
black music. "Elvis's immersion in black culture, both the blues and
gospel," as George (1998) observes, "was as deep as his Mississippi
background would allow" (p. 225). This analysis of Elvis's "white
negroism" (a term George adapts from Norman Mailer's essay on the
"White Negro") pinpoints his appropriation of various elements of
black style, including his clothing (purchased at a black store) and his
greased-back hair styled like the "negro conk" hair straightening
"process." George also notes the irony that the "conk" look Elvis
adapted was intended to make black hair look and act like white hair.
Eminem, a contemporary incarnation of this "love and theft" phenomenon, is promoted as the most lyrically adept white black rapper,
a judgment that depends upon elevating verbal virtuosity (lyrics), one
element of rap, over the holistic art of Spoken Word performance
(Fisher, 2003).

Abolitionists Frederick Douglass and John Brown

Critical Studyin's focus on the fight against slavery also illustrates
the need to rewrite knowledge and rethink the kind of authentic education required to address the unfinished legacy of Brown. If Frederick
Douglass is most often portrayed in school textbooks as a lone Black
hero who escaped from slavery, John Brown has usually appeared as a
lone white "madman" whose crazy scheme to disrupt slavery failed
(Loewen, 2005). The totality of the system of thought that justified
slavery is difficult to imagine from the vantage point of the 21st century.
Historical accounts generally fail to connect the critically engaged

moral agency of these abolitionists—one Black and one white—with African American ways of knowing and being that helped to inspire their ethical break with white supremacy racism.

Frederick Douglass. Although slavery meant that no enslaved person could legally learn to read, Frederick Douglass did learn to read and to write, and before his escape he taught others to read as well. Literacy gave him hope; it instilled in him a "life-giving" determination to reclaim his humanity (Douglass, 1963, p. 84). Douglass presented his own life experience as a public testimony of the truth about the barbarity of slavery. His life also represented the enslaved community whose cultural resistance nurtured his defiance. As an internationally prominent abolitionist orator, writer, and newspaper publisher, his eloquent and courageous speechmaking refuted claims about the innate incapacity of Africans and their willing acquiescence to enslavement. Missing from standard narratives of Douglass's life is any reference to the collective nature of his coming to consciousness or the cultural signs that make his extraordinary accomplishments intelligible as African. These cultural signs would include, for instance, the deep bonds of communal affection and ties of reciprocity and mutuality that existed between Douglass and his enslaved compatriots as they furtively and collectively contemplated freedom.

Another sign of this communal cultural reality can be "read" in Douglass's reverent encounter with African spirituality, in the form of a *root* given to him by Sandy, an older Black man who befriended and advised him. (To grasp the full meaning of this incident knowledge of indigenous African and African American "root-work" or spiritual-healing practices is needed.) Explaining the significance of this incident, Drake (1977) quotes Graham's (1947) account that describes Sandy giving Douglass a bag containing "Soil of Africa." After initially rejecting the bag's contents as "voodoo," saying, "I'm a Christian," Douglass reverently accepts this spiritual protection, feeling "as if a great hand lay on his heart" (Drake, p. 21).

John Brown. A contemporary of Frederick Douglass, John Brown acted decisively, violently, and without remorse, but also with religious conviction, to abolish slavery. Although Brown was white, he identified with Black people's suffering, so much so that he dedicated his entire family to a blood feud to fight to their deaths against it. Missing from standard textbook narratives is attention to Brown's profound understanding of the "price of repression" (Du Bois, 1909/2001); that is to say, the "culture-deep" (Muwakkil, 2005) problem slavery and racism posed for white people. Also omitted is information about Brown's practice of seeking advice from Black leaders and from his Black neighbors, among whom he *chose* to live at a time when Black people were thought to be less than human. What might John Brown have learned *from* Black people like those in the free black farming community of North Elba, New York—Black farmers who, according to one source, had the temerity to name their community "Timbuctoo" after the fabled city of the Songhoy Empire in West Africa (Du Bois, 1909/2001, p. 21)? His serious study of black history and culture, particularly black slave revolts, informed his conception of justice and propelled his abolitionism to the point of outright war against the slave system (Reynolds, 2005).

In his biography of John Brown, W.E.B. Du Bois (1909/2001) argues that Brown's emulation of black culture and self-liberation, by the Haitian Revolution and Nat Turner's rebellion, for instance, marked his greatness. Minimizing these understandings deprives students and teachers of opportunities to understand how black culture and resistance have repeatedly ignited the struggle for justice and human freedom. Diaspora Literacy and Heritage Knowledge illuminate these systematically neglected aspects of the empirical record. Black cultural influences shaped both Frederick Douglass's self-determination and John Brown's moral agency. Critical Studyin's focus on deciphering such examples is essential for rethinking education for human freedom.

Conclusion: The Unfinished Legacy of *Brown*

In order to construct societies based on social and economic justice, a new form of consciousness must emerge. (Clyde Woods, 1998)

The examples of Diaspora Literacy and Heritage Knowledge in this chapter show what and how students, teachers, and community educators can learn about the black experience in order to join efforts to fulfill the promise of *Brown* (Bell, 1994). The novelist John O. Killens (1971), a leading intellectual activist in the Black Arts Movement that coincided with the Civil Rights Movement, identified the "white problem" that Critical Studyin' addresses: "The Western world deliberately made black the symbol of all that was evil and ugly. Black Friday, blacklist, Black Plague, black look, blackmail . . ." (p. 388). Speaking directly to non-Black America, Killens summarized the crux of the argument for a liberatory praxis of Critical Studyin' for human freedom:

This distorted image of the Negro has its negative effect on your children, too. It gives them a distorted picture of this earth and of human potential and ill-equips them to live in a world, three-quarters of which is colored and fast becoming free and independent. (p. 388)

Both culturally informed memory work for liberating human consciousness from society's myths and rewriting knowledge are fundamental for human freedom. If justice—the goal of paramount importance to Ella Baker, the revered master teacher—*Fundi*—of the Black Freedom Struggle—is our objective, the praxis of Critical Studyin' offers a proven, morally engaged pedagogy for human freedom to "unbrainwash the entire American people" and the world (Killens, 1971, p. 379). This remains our challenge more than 50 years after *Brown*.

NOTE

1. This chapter expands upon an earlier, shorter version that appeared in King (2000) and that is further developed in King (2006).

REFERENCES

Anderson, S.E. (1995). *The Black Holocaust for beginners.* New York: Writers & Readers.

Aoishima Research Institute. (2005). Cultural literacy and the restoration of traditional values among youth. Retrieved September 30, 2005 from http://www.aoishima-research.com/custom.em?pid=206198.

Australian professor sparks racial flap. (2005, August 12). *Chronicle of Higher Education*, p. A-42.

Bailey, A.C. (2005). *African voices of the Atlantic slave trade: Beyond the silence and the shame.* Boston: Beacon.

Baldwin, J. (1955). *Notes of a native son.* Boston: Beacon Press.

Baldwin, J. (1996). A talk to teachers. In W. Ayers & P. Ford (Eds.), *City kids, city teachers: Reports from the front row* (pp. 219–227). New York: The New Press.

Banks, J.A. (2006). Democracy, diversity and social justice: Educating citizens for the public interest in a global age. In G. Ladson-Billings & W.F. Tate (Eds.), *Education and research in the public interest* (pp. 141–167). New York: Teachers College Press.

Brown, C.S. (Ed.). (1968). *Ready from within: Septima Clark and the Civil Rights Movement: A personal narrative.* Navarro, CA: Wild Tree Press.

Busia, A. (1989). What is your nation? Reconstructing Africa and her diaspora through Paule Marshall's Praisesong for the widow. In C. Wall (Ed.), *Changing our own words* (pp. 196–211). New Brunswick, NJ: Rutgers University Press.

Carney, J.A. (2001). *Black rice: The African origins of rice cultivation in the Americas.* Cambridge: Harvard University Press.

Clark, V. (1991). Developing diaspora literacy and marasa consciousness. In H. Spillers (Ed.), *Comparative American identities* (pp. 41–61). New York: Routledge.

Clarke, J.H. (1994). *Christopher Columbus and the Afrikan holocaust: Slavery and the rise of European capitalism.* Brooklyn, NY: A & B Publishers Group.

Cone, J.H. (1972). *The spirituals and the blues: An interpretation.* Maryknoll, NY: Orbis Books.

Davidson, B. (1961). *Black mother.* Boston: Little Brown.

Douglass, F. (1963). *Narrative of the life of Frederick Douglass: An American slave.* Garden City, NY: Dolphin Books.

Drake, S.C. (1977). *The redemption of Africa and Black religion.* Chicago: Third World Press.

Dubey, M. (1994). *Black women novelists and the nationalist aesthetic.* Bloomington: University of Indiana Press.

Du Bois, W.E.B. (1909/2001). *John Brown.* New York: The Modern Library.

Ellison, R. (1986). What would America be like without Blacks? In R. Ellison (Ed.), *Going to the territory: Essays by Ralph Ellison* (pp. 104–112). New York: Random House.

Farrow, A., Lang, J., & Frank, J. (2005). *Complicity: How the North promoted, prolonged and profited from slavery.* New York: Ballantine.

Fisher, M. (2003). Open mics and open minds: Spoken word poetry in African diaspora participatory literacy communities. *Harvard Educational Review, 73*(3), 362–389.

Fitzpatrick, E. (2002). *History's memory: Writing America's past, 1880–1980.* Cambridge: Harvard University Press.

Freire, P. (1971). *Pedagogy of the oppressed.* New York: Herder and Herder.

Flores, W.V., & Benmayor, R. (1997). *Latino cultural citizenship: Claiming identity, space and rights.* Boston: Beacon Press.

George, N. (1998). On white Negroes. In D. Roediger (Ed.), *Black on White: Black writers on what it means to be white* (pp. 225–232). New York: Schocken Books.

Glenn, D. (2003). Minority students with complex beliefs about ethnic identity are found to do better in school. *Chronicle of Higher Education.* Retrieved on June 2, 2003, from http://chronicle.com/daily/2003/06/2003060201n.htm

Gormley, M. (2005, August 11). Legislature again delves into racism lessons in schools. *Newsday*, p. 1.

Graham, S. (1947). *There once was a slave: The heroic story of Frederick Douglass*. New York: Julian Messner.

hooks, b. (1998). Representations of whiteness in the Black imagination. In D. Roediger (Ed.), *Black on white: Black writers on what it means to be white* (pp. 38–53). New York: Schocken Books.

Horton, M. (1990). *The long haul: Myles Horton, an autobiography*. New York: Doubleday.

James, C.L.R. (1970). The Atlantic slave trade and slavery: Some interpretations of their significance in the development of the United States and the Western world. In J.A. Williams & C.F. Harris (Eds.), *Amistad 1* (pp. 119–164). New York: Vintage Books.

Jensen, R. (2005). *The heart of whiteness: Confronting race, racism, and white privilege*. San Francisco: City Lights.

Killens, J.O. (1971). The Black writer vis-à-vis his country. In A. Gayle, Jr. (Ed.), *The Black aesthetic* (pp. 378–398). New York: Doubleday.

Kilminster, R. (1979). *Praxis and method: A sociological dialogue with Lukács, Gramsci and the early Frankfurt School*. London: Routledge & Kegan Paul.

King, J.E. (1990). Dysconscious racism: Ideology, identity, and the mis-education of teachers. *Journal of Negro Education*, *60*(2), 133–146.

King, J.E. (1992). Diaspora literacy and consciousness in the struggle against mis-education in the Black community. *Journal of Negro Education*, *61*(3), 317–338.

King, J.E. (1994). The purpose of schooling for African American children: Including cultural knowledge. In E.R. Hollins, J.E. King, & W.C. Hayman (Eds.), *Teaching diverse populations: Formulating a knowledge base* (pp. 25–44). Albany, NY: SUNY Press.

King, J.E. (1995a). Culture-centered knowledge: Black studies, curriculum transformation and social action. In J.A. Banks & C.M. Banks (Eds.), *The handbook of research on multicultural education* (pp. 265–290). New York: Macmillan.

King, J.E. (1995b). Race and education: In what ways does race affect the educational process? In J.L. Kinchloe & S.R. Steinberg (Eds.), *Thirteen questions: Reframing education's conversation* (pp. 159–179). New York: Peter Lang Publishers.

King, J.E. (1997). Thank you for opening our minds: On praxis, transmutation and Black Studies in teacher development. In J.E. King, E.R. Hollins & W.C. Hayman (Eds.), *Preparing teachers for cultural diversity* (pp. 156–169). New York: Teachers College Press.

King, J.E. (2000). A moral choice. *Teaching Tolerance Magazine*, *18*, 14–15.

King, J.E. (2004). Cultural knowledge. In S. Goodwin & E. Swartz (Eds.), *Teaching children of color: Seven constructs of effective teaching in urban schools* (pp. 53–61). Rochester: RTA Press.

King, J.E. (Ed.). (2005). *Black education: A transformative research and action agenda for the new century*. Mahwah, NJ: Erlbaum.

King, J.E. (2006). Perceiving reality in a new way: Rethinking the Black/White duality of our times. In A. Bogues (Ed.), *Caribbean reasonings: After Man toward the human. Critical essays on Sylvia Wynter* (pp. 25–56). Kingston, Jamaica: Ian Randle Publishers.

Leonardo, Z. (2002). The souls of White folk: Critical pedagogy, whiteness, and globalization discourse. *Race, Ethnicity and Education*, *5*(1), 29–50.

Lester, J. (2005). *Day of tears*. New York: Hyperion Books.

Loewen, J.W. (Ed.). (2005). *Lies my teacher told me: Everything your American history textbook got wrong* (2nd ed.). New York: The New Press.

Lott, E. (1993). *Love and theft: Blackface minstrelsy and the American working class*. New York: Oxford University Press.

Mays, B. (1967). *Born to rebel: An autobiography*. Athens: University of Georgia Press.

Munford, C.J. (2001). *Race and civilization: Rebirth of Black centrality*. Trenton, NJ: Africa World Press.

Muwakkil, S. (2005, August 1). So very sorry. *In These Times*, p. 13.

Payne, C.M. (2000). Education for activism: Mississippi's Freedom Schools in the 1960s. In W. Ayers, M. Klonsky, & G. Lyon (Eds.), *A simple justice: The challenge of small schools* (pp. 67–77). New York: Teachers College Press.

Plessy v. Ferguson, 163 U.S. 537 (1896).

Ransby, B. (2003). *Ella Baker and the Black Freedom Movement: A radical democratic vision*. Chapel Hill: University of North Carolina Press.

Rethinking Schools. (Winter 2001/2002). Resources for 9/11. Retrieved on May 26, 2006 from http://www.rethinkingschools.org/special_reports/sept11/16_02/reso162.shtml

Reynolds, D. (2005). *John Brown, abolitionist: The man who killed slavery, sparked the Civil War and seeded civil rights*. New York: Knopf.

Robinson, R. (2000). *The debt: What America owes to Blacks*. New York: Dutton.

Roediger, D. (1998). *Black on white: Black writers on what it means to be white*. New York: Schocken Books.

"Sixto Valencia Burgos" (2005). CNN.com. Retrieved on July 24, 2005 from http://www.cnn.com/2005/WORLD/americas/07/05/mexico.stamps.reut/

Smitherman, G. (1986). *Talkin and testifyin: The language of Black America*. Detroit: Wayne State University Press.

Weinburg, S. (1991). On the reading of historical texts: Notes on the breach between school and academy. *American Educational Research Journal, 28*(3), 495–519.

White, T.D., with Asfaw, B., DeGusta, D., Gilbert, H., Richards, G.D., Swua, G., & Howell, F.C. (2003, June 12). Pleistocene homo sapiens from Middle Awash, Ethiopia. *Letter to Nature, 423,* 742–747.

Wood, P.H. (2003). Slave labor camps in early America: Overcoming denial and discovering the Gulag. In C. Payne & A. Green (Eds.), *Time longer than rope: A century of African American activism, 1850–1950* (pp. 17–36). New York: New York University Press.

Woods, C. (1998). *Development arrested: The blues and plantation power in the Mississippi Delta*. London: Verso.

Woodson, C.G. (1933). *The miseducation of the Negro*. Washington, DC: Associated Publishers.

Wynter, S. (1984). The ceremony must be found: After humanism. *Boundary 2, 12*(3), 19–70.

Wynter, S. (1989, May). Beyond the word of Man: Glissant and the new discourse of the Antilles. *World Literature Today, 63*(4), 637–647.

Wynter, S. (1992). Rethinking "Aesthetics": Notes toward a deciphering practice. In M. Cham (Ed.), *Ex-iles: Essays on Caribbean cinema* (pp. 237–279). Trenton, NJ: Africa World Press.

Wynter, S. (1997). Alterity. In C. Grant & G. Ladson-Billings (Eds.), *Dictionary of multicultural education* (pp. 13–14). New York: Oryx.

Wynter, S. (2006). On how we mistook the map for the territory and re-imprisoned ourselves in our unbearable wrongness of being, of désêtre. In L. Gordon & J.A. Gordon (Eds.), *Not only the master's tools: African-American studies in theory and practice* (pp. 107–169). Boulder, CO: Paradigm Publishers.

CHAPTER 18

Building a Literocracy: Diaspora Literacy and Heritage Knowledge in Participatory Literacy Communities

MAISHA T. FISHER

The corner was our magic, our music, our politics. . . . The corner was our Rock of Gibraltar, our Stonehenge, our Taj Mahal, our monument, our testimonial to freedom, to peace and to love down on the corner. (Lynn, West, Oyewole, Bin Hassan, & Moore, 2005)[1]

Hip-hop can return to its original form
Slave spirituals and the African drum
50 Cent will only be in our pockets
And education and de-gentrification is what we will market.
                                                    (Naja, 12th grade student, 2004)[2]

In the poetics of struggle and lived experience, in the utterance of ordinary folk, in the cultural products of social movements, in reflections of activists, we discover the many different cognitive maps of the future, of the world not yet born. Recovering the poetry of social movements, however, particularly the poetry that dreams of a new world, is not such an easy task. (Kelley, 2002, pp. 9–10)

Historicizing "the corner" as a site for learning with purpose and permanence, legendary wordsmiths The Last Poets describe this everyday space as a "testimonial to freedom" for many black Americans in a recent collaboration with rapper Common. The Last Poets celebrate "monuments" such as "the corner" in the same way the Rock of Gibraltar, Stonehenge, and the Taj Mahal have become symbolic for others. In this context, "the corner" serves as a metaphor for social, cultural, and political institutions created in the absence of schools, literature,

Maisha T. Fisher is an assistant professor in the Division of Educational Studies at Emory University.

The author would like to thank Dale Allender, Cathie Wright-Lewis, and Ayanna McNeil for their continued support of this work.

and other outlets dedicated to knowledge and information focused on the lives and multiple experiences of "Africa's people here and there" (King, this volume, p. 345). However, Common's verses confront what "the corner" has become in many inner-city neighborhoods, where he asserts urban youth "write songs about wrong cause it's hard to see right" and are "dying just to make a living" (Lynn, West, Oyewole, Bin Hassan, & Moore, 2005). Together, Common and The Last Poets enter an intergenerational dialogue with the intent to [re]educate black youth about these local institutions, or "free spaces," that saw both the birth of Doo Wop in the 1950s and later hip-hop music and culture. In his study of the "Black radical imagination," Kelley (2002) argues "efforts to find 'free spaces' for articulating or even realizing our dreams are so rare or marginalized" (p. 10). Fifty years after *Brown v. Board of Education*, King [re]imagines the phrase, "If justice is our objective," by challenging educators and teacher educators to recognize the limitations of "ideologically biased knowledge" in literacy education and to create "free spaces" for literacy learning.

In this response, I revisit young men and women whose voluntary writing and visual literacy practices helped teachers, teacher educators, and literacy researchers rethink the "funds of knowledge" (Moll, Amanti, Neff, & González, 1992) urban youth bring to classroom communities. Although this review is not exhaustive, it calls attention to the pervasive need to recognize and cultivate the skills urban youths receive from their families and communities. Next, I examine transformations of everyday spaces into teaching and learning institutions by people of African descent in the United States. I show how the creation of "free spaces" to access both supplementary and alternative knowledge is part of a continuum, with black bookstore events and spoken word poetry venues as prime examples of 21st-century venues. Finally, in order to illustrate the significance of alternative knowledge or what King refers to as "Critical Studyin'" in literacy, I introduce a 12th grade student, Naja, and her teacher, Mama C (both pseudonyms), who were "studyin' freedom" in an urban public high school in Brooklyn, New York (Fisher, 2005a). Using the medium of spoken word poetry, Mama C helped her students in a predominately black school access both "Diaspora Literacy" and "Heritage Knowledge" (King, this volume). In Mama C's spoken word poetry class, student poets were practicing Critical Studyin' in an effort to reeducate themselves about their knowledge of Africa, the enslavement of Africans in the Americas, and contemporary portrayals of African Americans engaged in civil rights struggles. Building on King's argument that a true democracy depends on all citizens being literate in their own heritage, this final section unpacks how spoken word poetry provided "culturally informed ways of knowing and being" in a free space for young writers.

Literacy, Lyrics, and Lowriders: Accessing Students' "Funds of Knowledge"

In many ways, King's characterization of Critical Studyin' reflects the ideological model of literacy which views literacy as a "social practice," as opposed to "a technical and neutral skill" (Street, 2005). This perspective considers "knowledge" to be at the core of literacy, or as Street asserts, "The ways in which people address reading and writing are themselves rooted in conceptions of knowledge, identity, being" (p. 418). Studies examining literacy in the lives of ethnically and linguistically diverse youth have turned to spaces in which students in these communities have been engaged in reading, writing, and speaking. However, it has been appropriately noted that too much time has to be spent "documenting competence" in communities where "it should be simply assumed" that young people are knowledgeable and capable of making contributions to our understanding of literacy (Moll & Gonzalez, 2001).

Analyzing the voluntary writing of African American high school students, Mahiri and Sablo (1996) demonstrated how "Keisha" and "Troy" used writing as a "refuge" in out-of-school contexts (p. 174), arguing that the skills the two used in their voluntary writing (e.g., songs, poems, plays, and raps) "correspond to some of the behaviors and skills they need to develop and display in school" (p. 178). Similarly, Dyson (1999) examined the "official" and "unofficial" worlds of "Wenona" and "Marcel" (as well as their "brothers and sisters"). Elements of popular culture from the "unofficial" worlds of sports, film, and music "populated" their voices and ideas in the "official" world of the classroom during writing workshop and Author's Theater time. Dyson's research demonstrates how teachers can effectively build on students' "unofficial" worlds in their writing development. These studies and others have given literacy research a lens to view family and community ways of knowing, or "funds of knowledge," as a critical part of the learning experiences of ethnically and linguistically diverse students in American public schools (Gonzalez, Moll, & Amanti, 2005; Moll & Gonzalez, 2001).

For example, speakers of African American Vernacular English may use their home and community knowledge of language for literary interpretation in English classrooms (Lee, 1995). Moll and Gonzalez (2001) also maintain that the "social and labor history" of families is a resource for traditional classrooms (p. 160). In his study of visual literacies found in Chicano lowrider culture, Cowan (2004) described his journey as a teacher making discoveries about his students' art. When Cowan began his teaching career, school administrators dismissed Chicano student art as "gang-related." Using the history of Mexican immigrants in California, an analysis of "Lowrider" magazine, and most importantly, interviews with student artists and members of the Lowrider culture, Cowan demonstrated this art was a "socially constructed and culturally valued form of expression" (p. 52). Through "David" and "Sonny," Cowan also demonstrated the intergenerational tradition of Lowrider culture. Mahiri and Sablo (1996), Dyson (1999), and Cowan have introduced a more nuanced understanding of student literacies through the lives and work of Keisha, Troy, Wenona, Marcel, David, and Sonny. In addition to uncovering the "funds of knowledge" found in students' lives, these studies place the ideas and practices of these young people at the center, or as Dolby (2003) argues:

Youth culture researchers begin with young peoples' lives, and then reposition youth from passive receptors of popular culture to pedagogical actors who reshape the world through their everyday practices. (p. 268)

Like King's work with preservice teachers and curriculum development in California, these studies begin to underscore the complexities of ideologically biased knowledge and methods in teaching. Fifty years after *Brown*, these studies demonstrate that ethnically and linguistically diverse students still need classroom communities that reflect the ideals of democratic society that drove the vision of everyday people, activists, and leaders in the 20th century. Ironically, the classrooms in these studies, as well as the classroom of the study I introduce later in this chapter, were located in schools that were still segregated, based on ethnicity, socioeconomic status, or a combination of both. This being said, literacy research must continue to ask difficult questions about such contradictions before yet another 50 years bring us to *Brown*'s 100th anniversary.

Toward a Literocracy: Democratic Ideals in Literacy Learning

King calls attention to the critical role of out-of-school spaces in the education of black people. To be sure, King situates the values of "studyin' freedom" or Critical Studyin' in the tradition of Citizenship Schools and the Freedom Schools of the Civil Rights Movement. Evoking the literacy learning of Frederick Douglass, King contends the "hope" and eventual power of reading, writing, and orality gave Douglass fuel to fight for his freedom and eventually the freedom of others. Referred to as the "chain letter of instruction" (Holt, 1990), enslaved Africans pieced together literate identities through acts of reciprocity:

Just as Blacks maintained an invisible church, separate from the ones whites provided for them, they also maintained secret schools. These schools could be found in every major southern city and in countless rural communities and plantations. Their teachers were often barely literate themselves, but they passed on what little they knew to others in what one may call a chain letter of instruction. (p. 94)

Holt's description of the "chain letter of instruction" not only portrayed everyday people as teachers, but everyday sites as learning institutions as well. In other words, evidence of literacy teaching and learning for people of African descent may come from "unexpected sources" such as literary salons, writing groups, and book clubs organized outside formal academic institutions (McHenry, 2002, p. 11). In her comprehensive study of lost literary traditions for African Americans, McHenry examines how blacks organized their own literary clubs to promote reading, writing, and speaking while asserting the most important objectives: to cultivate the mind and be considered full human beings. Although African American literary societies substituted formal institutions for literacy learning in the early 20th century, men and women of color have continued to organize learning independent of American public schools for children and adults. Like the Citizenship Schools and Freedom Schools described in King's chapter, black men and women established Independent Black Institutions (IBIs) in the late 1960s and early 1970s to respond to a growing concern that children of African descent were still not receiving equal education in America's public schools (Fisher, 2004; Lee, 1992). Despite access to public schools and American universities, the movement to create and sustain IBIs was a reminder that in spite of the *Brown* decision some 20 years earlier, many black parents remained dissatisfied with their children's schooling experiences. It was believed that in the process of integrating schools, African American student experiences became marginalized and omitted from curriculum. Additionally, these grassroots learning communities sought to reconnect elders and youth in black communities (Fisher, 2004). Many IBIs like Uhuru Sasa (Brooklyn) and the New

Concept Development Center (NCDC) (Chicago) served multiple functions; Uhuru Sasa had a community center/performance space and both Uhuru Sasa and NCDC were connected to printing presses (see Fisher, 2004; Lee, 1992 for more history of IBIs). The tradition of multipurpose venues in the education of people of African descent continues in black-owned and operated bookstore events, spoken word poetry open mic venues, book clubs, and writers' collectives.[3]

In previous studies, I examined Participatory Literacy Communities (PLCs) of the African Diaspora in United States contexts (Fisher, 2003a, 2003b, 2004, 2006). Like King's concept of Diaspora Literacy, PLCs are partially situated in Freire and Macedo's (1987) understanding of the need to "read the word and the world":

> In our analysis, literacy becomes a meaningful construct to the degree that it is viewed as a set of practices that functions to either empower or disempower people. In the larger sense, literacy is analyzed according to whether it serves to reproduce existing social formations or serves as a set of cultural practices that promotes democratic and emancipatory change. (p. 141)

Although this idea is represented in many sociocultural studies of literacy, literacy educators still seek its wisdom and practical application. I would argue that PLCs differ from ideologically biased knowledge and the presentation of that knowledge by revisiting who and what can be considered valid (re)sources. Two types of PLCs in particular, black bookstores and spoken word poetry open mic events, offer an exchange of poetry, prose, and music in a forum-like setting, blurring boundaries of orality and the written word. In my study of "chosen" literacy spaces, I explored values associated with literacy learning in these communities as well as the roles of all participants, including featured poets/authors, members of the audience, event hosts, and organizers. In sum, participants sought these alternative knowledge spaces in an effort to supplement their schooling experiences (Fisher, 2006). Ultimately, I thought that if I could understand the reasons men and women of African descent participated in PLCs, I could help literacy educators think about how the English/Language Arts classroom was conceptualized. In an effort to understand how classroom teachers might adopt the out-of-school literacy practices found in PLCs, I conducted an ethnographic study of two spoken word poetry classes housed in two urban public high schools. Similar to the engagement found in open mic venues, I found teacher/poets in New York City who were engaged in a "literocracy" or "an intersection of literacy and democracy to signal the connection between student choice and the practice of literacy" (Fisher, 2005a, p. 92).

According to Kinloch (2005), Democratic Engagement invites collaborative activities for students including peer feedback and group performance:

Democratic Engagement advanced the argument that the ideals of education, the values in literacy acquisition, and the principles of creative pedagogies are based in the conversations and relationships people have with one another in multiple spaces of interaction. (p. 109)

At this intersection, literacy practices are cultivated relationships and a fostered intimacy around reading, writing, and speaking. Teachers in my study adapted open mic culture from the coffee house into the schoolhouse by inviting students to read original work and by encouraging peers to give each other feedback in a supportive and interactive environment (Fisher, 2005a, 2005b). In addition to developing students' skills in reading, writing, vocabulary, and knowledge of "Standard American English," students learned to listen to each other and acknowledge their multiple and shared truths.[4]

Diaspora Literacy, Heritage Knowledge, and the Spoken Word in Action

King argues for students, especially students of color, to have opportunities to be "literate in one's own heritage" (King, this volume, p. 338). She further asserts that information about Africa and the enslavement of Africans in the United States is the most "distorted" in public school education:

The way Africa and Black experience and culture are taught normally institutionalizes a dangerously incomplete conception of what it means to be African and what it means to be human, which obstructs Black students' opportunities to identify with their heritage. (King, this volume, p. 343)

In fact, some hip-hop artists have taken on this miseducation, giving youth culture a space to voice their frustrations with the public education system. In their anthem "Dirty South," the Atlanta-based hip-hop group, Goodie Mob, contends "In the third grade this is what you told. You was bought. You was sold" (Organized Noise, Bell, Gipp, & Patton, 1995). Goodie Mob's assessment of their schooling experiences was simple—the lives of black Americans began and ended in enslavement. Similarly, the Brooklyn-based Dead Prez critique representations of black Americans in the curriculum in their song "They schools": "I tried to pay attention but they classes wasn't interestin'. They seemed to only glorify the Europeans/Claiming Africans were only three-fifths a human being" (Gavin et al., 2000). Purposefully using African American Vernacular English ("they schools" and "they classes"), Dead Prez demonstrate their unwillingness to buy into ideologically biased knowledge. They also situate themselves on the periphery of a public school system they believed had no interest in them as young, African American males. Other hip-hop groups like Black Star (Mos Def and Talib Kweli) urge urban youth to uncover the privilege of "K.O.S." or "Knowledge of Self-Determination." In this context, Black Star does not criticize schools; instead they consider schooling at the core of one's educational journey. Black Star view K.O.S as a personal evolution: "That's why, Knowledge of Self is like life after death/Apply it, to your life, let destiny manifest" (Kweli, 1999).

Similarly, Mama C's spoken word poetry class at the Community School (CS) (a pseudonym) in Brooklyn pushed the boundaries of ideologically biased knowledge represented in Goodie Mob's and Dead Prez's lyrics by promoting what Black Star refer to as "knowledge of self." Twice a week, Mama C's "spoken wordologists," also known as "The Runaway Slaves of the 21st Century" (see Fisher, 2005b), voluntarily met in their spoken word poetry class to read, write, and "cipher" after school. In the final section of this chapter, I argue that Mama C used Diaspora Literacy and Heritage Knowledge in an effort to foster well-informed students who became independent readers, writers, and thinkers.

Sites and Participants

A product of "resegregation" or a "resegregated society" (Alim, 2005), approximately 89.2% of CS's 670 students identified themselves as black. According to Mama C, the literacy coach for CS, the school was originally slated to be an all African American male school. However, when this exclusively male student configuration was declared illegal, the school enrolled male and female students. Mama C, a native daughter of Brooklyn, attended segregated schools in the same district some 30 years prior to entering the teaching force, only to find herself in segregated schools once again. At the time of the study, Mama C, as a literacy coach, worked closely with the English teachers and students in the writing center. Mama C also taught courses such as the history of spoken word and children's literature part-time at a nearby college to preservice and in-service teachers. Her passion, however, remained with her high school students; teaching the spoken word poetry class was above and beyond her responsibilities at CS. I learned about Mama C's work at a National Council of Teachers of English convention from a colleague, Dale Allender, who knew of my work examining spoken word poetry in out-of-school contexts. I made an appointment with Mama C to meet at CS. She welcomed the idea of my study of her classroom. The first student Mama C introduced me to was Naja, a prolific student poet who had written and performed with Mama C since her sophomore year. Naja, born in Savannah, Georgia and raised in Brooklyn by parents of Barbadian and African American heritage, attended Mama C's class even after she completed all of her graduation requirements at the end of the fall semester.

Because CS had a high black student population (including African American, West Indian, and African students), faculty, staff, and administration were committed to increasing student self-awareness. The Brazilian, Nigerian, Cuban, and Barbados flags were among those proudly displayed in the school foyer, representing the African Diaspora. A large banner reading "You are the author of your own life story" stood out among the sea of flags. In an enclosed case displaying the names of the school and district administrators was yet another quotation: "Our children may learn about the heroes of the past . . . our task is to make ourselves architects of the future."[5] Mama C's after school class was an extension of the commitment in this quotation to prepare confident, emotionally healthy black children for life beyond high school.

Data Collection and Analyses

During the 2003–04 academic year, I volunteered in the CS writing center helping individual students and I was a participant observer in Mama C's after school spoken word poetry class. My initial research question was: How are high school English/Language Arts teachers adapting out-of-school literacy practices such as spoken word poetry in school contexts? Using ethnographic field notes and video, I collected data on Mama C's weekly class and developed a coding system to analyze this data. I interviewed Mama C and her students at different intervals in the academic year. Originally, I set out to study the literacy practices of this group of young poets; however, I discovered there was a strong history and social studies presence. The purpose of Mama C's spoken word class was to cultivate a new generation of readers, writers, and thinkers, as well as educate young black students about American history and the role of their ancestors. Mama C's approach to this after school class employed King's concepts of Diaspora Literacy and Heritage Knowledge. Student poets were encouraged to link their lived experiences with the histories of black people locally, nationally, and globally.

Mama C, a poet and writer outside of the classroom, encouraged the school administration to take advantage of the district's "poets in the schools" program. Through this opportunity, Mama C's students got to meet and share their poetry with Abiodun Oyewole, a member of The Last Poets, at a black-owned and operated bookstore in Brooklyn. During this fall 2003 session, Oyewole underscored what he considered a continuum between student work and the history of language for African Americans:

We have been living in a world of bastardization of words for some time where we are not really getting the sacredness out of the words we deserve—that we need. And poetry is the only sacred language we've got left. But the fact is we have a lot of folks who need to express themselves and poetry is still that language that allows us to tell the truth and at the same time give it some flavor and some spice. (Matsuoka, 2003)

Known for their uncensored testimonials to black life during the 1960s and 1970s in inner-city neighborhoods throughout the United States, The Last Poets are often hailed as the forefathers of hip-hop. Oyewole's service to New York City public schools is consistent with his advocacy on behalf of youth. Naming poetry as the vehicle for preserving the "sacredness" of words, Oyewole acknowledged the "need" for such expression throughout the history of Africans in the Americas. Referring to poetry as a language, Oyewole further noted the power in telling the "truth" with "flavor" and "spice." His characterization—the "bastardization of words"—referred to the strategic scattering of African people disrupting language patterns in an effort to minimize communication among and between enslaved Africans. Students like Naja understood Oyewole's poetry and Mama C's after school movement to be a history course as well as a writing seminar:

You have spoken word and spoken word is a tool to relate a message. And it's not just when you go to history class and someone gives a lecture on history. Most people feel threatened by a lecture but spoken word is an art. You can give them a message and so much meaning. (Naja, personal interview, April 20, 2004)

Naja viewed spoken word as a method to teach history, but she contrasted the style and delivery of spoken word to a history class lecture. According Naja, a lecture could be threatening "to most people" whereas spoken word could "relate a message" through art. Embedded in Naja's feedback is her belief that art makes learning more accessible. Naja's statement also critiques the "banking model" concept of education where the teacher "deposits" information into students (Freire, 2003):

Spoken word is history itself. Like it started, [Mama C] started teaching us the tradition of griots[6] and it starts with the word of mouth. All history started with the word of mouth. Every story that was told, every fable, every myth started with the word of mouth. That's what spoken word is. We're just continuing that tradition. It's evolved and it's growing into a whole industry now but its origins are in history. It's used to tell history, to preserve history. That's why it's such a powerful tool because it is history. (Naja, personal interview, April 20, 2004)

In his study of griots and griottes, Hale (1998) contends that the "texts" of griots "provide deep insights into the values of a people and their social structure" (p. 23). Hale also argues that contributions from griots to African history cannot be minimized solely because they are "oral rather than written" (p. 24). Naja considered her poetry and the writing of her peers as "continuing that tradition" while acknowledging the increased popularity of spoken word in television programming and anthologies (Fisher, 2004). She ultimately linked the medium of spoken word to oral histories while demonstrating an understanding of the role of griots in West Africa as well as the power of orality. A commitment to taking written words from the page and giving them life through performance and spoken word provided a starting point for Mama C and her students.

Mama C's focus on history emerged from her teaching experiences in public schools; according to Mama C she "always" had students who were unfamiliar with "their history," African American students in particular (see Fisher, 2005b). Mama C believed that the confidence students gained from knowing more about their families and their heritage prepared them for academic success. Consistent with King's beliefs that the affirmation of Heritage Knowledge helped students "participate fully" as capable and contributing humanitarians, Mama C set the tone for class by introducing the following people and topics:

- Assata Shakur: Students began the fall semester by reading *The Autobiography of Assata Shakur* (Shakur, 1987). In addition to reading the text on their own, students read passages together in class and worked on projects related to the reading. All students had to write a poem responding to Shakur's autobiography, which was integrated with her original poetry.
- Slavery in New York City/African Burial Ground: During the 2003–04 academic year, the New York City African Burial Ground was formally unveiled to the public. The Spoken Wordologists were asked to read about the African Burial Ground Project and stay current with any news related to the project and events that took place in its honor.
- Ghana, West Africa: Each year CS teachers led a trip to a different country or region in Africa. Mama C made it a point to attend this year because Naja committed to going on the trip. They both kept journals with poetry and shared them with the class upon their return.

Assata Shakur. Mama C explicitly addressed these topics and urged students to get "fired" up, signifying on Sonia Sanchez's poem "Catch the Fire,"[7] through their writing and reading of texts. In the fall semester, Mama C introduced student poets to *The Autobiography of Assata Shakur.* Shakur, living in political asylum in Cuba, remains a controversial figure in American history. Written in poetry and prose, Shakur's autobiography details her life experiences as an activist and member of the Black Panther Party.[8] Shakur's autobiography was to be a starting point to discuss the constant policing of young black and brown people in Brooklyn;[9] this was one of the foremost concerns in the Black Panther Party Platform. In addition to reading the text, Mama C invited students to choose a project like explications of Shakur's poems, writing a journal from the perspective of Shakur, or creating a multimedia timeline that required additional research. All students were invited to include a poem to Shakur. Responding to the renewed interest in Shakur's life, as seen in popular magazines such as *VIBE,* Mama C created an opportunity for students to learn more about Shakur's story. Naja immediately responded to the text with this poem:

WHO SHOT YA, ASSATA?
My African queen
Whose jewels have been tarnished and twisted
Yet your feet

God has kissed your feet
You've escaped
The slave masters who have yet to master
The magic of your magnificent departure
RUN BUTTERFLY RUN

In her poem, Naja compared Shakur's escape from prison to the efforts of runaway slaves; after reading Shakur's autobiography, Naja began to refer to her as a "Runaway Slave of the 21st Century." Referring to the prison guards as "slave masters," Naja documented "the magic" of Shakur's "magnificent departure" as similar to the way a butterfly was transformed in a cocoon. Using alliteration, Naja explored the possibility that Shakur's story could have been "tarnished and twisted." As the academic year progressed, Naja continued to keep Shakur in her writing throughout the semester. After reading a collection of poetry by Gerren Liles (2000), Naja made connections between Liles's poem and her prior reading of Shakur's autobiography:

The enslaved mothers were the ones who emancipated the rest
They cooked, taught, and cleaned up our mess
There were so many Rosas, Assatas, or Corettas that it was pointless
To ever accept the fact we are "hoes" or "bitches"
We were God sent

Here, Naja contemplated a shift in values across generations (see Appendix for the complete poem, reprinted by permission of the author). In spite of the difference in responses to racial injustice from the Black Panther Party and the nonviolence sector in the Civil Rights Movement, Naja situated Shakur with the "Rosas" (Rosa Parks) and the "Corettas" (Coretta Scott King).

The African Burial Ground Project. Mama C's spoken word poetry class addressed the discovery of the remains of enslaved Africans, mostly children, near Wall Street in New York City. The African Burial Ground project, in conjunction with the Schomburg Center for Research in Black Culture,[10] provided materials for educators, including timelines, maps, and a wealth of information about the excavation. Mama C refused to let this learning opportunity get by students. She devoted class sessions to conversations about the African Burial Ground. With desks arranged in a circle, Mama C gave students time to read through materials at their own pace, talking to each other and asking questions. King critiques the lack of such opportunities for students to discuss African American experiences with dignity:

The way Africa and black experience and culture are normally taught institutionalizes a dangerously incomplete conception of what it means to be African and what it means to be human, which obstructs Black students' opportunities to identify with their heritage. (King, this volume, p. 343)

Ghana and Senegal. Mama C wanted to create meaningful interactions in learning history and language arts; she did not view these as independent content areas. Through fund raising and student programs, Naja and Mama C attended the school trip to Ghana and Senegal in West Africa. Because Naja went on this trip with a particular awareness following the reading and discussions of slavery in New York City, she was disappointed in her peers who showed more interest in shopping than in visiting the preserved holding caves for enslaved Africans being sent to the Americas. Naja expressed this disappointment through her poem "Shopping Spree":

Money flashing, lies and deceptions
The Miseducation of these Negroes
Who rather sing Lauryn Hill on buses
Instead of visiting slave castles
And questioning why their titles are not dungeons
And in 50 years I fear
My experience of Senegal will be
In the lost and dumbfounded

Signifying on Carter G. Woodson's (1990) classic text *The Miseducation of the Negro* and rapper/singer Lauryn Hill's album "The Miseducation of Lauryn Hill," (1998) Naja questioned her peers who had a lack of interest in visiting the "slave castles" in Senegal. Naja was even more "dumbfounded" by her peers' inability to question why "slave castles" were not called "dungeons." Mama C encouraged Naja to read her poem at a school event to begin a schoolwide discussion. In the closing of her poem, Naja hypothetically asks a Senegalese craftsmen "How much for a piece of dignity?" This final question demonstrated Naja's exasperation with the trip becoming a "shopping spree." Naja, in a very sophisticated manner, confronted complicated issues about capitalism and the enduring exploitation of African countries. Her courage and insight grew out of the support she received in the spoken word class. It was in the poetry circle that Naja asked for feedback and generated strategies to prepare students for future travel/study programs.

It is important to note that Naja saw her participation in the spoken word poetry class as an opportunity to work on her writing skills across genres and content areas, in addition to being a history course. Poetry helped Naja gain writing confidence; she began to approach her writing from the perspective that if she could get comfortable with language, using words to work for her, then writing would be more enjoyable:

For me personally, I love writing all different kinds of writing. I don't shy away from having to write an essay but essays are boring sometimes. So with the use of poetry, and you know poetry doesn't have to rhyme, so you can have poetry in your essays and you can manipulate words that other people can't do because they don't get the opportunity to play with words like I do. . . . *The most important tool is knowing the English language and knowing how to use it because people who know how to use the English language won't get confused by it* [emphasis added]—won't get trapped by it. (Naja, personal interview, April 20, 2004)

Naja identified the trappings of being unfamiliar and uncomfortable with language. Through writing poetry, Naja began to "manipulate words." I think what is most compelling is Naja's "play" with words, which gave her a sense of ownership and extinguished any fear associated with writing. In an early stage in her academic career, Naja was already ascribing a sense of power to language and the sense of "sacredness" projected by Oyewole's visit with Mama C's class. Naja also believed being a poet helped her in an oratorical competition; once again she acknowledged the links between spoken word poetry and history:

I might say something in my essay that sounds poetic and people will say That's so poetic. You can tell you're a poet. *Because I play with words and I switch around sounds and you don't have to start an essay off with "My essay is about" or "My thesis statement is." You use the language, use the words that you're taught in school* [emphasis added]. I remember I had to do an oratorical competition and the last sentence we had to talk about a figure so I talked about Harriet Tubman and I said "Just as Harriet Tubman once did, I will venture out into the wilderness and face every obstacle and I will reach back to pull my generation to that Promised Land." And everybody said "That's so poetic." But it wasn't even a poem it was an essay. When you learn how to use words like how you want them and to enjoy words you'll have an easier time writing essays. (Naja, personal interview, April 20, 2004)

Naja almost presents a "cause and effect" method with her suggestion to "learn how to use words" and "have an easier time writing essays." She considered writing poetry an opportunity to use words "like how you want them" where she could "switch around sounds" and use different literary devices to convey her message. Even in her discussion of writing Naja still makes explicit links with history, using Harriet Tubman's life as a metaphor for her work with youth.

Discussion: What Can We Learn?

What can literacy research learn from Mama C, Naja, and their free space for learning, and what do literacy researchers and educators need to consider before the centennial celebration of the historical *Brown* decision? In this chapter, I respond to King's call to address the miseducation of students, teachers, and teacher educators through Mama C's praxis of Critical Studyin.' By contextualizing King's concepts of Diaspora Literacy and Heritage Knowledge in the tradition of IBIs and recent manifestations of such institutions, I attempted to show how an urban high school literacy teacher, Mama C, and one of her student poets, Naja, used Diaspora Literacy and Heritage Knowledge to foster a passion for reading, writing, and public speaking. Mama C created a democratic space for exploring, analyzing, and synthesizing ideas using the medium of spoken word poetry. Challenging ideologically biased knowledge, Mama C's after school class was both an alternative and a supplementary learning space with values rooted in Freedom School traditions. In the tradition of ingenious enslaved Africans who founded "secret schools" (Holt, 1990); African American readers and writers in the early 19th century who created literary societies (McHenry, 2002; McHenry & Heath, 1994); organizers of Citizenship Schools and Freedom Schools (King, this volume); parents who founded and maintained independent learning institutions (Fisher, 2004; Lee, 1992); and the caring found in African American schools of the segregated south (Siddle-Walker, 1996), Mama C deliberately introduced students to their histories and fostered a forum where they could exchange their ideas and a range of emotion through their poetry. Mama C did what countless parents did in the late 1960s and early 1970s; she redefined "within a community context the possibilities and gifts that black children offer the world" (Lee, 1992, p. 161). To be sure, Naja applied her poetry skills in other areas of her education by using writing to think critically about her community and eventually the world.

The irony is that CS remains a segregated public school, when students of all ethnic backgrounds should have access to the rich histories taught in Mama C's spoken word class. Using student writing to inspire dialogue is at the core of building a literocracy and is a tool that could be made accessible for all students. Mama C discussed another irony in her work at CS; she noted "it never failed" that black students did not know their ancestors' contributions to the development of the Americas. Similar to King's research on misrepresentations in curriculum, Mama C found students had never been introduced to scholarship that had African, African American, and West Indian experiences as their contexts. Therefore, she believed she had to "plant many seeds" in a short period of time. Mama C's efforts and the work of other literacy teachers should not be isolated in after school programs; I would argue these learning spaces need support from existing education infrastructures and, further, that all students in American public schools deserve to access their Heritage Knowledge across content areas.

Additionally, Naja's ideas and life experiences would be influential in diverse class settings. This was particularly striking for me when Naja visited my freshman seminar in a private university setting and volunteered to read a poem she wrote about the politics of popular culture and literacy. Out of 15 freshman from cities throughout the United States and abroad, Naja was the only African American student present, yet her words and ideas sounded through the class like an alarm, inciting one of the most powerful discussions we had during the semester. Literacy education cannot afford to wait another 50 years to integrate opportunities for Critical Studyin' and Heritage Knowledge. In honoring *Brown*, literacy education must include opportunities for students to view themselves as part of a continuum of important contributors to their neighborhoods, their communities, and eventually the world.

NOTES

1. This passage is from a poem performed by The Last Poets on rapper Common's song "The Corner" (Lynn et al., 2005).

2. Naja, a Kiswahili name with many meanings including "success," is a pseudonym. I have previously written about Naja and her teacher Mama C (Fisher, 2005b).

3. In the epilogue to McHenry's (2002) study of African American literary societies, she discusses the emergence of black bookstores which began with the frenzy surrounding Terry McMillan's blockbuster novel *Waiting to Exhale* (1992). The phenomenon of Writers Collectives is very much rooted in the tradition of literary societies. For example the NOMMO Literary Society, founded in New Orleans by poet/historian Kalamu ya Salaam, offered writers a weekly reading and exchange of writing. Salaam published many of the participants in poetry anthologies such as *360 Degrees: A Revolution of Black Poets* (1998).

4. In the context of my research, "truths" represent the many experiences students have. Here, "truth" is plural to underscore the fact that everyone has a story.

5. "CS" cited Jomo Kenyatta as the author of this quote.

6. Griots in western Africa have played many roles, including historian, storyteller, and praise singer. In this particular context, Naja compared a griot's ability to preserve history with the mission of spoken word poetry.

7. In his "cross-generational" poetry anthology titled *Catch the Fire!!!*, Gilbert (1998) discussed the inspiration for the title, which came from a Sonia Sanchez poem bearing the same name. According to Gilbert, Sanchez wrote the poem in response to a conversation she had had with Bill Cosby about his concern for black children and their future. Sanchez's poem urges black youth to "catch," "hold," "learn" their fire, which serves as a metaphor for passion.

8. After being charged with shooting a police officer and imprisoned, Shakur escaped and was granted political asylum in Cuba where she currently resides. Shakur's case still arouses controversy in the United States.

9. During the 2003–04 academic year, for example, a young African American man named Timothy Stansbury was shot and killed on the rooftop of his housing project by a police officer who claimed the unarmed youth startled him.

10. The Schomburg Center for Research in Black Culture is a part of the New York City Public Library. The Schomburg is committed to preserving the histories of people throughout the African Diaspora.

REFERENCES

Alim, H.S. (2005). Critical language awareness in the United States: Revisiting issues and revising pedagogies in a resegregated society. *Educational Researcher*, *34*(7), 24–31.

Cowan, P. (2004). Devils or angels? Literacy and discourse in lowrider culture. In J. Mahiri (Ed.), *What they don't learn in school: Literacy in the lives of urban youth* (pp. 47–77). New York: Peter Lang.

Dolby, N. (2003). Popular culture and democratic practice. *Harvard Educational Review*, *73*(2), 258–284.

Dyson, A.H. (1999). Coach Bombay's kids learn to write: Children's appropriation of media material for school literacy. *Research in the Teaching of English*, *33*(4), 367–401.

Fisher, M.T. (2003a). Choosing literacy: African Diaspora Participatory Literacy Communities. Unpublished Dissertation, University of California at Berkeley.

Fisher, M.T. (2003b). Open mics and open minds: Spoken word poetry in African Diaspora Participatory Literacy Communities. *Harvard Educational Review*, *73*(3), 362–389.

Fisher, M.T. (2004). "The song is unfinished": The new literate and literary. *Written Communication*, *21*(3), 290–312.

Fisher, M.T. (2005a). Literocracy: Liberating language and creating possibilities. *English Education*, *37*(2), 92–95.

Fisher, M.T. (2005b). From the coffee house to the school house: The promise and potential of spoken word poetry in school contexts. *English Education*, *37*(2), 115–131.

Fisher, M.T. (2006). Earning "dual degrees": Black bookstores as alternative knowledge spaces. *Anthropology and Education Quarterly*, *37*(1), 83–99.

Freire, P. (2003). *Pedagogy of the oppressed* (30th anniversary edition). New York and London: Continuum: International Publishing Group.

Freire, P., & Macedo, D. (1987). *Literacy: Reading the word and the world*. Westport, CT: Bergin & Garvey.

Gavin, C., Alford, L., Williams, V., & Mair, A. (2000). "They schools" [Recorded by Dead Prez]. On *Let's get free* [CD]. New York, Loud Records.

Gilbert, D.I.M. (1998). *Catch the fire: A cross-generational anthology of contemporary African American poetry*. New York: Riverhead Books.

Gonzalez, N., Moll, L., & Amanti, C. (2005). *Funds of knowledge: Theorizing practice in households, communities and classrooms*. Mahwah, NJ: Lawrence Erlbaum.

Hale, T.A. (1998). *Griots and griottes: Masters of words and music*. Bloomington and Indianapolis: Indiana University Press.

Hill, L. (1998). *The miseducation of Lauryn Hill* [CD]. New York, Ruffhouse Records.

Holt, T. (1990). "Knowledge is power": The Black struggle for literacy. In A.A. Lunsford, H. Moglen, & J. Slevin (Eds.), *The right to literacy* (pp. 91–102). New York: The Modern Language Association of America.

Kelley, R.D.G. (2002). *Freedom dreams: The Black radical imagination*. Boston: Beacon Press.

King, J.E. (2006). "If justice is our objective"—Diaspora Literacy, Heritage Knowledge, and the praxis of Critical Studyin' for human freedom. In A. Ball (Ed.), *With more deliberate speed: Achieving equity and excellence in education. Realizing the full potential of Brown v. Board of Education. The 105th yearbook of the National Society for the Study of Education, Part II* (pp. 337–360). Malden, MA: Blackwell Publishing.

Kinloch, V.F. (2005). Poetry, literacy and creativity: Fostering effective learning strategies in an urban classroom. *English Education*, *37*(2), 96–114.

Kweli, T. (1999). "K.O.S. (Determination)." [Recorded by Black Star]. On *Mos Def & Talib Kweli are Black Star* [CD]. New York, Rawkus Records.

Lee, C.D. (1992). Profile of an Independent Black Institution: African-centered education at work. *Journal of Negro Education*, *61*(2), 160–177.

Lee, C.D. (1995). A culturally based cognitive apprenticeship: Teaching African American high school students skills in literary interpretation. *Reading Research Quarterly, 30*(4), 608–629.

Liles, G. (2000). *On the road to Damascus*. New York: Division of Words.

Lynn, L., West, K., Oyewole, A., Bin Hassan, U., & Moore, L. (2005). "The corner." [Recorded by Common]. On *Be* [CD]. Santa Monica, CA, Geffen Records.

Mahiri, J., & Sablo, S. (1996). Writing for their lives: The non-school literacy of California's urban African American youth. *Journal of Negro Education, 65*(2), 164–180.

Matsuoka, B.M. (Executive Producer). (2003). The expanding canon: Critical pedagogy with Abiodun Oyewole and Lawson Fusau Inada [Television Broadcast]. New York, Thirteen/WNET.

McHenry, E. (2002). *Forgotten readers: Recovering the lost history of African American literary societies*. Durham and London: Duke University Press.

McHenry, E. & Heath, S.B. (1994). The literate and the literary: African Americans as writers and readers—1830–1940. *Written Communication, 11*(4), 419–444.

McMillan, T. (1992). *Waiting to exhale*. New York: Viking.

Moll, L., & Gonzalez, N. (2001). Lessons from research with language-minority children. In E. Cushman, E.R. Kintgen, B.M. Kroll, & M. Rose (Eds.), *Literacy: A critical sourcebook* (pp. 156–171). Boston: St. Martin's Press.

Moll, L.C., Amanti, C., Neff, D., & González, N. (1992). Funds of knowledge for teaching: Using a qualitative approach to connect homes and classrooms. *Theory into Practice, 31*(2), 132–141.

Organized Noise, Bell, F., Gipp, C., & Patton, A. (1995). "Dirty South" [Recorded by Goodie Mob]. On Soul Food [CD]. New York, LaFace Records.

Salaam, K., with Kwame, A. (1998). *360 degrees: A revolution of Black poets*. Washington, DC: BlackWords.

Shakur, A. (1987). *Autobiography of Assata Shakur*. Chicago: Lawrence Hill Books.

Siddle-Walker, V. (1996). *Their highest potential: An African American school community in the segregated south*. North Carolina: University of North Carolina Press.

Street, B.V. (2005). Recent applications of New Literacy Studies in educational contexts. *Research in the Teaching of English, 39*(4), 417–423.

Woodson, C.G. (1990). The mis-education of the Negro. New Jersey: Africa World Press.

Appendix: Corn Rows by Naja

Black people didn't always like corn rows
Or back lashing, sun beaming, and cotton barrels
They didn't find the word "nigger" compassionate
How could ancient kings and queens ever accept a term like that?
In fact, our men could never grow past the title of boy
And our women were forced to fill in the void
Of fatherhood, they became the sole provider
That's why sistahs are so comfortable being single mothers
Sagging pants, or the newest kicks
Were not our concern when we had fields to pick
And family was sacred and could not be captured on a television show
It was that love that made the sun glow

They didn't know about mad cows because the cattle had it better than them
A book was freedom
And their tragedies could not be caught on some Amistad film
The enslaved mothers were the ones who emancipated the rest
They cooked, taught, and cleaned up our mess
There were so many Rosas, Assatas, or Corettas that it was pointless
To ever accept the fact that we are "hoes" or "bitches"
We were God sent
But let's not forget, a family without a father has not been blessed
It wasn't Abe Lincoln who built our liberties, it was our enslaved kings
Who sweated determination under the rays of slavery
It was the granddaddies who schooled us on
The Temptations and The Emotions of voting
It's the fathers who stuck it out for you and me
And it was the brother who desired to one day be the producers of out babies
Hip-hop can return to its original form
Slave spirituals and the African drum
50 Cent will only be in our pockets
And education and de-gentrification is what we will market
And then we can put these armors down and settle down
And untangle the indoctrinating styles that have been titled full of soul
We will start wearing crowns instead of corn rows

Epilogue: The Implications of Brown v. Board of Education in an Increasingly Diverse Society

KENJI HAKUTA

It gives me great honor to use the many important issues raised in this volume as a way of looking back on the impact of *Brown v. Board of Education* as well as looking to challenges ahead. I write from perspectives shaped by my experiences as a researcher actively working at the interstices of policy and advocacy in two different arenas, both profoundly influenced by *Brown*. First, I have worked in the area of bilingualism and linguistic minority education, an area that has been virtually defined by another Supreme Court decision, *Lau v. Nichols*, based on Title VI of the Civil Rights Act, which of course is the most important legislative milestone downstream from *Brown*. As a beneficiary of *Lau*, I have always looked to *Brown* as its big brother, and stood in awe of the historical mantle. Second, I have worked on the issue of diversity in higher education in the post-*Bakke* environment, and tried to use social science research evidence to bear on the court battle over affirmative action, in particular the Supreme Court cases involving the University of Michigan (*Gratz v. Bollinger*, 2003; *Grutter v. Bollinger*, 2003). As a disclaimer, I should also state that I am somewhat iconoclastic and identify with neither the perspective of the normative, discipline-based social scientist, nor with that of the transformative educator, nor with that of the critical race theorist. I am mainly a pragmatist with a taste for useful research that uses strong methodology.

Seen through these lenses, the themes that have emerged in the chapters of this volume give rise to several reactions: an appreciation of legends and legacies—the giants on whose shoulders we stand; a fear of societal complacency in seeing the glass as half full; an anger at the mistaken shape that the public debate has taken; a sense of pragmatism to seek the next steps; and a hope that the cumulative nature of scholarship will give rise to a more promising future.

Kenji Hakuta is the founding dean of the School of Social Sciences, Humanities and Arts at the University of California, Merced. He is currently on leave from Stanford University.

Legends and Legacies

A history of *Brown* immediately reminds us of the giants of the field. Edmund Gordon refers to his direct contact with W.E.B. Du Bois and Kenneth Clark. Carol Lee rightly points out that Gordon himself is a giant, and I need to add, a most gentlemanly and classy giant. The scholars involved with the *Brown* plaintiffs were the pioneers of a mission-oriented, post-World War II social science, and included Otto Kleinberg, Jerome Bruner, and Mamie Clark, among others. The *Brown* lawyers included Thurgood Marshall, who was later appointed to the Supreme Court as the first black justice. Reconsiderations of *Brown* afford opportunities not just for celebrating the markers and players, but also for appreciating the fact that the decision is part of an epic struggle that spans centuries to rid the society of slavery and its consequences. We must appreciate the fact that the scholarship represented in this volume has taken its present shape because of this legacy—what Gordon in his chapter referred to as "science in the service of humankind and social justice" (this volume, p. 58–70).

Acknowledging legacies is also important in putting perspective on downstream events. I think particularly of events that assert the rights of language minorities and immigrants, including *Lau v. Nichols* in 1974 all the way up through the demonstrations around the reform of immigration law that are occurring at the time of this writing in spring 2006. In each of these cases, the issue of minority rights has been asserted—in the case of *Lau*, in the court of law, and in the case of immigration reform through the court of public opinion and pressure upon Congress. These are instances where inter-minority tensions can quickly rise to the surface if proper etiquette in acknowledging the historical role of the civil rights movement based in the African American population is not appropriately acknowledged. In a very real sense, every action taken on behalf of civil rights in our history is a legacy of *Brown*.

Complacency

Charles Ogletree (2004) titled his autobiography "All Deliberate Speed"—the words used to condition the remedies to segregation—in order to highlight the dangers of complacency that could result from the symbolism of the *Brown* decision, and to point out the enormous challenges that continue to erode racial justice. Evidence gathered for school adequacy cases, such as *Williams v. State of California* (2004), provide stark evidence that students of color, especially African American and Latino students, continue to attend substandard schools with inadequate facilities, materials, and teachers. Evidence from higher education continues to show the need for race-conscious admissions into selective colleges and universities if racial diversity is to be attained. In the absence of affirmative action, the situation is nothing short of catastrophic. As Richard Atkinson, former President of the University of California, noted, "UCLA and Berkeley together admitted 83 African American men in 2004, nearly half of them on athletic scholarships" (Atkinson & Pelfrey, 2005, p. 8). This is hardly the moment for complacency, yet the campuses are relatively quiet and student protests sparse. Where is the outrage? Where is the activism? Why have we lost our focus on social justice?

Shape of the Public Debate

     . . . which brings the issue to the framing of the policy debates. In my own specialty of bilingual education, debate has tended to focus on the differences between English-only instruction versus bilingual education (Crawford, 2004). What is in reality bilingual education, though, is only of the transitional variety, where the native language is a temporary prop for the learning of academics until the student has learned English. As such, the debate has been over the efficacy of the program in attaining English proficiency, and over how long it takes kids to learn English. Only recently has the debate begun to shift to the fact that regardless of whether the native language is used or not, students who attend inadequately resourced schools are doomed to failure, a point that has become the source of legal action in school adequacy cases such as *Williams*. The advantage of shifting the debate away from English-only versus bilingual education is that this provides a common policy agenda for advocates for a better *Brown* and for a better *Lau*.

     The shape of the debate for affirmative action in higher education is in even greater need for a new focus. The argument made in the Michigan cases was about the benefits of diversity for all students, and was not about social justice per se. This legal strategy was borne out of necessity because of the ever-narrowing court definitions of justice and remedies (Witt & Shin, 2003, provide an accessible summary of the history). After the Michigan decisions, we are down to Justice Sandra Day O'Connor's comments ("We expect that 25 years from now, the use of racial preferences will no longer be necessary to further the interest approved today") in order to make a diverse learning place possible for majority students. As important as the decision was in enabling affirmative action programs to continue, this is hardly what was envisioned after *Brown*. In order to bring the social and racial justice issues back into the public policy debate, the public will need to be reawakened to the realities of race, poverty, and justice in ways that lead to sustainable change.

Pragmatism and Cumulative Scholarship

What role can theory and scholarship play in advancing *Brown* and the civil rights agenda? The chapters in this volume are good examples of contributions that activist and thoughtful scholars can make to the enterprise. It is important to understand comparative perspectives through a better understanding of events in South Africa and the influences of *Brown* in educational reform (Jonathan Jansen, Neville Alexander). It is also important to think of transforming the roles of scholars in the area of social justice, as articulated elegantly by Gloria Ladson-Billings and Joyce King in their chapters. These perspectives lend important light to the changing roles and expectations of academics to issues of huge gravity.

How can we be sure that scholarship is being helpful in transforming our educational and social systems to address the issues of *Brown*? I would like to draw an analogy from what I have been advocating in the area of the education of language minority students, based on a federal court decision (*Castaneda v. Pickard*, 1981) that was helpful in providing a definition of "appropriate action" for school districts in addressing equal educational opportunity for language minority students. In this ruling, the judge outlined three "standards" against which the actions of a system can be judged:

1. Whether the school system is pursuing a program informed by *an educational theory recognized as sound* by some experts in the field, or, at least, deemed a legitimate experimental strategy.
2. Whether the programs and practices actually used by the school system are reasonably calculated to *implement effectively* the educational theory adopted by the school.
3. Whether the school's program is able, after a legitimate trial, to *produce results* indicating that the language barriers confronting students are actually being overcome.

A fourth piece not identified by the court, but important in its implementation across school districts, is that the implementation or the theory must be revised if desirable outcomes are not attained.

Applied to the current situation, I would like to suggest that, where we believe scholarship can be helpful in addressing different areas of struggle, this scholarship be charged with the task of developing their own "theory of the case," strategies for implementation to make change, and an explicit effort to monitor and evaluate the outcome after a period of time. In the half century since *Brown*, a number of approaches have been attempted, and progress has been made in some areas, yet as the chapters in this volume make amply clear there is much to be done. Through a systematic effort to make the theories of change explicit, and holding the theories and implementation accountable, my hope is that there will be more cause for celebration at the *Brown* centennial, and even more reason to celebrate the rich legacy of the continuing struggle for racial justice and equality that had its punctuating moment in 1954.

REFERENCES

Atkinson, R.C., & Pelfrey, P.A. (2005, May 18). *Opportunity in a democratic society: A national agenda*. Third annual Nancy Cantor Distinguished Lecture, University of Michigan. Retrieved April 27, 2006 from http://www.diversity.umich.edu/futuring/cantor.pdf

Castaneda v. Pickard, 648 U.S. (1981). F.2d 989.

Crawford, J. (2004). *Educating English learners: Language diversity in the classroom*. Los Angeles: Bilingual Educational Services.

Gratz v. Bollinger, 539 U.S. 244 (2003).

Grutter v. Bollinger, 539 U.S. 306 (2003).

Lau v. Nichols, 414 U.S. 563 (1974).

Ogletree, C. (2004). *All deliberate speed: Reflections on the first half century of* Brown v. Board of Education. New York: Norton.

Williams v. State of California, *supra*, 34 Cal. 3d at 26–28 (2004).

Witt, D., & Shin, C. (2003). Historical summary of affirmative action. In M.J. Chang, D. Witt, J. Jones, & K. Hakuta (Eds.), *Compelling interest: Examining the evidence on racial dynamics in colleges and universities* (pp. 185–201). Stanford, CA: Stanford University Press.

Subject and Name Index